Nigel Slater is the author of a collection of bestselling books and presenter of BBC 1's *Simple Cooking*. He has been food columnist for the *Observer* for twenty years. His books include the classics *Appetite* and *The Kitchen Diaries* and the critically acclaimed two-volume *Tender*. His award-winning memoir *Toast – the story of a boy's hunger* won six major awards and is now a BBC film starring Helena Bonham Carter and Freddie Highmore. His writing has won the National Book Award, the Glenfiddich Trophy, the André Simon Memorial Prize and the British Biography of the Year. He was the winner of a Guild of Food Writers' Award for his BBC 1 series *Simple Suppers*.

### Also by Nigel Slater

*Tender Volumes I* and *II*
*Eating for England*
*The Kitchen Diaries*
*Toast – the story of a boy's hunger*
*Thirst*
*Appetite*
*Nigel Slater's Real Food*
*Real Cooking*
*The 30-Minute Cook*
*Real Fast Food*

*For James Thompson*

# Acknowledgements

Thank you, as always, to Louise Haines, my editor for over twenty years, for your endless encouragement, guidance and patience. Without you there would be no book.

To Jonathan Lovekin for taking beautiful pictures of so much I have cooked over the years. Thanks, Jonnie. I am grateful to Harry Borden for kindly allowing my publishers to use his thoughtful portrait of me.

To James Thompson, producer, kitchen genius and confidant. He who holds it all together. James, thank you for everything, but especially for your sure hand with the recipes, guiding their journey from diary to table, published page and television screen. For your inspiration, enthusiasm, hard work and friendship, I can never thank you enough.

To my literary agent Araminta Whitley and my television agent Rosemary Scoular, to Harry Mann, Sophie Hughes, Wendy Millyard and everyone at LAW, United Agents, Breckman and Company and Mishcon de Reya for dealing with all the really important stuff that I don't understand.

To everyone at Fourth Estate, especially Victoria Barnsley, Michelle Kane, Georgia Mason and Olly Rowse. To David Pearson for helping to make this second volume of the diaries so beautiful and, as always, my thanks to Jane Middleton and Annie Lee for their eagle eyes and endless patience.

To everyone at the *Observer*, especially the wonderful Allan Jenkins, Ruaridh Nicoll, Martin Love, Gareth Grundy and John Mulholland. To Leah, Debbie, Helen and Caroline. And to Sarah Randell and Helena Lang. Thank you for your continued support.

To William, Sean and Mark and everyone at Fullers for all your hard work on the kitchen and to Steve Owens and everyone at Benchmark.

To Katie Findlay for helping to keep the garden in great shape; to Rob Watson at Ph9 for looking after nigelslater.com; to Dalton Wong and everyone at twentytwotraining for their endless encouragement and support and to Tim and Asako d'Offay and Takahiro Yagi for their wisdom and kindness.

And thank you to all the bookshops and those who work in them for their continued enthusiasm. And to everyone who enters their local booksellers and discovers the magic that lies on those creaking shelves and gets to know that there is nothing so beautiful as the feel and smell of a book in the hand.

# A few notes on television

I had no real intention to present a television series. I had enough on my plate with a long-running weekly newspaper column and my books, and, however much I enjoy watching 'celebrity chefs', had no wish to be part of that world. The idea of filming a cookery series was suggested to me by Jay Hunt, at the time controller of BBC1. She gently persuaded me that there was room for a series with calm and gentle presentation and understated and simple food.

Not only did the series turn out to be a success beyond our wildest dreams, I ended up rather enjoying myself, and as a result there have now been four of the 'Simple' series. I owe a huge debt to Jay and to Ian Blandford, to Alison Kirkham and Tom Edwards and of course to Danny Cohen. To the production team and everyone at BBC Bristol, especially Pete Lawrence, Simon Knight, Jen Fazey, Michelle Crowley, James Thompson and Gary Skipton. And to my awesome crew who have made the shows what they are: Richard Hill, Sarah Myland, Robbie Johnson, Conor Connolly, Cheryl Martin, Simon Kerfoot, Sheree Jewell, Sam Jones and Archie Thomas. And thank you to Rudi Thackeray and his team. A big shout out also to the guys at Kiss My Pixel and to Mark Adderley and Nadia Sawalha. Thank you all.

This book is not a traditional television 'tie-in' but versions of many of the recipes in *Simple Suppers* and *Simple Cooking* can be found between these pages. (Others are in *The Kitchen Diaries* volume I and *Tender Volumes I* and *II*.) Thank you to the millions of you who watch each programme, and send such heartwarming letters, emails and tweets. I cannot tell you how much the entire team appreciates it.

And to that vibrant, warm and encouraging community at Twitter @realnigelslater. You are a joy.

Nigel Slater, London, September 2012

www.nigelslater.com
Twitter @realnigelslater
www.4thestate.com

# A few words of introduction

I cook. I have done so pretty much every day of my life since I was a teenager. Nothing flash or showstopping, just straightforward, everyday stuff. The kind of food you might like to come home to after a busy day. A few weekend recipes, some cakes and baking for fun, the odd pot of preserves or a feast for a celebration. But generally, just simple, understated food, something to be shared rather than looked at in wonder and awe.

Sharing recipes. It is what I do. A small thing, but something I have done for a while now. As a cookery writer, I find there is nothing so encouraging as the sight of one of my books, or one of my columns torn from the newspaper, that has quite clearly been used to cook from. A telltale splatter of olive oil, a swoosh of roasting juices, or a starburst of squashed berries on a page suddenly gives a point to what I do. Those splodges, along with kind emails, letters and tweets, give me a reason to continue doing what I have been doing for the past quarter of a century. Sharing ideas, tips, stories, observations. Or, to put it another way, having a conversation with others who like to eat.

That is why, I suppose, each book feels like a chat with another cook, albeit one-sided (though not as one-sided as you might imagine). It is a simple premise. I make something to eat, everyone, including myself, has a good time, so I decide to share the recipe. To pass on that idea, and with it, hopefully, a good time, to others. For twenty years I have shared many of those ideas each week in my column in the *Observer* and in my books. They might also come dressed up a little nowadays, in the form of the television series, but it is still the same basic premise.

## The diaries

For years now I have kept notebooks, with scribbled shopping lists and early drafts of recipes in them. These are not, I hasten to add, a set of exquisitely bound Kitchen Chronicles, but a scruffy hotchpotch, a salmagundi, of anything and everything I need to remember, from shopping lists and baking temperatures to whether it was two or three eggs that went into the cake. The books also contain the endless lists that I have written, almost obsessively, since childhood.

The notes, sometimes carefully annotated, sometimes not, vary from neat essays in longhand in black fountain pen to a series of almost illegible scribbles on any bit of paper that was handy at the time. The notebooks have recently been replaced, unromantically, by notes typed on an iPad. A decision I now rather regret. These notes form the basis of this second volume of *The Kitchen Diaries*. More than a diary, this is a collection of small kitchen celebrations, be it a casual, beer-fuelled supper of warm flatbreads with pieces of grilled lamb scattered with toasted pine kernels and blood-red pomegranate seeds or a quiet moment contemplating a bowl of soup and a loaf of bread. We can either treat food as nothing more than fuel or relish its every quality. We can think of preparing it as something to get done as quickly and effortlessly as possible or as something to find pleasure in, something to enrich our everyday life, to have fun with.

I have always written about the minute details of cookery, the small pleasures that can make it enjoyable and worth our time. (The bigger picture, the science and politics of food, its nutrition, provenance and chemistry, I leave to others who can do it better.) What intrigues me about making something to eat is the intimate details, the small, human moments that make cooking interesting. Whilst I never forget that most cooking is about getting something on the table at the end of a working day, I see no reason why it can't be something to celebrate. The craft of making something with our hands, something for ourselves and others.

Between the pages of this book there are those days, hours and moments spent in the kitchen that I enjoyed enough to make notes about. The dish of quinces baking in the oven on a winter's day; a hastily assembled salad of chicken, fresh peas and their new shoots; a bowl of brilliant-orange sweet potato soup for a frosty evening; a steak tossed with chilli sauce and Chinese greens; little cakes of crab and fresh coriander to eat with a friend, straight from the frying pan. It is also a collection of jottings about kitchen kit, a shout-out to the pieces of equipment that have become old friends: the favourite knife for peeling vegetables, the wooden spatula or spoon that feels more comfortable in the hand than any other. The bits and pieces we gather together over the years for our kitchen tasks that have become a pleasure to use. Their place in my life, like the most comfortable trainers that have seen better days, or the pullover with holes in it that you can't bear to get rid of, is something I felt needed celebrating. These small pieces of equipment are part of my kitchen life.

## The recipes

I am not a chef and never have been. I am a home cook who writes about food. Not even a passionate cook (whatever one of those is), just a quietly enthusiastic and slightly greedy one. But, I like to think, a thoughtful one. Someone who cares about what they feed themselves and others, where the ingredients come from, when and why they are at their best, and how to use them to give everyone, including the cook, the most pleasure. Whilst a bit of cookery is simply magic (some of the food being produced by professional chefs at the moment is extraordinary, exciting and wonderful), most of it is essentially craft, a subject that holds great interest for me. The art of crafting something by hand – a sandwich even – for others to enjoy is something I can always find time for. Making a dish over and over again till it is how you want it, whether a loaf of bread or a pasta supper for friends, gives me a great deal of pleasure. As does making an economical one-off dish from the 'bits in the fridge'.

I'm neither slapdash nor particularly pedantic in the kitchen (I haven't much time for uptight foodies; they seem to have so little fun). Neither am I someone who tries to dictate how something should be done, and I am never happier than when a reader simply uses my recipe as an inspiration for their own. If we follow a recipe word for word we don't really learn anything, we just end up with a finished dish. Fine, if that's all you want. Does it really matter how you get somewhere? I don't think it does. Short cuts are fine, rule breaking is fine. What matters is that the food we end up with is lick-the-plate delicious.

I have never held the idea that a recipe should merely be a set of instructions (if that is what you want, there is plenty of it out there). I want more. The cookbooks dearest to me are those where the author has been more generous, adding notes and observations from their own kitchen. I like more than just an author's fingerprint on a recipe.

What can be of particular value is when a previous reader's notes come alongside those of the author. In a secondhand bookshop opposite Kew Gardens, I once came across a baking book by a well-known cookery writer. There were notes pencilled in the margin, alterations and occasional exclamation marks. A chocolate cake got three stars, the author's 'Moist Fruit Cake' had the terse note, 'No it isn't', scribbled across it.

Encouraging as it is when I find a well-used copy of one of my books in the kitchen, I am just as happy when readers tell me my book spends as much time on the bedside table. ('There are three of us in this marriage, Nigel,' is a sentiment I have heard more than once.) A good cookbook should be a good read, too. And that is what I hope this book will be to you. Recipes, yes, but also a collection of notes, suggestions and tips (though never, ever instructions or diktats) that I would like to pass on to others. All I want to do is share a good time through the medium of a recipe.

Let us never forget that we are only making something to eat. And yet, it can be so much more than that too. So very much more.

## A note on the chronology

The first volume of *The Kitchen Diaries* was a chronological record of what I had cooked and eaten over the course of a single year. This second volume is slightly different in that it is compiled from a collection of my notes taken over several years, so a piece dated June 3 or November 5 could be from one of two or even three years.

The specific dates are relevant because they give a clear and essential link between what I cook and the seasons, a way of eating that has long been dear to my heart, but also because of the structure they bring to the disparate and somewhat chaotic form in which the jottings in my kitchen diaries tend to appear.

January

## A humble loaf and a soup of roots

The mistletoe – magical, pagan, sacred to Norsemen and the Druids – is still hanging over the low doorway to the kitchen. Part of the bough I dragged back from the market the Sunday before Christmas, my hands numb from the cold. Its leaves are dull now, the last few golden-white berries scattered over the stone floor. Like the holly in the hearth, its presence was a peace offering to the new kitchen that still awaits its work surface, cupboards, sink, taps.

There is an English mistletoe fair at the market in Tenbury Wells each Saturday throughout December. Vast, cloud-like bunches are cut from local cider-apple orchards and sold along with holly and skeins of ivy. Mine came from an oak tree in Hereford, though nowadays much of the folklore-laden evergreen arrives by less-than-romantic truck from northern France. It is only the mistletoe grown on oak that is imbued with magical powers.

Empty glasses are scattered around the room, perched on shelves and window ledges from where we toasted the new, albeit unfinished kitchen. And there is just enough Champagne left in a bottle in the fridge for me to celebrate, in secret, the first morning of the New Year.

This January 1st is no different from all the others, in that I will make soup and a loaf in what is now an annual ritual. Kneading is a good way to start the year. Tactile, peaceful, creative, there is something grounding about baking a loaf on New Year's Day. We have baked bread since the New Stone Age.

There has been a decade of New Year's loaves in this house: a simple white bun, its surface softened with a bloom of flour; a dimpled foccacia that left our fingers damp with olive oil; a less than successful baguette, as thin as a wand; a brown, seeded loaf we ate for days like fruit cake; a flat-bread; a crispbread; and once a craggy cottage loaf, its top slid to one side like a drunk in a top hat. I forget the others.

This year's bread is the simplest of them all, a single, hand-worked loaf of strong white flour and spelt – the ancient cousin of wheat that is currently enjoying a renaissance. (This is less considered than it sounds: they are simply the flours I happen to have left in the cupboard after making mince pies.) Modern spelt is a hybrid of the emmer wheat and goat grass grown since the Iron Age, and has found favour with those who consider modern, commercial wheat heavy on the gut. I like it for the faintly nutty quality it brings to the party.

Making a loaf is cooking at its most basic – a bag of flour and a pinch of salt, some warm water and something to make it rise (baking powder, yeast, a home-made leaven). Yet there is more to it than that. There is something therapeutic about kneading live, warm dough. We do it in order to make the dough softer and more elastic, but the feel of dough in the hand makes you consider yourself a craftsman of some sort, which of course you are. I often knead my bread dough every twenty minutes or so, rather than the customary twice. Each kneading only lasts for about a minute. I do it gently too, without bumping or slapping. I am not sure any good can come from treating our food like a punch-bag.

I will attempt to achieve the yeasty sourness I want by using a glass of cider in place of some of the usual water and will get the crust crisp by punching the oven up to almost its highest setting. I want a crackling crust that shatters over the table when you break it, and a soft wholemeal crumb within. A good plain loaf that smells slightly sour and faintly lactic, yeasty, with a subtle fruitiness to it – a quiet and humble loaf with which to start a new year.

# A cider loaf

Makes one medium-sized round loaf that will keep for two days and is still good for toast after four.

| | |
|---|---|
| wholemeal spelt flour: 250g | honey: a teaspoon |
| strong white bread flour: 250g | fresh yeast: 35g |
| sea salt: a lightly heaped teaspoon | dry cider: 250ml |
| whole milk: 150ml | |

Warm a large, wide mixing bowl (I pour in water from the kettle or hot tap, leave for a minute, then drain and dry). Weigh the flours into the bowl – there is no point in sifting – then stir in the salt. Warm the milk in a small saucepan. It should be no hotter than your little finger can stand. Stir in the honey until it dissolves. Cream the yeast with a teaspoon in a small bowl, slowly pouring in the warm milk and honey. When it is smooth and latte coloured, pour it on to the flours together with the cider and mix thoroughly. I use my hands, though the mixture can be sticky at this point, but a wooden spoon will work too. When the dough has formed a rough ball, tip it out on to a lightly oiled or floured surface. Knead gently for one minute by firmly but tenderly pushing and stretching the dough with the heel of your hand, turning it round and repeating. Lightly flour the bowl you mixed the dough in and place the kneaded dough in it. Cover with a clean, preferably warm cloth and leave in a warm, draught-free place for an hour. Close proximity to a radiator will do, though not actually on it, as will the back of an Aga, a shelf in the airing cupboard or indeed anywhere the yeast can work.

Remove the dough, scraping off any that has stuck to the bowl, and knead lightly for one minute. Return to the bowl, cover and replace in the warm for twenty-five to thirty minutes, until the dough has risen once again.

Set the oven at 240°C/Gas 9. Knead the dough once more, this time forming it into a ball, then place it on a floured baking sheet and dust it generously with flour. Cover with a cloth and keep warm for a further fifteen to twenty minutes.

Put the dough in the oven and bake for twenty-five minutes. If it is nut-brown and crisp, remove it from the oven, turn it upside down and tap the bottom. Does it sound hollow, like banging a drum? Then it is cooked. Cool on a wire rack.

# A soup of bacon and celeriac

Celeriac has long been part of the European kitchen, most notably in celeriac remoulade – a classic accompaniment to thinly sliced meats (a few slivers of air-dried ham, a couple of gherkins and a mound of mustardy remoulade is often a winter lunch in our house). The knobbly, ivory root has taken longer to find friends in this country, and we still have no classic British recipe that exploits its clean, mineral qualities. I use it for cold-weather soups, setting it up with bacon, mustard and either thyme or rosemary. The result is deceptively creamy.

medium onions: 2
butter: a thick slice, about 25g
smoked bacon: 120g
celeriac: 800g (1 large root)
thyme: the leaves from 3 small
   sprigs

chicken or vegetable stock: 500ml
water: 1 litre
grain mustard: 4 teaspoons
parsley: a small bunch

Peel the onions and roughly chop them. Melt the butter in a large, heavy-based saucepan and add the onions. Let them cook for ten to fifteen minutes or so, till translucent. As they cook, cut the bacon into short strips or dice and add them to the pan. Leave over a moderate heat, stirring occasionally, till the bacon fat is pale gold and the onions are soft.

While the onions and bacon are cooking, peel and coarsely grate the celeriac. Stir it into the onions, add the thyme leaves and a little salt, then pour in the stock and water. Bring to the boil, lower the heat and cover with a lid. Leave to simmer for thirty minutes, then stir in the mustard. Chop the parsley and add it to the soup with a seasoning of salt and black pepper. Simmer for five minutes, then remove from the heat.

Remove half the soup and blitz in a blender or food processor till almost smooth. You may need to do this in several batches, so as not to overfill the blender jug. Return the liquidised soup to the remaining soup in the saucepan. You will probably find the result is creamy enough, but if you wish to add some cream, then this is the point at which to do it. Check the seasoning and serve.

Enough for 6

# A bunch of parsley

Few herbs have much to offer in winter, save bay. Even that is more aromatic when it is dried. They need the heat of the sun to concentrate the aromatic oils that lurk in their leaves and, sometimes, their stems. Parsley, though, has plenty of flavour even in the dead of winter, unless it has frozen in the ground. Parsley heals (John Gerard, the sixteenth-century herbalist, used it to quell stomach complaints) and has a high vitamin C content. Where basil stirs the senses, parsley brings us back to earth.

There is much talk about parsley stems and where they are useful. I don't mind them in a leaf salad if they are fine and young, no thicker than a needle, but I don't include them in 'chopped parsley', rough or otherwise. The stem occasionally carries an inherent bitterness and can be string-like too. Fastidiously stripping the leaves from their stems is something worth doing.

The stalks add a pleasing mineral quality to stock and soup (they possess a long tap root, like horseradish, that can stretch a foot or more into the earth) but you might prefer to add them towards the end of cooking, otherwise they will introduce a cabbagy note. Twenty minutes is time enough.

Wasted in its usual role as a garnish, if not downright pointless, this biennial, slow-germinating herb prefers rich soil, ideally slightly alkaline. Liking a little shade and winter shelter, it does well in my dampest bed, under the medlar tree. You can grow it from seed if you have the patience. I 'rescue' large pots of it from the supermarket and plant it in the garden just as others rescue battery hens.

There is little of interest in the cupboards and the fridge is as bare as I have seen it. But there is a granite-like lump of Parmesan in an airtight box in the fridge, a packet of rice in the cupboard and therefore the possibility of risotto. Parsley makes a surprisingly luxurious addition to rice as long as you are generous with the butter and cheese.

# A parsley risotto with Parmesan crisps

Timing wise, you can manage to give the risotto its last ladle of stock, then start on the crisps. They will stay warm and crisp(ish) for long enough.

flat-leaf parsley: a good 50g
hot stock (chicken, turkey, vegetable at a push): a litre
a shallot or very small onion
butter: a thick slice
Arborio rice: 300g
a small glass of white wine or vermouth

*To finish:*
butter and grated Parmesan

*For the Parmesan crisps:*
finely grated Parmesan: 4 heaped tablespoons

Prepare the parsley. Pull the leaves from their stems, crack the stems with the back of a knife – their mineral scent is worth inhaling – then put them in a pan with the stock and bring to the boil. As the stock boils, turn the heat down to a low simmer. Finely chop the parsley leaves.

Peel and very finely chop the shallot and let it cook in the butter in a saucepan, without taking on any colour. Add the rice, turn the grains briefly in the butter till glossy, then pour in the wine and let it cook for a minute or two. Add a ladle of the stock. Stirring almost constantly, add another ladle of stock and continue to stir until the rice has soaked it all up. Now add the remaining stock, a ladle at a time, stirring pretty much all the time till the rice has soaked up the stock, the grains are plump and the texture creamy.

Stir in the chopped parsley, a thick slice of butter and a couple of handfuls of grated Parmesan. Season carefully.

For the Parmesan crisps, simply put heaped tablespoons of the grated Parmesan into a warm, non-stick frying pan. Press the cheese down flat with a palette knife and leave to melt. As soon as it has melted, turn once and continue cooking for a minute or so. Lift off with the palette knife and cool briefly. They will probably crisp up in seconds. Place on top of the risotto and serve.

Enough for 4

# A crisp salad for a winter's day

There are some pears and cheese left from Christmas, a couple of heads of crisp, hardy salad leaves still in fine fettle, and a plastic box of assorted sprouted seeds in the fridge. I put them together almost in desperation, yet what results is a salad that is both refreshing and uplifting, clean tasting and bright.

## A salad of pears and cheese with sprouted seeds

Crisp, mild, light and fresh, this is the antidote to the big-flavoured salad. I prefer to use hard, glassy-fleshed pears straight from the fridge for this, rather than the usual ripe ones. Any sprouted seeds can be used, such as radish seeds, sunflower or mung beans. The easy-to-find bags of mixed sprouts are good here, too. The cheese is up to you. Something with a deep, fruity flavour is probably best, though I have used firm goat's cheeses on occasion too. Rather than slicing it thickly, I remove shavings from the cheese with a vegetable peeler. A sort of contemporary ploughman's lunch.

crisp pears: 2
bitter leaves such as frisée or
    trevise: 4 handfuls
firm, fruity cheese such as
    Berkswell: 150g
assorted sprouts (radish, alfalfa,
    sunflower, amaranth, etc.):
    a couple of handfuls

*For the dressing:*
natural yoghurt: 150ml
olive oil: 2 tablespoons
herbs, such as chervil, parsley,
    chives: a handful

Put the yoghurt into a bowl and whisk in the olive oil and a little salt and black pepper. Chop the herbs and stir them into the yoghurt.

Halve the pears, remove the cores and slice the pears thinly, then add them to the herb and yoghurt dressing.

Put the salad leaves in a serving dish. Pile the pears and their dressing on top. Using a vegetable peeler, shave off small, thin slices of the cheese and scatter them over the salad with the assorted sprouted seeds.

Enough for 2

## Twelfth Night

The day that precedes Twelfth Night is often the darkest in my calendar. The sadness of taking down The Tree, packing up the mercury glass decorations in tissue and cardboard and rolling up the strings of tiny lights has long made my heart sink. Today I descend further than usual.

The rain is torrential and continuous. I clean the bedroom cupboards, make neat piles of books and untidy ones of clothes ready for the charity shop and make a list of major and minor jobs to do in the house over the next few months.

The local council collects discarded Christmas trees and recycles them for compost. I keep mine at home, cutting every branch from the main stem with secateurs and packing them into sacks. Over the next few weeks, the needles will fall and end their days around the blueberries and cloudberries in the garden. There is much that appeals about this annual cycle of the tree going back into the earth.

You would think that this day of darkness would be predictable enough for me to organise something to lift the spirits – dinner with friends or a day away from home. But the consequences of evergreens left in the house after Twelfth Night is too great a risk, even though this superstition is quite recent. So a day of dark spirits it is.

## Epiphany

After yesterday's darkness and self-indulgence, I open the kitchen door to find the garden refreshed after the rain. The air is suddenly sweet and clean, you can smell the soil, and the ivy and yew are shining bright. The dead leaves are blown away, the sky clear and white. There is a new energy and I want to cook again.

Today is an important day for those who grow their vegetables bio-dynamically, when the Three Kings preparation – a stir-up containing gold, frankincense and myrrh – is ground for an hour, then made into a paste with rain or pond water and offered to the land. Jane Scotter at Fern Verrow, the

Herefordshire farmer from whom I buy the vegetables I cannot grow for myself (for which read most), says it smells 'like a fine fruity Christmas cake'. 'We do this to invite elemental life forces to help and guide us for the coming growing season. We ask for good things to happen and give the preparation as an offering to the earth and to give thanks for what the universe provides. It is a lovely thing to do and a chance to walk around the farm on a route not usually taken, holding thoughts of thanks and wishes to the farm on a spiritual level.'

Hippy-dippy hocus-pocus it may sound, but I have far less of a problem believing in this than I do many of the religious ceremonies practised by millions. Actually, much less so.

My energy and curiosity may be renewed but the larder isn't. There is probably less food in the house than there has ever been. I trudge out to buy a few chicken pieces and a bag of winter greens to make a soup with the spices and noodles I have in the cupboard. What ends up as dinner is clear, bright and life-enhancing. It has vitality (that's the greens), warmth (ginger, cinnamon) and it is economical and sustaining too. I suddenly feel ready for anything the New Year might throw at me.

## Chicken noodle broth

chicken pieces and wings: 400g
black peppercorns: 8
star anise: 2
half a cinnamon stick
palm sugar: a scant teaspoon

fresh ginger: a small lump
fine, rice noodles: 200g
greens: about 400g
Thai or Vietnamese basil: a small
 handful

Make the chicken broth: put the chicken pieces and wings in a deep pan with the whole peppercorns, star anise, cinnamon stick and palm sugar. Peel the ginger, cut it into coins and add to the pan. Pour in a litre of water and bring to the boil. Turn down the heat and leave to simmer, at a gentle bubble, for twenty-five minutes. Remove from the heat and set aside.

Cook the noodles according to the instructions on the packet, then drain and set aside. Trim, wash and lightly steam the greens, then refresh under cold running water.

Divide the hot broth between four bowls, add the noodles and greens and finish with the basil.

Enough for 4

## An old-fashioned ham, a new sauce

We have never been what you might call a 'close' family. A mother and father dead by the time I reached my late teens; a brother who emigrated; an uncle distanced by his obsession with religion. The family member I was closest to was a mischievous, twinkly-eyed aunt whose diet consisted solely of Cup-a-Soup, Bailey's Irish Cream and a regular swig of Benylin. She lived to be a hundred, which puts the healthy-eating lobby firmly in its place.

When I was a child, she would take me to see my grandmother, a tiny, bent woman (I have inherited her shoulders), whose curtains were permanently drawn. My grandmother's kitchen always had a pot on the stove and condensation running down the windows. The room was dark and smelled of boiling gammon and the smoke from the coal fire in the parlour. Yet despite the suggestion of food on its way, the scene was less than welcoming. No jolly granny with a laden tea table here, just a tired old lady, exhausted from a hard life spent bringing up five children on her own.

The smell of a ham puttering away in my own kitchen still reminds me of her – I suspect it always will – but now comes with a welcome. Thinly cut ham, warm from its cooking liquor, is a dish I too bring out to feed the hordes. Reasonably priced, presented on a large, oval plate with a jug of bright-green sauce, it seems to go a long way. A piece weighing just over a kilo will feed six, with leftovers for a winter salad the following day.

Parsley sauce is the old-school accompaniment to a dish of warm ham, but far from the only one. This week I put a bag of knobbly Jerusalem artichokes to good use, serving them roasted as a side dish to the ham and to add interest to the accompanying parsley sauce. Artichokes and parsley have an affinity with pork and with each other – I like to add bacon and the chopped herb to the roasted tubers, and snippets of crisp smoked streaky often find their way on to the surface of a bowl of parsley-freckled artichoke soup.

Any large lump of ham will do for slow cooking in water (I sometimes use apple juice). A 'hand' of pork, which comes from the top of the front legs and is what the French call *jambonneau*, is a sound cut for those who want to cook theirs on the bone. A piece of rolled and tied leg is easier to carve for a large number. A cut cooked on the bone shouldn't give any trouble after an hour and a half on the stove. The meat should fall away with just a tug from a fork.

This is an unapologetically old-fashioned dish and the best accompaniments are those of a gentle nature: a quiet, cosseting sauce, some floury steamed potatoes and possibly the inclusion of some mild mustard, either in the sauce or on the edge of the plate. The recipe can be energised a bit in summer, when it will benefit from a bright-green, olive-oil- and herb-based sauce. But on a day as bone chilling as this, it needs an accompaniment as comforting as a goose-down duvet. We passed round a plate of apples and a lump of milky Cotherstone afterwards.

## Ham with artichoke and parsley sauce

Some cooks like to soak their ham before cooking – a precaution against a salty ham. Overly salted hams seem to be a thing of the past, so I don't bother. It is worth doing if you are unsure of your ham. I'm not convinced the sauce needs any cream but, should you wish to soften it further, 3 tablespoons of double cream will be enough. Serve with the roast artichokes below and large chunks of steamed potato.

a piece of boiling ham weighing
   about 1.5kg
onions: 2
bay leaves: 2
thyme: 4 short sprigs
black peppercorns: 15 or so
parsley stalks: 6–8

*For the sauce:*
Jerusalem artichokes: 250g
butter: a thin slice, about 20g
the onions from the ham liquor
parsley: a small bunch, about 15g
grain mustard: a tablespoon
a squeeze of lemon juice

Put the ham in a very large pot. Peel and halve the onions, then tuck them around the meat with the bay leaves, thyme sprigs and peppercorns (reserve the parsley stalks for adding later). Pour in enough water just to cover the meat – a good 2 litres. Bring to the boil, skim off the froth that rises to the surface, then leave to boil for a few minutes before turning down the heat to a simmer. Keep the liquid just below the boil (at a gentle simmer), partially covered with a lid, for an hour. Add the parsley stalks, then let it cook for a further half hour.

About half an hour or so before you are due to serve the ham, make the sauce (timing is not crucial here; both ham and sauce can keep warm without harm). Scrub and chop the artichokes. Warm the butter in a medium saucepan. Remove the onions from the ham pot with a draining

spoon and put them into the butter with the artichokes. Let the artichokes cook for three or four minutes, then pour in 750ml water (you could add some of the ham cooking water if you wish, but no more than a third) and bring to the boil. Add a little salt, then turn the heat down and continue to let the artichokes simmer enthusiastically for twenty minutes or until they are on the verge of falling apart.

Roughly chop the parsley and add just over half of it to the artichokes, holding back the rest for later. Grind in a little black pepper. Simmer for five minutes or so, then remove from the heat. Whiz the sauce in a blender (never more than half filling it) till smooth and pale green. Check the seasoning, adding salt, pepper, the mustard, the reserved chopped parsley and a squeeze of lemon juice, if you wish (if you are adding cream, then you can add it now). Set aside till needed. It will take just a few minutes to reheat.

Remove the ham from its cooking liquor. Slice thinly and serve with the sauce and the roast artichokes below.

Enough for 6


## Roast artichokes

You only need a couple of artichokes each. Trust me.

| | |
|---|---|
| Jerusalem artichokes: 12 (about 800g) | olive oil the juice of half a lemon |

About an hour before the ham is due to be ready, set the oven at 180°C/Gas 4. Scrub the artichokes, slice them in half lengthways and put them in a baking dish. Pour over about 4 tablespoons of olive oil – just enough to moisten them – squeeze over the lemon, then grind over a little salt and black pepper. Toss gently and settle the artichokes cut-side down. Place in the preheated oven and bake for fifty minutes or until the outsides of the artichokes are golden and the insides meltingly soft.

# Juniper – a cool spice for an arctic day

I consider leftovers as treasure, morsels of frugal goodness on which we can snack or feast, depending on the quantity. A few nuggets of leg meat from Sunday's roast chicken are likely to be wolfed while standing at the fridge, but a decent bowlful of meat torn from the carcass could mean a filling for a pie (with onions, carrots, tarragon and cream). Today there is a thick wodge of leftover ham, its fat as white as the snow on the hedges outside, still sitting on its carving plate. A little dry round the edges from where I forgot to seal it in kitchen film, it is nevertheless going to be a base for tonight's supper. On a warmer day, I might have eaten it sliced with a mound of crimson-fruited chutney and a bottle of beer, but the temperature is well below freezing and cold cuts and pickles will not hit the spot.

I am probably alone in holding juniper as one of my favourite spices. Its clean, citrus 'n' tobacco scent is both warming and refreshing. Where cumin, cinnamon and nutmeg offer us reassuring earthiness, juniper brings an arctic freshness and tantalising astringency. Growing on coniferous bushes and trees throughout the northern hemisphere and beyond, the berries, midnight blue when fresh, dry to an inky black. I delighted in finding them growing in Scotland amongst the heather. In a stoppered jar in a dark place, they keep their magic longer than almost any other spice.

The gin bottle aside, the berries are best known for their appearance in the fermented cabbage dish, sauerkraut (though I first met them in a dark, glossy sauce for pork chops). Their ability to slice through richness has led them to a life of pork recipes, from Swedish meatballs to pâté. I sometimes add them to a coarse, fat-speckled terrine for Christmas, dropping them into the mixture instead of the dusty-tasting mace. But their knife-edge quality makes them worth using with oily fish too, as in a marinade for fillets of mackerel (with sliced onions, cider vinegar, salt and dill) and a dry cure for sides of salmon (sea salt, dill and finely grated lemon zest).

Juniper berries are best used lightly squashed rather than finely ground. Crush them too much and they will bite rather than merely bark. Something you learn the hard way. A firm pounding with a pestle or the end of a rolling pin is all they need to release their oil. Their affinity with rich flesh is not confined to fat pork and oily fish. The berries have long been used to season game birds, especially towards the end of the season, when pigeon and partridge toughen and are brought to tenderness in a stew.

This (freezing) evening, as I crush the coal-black beads with the round end of a pestle, the piercing citrus notes come off the stone in cold, Nordic waves. They will invigorate my leftover ham, ripped into thick shards and tossed with onions and shredded white cabbage. Seasoned with sharp apples, brown sugar, cloves and white vinegar, my quick ham and cabbage fry up has its roots in the altogether more sophisticated sauerkraut.

## A ham and cabbage fry up

A bottle of very cold beer would be appropriate here, if not downright compulsory.

butter: 30g
an onion
cloves: 4
juniper berries: 15
a large, sharp apple: about 250g
white wine vinegar: 2 tablespoons

demerara sugar: a tablespoon
a hard, white cabbage: about 800g
leftover cooked ham: 250g
balsamic vinegar: a tablespoon
parsley: a small handful, roughly
    chopped

Melt the butter in a large, heavy-based pan over a low to moderate heat. Peel the onion and thinly slice into rounds, then add it to the butter. Throw in the cloves and the lightly crushed juniper berries (squash them flat with the side of a kitchen knife or in a pestle and mortar) and cover with a lid. Leave to cook, still over a low to moderate heat, with the occasional stir, for seven to ten minutes. The onion should be soft and lightly coloured.

Halve, core and thickly slice the apple. There is no need to peel it. Add it to the pan, then pour in the white wine vinegar and the sugar. Season with salt and pepper.

Shred the cabbage, not too finely, add it to the pan and mix lightly with the other ingredients. Cover with a tight lid and leave to soften over a lowish heat for about twenty minutes. The occasional stir will stop it sticking.

Tear or chop the ham into short, thick pieces. They are more satisfying if left large and uneven. Fold them into the cabbage, continue cooking for five minutes, then pour in the balsamic vinegar and toss in the chopped parsley. Pile into a warm dish and serve.

Enough for 2

# The cook's knife

There have been surprisingly few kitchen knives in my life. One, a thin, flexible filleting knife, has been with me since my cookery-school days; another from that era, its thin tang having come loose from the handle, is now used to gouge grass from between the garden paving stones. There is a fearsome carving blade from Sheffield, long the home of British knife making; a medium-sized, much-used Japanese knife that I regard as the perfect size and weight for me; and a tiny paring knife with a pale wooden handle that I hope stays with me to the grave.

The most used blade in my kitchen belongs to a heavy, 20cm cook's knife. Thicker than is currently fashionable, its blade is made from carbon steel rather than the more usual stainless, which immediately marks me out as something of an old-fashioned cook. So be it. The blade, a mixture of iron and carbon, is the dull grey of a pencil lead, and heavily stained from years of lemon juice and vinegar. Its biggest sin is its habit of leaving an unpleasant grey streak on apples or tomatoes I have sliced with it, and occasionally on lemons too, but that, and the need to dry it thoroughly to prevent it rusting, is a small price to pay for a tool that is so 'right' it actually feels part of my body.

Picking up the right knife is like putting on a much-loved pullover. It may well have seen better days but the odd hole only seems to add to its qualities – like the wrinkles on a close friend. Price has little to do with it. My trusty vegetable peeler cost less than a loaf of bread and has dealt with a decade of potatoes and parsnips. And even if an expensive top-of-the-range Japanese knife is a pleasure to hold in the hand, it may not work any better for you than something as cheap as chips from the local ironmonger's.

A strong, long-bladed implement is the only way to gain entry to tough-skinned squashes such as the winter pumpkins, though I have been known to take a garden axe to the odd Crown Prince variety. You need a strong blade to get through celeriac too, and sometimes the larger, end-of-season swede. A serrated bread knife might just stand in its stead, but it is rarely man enough for the job.

I brought the 20cm cook's knife back from Japan a while ago. It is the tool I use for slicing vegetables, chopping herbs, dicing meat. I know every nick and stain on its blade. It seems inappropriate to say that the right knife is like a comfort blanket, you feel safe with it in your hand, but that is how it is.

I do, though, find it mildly disturbing to find comfort in something with which you could so easily kill someone.

## Hot, sweet baked pumpkin

Initially, this was a side dish to go with a flash-fried steak. But its sticky, sweet-sharp qualities led me to serve it as a dish in its own right. In which case there is a need for a dish of steamed brown rice to go with it. This is a genuinely interesting way to combat the sugary, monotonous note of the pumpkin. The colours are ravishing.

pumpkin or butternut squash, 1.5 kg (unpeeled weight)
butter: 50g

*For the dressing:*
caster sugar: 4 tablespoons
water: 200ml

ginger: a thumb-sized lump
large, medium-hot red chilli: 1
limes: 2
fish sauce: 2 capfuls
coriander: a small bunch, finely chopped

Set the oven at 200°C/Gas 6. Peel the pumpkin, discard the seeds and fibres and cut the flesh into small pieces about 3cm in diameter. Put them in a roasting tin with the butter and bake for about an hour, turning them occasionally, till soft enough to take the point of a knife. They should be completely tender.

Put the sugar and water in a shallow pan and bring to the boil. Turn the heat down and leave to simmer enthusiastically till the liquid has reduced by about half. Meanwhile, peel and roughly chop the ginger and put it in a food processor. Halve the chilli lengthways and chop roughly, removing the seeds if you wish for a less spicy seasoning (I tend to leave them in for this recipe). Add the chilli to the ginger, then grate in the zest of the limes. Squeeze in the juice from the limes, then process everything to a coarse paste, pushing the mixture down the sides of the bowl from time to time with a spatula.

Stir the spice mixture into the sugar syrup and continue simmering for a minute. Add the fish sauce and coriander and remove from the heat.

When the pumpkin is fully tender, spoon most of the chilli sauce over it, toss gently to coat each piece, then return to the oven for five to ten minutes. Toss with the remaining dressing and serve.

Enough for 6 as a side dish

## A slow-cooked bean hotpot. And a quick version

A dry day, warm enough to garden without a jacket. The earth, dark and moist from the week's rain, crumbles in textbook fashion under the garden fork. There is still a scattering of bronze leaves and here and there the odd medlar that melts in your hand, leaving behind the ghost of wine dregs in a glass. Anyone with a scrap of land will value January days like these for getting the earth turned, roses pruned and stray leaves collected.

I spend a couple of hours tugging out the last of the borlotti beans, their dried stems still twisted around the hazel poles. This should have been done in December and both the bean stems and precious hazel supports snap like icicles. The odd purple-skinned potato and (useless) radish come to the surface as I fork the soil. Before I go in, I move a patch of soggy brown leaves from under the medlar tree and find three rhubarb tips poking teasingly through the soil. Their carmine rudeness against the chocolate-brown soil at first startles, then delights.

Technology excites me (be it Japanese Shinkansen trains or the next thing that Apple throws our way) but so does the celebration of slow, time-honoured rituals. The way of living that hasn't changed in centuries. Houses built or restored using traditional methods, treading grapes to make wine (yes, a tiny number of vineyards still do it) and anything hand made. Last night I soaked beans for a hotpot. I could have opened a can of course, and sometimes I do, but the idea of doing something just as it has been done for thousands of years appeals to me. So I soak them, a mixture of small white haricot and black-eyed beans. You can soak different varieties of bean together if they are the sort that enjoy the same cooking time (long, oval flageolet take less than the rounder beans). Covering the beans with an equal volume of water is usually enough. But they should be drained and rinsed the following day. This will effectively reduce the oligosaccharides, those complex, indigestible sugars that make us fart. More importantly, it cuts down the cooking time.

# A crisp-crusted hotpot of aubergines and beans

If you haven't soaked beans the night before, or simply can't be bothered, then use canned haricot or black-eyed beans for this. You will need three 400g cans, drained and rinsed.

dried haricot or black-eyed beans:
  450g
bay leaves: 2
aubergines: 2 (about 500g in total)
olive oil
onions: 2
garlic: 3 cloves
rosemary: 3 stems
dried oregano: 1 tablespoon
chopped tomatoes: two 400g cans

*For the crust:*
white bread, not too crusty: 125g
a clove of garlic, peeled and
  crushed
grated Parmesan: 30g
a lemon
rosemary: 2 or 3 sprigs
dried oregano: 1 teaspoon
olive oil: 3 tablespoons

Put the beans into a deep bowl, cover with cold water and leave overnight. In the morning, drain off any remaining water, rinse the beans, then tip them into a large saucepan and cover with at least 2 litres of water. Bring to the boil, then skim off the froth that rises to the surface. Lower the heat to a jolly simmer, add the bay leaves and partially cover the pan with a lid. Leave the beans to cook for forty-five minutes, till almost tender. They should give a little when squeezed between finger and thumb. Drain the beans and set aside.

Cut the aubergines in half lengthways, then cut each half into about 8 thick slices. Warm 4 tablespoons of olive oil in a casserole. Fry the aubergines, in two or three batches, till pale gold on both sides and soft in the middle, then remove and drain on kitchen paper. Add more oil to the pan and lower the heat as necessary for each batch. The pieces of aubergine must be soft and tender.

Set the oven at 200°C/Gas 6. Peel and roughly chop the onions. Add to the empty casserole with a tablespoon or two of olive oil and leave over a moderate heat till they have softened. While the onions are cooking, peel and thinly slice the garlic and finely chop the needles from the rosemary stems. Add to the onions with the oregano and leave to soften. The onions shouldn't colour.

Add the tomatoes to the onions and garlic and bring to the boil, then stir in the drained beans and the aubergines. Fill an empty tomato can with water and pour it into the pan. Once the mixture has returned to the boil, turn off the heat. Cover the pan, transfer to the oven and bake for 45 minutes.

Make the crust by reducing the bread to coarse crumbs in a food processor. Add the garlic and the Parmesan cheese, then season with black pepper and a little salt. Finely grate the lemon zest and add it to the crumbs. Remove the rosemary needles from their stems and chop them finely. Stir into the crumbs with the dried oregano. Pour the olive oil into the breadcrumbs and toss gently; you want them to be lightly moist.

Remove the bean dish from the oven and spoon the crumbs on top. Return to the oven, uncovered, and bake for twenty to twenty-five minutes or until the crust is crisp and the colour of a biscuit.

Enough for 4

## JANUARY 18

## Cheating with puff pastry

There are two ways of making a savoury puff pastry crust. I sometimes take a quiet afternoon to blend flour and butter and roll, fold, chill, roll and roll again. With Radio 4 on in the background, making puff or rough puff pastry is as much therapy as cooking. I use the ready-made stuff from the freezer, too. It's a cop out, a cheat, but really, who cares? The brands made with butter have a good flavour, are crisp and light and often, helpfully, come ready rolled into sheets. It means I can have a pie such as tonight's chicken and leek without making my own pastry.

### A hearty pie of chicken and leeks

chicken thighs on the bone: 350g
chicken breasts: 350g
half an onion
peppercorns: 8
a bay leaf
milk, to cover
butter: 30g
smoked streaky bacon: 6 rashers

leeks: 2 medium
plain flour: 3 lightly heaped
   tablespoons
Dijon mustard: 3 teaspoons
puff pastry: a 375g sheet
a little beaten egg and milk
grated Parmesan

Put the chicken pieces into a large saucepan, together with the half onion, peppercorns, bay leaf and enough milk just to cover the chicken. Bring to the boil, then, just when it starts to bubble, lower the heat and leave to simmer, partially covered by a lid, for twenty minutes. Remove the chicken, reserving the milk, and pull the meat from the bones. Cut it into small, plump pieces.

Set the oven at 200°C/Gas 6. Melt the butter in a large saucepan, add the bacon, cut into small pieces, and let it soften without colouring over a moderate to low heat. Slice the leeks into pieces roughly 1cm thick. Wash them very thoroughly, then add them to the bacon and continue cooking for about fifteen minutes, till they are totally soft.

Stir the flour into the leek and bacon, continue cooking for a couple of minutes, then gradually strain in enough of the warm milk to make a thick sauce. Fold in the chicken and check the seasoning, adding the mustard and a generous grinding of salt and pepper.

Roll one half of the pastry out into a rectangle 27cm x 37cm and transfer it to a baking sheet. Spoon the filling on to the pastry, leaving a wide rim all the way round. Brush the rim with beaten egg and milk. Roll out the second piece of pastry to the same size as the base and lower it over the filling. Press and crimp the edges together firmly to seal them. It is worth making certain the edges are tightly sealed, otherwise the filling may leak.

Brush the pastry all over with the beaten egg wash and scatter a handful of grated Parmesan over the surface. Bake for thirty-five minutes or till golden.

Enough for 6

## Poached apples with ginger and anise

Warm apples in a gently spiced syrup are useful as both a breakfast dish and a dessert. Sweet but refreshing, and pleasingly simple, these poached fruits are also good served thoroughly chilled. A nice change from creamy desserts. Odd as it seems, we ate this outside in the snow. The ginger-scented warmth and clarity of the juice encouraged us to eat it standing up in the garden, marvelling at the tall hedges weighed down with snow and the slowly darkening sky.

small to medium dessert apples: 3
the juice of half a lemon
unfiltered apple juice: 400ml
golden caster sugar: 2 tablespoons

star anise: 2
ginger preserved in syrup: 40g
syrup from the ginger jar:
    4 tablespoons

Peel the apples, halve them and remove their cores. Toss gently in the lemon juice. Pour the apple juice into a pan large enough to accommodate the apples, then add the caster sugar, star anise, the ginger, sliced into coins, and the ginger syrup. Bring to the boil, then lower the heat so the liquid simmers gently.

Lower the fruit into the simmering syrup and leave, partially covered with a lid, until they are tender. They are ready when a skewer will glide effortlessly through their flesh – fifteen to twenty minutes or so.

Lift the fruit from the syrup with a draining spoon and place on a serving dish or in smaller individual dishes. Turn up the heat and bring the syrup to the boil. Serve warm, three halves of fruit per person, in little dishes or glasses with some of the apple- and spice-scented syrup spooned over.

Enough for 3

## JANUARY 20

## A golden fruit

A need for something sweet so I walk along London's Edgware Road, with its Lebanese grocer's and pastry shops. On a winter's afternoon, this road north of Marble Arch is where I go to stock up on what we used to call sweetmeats – the tiny, sugary fruits and pastries that mark the end of a meal. Though I should add that they come out with coffee too, mid morning.

Today there are boxes of darkly sticky dates, powdery lokum, the Turkish delight whose chewy translucency comes scented with rose, pistachio and lemon, and crates of fat, gritty figs. Any of these will signify the full stop at the end of dinner as effectively as a slice of pie (though I would rather have the latter, if I'm honest). There are crimson pomegranates too, lemons on the twig, and tangerines sold with their leaves. There are pale and milky walnuts in their shells, sugared almonds and sultanas the colour of Sauternes.

Today I come back with a small box of honey-soaked pistachio pastries, a bag of fudge-textured dates, some thick, snow-white Lebanese yoghurt and a polystyrene tray of lamb chops the size of a baby's fist. They will be grilled and dipped into hummus. Almost absentmindedly, I also pick up a handful of golden, pear-shaped quinces.

Despite its delicate fragrance, the quince is a harsh taskmaster. You need a strong wrist and a good knife to get through its hard flesh, and patience

to see it cook through to tenderness. Your efforts will be rewarded though. Cooked slowly, this rock-hard fruit will be transformed into one of glowing colour and gently honeyed flavour. If you leave one to simmer with sugar and water, it will eventually turn a deep, translucent crimson.

Just two quinces in an apple pie are enough to imbue the entire filling with their scent and flavour. The quince's flesh is considerably drier and more grainy than the apple, and needs additional moisture and time in which to cook. I put them on first, adding the apples only once the quince is showing signs of softness. In *Tender*, I used them in a pickle, a crumble and to sweeten a dish of slow-cooked lamb, but I spent today working them into a pie. Instead of a pastry crust, I have enclosed them in a loose form of crumble, so that the amber fruit shows through.

This tart needs a good hour or more of our time, but is really rather good. Serve it with a jug of cream or a scoop of crème fraîche.

## Quince and apple tart

a lemon  
quinces: 500g  
caster sugar: 2 tablespoons  
maple syrup: 3 tablespoons  
sweet apples: 750g  

*For the top:*  
plain flour: 150g  
butter: 75g  
demerara sugar: 75g  
an egg, lightly beaten  

*For the crust:*  
butter: 100g, at room
    temperature  
caster sugar: 80g  
an egg, lightly beaten  
plain flour: 200g  

Make the pastry crust: dice the butter and put into a food mixer or processor with the sugar. Cream till light and fluffy, then add the egg and mix thoroughly. Spoon in the flour, bring the dough into a ball – it will be quite soft – then place on a generously floured work surface or board. Knead briefly; this will make it easier to work. Roll out the dough to fit a 22cm tart tin with a removable base, pushing it carefully into the corners and up the sides, patching any tears as you go. Refrigerate for twenty minutes.

Put a baking sheet in the oven and set it at 200°C/Gas 6. To make the filling, squeeze the lemon into a mixing bowl. Peel and core the quinces, then chop them into small pieces, tossing them in the lemon juice as you go to stop them browning. Place them in a deep saucepan, add the sugar and maple syrup, cover with a lid and leave over a low heat for fifteen minutes, until tender enough for you to insert a metal skewer into them easily. Check regularly and lower the heat if necessary, particularly towards the end of cooking when the syrup has reduced.

Meanwhile, core and dice the apples – there is no need to peel them. Stir them into the quinces as soon as the quinces are almost tender. Continue cooking, covered, for five to ten minutes or until the apples are just soft. Set aside.

Make the topping: put the flour and butter into a food processor and blitz till they resemble fine breadcrumbs. Alternatively, rub the butter into the flour with your fingers. Add the sugar and the egg and mix briefly to a moist, crumbly texture.

Fill the uncooked tart case with the apple and quince mixture, setting aside any juice, then scatter the crumble topping over. Some of the fruit will show through. Lift on to the hot baking sheet and bake for thirty minutes, till the crust and pastry are crisp and golden. Allow to settle a little before serving with a trickle of the reserved juices and some cream or crème fraîche.

Enough for 6–8

## JANUARY 21

## Browning meat. More quinces

Putting a piece of meat into a shallow layer of sizzling-hot fat, butter, duck fat, dripping or oil will do wonders for its flavour. Whilst it won't actually 'seal in' the juices, as is often suggested, getting the cut surfaces of the meat to brown will enrich both the flavour of the meat and, rather importantly, the juices in the pan. It is worth doing. But here's the rub. The meat must be given time to brown properly, and that means we need to leave it alone. I have lost count of the number of times I have seen meat, particularly beef, moved constantly round with a spoon or spatula. Hard as it is not to tinker, we must leave it alone long enough for the cut surfaces to colour appetisingly, otherwise the action is pointless.

## Quick, mildly spiced beef

rapeseed oil
cubed beef (e.g. chuck steak):
   500g
onions: 2 large
garlic: 3 cloves
ground cumin: 2 teaspoons

ground coriander: 2 teaspoons
garam masala: 1 tablespoon
vegetable or beef stock: 500ml
grain mustard: a tablespoon
double cream: 200ml

Warm a little oil in a heavy, shallow casserole. Season the beef with salt and black pepper, then colour on all sides in the oil, turning only occasionally. Remove from the pan with a draining spoon.

Meanwhile, halve, peel and thinly slice the onions. Peel and thinly slice the garlic. Add the onions and garlic to the pan, letting them soften a little but not brown beyond pale honey colour. Stir in the ground cumin, coriander and garam masala, then continue cooking for five minutes before returning the meat and any juices to the pan. Pour in the stock, bring to the boil and simmer for ten minutes, till the liquid has reduced by half.

Stir in the mustard, pour in the cream and bring to the boil. Check the seasoning and serve.

Enough for 4

## Baked quince with orange and mascarpone ginger crunch

The quince once seemed so impenetrable. Mentions of membrillo and quince liqueur did nothing to invite entry to the rock-hard, yellow fruit that resembled a dumpy papaya. Ten years on, I take a deep casserole from the oven, the five fruits split, their soft, almost fluffy, pink flesh peeping through, and marvel at their beauty. There is orange in there too, vanilla in its sticky pod and a single cinnamon stick. The steam beguiles and amuses with its notes of amber, orange blossom and spice. The quince has come a long way in this kitchen. I guess we all have.

quinces: 4 large
oranges: 3
a cinnamon stick
a vanilla pod

*For the mascarpone ginger crunch:*
ginger biscuits: 75g
mascarpone: 200g

Set the oven at 200°C/Gas 6. Put the quinces in a deep casserole, piercing them here and there with a small knife or skewer as you go.

Halve and juice the oranges and pour into the casserole, add the cinnamon stick and vanilla pod and then cover with a lid. Bake for an hour or so, till the skins have wrinkled and the flesh is tender to the point of a knife.

For the ginger crunch, crush the biscuits, either in a plastic bag with a rolling pin or in a food processor, but not too finely. They should have a mixture of textures from gravel to coarse sand. Fold the biscuits into the mascarpone.

Remove the quinces from the juice, place on small plates and serve with the pan juices and the mascarpone ginger crunch.

Enough for 4


## JANUARY 22

## A potato crust for a fish pie…

I do love a fish pie, with its flaky, undulating pastry crust or deep, furrowed lid of mashed potatoes crisped in the oven. For an everyday fish pie, the sort I might make for a midweek supper, I take a shortcut with the crust, using breadcrumbs and herbs blitzed in the food processor or thin slices of potato. That way I get a crisp lid as a contrast to the softness underneath without having to make and roll pastry. When time is of less importance, at the weekend, say, I use a more traditional crust of butter and flour or potatoes whipped up with parsley and butter to contrast with the deep, creamy, piscine filling.

Which fish I use for a pie will change according to supply, whim and conscience. Fish is rarely a cheap eat, but we can trim the bill a little by choosing the less popular varieties such as ling and whiting and, if it is to our taste, coley (try as I might, I can't find much excitement in a piece of coley). A sustainable alternative to the knee-jerk varieties is crucial and I have had much success with pollack and line-caught haddock. I'm getting used to gurnard too, a bit of an ugly bugger but with a reasonable flavour. A firm-textured fish once used as lobster bait and now appearing on menus everywhere, from Moro to Rick Stein's restaurants in Padstow, the gurnard responded well to being baked with cream and basil. I introduced a potato top, neat slices laid one overlapping the next, a way of padding out a few fish fillets to make them go a bit further. It's a sweet and gentle pie, without the stodge of one crowned with mashed potatoes (good though they can be). Something to serve with steamed purple sprouting broccoli or the salad that follows.

# Gurnard, basil and potato pie

potatoes: 400g
a large onion
olive oil: 2 tablespoons
gurnard or similar white fish:
    4 large fillets (about 450g),
    skinned

basil leaves: 15g
double cream: 250ml
butter

Peel the potatoes, slice them roughly the thickness of a pound coin, bring them to the boil in lightly salted water, then leave to cook at a gentle boil for five or six minutes. Drain and set aside. Set the oven at 200°C/Gas 6.

Peel and finely slice the onion, then let it cook in the oil in a shallow oven-proof pan for five to ten minutes, till it has softened but not coloured. Switch off the heat. Season the fish fillets with salt and black pepper, then place them on top of the onion. Shred the basil leaves and stir them into the cream with a light seasoning of salt. Pour the cream over the fish, then lay the sliced potatoes on top, neatly and slightly overlapping. Season and dot the surface with butter.

Bake for thirty to forty minutes, till the potatoes have lightly browned.

Enough for 2

## …and the beauty of a winter salad

The crisp, winter leaves – trevise, radicchio, in fact all the chicories – have a beauty not present in the lush green leaves of summer. Their wayward curls, like tendrils of squid, the flashes of magenta, rose and blood-red on white as if they have been painted by hand, all lead us to want to use these leaves whole rather than chopped or torn. The shape of the leaves is as much a part of their attraction as their flavour, their dazzling colours only becoming clear and bright in cold weather. Just as importantly, there is a bitterness to the winter leaves that makes them a perfect match for the sweetness of walnuts, mild cheeses (the Gloucesters, the Beaufort family) and bacon.

I find something endearing about the fact that the sweeter leaves are those nearest the heart. The most bitter – and the ones I like the most – are the ones that grow on the outside. The more light they receive, the deeper their pungency. The intensely coloured, rabbit-eared raddichios are especially hand-some on a white plate. The one that melts people's hearts is the Castelfranco variety, with its cream, rough-edged leaves speckled with maroon and pink. It's a rare find, but a showstopper on the plate, perhaps with slices of Russet apple.

I grow several varieties of winter lettuce in pots in the cold frame. They seem to sit there sulking, then take me by surprise by appearing as fist-sized whorls of beautiful, rose-tinted leaves with freckles of deepest burgundy. The cold spurs on their growth, just as it does the snowdrops and narcissi in the garden. There is the curiously waxy claytonia, sometimes known as winter purslane, landcress with its iron-rich flavour, buttery lamb's lettuce, and all of them can be grown outdoors, even when there is frost on the ground. Sow in August and harvest all winter.

The dressings for winter salads are something I tend to introduce a touch of sweetness to, in the form of walnut oil or balsamic vinegar, as a knee-jerk contrast. Occasionally it is worth flying more dangerously and adding other pungent flavours – capers, gherkins, mustard and salty, palate-cleansing cheeses – to the leaves too. The shock of the bitter, the sour and the pungent, together with the crunch of the leaves, makes for refreshing, sense-awakening eating.

## Winter leaves with gherkins and mustard

white chicory, frisée or other
    crisp, bitter winter leaves:
    4 double handfuls
watercress: a large bunch

*For the dressing:*
a large egg yolk
Parmesan: 50g, finely grated
Dijon mustard: a teaspoon
white wine vinegar: a teaspoon
mild olive oil: about 100ml
gherkins: 2 tablespoons, finely
    chopped
capers: a teaspoon, rinsed

To make the dressing, put the egg yolk into a food processor, add the grated Parmesan, mustard and wine vinegar and switch the machine on. Pour in the oil rather slowly, as if you were making mayonnaise. Stop adding it when you have a smooth sauce that is thin enough to fall slowly from a spoon. Stir in the chopped gherkins and rinsed capers. Add no salt.

Rinse and trim the salad leaves, removing any tough stalks from the watercress. Spin or shake dry. Gently toss the leaves in the dressing and pile on to plates.

Enough for 4

# Using up the marzipan

There is some marzipan left over from Christmas. It's the uncoloured sort, a soft shade of buttermilk, which I brought back from a trip to Oslo at the beginning of Advent. Made from ground almonds, sugar and egg moulded into a stiff paste, marzipan is a like-it or loathe-it thing. I like it best coated with bitter chocolate, partly because the coating keeps the almond paste moist but also because of the contrast of crisp chocolate and soft, sweet marzipan. I must admit to a curious soft spot for those slightly stale-tasting marzipan fruits and vegetables from Palermo (carrots, apples, peaches and even cauliflowers) that you can buy at Christmas.

Although marzipan originated in Persia, where it is often flavoured with orange flower water, almost every almond-producing country has its own version. The almond paste is linked to any manner of ceremonies, from the wedding feasts of the Aegean to All Souls' Day – *il giorno dei morti* – in Palermo. But mostly, marzipan, *massepain* (French), *mazpon* (India) or *mazapan* (Philippines), is just as much a part of Christmas as mince pies.

I bought mine in Norway only because I had browsed a little too long in a cake-decorating shop and felt guilty not making a purchase, but it is essential to read the packet. A few versions sold abroad are made with peanuts or cashews instead of almonds. I have yet to taste persipan, the version made from peach kernels. It sounds fun.

The marzipan from Lübeck in Germany is reputed to be the finest, partly because of the high percentage of almonds to sugar. A general rule is that the more gaudy the presentation, the lower the quality is likely to be. The cheaper brands tend to contain sugar syrup and a hefty dose of colouring and flavouring.

I sometimes make my own, combining finely ground almonds with a mixture of icing and caster sugar, egg yolk and a little grated orange zest. It's a pleasing sugar and spice job, something for a frosty or even snowy afternoon.

Whilst in Norway, I came across some shallow, moist almond cakes studded with dark berries that had a little almond paste in them. Once home, I set about tinkering with my classic almond sponge mixture and some frozen blackcurrants and blueberries, but it was only once I added some crumblings of marzipan that my cakes approached those I had eaten rather too many of in Oslo. Recipes like this are trial and error, but I eventually got it to where I wanted it to be: the cake crumb moist and slightly squidgy, the fruit seeping its sharp juice, and here and there sweet nuggets of almond paste.

## Almond, marzipan and berry cakes

My version of the sweet, almond-scented cakes I ate in one of Oslo's most popular new-wave bakeries.

You will need six shallow round cake tins about 10cm in diameter or rectangular baking tins, about 8cm x 10cm.

butter: 180g
caster sugar: 180g
eggs: 2, lightly beaten
plain flour: 80g
ground almonds: 150g

marzipan: 100g
berries (assorted blueberries and currants), fresh or frozen: 200g
icing sugar

Line the cake tins with baking parchment. Set the oven at 180°C/Gas 4.

Using an electric beater, cream the butter and sugar together till pale and fluffy. Gradually beat in the eggs, then slowly introduce the flour and ground almonds. Once they are incorporated, stop the machine immediately.

Break the marzipan into small pieces about 1–2cm in diameter. Stir these into the mixture. Divide it between the baking tins, then scatter the fruit over the top of each. Bake for forty minutes, till lightly firm to the touch. Remove from the oven, dust with icing sugar and leave to cool before serving.

Makes 6

# JANUARY 30

# And using up the marmalade

The opened jars of sweet preserves in the fridge seem to be multiplying. I don't mind, I think of them as treasure. Right now there are blackcurrant, damson and mulberry jams; a pot of lemon curd and another of damson jelly; French apricot jam, some Lebanese rose petal jelly and three different marmalades. Three. One of these jars of orange preserve I proudly made

myself last February from organic, green-tinged Seville oranges, the other two were gifts, finer than my own and with fewer strips of peel. I have the urge to use all three up, scraping out every last amber mouthful with a teaspoon, getting my knuckles sticky in the process, and use the sweet-sharp jelly in an ice cream. The recipe is an experiment, a marriage of shards of bitter chocolate and orange preserve. I end up with beautiful, custard-coloured, soft-scoop ice cream of which I am almost absurdly proud.

Ice cream, when it is home made, has a habit of setting like a brick. Many is the time I have sat, well beyond midnight, chipping off little shards and flakes with a teaspoon. The classical way round this is to add some glucose syrup to the mix, resulting in a soft-scoop texture. Adding marmalade turns out to work much the same magic, only in a way that seems more wholesome. The ice is the most silkily textured I have ever made. The flavours are stunning. If only cooking was always like this.

## Marmalade chocolate chip ice cream

single or whipping cream: 500ml
egg yolks: 4
golden caster sugar: 2 tablespoons

marmalade: 400g
dark chocolate, 100g, roughly chopped

Bring the cream to the boil. Beat the egg yolks and sugar in a heatproof bowl till thick, then pour in the hot cream and stir. Rinse the saucepan and return the custard to it, stirring the mixture over a low heat till it starts to thicken slightly. It won't become really thick. Cool the custard quickly – I do this by plunging the pan into a shallow sink of cold water – stirring constantly, then chill thoroughly.

Stir the marmalade into the chilled custard. Now you can either make the ice cream by hand or use an ice-cream machine. If making it in a machine, pour in the custard and churn according to the manufacturer's instructions. When the ice cream is almost thick enough to transfer to the freezer, fold in the chopped chocolate, churning briefly to mix. Scoop into a plastic, lidded box and freeze till you are ready.

If you are making it by hand, pour the custard and the chopped chocolate into a freezer box and place it in the freezer, removing it and giving it a quick beat with a whisk every hour until it has set.

Enough for 6

February

# FEBRUARY 4

It wasn't, on reflection, the wisest of days to make marmalade. I had pruned the roses, the temperature was a degree or two below freezing, and the skin around my thumbnail had cracked open in the cold. Each drop of bitter orange juice, each squirt of lemon zest sent shots of stinging pain through my thumb. But the Seville orange season is over in the blink of an eye and sometimes you just have to shut up and get on with things.

Marmalade making is about as pleasurable as cooking can get. It isn't something for those whose only reason for cooking is the finished product. If the process of peeling oranges, painstakingly cutting their skin into fine strands and constantly checking their progress on the stove is a chore, then don't do it. There is enough exceptionally good cottage-industry marmalade out there. Go and buy it. Making marmalade is a kitchen job to wallow in, to breathe in every bittersweet spray of zest, enjoy the prickle of the fruit's oils on your skin and fill the house with the scent of orange nectar (or, of course, screech with pain as the bitter juice gets into your wounds).

Each stage, and there are several, carries with it waves of extraordinary pleasure. I say extraordinary because it is not every day you get the chance to fill the house with a lingering smell that starts as bright and clean as orange blossom on a cold winter breeze and ends, a day later, with a house that smells as welcoming as warm honey. There is something heart-warmingly generous about marmalade makers. I can't tell you how many jars I have been given over the years. In my experience they like nothing more than passing their golden pots of happiness on to others.

There must be hundreds of recipes, but it is the method that changes rather than the ratio of ingredients. Some cooks swear by boiling the oranges whole, then chopping them; others cut the fruit into whole slices, others still include the pith in the jam itself, while some nitpickingly remove it. I have met cooks who chuck their boiled peel in the food processor, some who add a lemon or two, and those who introduce a couple of sweet oranges. It probably goes without saying that there is someone out there making it in minutes in the microwave (and surely missing the whole damn point).

The method you choose will depend on how you like your marmalade. Don't probe a marmalade fan on the subject of texture unless you are actually in need of a Mogadon. Some of us like ours soft and syrupy, others prefer a jam that will stand to attention on the spoon. I like my peel in thin,

hair-like strips, while friends insist on juicy chunks. Then there are those who leave the fruit in whole slices or cut it into fat nuggets. In my experience the latter produces the marmalade most likely to fall off your toast while you are engrossed in Nancy Banks-Smith or the 'Today' programme. Lastly, there's the lot who insist on sieving their pith out altogether. And the lovely thing is that each and every one of us is right.

I like my marmalade to shine in the morning sun. A bright, jewel-like mixture with thin strands of peel, quivering, but not so loosely set that it drips down the sleeves of my dressing gown. The point of this golden jam is its bittersweet quality. It's a wake-up call in a jar. That is why we eat it first thing in the morning. The bitter oranges you need are available for a short season in January and February.

I know I am stepping into deep water giving a marmalade recipe, which is partly why it has taken me twenty years to get round to offering you one, but marmalade recipes are very personal things and we marmalade makers are a proud bunch (which is possibly another reason why we give so much of it away). But here it is, a little pot or two of bright, shining happiness, full of bittersweet flavour and stinging thumbs.

## Seville orange marmalade

I made two batches this year. One with organic fruit, the other not. The flavour of the organic one shone most brilliantly and took less time to reach setting point.

Makes enough to fill about 5 or 6 jam jars.

Seville oranges: 1.3kg        golden granulated sugar: 2.6kg
lemons: 2

Using a small, particularly sharp kitchen knife, score four lines down each fruit from top to bottom, as if you were cutting it into quarters. Let the knife cut through the peel without piercing the fruit. Remove the peel, cut each quarter of peel into fine shreds (or thicker slices if you like a chunkier texture) and put into a large bowl. Squeeze in the juice from the peeled oranges and lemons with your hands, chop the pulp and add it, removing the pips. Add 2.5 litres of cold water. Tie the pips in a muslin bag and push into the peel and juice. Set aside in a cold place and leave overnight.

The next day, tip the mixture into a large stainless steel or enamelled pan (or a preserving pan for those lucky enough to have one) and push the muslin bag down under the juice. Bring to the boil, then lower the heat so that the liquid continues to simmer merrily. It is ready when the peel is totally soft and translucent. This can take anything from forty minutes to a good hour and a half, depending purely on how thick you have cut your peel (this time, mine took forty-five minutes).

Once the fruit is ready, lift out the muslin bag and leave it in a bowl until it is cool enough to handle. Add the sugar to the peel and juice and turn up the heat, bringing the marmalade to a rolling boil. Squeeze every last bit of juice from the reserved muslin bag into the pan. Skim off any froth that rises to the surface (if you don't, your preserve will be cloudy). Leave at a fast boil for fifteen minutes. Remove a tablespoon of the preserve, put it on a plate and pop it into the fridge for a few minutes. If a thick skin forms on the surface of the refrigerated marmalade, then it is ready and you can switch the heat off. If the tester is still liquid, then let the marmalade boil for longer, testing every ten to fifteen minutes. Some mixtures can take up to fifty minutes to reach setting consistency. Ladle into sterilised pots and seal immediately.

## Fish, some new thoughts

I like February, with its grey-white skies and snowdrops. In the kitchen it is the time for long-cooked dishes of earth-coloured pulses, meat on its bones and home-made cakes. A month of beans, bones and baking. But it is also the month I go on holiday. Not towards warmth and bright sunshine, but places cold and icy, with crisp air that reminds you that you are alive.

Little feels more right than eating fish within a few steps of the sea. A lunch in Oslo, now a favourite place to escape, of fish soup flavoured with basil, eaten within sight of seventy white masts in a harbour with water like a black mirror, feels about as right as any meal I have ever eaten. Even more so as I saw the fish arrive barely twenty minutes before.

I have eaten nothing but fish for several days now – give or take the odd marzipan-filled, cardamom-scented maple syrup bun. The most curious was my lunch yesterday, of Arctic char served with chestnuts, bacon and apple purée. You feel it shouldn't work, the flavours being more suited to pork or perhaps reindeer, but it does. A dish ordered partly out of novelty, partly out of disbelief. It's clever, because the apples are cut into the tiniest imaginable dice and mixed with celery before being fried and served with the fish. It is a bit of a nancy presentation, but it leaves me inspired enough to have a go at home.

I have always loved the colour grey. Peaceful, elegant, understated; the colour of stone, steel and soft, nurturing rain. The view from the window across the harbour has every shade, from driftwood to charcoal: the lagoon, the restaurant's weathered cedar cladding, the moored boats, the trees on the opposite shore, all in delicate shades of calming grey.

The monotones through the window aren't altered by my plate of scallops, two if we are being precise, shallow fried, with a julienne of apple on top. Creamy, buttery cauliflower purée, black pepper and tiny bits of fried cauliflower complete the dish. It's a study in cream and white on a white plate, eaten under a stainless sky. A scene of such subtlety it makes everything else look gaudy and crass. There is risotto too, a blissful combination of smoked cod and spinach. As soon as I am off the plane, back in my own kitchen, I will ape that restaurant's sublime risotto.

# A risotto of smoked cod and spinach

And I did . . .

| | |
|---|---|
| milk: 450ml | a small onion |
| smoked cod or haddock: 400g | butter: 50g |
| bay leaves: 2 | Arborio or other risotto rice: 250g |
| black peppercorns: 6 | a glass of white wine |
| hot stock: 450ml | spinach leaves: 2 handfuls |

Pour the milk into a saucepan large enough to take the fish. Place the fish in the milk, add the bay leaves and peppercorns, then bring to the boil. As soon as the milk shows signs of foaming, lower the heat and simmer for ten minutes. Turn off the heat and leave the milk to infuse with the fish and aromatics. Heat the stock in a saucepan; it should simmer lightly whilst you are making the risotto.

Peel and finely chop the onion, then fry gently in the butter in a broad, heavy-bottomed pan. When the onion is soft and translucent, and before it colours, add the rice and briefly stir it through the butter to coat the grains. Pour in the wine, let it evaporate, then add the stock a ladleful at a time, allowing each one to be soaked up by the rice before adding the next, stirring continually and keeping the heat moderate to low. Once the stock has been used up, change to the milk, strained of its peppercorns. By the time almost all the milk has been absorbed, the grains should be soft and plump yet with a firm bite to them. Season carefully. The total cooking time will probably be about twenty minutes, maybe a few minutes longer.

Wash the spinach leaves, tear them into small pieces, then stir them into the rice. Break the fish into large, juicy flakes and add them to the rice, folding them in but keeping the flakes as whole as possible. Check the seasoning and serve.

Enough for 2 generous servings

## A little brown stew for a little brown day

A certain calm comes over the kitchen when there is any sort of grain simmering on the stove. The steam from brown rice, spelt or pot barley brings with it a quiet benevolence that I am grateful for on a grey-brown day like today. With a house in turmoil (I remain holed up in my tiny study while the plasterers plaster, painters paint and welders weld) the homely smell of boiled rice is somehow reassuring.

All the grains appeal to me but I am becoming partial to the quiet pleasures of pearled spelt (think pearl barley but made from wheat). The pale-brown wheat grain makes a pleasing change from Arborio rice in a risotto and adds a chewy note to a herb salad, but is something to consider for bulking up a casserole, too. The small, oval grains plump up like Sugar Puffs with the aromatic cooking liquor from a stew, taking on a velvety texture whilst making the dish both more substantial and more economical.

The mushroom stew on the hob today is rich and earthy enough but is hardly going to fill anyone. A couple of handfuls of spelt, boiled in lightly salted water and drained, will help turn what is essentially an accompaniment into something resembling a main course. Mushroom sauce becomes mushroom stew.

Spelt is said to be easy on the digestion and I have to agree. Some of us who find modern wheat heavy and soporific have no such trouble with the modern versions of ancient strains such as spelt. The ancestors of this mild, nubby grain spread across central Europe during the Bronze Age and were in common use in southern Britain by 500BC. Available for years in the sort of food shops that smell of brown rice and massage oil, spelt has recently taken a step towards the mainstream.

The sense of peace and humble bonhomie you get from simmering grain (akin, I think, to Chinese dumplings steaming in their bamboo baskets) is slightly lost when pearled spelt is stirred into a risotto but is there in spades when it is simmering in water, its steam rising in soft clouds. Like brown rice, it has an affinity with mushrooms, onions and the more earthy spices, but has less of the hardcore 'wholemeal' character.

# A little brown stew of mushrooms and spelt

Use fancy mushrooms if you wish, but I rather like this made with an every-day mixture of flat 'field' mushrooms and the small chestnut variety. Add the mushrooms according to their size and thickness, leaving anything particularly small and delicate till last. By field mushrooms I mean the wide, flat variety that are usually served on toast.

| | |
|---|---|
| dried mushrooms: a tablespoon (8g) | garlic: 2 cloves, crushed |
| pearled spelt: 250g | assorted fresh mushrooms: 850g |
| a medium onion | tomato purée: a tablespoon |
| olive oil: 4 tablespoons | plain flour: a tablespoon |
| | dried chilli flakes: ½ teaspoon |

Put the dried mushrooms in a heatproof bowl, cover with 500ml hot water from the kettle and set aside.

Boil the spelt in lightly salted water for fifteen minutes, then drain and set aside.

Peel and roughly chop the onion. Warm the olive oil in a large pan. Add the onion and leave to soften, with the occasional stir to stop it burning, over a moderate heat. When it is pale gold – a matter of ten to fifteen minutes – add the crushed garlic and continue cooking for two or three minutes.

Finely slice the fresh mushrooms. Stir them into the onion and continue cooking for about five minutes, till they are starting to colour.

Stir in the tomato purée. Cook for two or three minutes, then stir in the flour. Pour in the dried mushrooms and their soaking water and bring to the boil. As soon as the liquid is boiling, lower the heat, season with salt and black pepper and stir in the dried chilli flakes. Leave to simmer for ten minutes, then add the cooked spelt. Cook for a further ten to fifteen minutes, until the mushrooms are soft and silky and the sauce is rich and lightly thickened. Serve in shallow bowls.

Enough for 4

# Down to the bone

Having work done on the kitchen has given me the privilege of seeing the bones of this house. Not just the oak laths and plaster but the long joists that form the skeleton of the old girl. Peering beneath the sagging ceilings, walls and floors has given me a clue as to how the building, and particularly the kitchen, was built. There is something empowering about knowing how something was put together – a toy plane (yes, I was one of those Airfix kids), a house, a car and most of all, a recipe.

I get pleasure from cooking with the bits of an animal that clearly show their function – what they do and where they fit in. The neck, tail, shanks and shoulders all allow you to see form and function (I particularly like cutting the string on a neatly butchered ring of oxtail and sorting the strong, broad bones from the tiny cartilaginous ones at the flicking end). Getting to know what a piece of an animal did can help us cook it appropriately. It is probably a generalisation to suggest that the more work a joint of meat had to do, the longer it will need to cook, but it is true that the hard-working shanks and neck will take longer to come to tenderness than the fillet, which never did a day's work in its life. A chop from the loin will cook quicker than a chop from the ever-bending neck.

The butcher had some neck of lamb this week. This is a joint that gets much use – I have rarely seen a sheep that wasn't eating. Awkward and lumpy, the neck is a cut to be valued for its cheap price, sweet fat and almost indestructible nature. The fact that I can make a fragrant, even luxurious supper out of something some people boil up for the dog makes me warm to it all the more. Tucked up in a heavy pan with earthy spices and sweet onions, the untidy lumps of meat can cook on a low heat for anything up to a couple of hours, its tough flesh and gristle breaking down to soft, spoon-able meat and wobbly fat. Did I ever tell you my name is an anagram of lean gristle? Well, it is. I was slightly saddened this week to find the major supermarkets shunning this richly flavoured cut in favour of the neck fillet at over 12 quid a kilo. A decent butcher is always the best bet for the tougher cuts, until they become fashionable again like shanks.

As good as slow-cooked meat on the bone can be, it's the gravy that forms in the pan that is the real prize. I invariably start with onions, but this time I am throwing the spice rack at them, with whole cumin seeds, ground coriander, a cinnamon stick and just a pinch of crushed chilli. The weather being as it is, I am keen to add some sweetness, and do so in the form of dried apricots, though it could have been figs or raisins.

Sometimes, I drop a few floury potatoes into a slow-cooked supper to bolster it up a bit and make it even more economical, but I am also tempted by other starchy fillers, such as couscous, barley and spelt. My starch of the moment is the fat, pearl-like mograbia, occasionally known as Lebanese or pearl couscous. It responds best to a spirited boil rather being steamed like the usual fine couscous. Some of the supermarkets sell it labelled as giant couscous, and it is easy to find in Middle Eastern grocer's shops.

If mograbia remains elusive, then this rich, bargain-basement stew will feel just as comfortable with steamed fine couscous, quinoa or rice. I would add a little cinnamon to these, maybe some black pepper and some finely grated lemon zest and melted butter.

## Braised neck of lamb with apricots and cinnamon

Something sharp to cut the fat is good here. Dried apricots have a pleasing tang that works well. Like cooking apples work well with pork. Neck of lamb is my first choice for this treatment, but I would also recommend small shanks. They are easier to get hold of. You may need to turn them once or twice during cooking, as they will sit proud of the sauce.

I usually reckon on at least 300g neck of lamb per person. This sounds quite a lot, but we are talking about one of the most bone-rich cuts of meat, so the quantity of meat should be just about right. The hands-on work is very straightforward.

middle neck of lamb: 1.25kg
  (8 pieces)
plain flour: 3 tablespoons
groundnut or olive oil: 2 tablespoons, plus a little more
onions: 2 medium to large
cumin seeds: 1 teaspoon
ground coriander: 2 teaspoons
crushed dried chilli: half a
  teaspoon or so

garlic: 2 cloves
fresh ginger: a 3cm lump
lemon zest: 2 strips, about 6cm long
a cinnamon stick
dried apricots: 250g
stock or water: 750ml

*To serve:*
chopped mint: 2 tablespoons
finely grated lemon zest: a teaspoon

Dust the lamb with the flour and season with salt and black pepper. Heat a couple of tablespoons of oil in a large, heavy-based casserole to which you have a lid. Add the lamb to the pan and let the pieces brown lightly on both sides. You will probably need to do them in two batches. Remove them from the pan, leaving behind any oil (if the oil has blackened, wipe out the pan and start again with fresh oil). Set the oven at 160°C/Gas 3.

Peel the onions and roughly chop them. Add them to the pan and let them soften for ten minutes or so over a moderate heat. Stir in the whole cumin seeds and ground coriander. Sprinkle in the dried chilli, adding a little extra if you want more warmth (I don't think the dish should be hot, just warm and fruity). Peel the garlic and slice it finely, then add it to the onions. Peel the ginger, shred it finely and add it to the pan together with the lemon zest and cinnamon stick.

Add the dried apricots to the onions, then pour in the stock or water. Return the lamb to the pan, tucking it in amongst the rest of the ingredients. Season carefully. Bring to the boil, cover with a lid and place in the oven for one and a half hours, until the lamb is tender enough to come away from the bone easily.

As you serve, scatter the surface with fresh mint and lemon zest.
Enough for 4


## Mograbia

Also known as giant or Lebanese couscous, the pearl-sized grains should be cooked till they are soft but retain a little bite, too.

| | |
|---|---|
| half a cinnamon stick | a little butter, melted |
| mograbia: 250g | a small lemon (optional) |
| parsley: a few sprigs | |

Put a large pot of water on to boil (the mograbia likes to move around as it cooks, like pasta). Salt the water quite generously, as you would for pasta, and add the cinnamon stick.

Tip in the mograbia and leave to come back to the boil. Turn the heat down slightly, then let it simmer merrily for ten for fifteen minutes, till al dente, rather as you would like pasta to be.

Remove the parsley leaves from their stalks and chop them quite finely. Stir them into the melted butter, adding pepper and a little grated lemon

zest if you wish. Drain the mograbia, discard the cinnamon stick, then toss in the melted butter and parsley. Serve with the braised lamb above.

# The perfect marriage of smoked fish and cream

I am not especially fond of cream in main courses, but there are a few dishes in this book – rabbit with tarragon, gurnard with potatoes, pork chops with pears, to pick randomly on three – where it features with good reason. Tarragon is often overwhelming without the calming notes of dairy produce; a dose of double cream brings the fish and potatoes together; the pork dish uses the cream to deglaze the pan, giving the dish a velvety texture. The cream is not essential but it has a clear purpose.

Tonight I make the most of the masterful marriage of smoked fish and cream. Cream and smoke produce a calm and gentle partnership, working in dish after dish.

## Smoked haddock with potato and bacon

unsmoked streaky bacon:
  6 rashers
rapeseed oil: 3 tablespoons
medium potatoes: 400g
smoked haddock fillets: 500g

double cream: 500ml
bay leaves: 2
black peppercorns: 6
finely chopped curly parsley:
  2 tablespoons

Cut the bacon into pieces roughly the size of a postage stamp. Warm the oil in a non-stick frying pan and add the bacon pieces, letting them colour lightly.

Cut the potatoes, without peeling them, in 1cm-thick slices, then cut each slice into short pieces, like tiny chips. Tip them into the pan with the bacon and fry for about fifteen minutes, until golden and cooked right through.

Meanwhile, put the smoked haddock into a pan with the cream, bay leaves and peppercorns. Bring almost to the boil, then turn down the heat and simmer for fifteen minutes. Put the lid on and leave to infuse for five minutes or so.

Divide the potatoes and bacon between two warm plates, lift the haddock out of the cream and place a fillet on each plate. Stir the chopped parsley into the cream, then spoon it over the fish and serve.

Enough for 2

## Sharing a pudding

Sharing comes naturally to me. It is, after all, at the heart of what I do. Writing down a recipe is a way of passing something you enjoy on to someone else. A gift, yes, but also a way to make a living. And whilst I like sharing plates of dim sum, tapas and boxes of chocolates (though I generally stop short of double-dipping), I find myself divided over the merits of sharing a pudding. Nothing makes my heart sink like a restaurant order of one pudding and four spoons. I have no wish to sound greedy but I would really rather everyone ordered their own.

At home, I can never make up my mind whether I prefer a large, dig-in type of pudding or an individual one. As much pleasure as can be had in doling out generous spoonfuls of trifle or steamed treacle pudding to a gathering of friends, family and assorted appetites, there is something rather delightful in having a tiny pudding all to oneself.

Today is cold and wet. A sponge-pudding kind of day. I make a cluster of little puddings with brown sugar and soft prunes that I soak in sherry. Baked not boiled, they turn out moist, caramel sweet, and cute and plump as cherubim. So much more charming than a whole one cut into portions.

### Little prune puddings with caramel sauce

The accompanying brown sugar and cream sauce seems, at first, to taste rather sweet, but once it shares a spoon with the fruit pudding its inclusion is suddenly explained. I have used soft, ready-to-eat Agen prunes here but ready-to-eat dried apricots could be good too. I would suggest you use medium eggs rather than large ones, which may result in the mixture slightly bubbling over the top.

ready-to-eat Agen prunes: 10
medium-dry sherry: 2 tablespoons
butter: 120g
light muscovado sugar: 70g
caster sugar: 70g

eggs: 2, lightly beaten
self-raising flour: 120g

*For the sauce:*
light muscovado sugar: 50g
double cream: 250ml

Butter and lightly flour four 200ml pudding tins. Don't be tempted to skip this step, otherwise your puddings may stick. Roughly chop the prunes and pour the sherry over them. Set aside. Set the oven at 160°C/Gas 3.

Cream the butter and sugars together till light and fluffy. Add the beaten eggs a little at a time (introduce a spoonful or two of flour if the mixture looks as if it might curdle), then gently fold in the flour.

Stir in the chopped prunes and any liquid. Divide the mixture between the pudding bowls – it should fill them by two-thirds – and bake in the pre-heated oven for forty to forty-five minutes, until springy and golden. To turn the puddings out, run a tiny palette knife around the inside of the tins, then invert them and shake firmly.

For the sauce, put the sugar and cream in a saucepan, bring to the boil and simmer for two minutes. Serve with the puddings.

Enough for 4

## Chicken with potatoes and dill

A mild treatment for chicken, with soft flavours. Steamed rice, possibly brown basmati, would work nicely here.

| | |
|---|---|
| butter: 30g | small potatoes: 400g |
| olive oil: a tablespoon | cider: 500ml |
| a chicken, jointed into 8 pieces | double cream: 150ml |
| small chestnut mushrooms: 250g | a small bunch of dill |

Melt the butter in a casserole and add the oil. When it starts to sizzle, put in the chicken pieces. Season with salt and pepper, then leave to cook over a moderate heat until the chicken is pale gold on both sides. Remove from the pan and set aside.

Halve or quarter the mushrooms, depending on their size, and add them to the pan. Let them soften, adding a little more butter or oil if necessary. Scrub and halve or quarter the potatoes. Add them to the pan and leave till lightly coloured, then pour in the cider. Return the chicken to the pan and bring to the boil. Immediately the liquid is boiling, lower the temperature so that it simmers gently.

Cover with a lid and leave to cook for thirty minutes or until the chicken is cooked right through. Check by pushing a skewer into the thickest part; if the juices run clear, then it is done.

Remove the chicken. There will be a lot of liquid. Turn up the heat and boil to concentrate the flavours, letting the quantity of liquid reduce by about a third. Stir in the cream and the chopped dill, then season to taste. Wait for a minute or two, then remove from the heat and serve.

Enough for 4

# FEBRUARY 17

## A can of butter beans

There are some who turn their noses up at a can of beans. As indeed I do on occasions, when I am in the mood for soaking, draining, boiling, skimming, testing, draining, cooling and dressing dried beans. But a can or two of butter beans (or the oval, green flageolet; tiny, bead-like haricot; or white cannellini, the dragée of the bean world) has got me out of jail more times than I can shake a wooden spoon at.

Rinsing the beans will rid them of the slimy canning liquor but it is best done under a softly running tap if you are not to mash them to a watery hummus. Butter beans are the meatiest of the canned beans, the ones you can roll over in your mouth like the golden toffees in a tin of Quality Street. They are similar to, but not quite the same as, the delicious lima beans that are so popular in the US.

I wouldn't argue with those who say a lovingly made bean bake, simmered and then cooked in a low oven, is better than the quick canned-bean supper I made tonight, but I am not after perfection here, I'm after something good to eat following a long day at my desk.

### Butter beans with mustard and tomato

onions: 3
garlic: 3 large cloves
olive oil: 3 tablespoons
thyme: a few sprigs
bay leaves: 2
crushed tomatoes (or tomato
 passata): two 400g cans

butter beans: two 400g cans,
 drained
medium chillies: 2, deseeded
 and chopped
black treacle: 2 tablespoons
grain mustard: a tablespoon
smooth French mustard:
 a tablespoon

Peel and roughly chop the onions and garlic, put them in a heavy-based casserole with the olive oil and cook over a moderate heat till they are soft and pale gold. An occasional stir will prevent them sticking to the pan.

Add the thyme, bay leaves, tomatoes, drained beans and 250ml water and bring to the boil. Season with salt and black pepper and stir in the chillies, treacle and mustards. Partially cover with a lid and leave to simmer gently for thirty minutes or so, until the sauce has thickened a little. Serve hot.

Enough for 4

## FEBRUARY 18

## Little cakes – getting a good start

It is the creaming together of the butter and sugar that tends to get overlooked by those new to cake making. Yes, the raising agent – baking powder or self-raising flour – plays an essential part in the texture of your cake, but the amount of time you give to the initial creaming should never be underestimated.

The right beater helps. A wooden spoon and elbow grease will work, but things have moved on, and a machine of some sort will give a quicker and frankly better result. A hand-held electric beater or an electric mixer has the power to produce a vastly superior mixture, where the sugar and butter are whipped up into something resembling soft ice cream, like an old-fashioned Mr Whippy.

Little cakes are a good place to start. Individual cakes are usually better-natured than a larger, family-sized sponge, and any shortcomings can be more easily masked. Not for nothing the success of the ubiquitous buttercream-crowned cupcake.

I'm guessing here, but I suspect the world doesn't need another cupcake recipe, which is why I set about making something with a little more heart and soul. A cake with a backbone, not to mention an interesting texture, which comes from rolled oats and dried apricots. It's as near as I can get to giving you a cupcake recipe.

# Little apricot and oat cakes

You will need about 16 paper muffin cases and a couple of muffin trays or tart tins to hold them.

butter, at room temperature: 225g
golden caster sugar: 225g
eggs: 3
dried apricots: 160g
self-raising flour: 225g

chopped mixed candied peel:
 a tablespoon
the grated zest of an orange
rolled oats: 3 tablespoons
a little demerara sugar

Set the oven at 180°C/Gas 4. Put the butter into a food mixer with the sugar and beat together until light and fluffy. The mixture should be pale, almost the colour of double cream. Break the eggs and beat them lightly, just to break them up, then beat them into the butter and sugar mixture a little at a time. Chop the apricots in a food processor till they resemble fine orange grit.

Add the flour to the cake mixture, through a sieve if you wish, stirring gently with a large metal spoon until no flour is visible. Stir in the chopped apricots, peel and orange zest.

Divide between the paper muffin cases, scatter with the oats and a good pinch of demerara sugar and bake in the preheated oven for twenty to thirty minutes, until risen (they may sink slightly in the centre) and golden brown.

Makes about 16

## FEBRUARY 19

# The beauty of kale

When it is touched with frost, it is hard to picture a leaf so beautiful as kale, even more than a nasturtium with morning dew caught in its veins. But there is more to it than that. The frost will sweeten the strident notes of the brassica, just as it does with sprouts and parsnips.

Cabbage and pork is an age-old marriage that I am still finding new versions of. Brussels sprouts, fried and tossed with bacon and cream, was a recent one; white cabbage with crumbled black pudding; a salad of sprouted broccoli and shredded coppa. All variations on a theme that works brilliantly. Chorizo has a spiciness that goes nicely with kale but, more importantly, it has great pearls of fat that will work the same magic with the dark, bitter leaves as sausages do for sauerkraut and streaky bacon does for Brussels sprouts.

## Kale with chorizo and almonds

Good-quality cooking chorizo is not the cheapest of meats but I find a little goes a long way. When this recipe was first published in my column I was asked why I suggested discarding the oil, especially as it contains so much chorizo flavour. A good point, but I felt there was enough fat in the dish already. So the suggestion is just that. Leave the spicy, orange, liquid fat in, if you wish.

| | |
|---|---|
| curly kale: 250g | a little groundnut or sunflower oil |
| soft cooking chorizo: 250g | a clove of garlic, peeled and |
| skinned whole almonds: 50g | crushed |

Wash the kale thoroughly – the leaves can hold grit in their curls. Put several of the leaves on top of one another and shred them coarsely, discarding the really thick ends of the stalks as you go.

Cut the chorizo into thick slices. Warm a non-stick frying pan over a moderate heat, add the slices of chorizo and fry until golden. Lift them out with a draining spoon on to a dish lined with kitchen paper. Discard most of the oil that has come out of the chorizo (better still, keep it for frying potatoes) and wipe the pan clean. Add the almonds and cook for two or three minutes, till pale gold, then lift out and add to the chorizo.

Warm a little oil in the pan, add the crushed garlic and shredded greens and cook for a couple of minutes, turning the greens over as they cook, till glossy and starting to darken in colour. Return the chorizo and almonds to the pan, add a little salt and continue cooking till all is sizzling, then tip on to hot plates.

Enough for 2 as a light main course, 4 as a side dish

# The pancetta question

Modern cookbooks, mine included, are awash with pancetta – to start a sauce, flavour a soup, add protein to a leaf salad or simply give depth and savour. But could we not use bacon?

Though both bring a similar note to a recipe, pancetta has a few advantages over bacon. Most bacon in the UK is sold in rashers, while pancetta is more often found in useful cubes (often labelled as cubetti), which give more body to a sauce than strips of wafer-thin bacon. Most cures are less salty than our own back or streaky, and seem to have a faintly herbal note to them. (In practice they don't, but most pancetta is more subtly aromatic.)

It is this subtlety that makes pancetta more suitable for so many recipes. It tends to become part of the backbone of a dish, rather than intrude as bacon can occasionally do. But that is not all. The reason it is so often specified over bacon is that it is a more consistent product. Suggest chopped bacon for a recipe and you can get any one of a hundred different cures, ranging from pale and watery to deeply smoky and dry. Although there are most certainly differing qualities of pancetta available, it is by and large consistent and therefore a safer bet.

A block of pancetta bought from an Italian deli will keep in decent condition in the fridge for a week. Bacon rashers less so. I regard a lump of the stuff, dirty rose pink in colour, thickly ribbed with white fat, as one of the kitchen essentials – like lemons, Parmesan and olive oil. A meal it does not make, but the difference it adds to even a few lettuce leaves or a bowl of soup is extraordinary. Today's bean and spaghetti soup is a case in point.

# Pancetta and bean soup with spaghetti

The one good thing about having little in the larder is that it prompts experimentation.

| | |
|---|---|
| pancetta in the piece: 175g (you can use pancetta cubetti at a push) | chickpeas or other large, firm pulses: a 400g can, drained |
| a little olive oil | spaghetti: 250g |
| garlic: 2 small cloves | parsley: a small bunch |
| chopped tomatoes: two 400g cans | extra virgin olive oil |

Chop the pancetta into small pieces, then fry for a minute or two in the olive oil over a moderate heat. Once the pancetta starts to turn golden, peel and crush the garlic and add to the pan, followed by the chopped tomatoes, 400ml water and the drained canned chickpeas or beans. Bring to the boil and season with salt and black pepper. Lower the heat so that the mixture simmers gently, thickening slowly, for about fifteen to twenty minutes.

Break the spaghetti into short lengths and boil in deep, generously salted water for eight or nine minutes, till tender, then drain. Roughly chop the parsley and stir into the soup together with the spaghetti. I add a trickle of really good olive oil to each bowl at the table.

Enough for 4

## FEBRUARY 21

# A family cake

Don't you just hate lining cake tins? I know you don't have to any more with the ready-made paper liners available from cookware shops, but they have the habit of making everything come out looking like a shop-bought cake.

The truth is that cakes rarely stick round the sides, and if they do they can be loosened with a palette knife (run the knife smoothly around the edge, pressing firmly against the side of the tin, without digging into the cake). I now line only the base, cutting a simple disc of brown baking parchment or grease-proof paper to fit the base of the tin. It takes thirty seconds, stops the cake attaching itself to the base and leaves your handiwork looking homemade.

# An apricot crumble cake

This is the grown-up version of the little cakes I made a week or so ago (see page 75). A family cake, suitable for tea or dessert, in which case it will benefit from an egg-shaped scoop of crème fraîche.

dried apricots: 250g
softened butter: 175g
golden caster sugar: 175g
eggs: 2
ground almonds: 80g
self-raising flour: 175g
ground cinnamon: a pinch
vanilla extract: a few drops

*For the crumble:*
plain flour: 100g
butter: 75g
demerara sugar: 2 tablespoons
jumbo oats: 3 tablespoons
flaked almonds: 2 tablespoons
a little cinnamon and extra demerara sugar for the crust, and perhaps a little icing sugar to finish

Preheat the oven to 160°C/Gas 3. Line the base of a 22cm round cake tin with baking parchment.

Put the apricots in a saucepan, cover with water and bring to the boil. Turn down the heat and simmer for twenty minutes, then turn off the heat and leave them to cool a little.

Beat the butter and sugar in a food mixer for five to ten minutes, till light and pale-coffee coloured. Break the eggs, beat them gently just to mix the yolks and whites, then add them gradually to the mixture with the beater on slow. Fold in the ground almonds, flour and cinnamon, then add the vanilla extract. Scrape the mixture into the tin and smooth the surface.

Drain the apricots and add them to the top of the cake mixture. Make the crumble topping: blitz the flour and butter to crumbs in a food processor, then add the demerara sugar, oats and flaked almonds and mix lightly. Remove the food processor bowl from the stand and add a few drops of water. Shake the bowl a little – or run a fork through the mixture – so that some of the crumbs stick together like small pebbles. This will give a more interesting mix of textures. Scatter this loosely over the cake, followed by a pinch of cinnamon and a little more demerara. Bake for about an hour, checking for doneness with a skewer; it should come out clean.

Remove the cake from the oven and set aside. Dust with a little icing sugar if you wish and slice as required. The cake will keep well for three or four days.

Enough for 8

## Desperate for dessert

There are apples that fluff up when they are cooked and apples that keep their shape. But you know that, if you have read the apple chapter in *Tender Volume II*, or indeed have ever made apple sauce or baked an open apple tart.

What I find particularly useful are recipes that work with 'fruit bowl' apples, the sort you tend to have knocking around. This is such a recipe. It's a pudding for when you didn't intend to have a pudding, until someone asked for one.

### Fried apples with brown sugar and crème fraîche

The apples should be cooked over a fairly low heat so they soften but don't colour too much before you add the sugar. Once the sugar is added, things happen quite quickly, so don't be tempted to take your eye off the pan. The Calvados is a suggestion. You can add a straightforward cognac if you prefer, or leave it out altogether. If there is no crème fraîche around, use ordinary double cream – though the result will be a little sweeter.

| | |
|---|---|
| a large apple | butter: 50g |
| a little lemon juice | Calvados: 1 tablespoon |
| light muscovado sugar: 2 tablespoons | crème fraîche: 2–3 tablespoons |

Cut the apple into quarters and remove and discard the core and pips. I don't peel my apples for this recipe, but it is up to you. Cut the apple into thick slices, put them in a basin and squeeze over a little lemon juice, just enough to stop them browning.

Melt the butter in a shallow, non-stick pan. Add the apple slices and let them cook over a moderate heat for about ten minutes, turning them as necessary and lowering the heat if they colour too quickly. When they are soft and golden, scatter over the sugar and let it melt in the butter. As it starts to turn to caramel in the pan, add the Calvados and crème fraîche. Once the cream has melted around the apple, serve immediately.

Enough for 2

# Pumpkin, tomato and cannellini soup

This is quite a substantial soup and could easily double as a main dish. To make a quick version, use canned beans. Drain them of their canning liquid and rinse them thoroughly, then add them to the soup once the tomatoes have simmered down to a slush. You could use any bean, but the cannellini type has a good contrast of texture to the soft vegetables and tends to stay quite firm during cooking. The soup can be kept in the fridge for several days.

dried cannellini beans: 250g
onions: 2
olive or rapeseed oil: 2 tablespoons
garlic: 2 or 3 cloves
rosemary: a small sprig
tomatoes: 400g

pumpkin: 800g (about 650g prepared weight), peeled and cut into chunks
parsley: a small bunch
a little extra virgin olive oil

Soak the dried beans in cold water overnight. Drain and rinse, then tip into a large, deep pan and cover them with water. Bring to the boil, partially cover with a lid, then turn down the heat so they cook at an enthusiastic simmer. Don't be tempted to add any salt at this point, as it will toughen the beans. Skim off any froth that rises to the surface as they cook, and occasionally check the water level and top up from the kettle if necessary. Test for doneness after forty-five minutes or so; they should be tender but not soft. Drain and set aside.

Peel and roughly chop the onions. Warm the oil in a deep pan, add the onions and cook for about ten minutes, until soft. While the onions cook, peel and slice the garlic and add to the pan, together with the rosemary needles, roughly chopped. Cut the tomatoes in half and stir them into the onions. Continue cooking for five minutes, then pour in 750ml water and bring to the boil. Add the pumpkin pieces to the pan, season with salt and black pepper and leave to simmer gently for thirty to forty minutes, until the pumpkin is tender to the point of a knife.

Tip the drained beans into the pan and continue cooking for ten minutes. (If you want to cool everything at this stage and put the soup in the fridge overnight, it will be all the better for it.) Remove the leaves from the parsley and chop roughly, then stir them into the soup. Ladle into deep bowls, trickle a little extra virgin olive oil over the top and serve.

Enough for 4

# The old wok

I have three woks. The oldest is cheap, thin, and has been a friend for longer than I can remember. A purchase from Chinatown, now blackened from years of use and, if I am honest, a little rusty here and there. Its diameter is 40cm, which will make a stir-fry (mushroom and broccoli, prawn and fat, fresh noodles, chicken and choy sum) for two.

The trendy thick woks with famous names are rubbish. Leave them in the shops. Never pay more than a few quid for a wok. Go for one made from steel no thicker than a ten-pence piece. It will take more looking after (it needs seasoning to stop it rusting) but it will reward you with a better stir-fry. The whole point of a stir-fry is the speed at which the meat cooks. A slow stir-fry where the pan is too thick or the heat too low simply isn't a stir-fry. It's a stew-fry.

Woks will eventually season themselves. They will develop a surface patina of burned-on oil that will be both non-stick and non-rust. I speed the matter up by putting a new wok, coated in groundnut oil, into a hot oven and leaving it for an hour or so for the oil to burn on. I then wipe the surface with kitchen paper without washing it and let the wok cool. I sometimes do this several times, depending on the progress. If the wok has a wooden handle, then it's a case of doing it on the hob. A smoky business.

Oyster sauce, in particular the Lee Kum Kee brand, is one of the sauces that are always present in my fridge. Dark, velvety and not as fishy as it sounds, it keeps in good condition for a few weeks. Its destination is usually a last minute stir-fry – tonight, one of cubes of pork, too much garlic and some mushrooms. As a simple supper, it is difficult to beat.

## Pork with garlic and oyster sauce

Plus greens somewhere.

flavourless oil: 5 tablespoons at least

cubed pork shoulder or fillet: 350g

garlic: 3–4 cloves

shallots: 2

small, hot red chillies: 4

mushrooms, shiitake, chestnut, whatever: 150g

oyster sauce: 3 heaped tablespoons

Shaoxing wine: 3 tablespoons

Heat the wok. Add 2 tablespoons of oil. When it starts to smoke, add half the meat and let it colour, removing it as it turns golden at the edges. Repeat with the second batch of meat, using a little fresh oil if you have to.

Meanwhile, peel and finely chop the garlic and peel and slice the shallots. Finely chop, but do not seed, two of the chillies. Leave a couple whole to add a deeper, subtler flavour. Get the wok hot, pour in the remaining oil and let it start to smoke, then add the chopped garlic, shallots and chillies, stirring as they cook. Fry them for a minute or two till they start to colour. Add the mushrooms, whole or torn up if they are large. Continue stir-frying till they are soft and lightly coloured, then return the meat to the pan. Once the meat is thoroughly hot, stir in the oyster sauce and the wine and bring to the boil. Let the resulting sauce reduce for a minute, maybe two, then serve.

Enough for 2

## FEBRUARY 25

# In the squeezing of a lemon

A warm lemon will yield more juice than a cold one. So it is better to keep them at room temperature than in the fridge. More importantly, a ripe or even slightly overripe fruit will give up more juice than one so hard you can barely squeeze it. Many lemons are sold unripe. A ripe lemon is often a deeper yellow, and yields gently under pressure. I roll my lemons on the work surface before juicing them, pushing firmly down on them with the palm of my hand. I seem to get even more juice that way.

The standard domestic glass lemon squeezer, the one with a moat to catch the juice and tiny beads to hold back the pips, works well enough. The deeper, stainless steel versions are good too, letting the juice fall through into the base. Yet I get the best results with a wooden lemon reamer. The simplicity appeals, a pointed ridged cone with a beech or olive wood handle, and the fact that it has been made by hand rather than machine. Some are made from one piece of wood rather than two (the handle is often made separately from the ridged cone). But what sets it apart from the others is its simplicity and, in some cases, its beauty. Of course, the pips escape into the juice. You simply fish them out with your fingers.

## Lemon tart

The tart case needs to be made with care, so the edges don't shrink as they cook, otherwise it will leak once the filling goes in. I keep a little bit of pastry aside for patching, so that if any cracks or gaps appear I can patch them before I add the lemon custard.

*For the pastry:*
plain flour: 180g
butter: 90g
caster sugar: a tablespoon
a large egg yolk
a little water

*For the filling:*
eggs: 4, plus 1 extra egg yolk
caster sugar: 250g
zest of 2 unwaxed lemons
zest and juice of a small blood orange
lemon juice: 160ml
double cream: 180ml

Make the pastry: put the flour into a food processor, add the butter, cut into pieces, and blitz to fine breadcrumbs. If you prefer, rub the butter into the flour with your fingertips. Add the sugar and egg yolk and just enough water to bring the mixture to a firm dough, either in the machine or by hand. The less water you add, the better – too much will cause your pastry case to shrink as it bakes.

Tip the dough on to a floured board, pat it into a round, then roll it out a little larger than a 24cm loose-bottomed tart tin. Lift the pastry carefully into the tin, pushing it well into the corners and making certain there are no holes or tears. Trim away any overhanging pastry, then place in the fridge for twenty minutes.

Set the oven at 200°C/Gas 6. Put a baking sheet in the oven to heat up. Line the pastry case with foil, fill with baking beans and slide it on to the hot baking sheet. Bake for twenty minutes, then remove from the oven and carefully lift out the beans and foil. Return the pastry case to the oven for five minutes or so, until the surface is dry to the touch. Remove from the oven and set aside. Turn the oven down to 160°C/Gas 3.

Make the filling: break the eggs into a bowl and add the egg yolk and caster sugar. Grate the lemon and orange zest into the eggs. Pour in the orange and lemon juice. Whisk, by hand, until the ingredients are thoroughly mixed, then stir in the cream.

Pour the mixture into the baked tart shell and slide carefully into the oven. Bake for thirty-five to forty-five minutes till the filling is lightly set. Ideally, the centre will still quiver when the tray is shaken gently.

Enough for 8

## FEBRUARY 26

## A little meal of peace

Sometimes, I rather like noise. The testosterone-fuelled roar of a football match heard from my back garden; the tired and blissfully happy sounds of a crowd singing along at a festival; the swoosh of a barista's steam wand. But most times I prefer peace and quiet. The sound of snow falling in a forest is more my style – something I have yet to hear this year.

There is quiet food, too. The tastes of peace and quiet, of gentleness and calm. The solitary observance of a bowl of white rice; the peacefulness of a dish of pearl barley; running your fingers through couscous. The thing these have in common is that they are grains or something of that ilk. What is it about these ingredients that makes them so calming? Could it just be that they bring us gastronomically down to earth, show us how pure and simple good eating can be? This is food pretty much stripped of its trappings. It is, after all, the food that many people survive upon.

The peacefulness of grains, their earth tones and the fact that they don't snap or crunch between the teeth, is what makes them food to eat when we are looking for solace and calm. The fact they are not from a dead animal probably has something to do with it, too.

More and more, I make a main course of what is generally thought of as an accompaniment. Tonight, I make a dish of pale bulgur wheat, cooked

with chopped onions, bacon, mushrooms and dill. It is a bit of a hybrid (pork and bulgur are not often found sharing a plate) but it turns out to be one of those ridiculously cheap meals that hits all the right notes.

## Bulgur and bacon

I sometimes spoon a little seasoned yogurt – salt, pepper, paprika – over this at the table, stirring it into the grains. But mostly I leave the pilaf as it is, enjoying the warm, homely grains and juicy nuggets of mushroom as they are.

smoked streaky bacon: 200g
onions: 2
olive oil
garlic: 2 cloves
small mushrooms: 250g
bulgur wheat, medium fine: 250g

boiling water from the kettle: 400ml
sprigs of parsley: 3–4
dill: 6 sprigs
butter: 60g

Cut the bacon rashers into short, thick pieces. Peel the onions and slice them thinly. Warm a couple of tablespoons of olive oil in a large, shallow pan over a low heat, add the sliced bacon and stir occasionally till the fat has turned pale gold. Peel and finely chop the garlic. Add the onions and garlic to the pan and leave till soft, golden and translucent, stirring from time to time.

Quarter the mushrooms and add them to the softening onions. Leave them to cook for five minutes or so, with the occasional stir. Add the bulgur with a pinch of salt, then pour in the boiling water. Cover tightly, switch off the heat and leave for fifteen minutes.

Roughly chop the parsley leaves and dill. Lift the lid from the pan and add the butter, herbs and a little salt and pepper. Stir till the grains are glossy with butter, then serve.

Enough for 4

## Coconut cream

One of the reasons I have stayed put for more than a decade is because of the way this house floods with light in the mornings. Softened by closed blinds, the sun that comes in from the east wakes you gently, if a little earlier than you would like. This morning, the rooms fill with honeyed light, like a Hammershoi painting. I suddenly realise how much I have missed it these last few weeks.

Sunlight, even on a relatively cold day, has a habit of changing my appetite. Pasta, potatoes and grains feel inappropriate and heavy. The brown food that has provided such homely comfort on the grey days since the year's start suddenly looks out of place.

Coconut is one of those ingredients that tend to walk hand in hand with sunshine. It smacks, albeit softly, of trips to Kerala and Thailand, of tiny scented pancakes for breakfast on sun-filled terraces, of lime juice and chillies and, of course, sun-tan oil. All of which is about as far as you can get from a February day within a ball's throw of Arsenal Stadium.

I met coconut first in the form of a neat, sweet Bounty bar, and as a coating, along with raspberry jam, for the tiny, castle-shaped sponges we wrongly called madeleines. Later, it became the principal seasoning of a holiday in Goa and then, a decade on, of the deep, pale-green soups of Thailand. For an ingredient of which I am not particularly fond, the flesh of the coconut is laden with happy memories.

The finely desiccated coconut that covered my childhood like snowflakes, on everything from jelly mushrooms to fairy cakes and marshmallows, has never set foot in my adult kitchen. It is a flavour I seem to have left behind, like a school blazer that no longer fits. I keep coconut in two forms: as a can of creamy, brilliant-white milk for soups and curries and as coconut cream, a thicker, more concentrated version made from the top of the milk. This latter form is useful when you want the flavour of the nut without introducing too much liquid. Spiked with ground cumin, cardamom and turmeric, it makes a simple marinade for prawns or chicken. It comes in jars and small cans, like the mixers on the drinks trolley of a plane, and is not to be confused with 'cream of coconut' whose principal use is in a rum-spiked piña colada.

Coconut cream is the thick, almost paste-like gloop that rises to the top of the pot when coconut milk is produced. You can make your own by adding water to shredded, fresh coconut, bringing it to the boil and letting it cool. On refrigeration, the cream will rise and can be scooped off.

As well as introducing a nutty sweetness, coconut cream works as a balm. I often add the contents of a small can to knock the edge off an exceptionally spicy lamb curry, or indeed to any dish in which I have misjudged the chilli quotient and left everyone breaking out in a sweat.

## Chicken wings with coconut cream

You could serve this with plenty of the brick-red, coconut-scented sauce and some steamed rice, but I prefer to reduce the sauce over a high heat, stirring almost continuously to prevent it sticking to the pan, till it is thick enough to coat the chicken wings.

groundnut oil: 2 tablespoons
chicken wings: 16 (or 12 large ones)
fresh ginger: a 60g knob
garlic: 2 large cloves
ground chilli: half a teaspoon
ground turmeric: half a teaspoon

ground coriander: a teaspoon
small 'new' potatoes: 250g
chopped tomatoes: a 400g can
coconut cream: up to 320ml
coriander leaves: a small handful

Warm the oil in a deep frying pan. Season the chicken wings with salt and pepper, add to the pan and leave them to colour on both sides. Remove to a plate once they are golden brown.

Peel the ginger and garlic and blitz them to a rough pulp in a food processor. Blend in the ground chilli, turmeric and coriander. Cut the potatoes into thin 'coins'. Return the empty chicken pan to a moderate heat and add the spice mix from the processor. Once it starts to sizzle and its fragrance rises, add the potatoes and 200ml water. Continue cooking, with the occasional stir, for ten minutes or until the potatoes are approaching tenderness. Stir in the tomatoes, bring to the boil and simmer for five minutes.

Pour in the coconut cream (start with 160ml, then add more as you wish). Season with salt, stir well, return the chicken and any juices on the plate to the pan and leave to simmer for fifteen to twenty minutes, allowing time for the liquid to reduce a little. Turn up the heat and, stirring almost continuously, let the sauce bubble till it has thickened considerably. Scrape away at the bottom of the pan with a wooden spoon as you go to stop the sauce sticking. It should be thick and should easily coat the chicken. Stir in a little chopped coriander, if you wish.

Serve in shallow bowls or deep plates and, being best eaten somewhat messily with the hands, provide something for everyone to wipe their fingers with.

Enough for 4


## FEBRUARY 28

# Hand to mouth

I have always regarded mopping food from my plate with a piece of bread as one of life's better moments. No doubt it is made twice as enjoyable by the fact I was forbidden from doing it as a child. Those last few puddles of sauce sponged up with anything from a wodge of floury bap to a jagged shard of warm pitta form a natural conclusion to my day's cooking, a form of delicious closure. Given half the chance, I would be happy to transfer an entire meal from plate to mouth in pieces of warm bread.

Any soft dough, flat or bun-like, can be used to scoop sloppy, spicy or stew-like things from our plates. Yes, the bread adds substance to our supper, but the real point – for me at least – is the tactile pleasure to be had from holding the hot sauce in a piece of damp bread. It feels as good as it tastes. More than just an edible receptacle with which to trap our food, the bread, saturated with juices, becomes part of the dish – more than you can say for a knife and fork.

I sometimes make flatbreads at home, the kind of slipper-shaped breads you can split and stuff, or tear into rough pieces to dunk into taramasalata, puréed chickpeas or chunkily textured tomato sauce. They are perhaps my favourite of all for cleaning my plate. The most straightforward is a flour, yeast and water dough rolled into small ovals and baked. They often leave the oven crisp, so in order to make them soft enough to wipe a plate, I cover the warm breads with a tea towel, which leaves them suitably pliable.

Today I made a sort of gloopy stew with chickpeas and tomatoes, sharpened with pickled lemon, leaving them to cook long enough to make the juices thick and rich. To introduce a bit more depth, I roasted the tomatoes first, tossed around with a chopped ripe pepper and a few cumin seeds, adding a deceptively smoky quality. Just the stuff for a bit of bread.

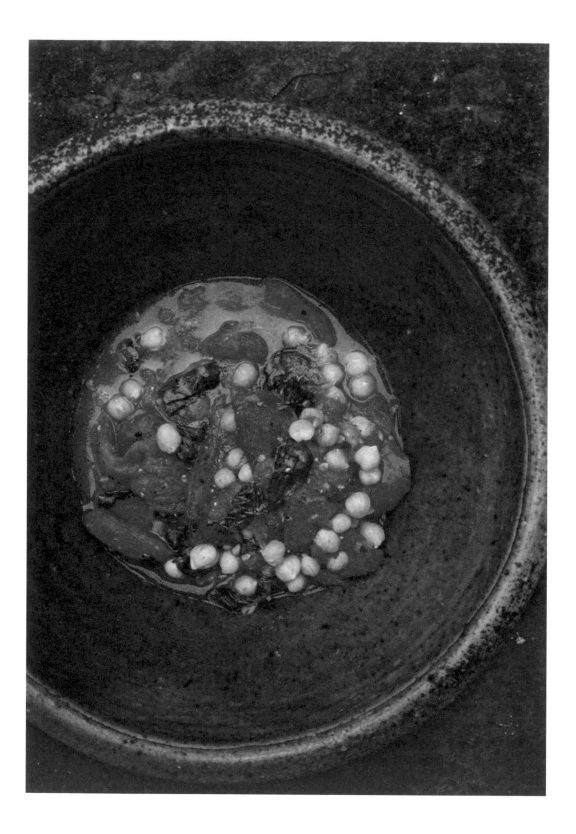

# Chickpeas with tomatoes and harissa

A vegetable-based stew to serve with rice or bread.

tomatoes: 800g
red peppers: about 500g
olive oil: 110ml
red wine vinegar: 3 tablespoons
cumin seeds: a teaspoon
chickpeas: two 400g cans

preserved lemons: 60g
harissa paste: a teaspoon
basil leaves: a handful
soft, Middle Eastern-style bread,
  to serve

Set the oven at 200°C/Gas 6. Remove the tomatoes from their stalks, cut each into six and put them in a baking dish. Cut the peppers in half, tear out their stalks and seeds, cut the flesh into short chunks, then add to the tomatoes.

Add 75ml of the oil, plus the vinegar, cumin seeds and a generous grinding of black pepper and sea salt. Roast for fifty minutes to an hour, until the peppers are tender and the tomatoes are soft and juicy. If the edges have caught slightly, then all to the good.

Transfer the tomatoes and peppers from the baking dish to a saucepan. Drain the chickpeas of their canning liquor and rinse them under the cold tap. Mix the drained chickpeas with the tomatoes and peppers.

Chop the preserved lemon, discarding the soft inner pulp. Stir the harissa, chopped lemon and remaining olive oil into the chickpeas, place the pan over a moderate heat and leave to simmer for ten minutes or so, till it is thoroughly hot and juicy. Season with salt and coarse black pepper.

Fold the basil leaves, whole, into the mixture, letting them wilt in the heat. Transfer to a serving dish and serve with warm bread.

Enough to serve 4, generously, as a main course

# A spurtle, some oats and a beautiful bowl

I have been using my spurtle the wrong way round. This came to light last year, when I took a porridge-making lesson with Ian Bishop in Carrbridge, Scotland. This morning, under a beautiful, grey-white winter sky, Ian's softly spoken words come back to me.

A spurtle, spirtle, theevil or, as it used to be known in Shetland, gruel-tree, is a thick wooden stick purely for stirring porridge in its pan, and seems like one piece of kit too many, especially to someone with a pathological dislike of unnecessary gadgets. But the gentle sound of warm oats and water being stirred in a thick pan on a freezing morning is a noise of ancient comfort, like the soft crackle of an open fire in an old hearth. I have loved porridge since I was a boy, but my mother made it with milk and sugar whereas I make mine with water and salt.

Ian taught me to use three cups of water to one of pinhead oats. I use the same oats as him now, an organically grown medium oatmeal, and only slightly less salt. He insisted, politely, on a teaspoon of salt to a cup of oats, and I follow his lead, aware that it is almost my entire salt ration for the day. Just as it does in a batch of flapjacks, the salt brings out an almost toasted flavour in the oats. I stir them clockwise only, lest the devil get me, and embellish them with cream and a dark berry jam such as blackcurrant, just as my teacher does.

A bowl of porridge is a quiet breakfast (no snap, crackle or pop) that sets me up for the day. I feel a sense of calm and wellbeing after a breakfast of porridge. I should add that mine now comes in a wooden bowl. I regard my porridge bowls as some of the most beautiful items in my kitchen. They are made by Guy Kerry at his croft in the Black Isle, with ash wood from a tree blown down in a storm.

The recipe is straightforward, and I owe it entirely to Ian. I bring three cups of water to the boil, pour in a cup of medium pinhead oatmeal in a steady flow (let it fall in a steady rain, is how Marian McNeill puts it in *The Scots Kitchen*), stirring all the time in a clockwise direction. It is done in five minutes, no longer, a scant teaspoon of salt added in the last minute of cooking. As it slides into the wooden porridge bowls, I spoon in a smudge of damson or blackcurrant jam and, if there is any around, some cold single or double cream, avoiding the temptation to write my initials with maple syrup. Tradition prefers us to stand. I hope that leaning against the kitchen sink isn't going to induce the wrath of the devil.

March

# The cast-iron casserole

A casserole is a cooking vessel rather than the food cooked in it. Nevertheless, the word has come to mean a thick, sloppy stew cooked in a covered pot. I'm no pedant and that is fine by me. Once under the ownership of the frugal home cook, such recipes are now standard gastropub fare, and in particular those involving lamb shanks.

The shank, no longer the cheapest of meats, is the hard-working cut from the top of the front leg. The muscles and sinews of the shank can soften or tighten as the mood takes them, so it is best cooked slowly, in liquid, and in a low oven. Frustratingly, the flesh can fall easily from the bone or not, so exact timing in a recipe is almost impossible. They may need an hour or three. Of course, modern cooks demand a recipe that is done in the time it states, but with the lamb shank we must enter a different mindset, one where something is done when it feels like it, not when a recipe says it should be.

Size isn't necessarily an issue, but the smaller the shank, the quicker it may come to tenderness. No guarantees though; I have met the odd tough little bugger before now. Covering with a lid or foil will help the meat to steam as well as bake, which should encourage it down the path towards tenderness. But the most likely way to guarantee your meat falling from the bone in a sinewy, velvety mound is to sink it in plenty of liquid – stock, wine, cider, whatever. Just keep the meat covered. This is no mean feat with a large shank, so regular turning during cooking is essential to keep as much of the flesh covered for as long as possible.

I have several casseroles – by which I mean the pots, not their edible contents. A couple are scarred from bean-based recipes forgotten in the oven (chickpeas leave bubblewrap-type rings on the base; cannellini the sort of snow you get on an untuned television screen), whilst many have cream or grey linings that have taken on the hue of red wine sauce. That'll be boeuf bourguignon, or perhaps oxtail. There is a beautifully understated matt-black one, solid cast iron, which I use for stock and occasionally for a breadcrumb-topped stew. If I were a different sort of cook, it would have been used like those in Castelnaudary, the French home of cassoulet, with its bits of pork, goose and beans. But mine gets used for macaroni cheese, chicken casserole with tarragon and potatoes and, today, a heart-warming dish of lamb shanks cooked with thyme, garlic, onions and black-eyed beans, or other beans if you wish. The sort of recipe that looks as if it took days to make, that warms like no other and makes you feel like a real cook. Whatever one of those may be.

## Lamb shanks with black-eyed beans

I say black-eyed beans, but you could use haricot beans or chickpeas if that is what you have to hand.

dried black-eyed beans: 500g
bay leaves: 2
olive oil
lamb shanks: 4
onions: 3
thyme: 4 small sprigs
garlic: 4 plump cloves, finely
  sliced

plain flour: 4 lightly heaped
  tablespoons
stock or, at a push, water: 750ml

*For the crust:*
fresh white breadcrumbs: 150g
a handful of chopped parsley
olive oil

Soak the beans in cold water overnight to plump them up. The next day, drain and rinse them, then bring to the boil in deep water, together with the bay leaves and a good glug of olive oil. Boil hard for ten minutes, then reduce the heat so they simmer merrily till they are just tender yet retain their shape and some bite – a matter of thirty to thirty-five minutes or so. Drain the beans in a colander and set aside.

Season the lamb shanks and lightly colour them in a little oil – 2 tablespoons should do – in a heavy-based casserole. Once they are pale gold, remove them, but leave their cooking fat behind. Peel the onions, cut them in half and then cut each half into thick segments. Let these soften in the pan over a medium heat, adding a little more oil if there is less than a couple of spoonfuls of fat left. As the onions soften, add the thyme sprigs and the garlic. When all is soft and translucent, stir in the flour and leave to colour lightly for two or three minutes. Gradually stir in the stock to make a thick, oniony sauce. Set the oven at 180°C/Gas 4.

Tip the drained cooked beans in with the onions, then tuck in the lamb and any juices from the plate and season with salt and black pepper. Simmer for thirty minutes, partially covered with a lid, stirring from time to time to check the beans are not sticking. Add more stock if you feel it needs it, then remove from the heat.

Mix the breadcrumbs and parsley with 3 or 4 tablespoons of olive oil, then scatter them over the top of the casserole. Cover loosely with foil, transfer to the oven and cook for an hour and a half or until the meat can be persuaded to part company from its bones. Remove the foil and cook for a further ten to fifteen minutes to let the crust crisp up.

Enough for 4

# Getting passion fruit right

The passion fruit offers us the crunch of a hundred seeds, a dab of golden jelly surrounding each one and a little (very little) piercing saffron juice. Sour, sweet, soft, crisp, the passion fruit gives us a hit of bracing freshness to brighten a grey day.

The dark, spherical fruit is most usually sold unripe – that is, completely smooth, a dull purple mauve, either in packs of four from the supermarket or loose in a cardboard box from the greengrocer's. Keep them till the skin has thinned and its surface is covered with dimples, like a golf ball. Like us, the passion fruit is better for a few wrinkles.

As your fruits progress towards ripeness, their skin will shrivel and become a little brittle. Though small, they should feel heavy for their size. Lightness is generally an indication of dryness within. Catch it before the casing collapses on one side, which is the fruit's last gasp.

Eaten too early, the passion fruit has an astringency that will remind you of the pomegranate, and the juice will be watery and pale. Kept till ripe, it will give you intense fruit flavours and bright, clean, fresh-tasting juice and seeds, to be eaten first thing on a cold morning, with a teaspoon, like a boiled egg. A little cup of sunshine.

This morning the greengrocer has a box of them that are spot on (I have a feeling they were about to be thrown out). I get them cheap and use their knife-sharp juice to make tiny pots of golden cream no bigger than espresso cups. Just four or five teaspoons per person with which to end tonight's dinner.

## Passion fruit creams

| | |
|---|---|
| passion fruit: 16 | caster sugar: 150g |
| double cream: 500ml | lemon juice: 35ml |

Cut the passion fruit in half and scrape out the seeds and juice into a small sieve balanced over a measuring jug or bowl. Let the juice from the fruit drip through, then rub the seeds against the sieve with a teaspoon to get as much of the pulp through as you can. Set the juice aside in a cool place and reserve the seeds for later.

Put the cream and caster sugar in a saucepan and bring to the boil, stirring occasionally to dissolve the sugar. Lower the heat and leave to bubble for three minutes, stirring from time to time. Put the lemon juice in a measuring jug and make the quantity up to 75ml with the reserved passion fruit juice. Keep the remaining juice cold.

Remove the cream mixture from the heat, stir in the lemon and passion fruit juice and leave to settle for a few minutes. Pour into 6 or 8 espresso cups or very small glasses. I like to stir a few of the reserved passion fruit seeds into the mixture for a contrast in texture (say, half a dozen per cup) but that is up to you. Cool, then refrigerate for at least a couple of hours.

Just before you serve the creams, spoon a little puddle of the passion fruit juice over the top. As each diner digs in with their teaspoon, the juice will trickle down into the depths of the cream.

Makes 6–8 espresso cups


## MARCH 6

# Beans on toast again

Being compiled from my dog-eared, chaotic notebooks rather than a meticulously kept and chronologically perfect diary means that many of my everyday meals, those I tend to do almost on autopilot, rarely get their fifteen minutes in the limelight. This is a shame because they are often jolly good eating.

Such meals tend to get taken for granted, like very close friends. One of my favourite quick fixes has always been beans on toast. I like the sweet commercial sauce and the thick toast, which, just for the record, I always butter. The joy of richly sauced beans and hot toast is not confined to the turquoise tin though, and I often make a home-made version, with cans of beans that I put in my own sauce, stirring in bacon, mushrooms or whatever is to hand (chorizo and black pudding are favourite additions).

Today, even with my woolly hat on (I now have three, and every one of them makes me look as stupid as the other), the biting-cold wind is making my ears numb. The idea of going home to sweet, sticky beans with a wodge of warm sourdough bread appeals more than almost anything I can think of. I could cop out with my mate Heinz, embellishing them with chilli or Marmite, or even a bit of bacon, but instead decide to take an extra thirty minutes to make a down-home version. It does the trick.

## Beans on toast

A little more trouble than opening a can, but much more satisfying when you have the time.

lardons or cubed bacon or pancetta: 200g
an onion
a little rapeseed or olive oil
a rib of celery
carrots: 2 small to medium
chopped tomatoes: two 400g cans
canned beans (pinto, haricot, butter beans etc): two 400g cans
black treacle: 1 teaspoon
a lump of sourdough loaf

Fry the lardons in a deep pan over a moderate heat. Peel and roughly chop the onion. When the lardons and their fat are golden, add the onion, together with a little rapeseed or olive oil if there seems too little fat in the pan. Chop the celery and carrots, add to the pan and leave to cook for a full five minutes, till fragrant and starting to soften. Add the tomatoes, simmer for ten minutes, then stir in the drained beans and simmer for another ten minutes. Season with the treacle, a little black pepper and some salt.

Warm the bread in the oven, tear into chunks and serve with the beans.
Enough for 2

## A tropical marinade and a shoal of sea bass

For some time now I have been curious about glass, and why some is more beautiful to look at, and look through, than others. Windows made from old 'crown' glass have soft waves and little bubbles, like tiny seeds to catch the light, while drinking glasses that are uneven in the hand, with ripples and furrows, make the water within sparkle. Small things, but they matter to me. I like drinking water from a hand-made tumbler with dimples and folds.

Aesthetics aside, glass is a useful object in the kitchen because it has a neutral effect on the food we put in it. Unlike aluminium, glass is unaffected by acid ingredients such as rhubarb, lemon and vinegar. Leave a batch of poached rhubarb in a glass bowl and it will taste the same after a night or two in the fridge. Use aluminium and your fruit will have taken on an unpleasant taint from the dish. It is one of the reasons glass has been used for centuries for storing acid-based preserves such as pickles and relishes.

I also use glass to marinate meat and fish. Not only is it non-reactive but you can see the changes taking place in the food more easily. Make a ceviche in a glass dish and you can see whether the fish has turned opaque from the lime juice. I can't be the only person who finds measuring liquid in a glass jug more accurate than in one made from china. I particularly like making the classic lemon surprise pudding in a Pyrex bowl so I can see the distinct layers of sponge and lemon sauce.

Today I work on a recipe for a television programme for next Christmas (such is the life of a cookery writer). It is not my recipe, but comes via The Rebel Dining Society. It's fresh, clean, smart and uses up the rest of the passion fruit.

# A ceviche of sea bass and passion fruit

| | |
|---|---|
| passion fruit: 4 | a red chilli |
| limes: 2 | a small yellow or orange chilli |
| an orange | chives: 4 or 5, snipped into short |
| a vanilla pod |     pieces |
| sea bass fillets: 4 | coriander leaves: a small handful |

Squeeze the juice of the passion fruit, seeds and all, plus the limes and the orange into a bowl. Scrape in the seeds of the vanilla pod and mix gently.

Skin the sea bass fillets, then cut the flesh into thin slivers and arrange them neatly on a large plate or in a glass bowl. Pour over the juice, almost submerging the fish. Scatter over very fine slices of red and yellow chilli and cover the plate with a piece of cling film. The sea bass will be 'cooked' by the acidity in the dressing, so leave in the fridge for a good three or four hours or even overnight. Scatter the chives and coriander leaves over the fish and serve.

Enough for 4 as part of a light lunch

# MARCH 8

# A jar of capers

The door of the fridge holds many treasures, but mostly rows of opened jars. Today the list is typical: a bottle of Vietnamese chilli paste, a block of tamarind, two packets of butter, a tube of harissa paste and another of wasabi, a bottle of damson gin and a jar of damson jam, two opened jars of marmalade, four bottles of tonic water, a bottle of apple juice I use for my breakfast smoothies, a bottle of Vietnamese fish sauce and another of rice wine, four bottles of sparkling Norwegian mineral water and a jar of salted capers. Of course, the capers don't need refrigerating, but the oversized fridge has become the modern-day larder.

Capers generally come in brine or salt. The latter is considered to be better, mostly because the capers are plumper and, although salty, the seasoning stays on the outside and can be washed off – unlike the brined version, where the capers soak up the salt-water solution like little sponges.

Their qualities of sourness and salt tend to polarise people, but they are without doubt one of the most used seasonings in my kitchen, finding their way into sauces for steak and fish, a dressing for many a salad, and tossed with warm, partially melted butter for a pasta sauce.

The caper is the cook's first call for piquancy. Bitter, sharp and salty, it has the ability to bring out the flavour of any ingredient it is partnered with. A dull nugget that makes other flavours shine. Generally, I suggest a caper is only warmed, never cooked, as it can become inedibly bitter, though once it is dunked in a pool of tomato sauce on a pizza the average caper is probably fairly safe.

The caper is a flower bud, pickled or salted before it becomes a small, creamy-white flower. Italian ones are probably the best known but they are grown in Morocco and Turkey too. Caper berries, incidentally, are fatter than capers – almost the size of an olive – and are eaten with their stalk, with a distinctive crunch to them. They are the fruit of the caper bush that is produced after the buds have flowered.

Despite all the culinary partnerships that intrigue or delight, there are very few that actually make the mouth water. Mouthwatering, that over-used term that I have banned from any piece of writing or programme that bears my name, is a particular horror of mine, like the word 'crispy'. Yet occasionally the word is accurate, such as when it is used to describe the partnership of capers with lemon. A recipe for culinary fireworks. The two have almost magical powers when they appear with fish.

## Sea bass with rosemary and capers

| | |
|---|---|
| sea bass: 2 small ones, cleaned | capers: a tablespoon, rinsed |
| new potatoes: 500g | the juice of a small lemon |
| olive oil | garlic: 2 cloves |
| rosemary: 4 bushy sprigs | parsley: 4 large sprigs |
| a long, hot red chilli | a lemon, to serve |
| sherry vinegar: a tablespoon | |

Set the oven at 200°C/Gas 6. Rinse the fish and wipe them dry with paper towel.

Peel the potatoes, then cut them into slices about the thickness of a pound coin. Warm a couple of tablespoons of olive oil in a large, shallow pan or roasting tin set over a moderate to low heat and slide in the potatoes.

Let them cook slowly until their edges are starting to colour – a matter of ten minutes. It is worth stirring them and turning them over now and again, so they don't stick to the pan.

As the potatoes cook, make the dressing: remove the needles from the rosemary twigs, chop them finely, then put them into a mixing bowl. Halve the chilli lengthways, scrape out and discard the seeds, then chop the flesh finely. Add it to the rosemary together with the sherry vinegar, the rinsed capers, the lemon juice and a grinding of black pepper. Peel and finely chop the garlic, remove and chop the leaves from the parsley, then stir both into the dressing with three tablespoons of olive oil.

When the potatoes are ready, stir them again, then lay the fish on top of them and spoon over the dressing, tucking as much of it as possible into the open bellies of the fish. Transfer to the oven and bake for about twenty-five minutes, until the fish is tender, opaque and just cooked through to the bone.

Serve the fish by cutting off the heads and tails (you can do it with a spoon), then lifting the fish on to hot plates. Divide the potatoes between the plates and serve immediately, squeezing half a lemon over each at the table.

Enough for 2

## MARCH 10

# The usefulness of a rye loaf

In Helsinki, Stockholm, Copenhagen and Oslo, you will find trays of marinated pickled herrings in the market to buy by the kilo. Juniper, dill and onion are the usual flavourings, but some stallholders will push the boat out with a mustard dressing or perhaps beetroot and soured cream. A taste of sea spray.

At home, it is more usual to see these iridescent blue and silver fillets trapped in glass jars, stuffed with minced onion, each herring fillet bound round itself with two tiny wooden sticks. There is almost always a jar in the fridge for when I need a shot of their piercing sourness; a culinary slap in the face. My only gripe is that they usually contain too much onion.

A hint of sourness goes well in bread too, by which I mean the seemingly endless rye breads you find in Scandinavian bakeries, rather than the delightful but ubiquitous Californian-style or Parisian sourdough. One of the many delights of eating in Sweden, Finland and Norway has been the chewy, seed- and oat-laden rye loaves that turn up at breakfast and, particularly in Norway, for lunch. Some are made deliberately heavy and dark with a hint of molasses, the bitter-sweet 'treacle' removed during sugar production. Some are freckled with whole grains, others almost sponge-like, the colour of butterscotch. The detail they all have in common is their chewy quality and, of course, the note of sour that comes from the lightly fermented rye grains. And another good thing: you need only a slice or two to fill you up.

This evening, supper is 'something on toast'. A creamy puddle of chopped pickled herring, a scattering of dill and soured cream on rounds of rye toast from the St John Bakery in Bermondsey. I sometimes use the squares of sticky rye that come shrink-wrapped in tight, plastic packs from the corner shop, the sort that look like a treacle-coloured brick. Either way, the point is the marriage of sweet pickled fish and sour rye bread, Nordic to the core.

### Herrings, soured cream, rye toast

| | |
|---|---|
| cucumber: 250g | soured cream or labne: 200g |
| a small red onion | capers: 8 |
| dill leaves and stalks: 15g | rye bread: 4 slices |
| white wine vinegar or verjuice: | |
|    2 tablespoons | *For the top:* |
| pickled herring fillets: 300g | a few thin slices of red onion |

Peel the cucumber, removing only the tough outer skin. Slice the cucumber no thicker than a pound coin. Put the slices in a colander and scatter them generously with salt. Set the colander in the sink or over a bowl and leave for an hour. The salt will draw out some of the juices.

Pat the cucumber slices dry with kitchen paper and transfer them to a mixing bowl. Peel the onion and slice half of it very thinly, finely chopping the remainder. Chop the dill fronds and stalks and toss most of them in with the cucumber, the chopped onion and the white wine vinegar or ver-juice, then set aside. Reserve the remaining dill.

Pat the herring dry, removing any onion or spices that may come with it, and slice it into short 1cm-wide strips. Add these to the cucumber. Mix the soured cream or labne with the herring and cucumber, season with black pepper and the capers and set aside.

Toast the bread, then spread the herring mixture generously on top. Scatter with the reserved chopped dill and thinly sliced red onion.

Enough for 2 as a light lunch or supper

# Surf and turf

One of the most successful recipes to come out of the 'Surf and Turf' programme in the *Simple Cooking* series on BBC1 was the fillets of trout baked with Parma ham. The feedback was heartwarming. Today I make a similar dish with salmon and bacon, mostly because that is what I have brought back from the shops. My rashers are on the thick side, so I stretch them out by pressing them down on a chopping board with the flat side of a knife blade before wrapping the salmon in them.

## Bacon-wrapped salmon

salmon: two 250g steaks or fillets
thinly cut streaky bacon:
    4 rashers

lemon thyme: a couple of sprigs
a little oil

Set the oven at 200°C/Gas 6. Season the fish with black pepper and a very little salt. Wrap each piece in 2 rashers of bacon, tucking a sprig of thyme under the bacon. Brush with a little oil and bake for fifteen to twenty minutes, till the fish is cooked through and the bacon golden.
    Enough for 2

## A new mash

Cumulus-style potato mash, whipped up with butter and a heavy beater, seems perfect as an accompaniment to boiled gammon or grilled liver, where the parsley sauce or onion gravy is forked into the mashed potato. What ends up on your fork is part soft potato, part sauce. A luscious, perfect thing.

Occasionally, there is call for a butter-free mash, where the potato is forced through a ricer or coarse sieve, whose minute holes create airy, open-textured mash. It is the sort of thing to serve with something unctuous and possibly wine-imbued, such as a beef casserole. The suave, restaurant-style, olive-oil-enriched mashes so sloppy they almost ooze across the plate are what I make to accompany fish or lentil dishes, particularly grilled fillets of mackerel or baked hake with cream and parsley.

Tonight I produce a new mash, deliberately coarse textured (the mean-spirited might say lumpy), made using the tines of a fork rather than a flat metal beater or wooden spoon. The potato skins are left on, giving a rather wholesome, rustic quality. You could call it lazy mashed potato, but skipping the peeling is hardly the point. It is the earthy, rough-meadow feel of the potato that is the prize, the sort of topping I want for a creamy mushroom and leek pie. A classic mash would be too soft and bland in texture. As a crust for a soft filling of fungi, Marsala and cream, this rough-edged mash is darned well perfect.

## Leek and mushroom pie with skin-on mash

small leeks: 400g, untrimmed
    weight
olive oil: 2 tablespoons
butter: 30g
assorted mushrooms: 600g
plain flour: 2 lightly heaped
    tablespoons
dry Marsala: 3–4 tablespoons

vegetable or chicken stock: 300ml
tarragon: a small bunch
crème fraîche: 2 heaped
    tablespoons

*For the potatoes:*
floury potatoes: 1.5kg
butter: 50g

Trim the leeks, removing any dark green leaves (anything pale green or white is fine). Warm the olive oil and butter in a large casserole over a moderate heat. Thinly slice the leeks, then add them to the casserole. Cover with a lid and cook at a low to moderate pace for ten to fifteen minutes, until they are soft but not coloured.

Sort the mushrooms, dividing them into firm (chestnut, portabello, button) and the more fragile 'wild' varieties that will take less time to cook. Once the leeks are soft, remove them from the pan and set aside. Slice or quarter the firm mushrooms where necessary, add them to the pan and cook till they are lightly coloured, adding more butter or oil as you think fit. Return the leeks to the pan. Stir in the flour and continue cooking for two or three minutes, then pour in the Marsala, followed shortly by the stock. Leave to simmer for thirty to forty minutes.

Remove the tarragon leaves from their stalks, keeping them whole, and stir them into the sauce with the crème fraîche. Check the seasoning, remove from the heat, then pour the mixture into a large baking dish. Tuck in the raw fragile mushrooms (they will overcook if added during the initial cooking) and set aside.

Set the oven at 200°C/Gas 6. Cook the potatoes, unpeeled, in boiling salted water till tender, then drain. Mash roughly, skins and all, with the butter. Place in rough mounds over the mushroom sauce (don't be tempted to smooth the mash on top) and bake for forty-five minutes.

Enough for 6

MARCH 14

## Black bananas

No fruit's ripeness seems to divide people the way that of the banana does. And it is not simply a question of soft or firm. Oh deary me, no, nothing so straightforward. Within the boundaries of soft and firm are further categories, mostly easier to feel than to describe, where the exact level of ripeness becomes almost an art form. Even before we get inside, there are pointers, mostly to do with the level of mottling and about which some aficionados could probably write an essay, if not a short story. The feel of the banana (go carefully here) is crucial. It must yield like fudge, butter or, for some, be only just short of a smoothie. Some take it even further: their fruit must be the right shape. For heaven's sake. It's a banana.

I need a banana to be firm, crisp, almost underripe. Few things make me feel queasier than the smell of an overripe banana in a confined place (it's a school duffel bag thing, let's not go there). Occasionally, you do find the perfect fruit, in the optimum condition, but more often than not they are not quite right. Some, dismissed or simply forgotten, end up black.

Black bananas. Oh, yes please. Sugary to the point of sickly, their flavour has developed to such an extent that they will perfume a cake to perfection, providing the depth of flavour you always hope a banana cake will have but it so rarely does.

There is always one recipe that becomes the star of a television series, the one that more people make than any other. According to the monumental Twitter activity, this cake 'trended'. A cake 'trending'.

## Nigel's chocolate muscovado banana cake

| | |
|---|---|
| plain flour: 250g | ripe bananas: 400g (peeled weight) |
| baking powder: 2 teaspoons | vanilla extract: a teaspoon |
| butter, softened: 125g | eggs: 2 |
| muscovado sugar: 235g | dark chocolate: 100g |

You will also need a non-stick loaf tin approximately 24cm x 12cm x 7cm deep, lined with baking paper. Set the oven at 180°C/Gas 4. Sift the flour and baking powder together.

Using an electric mixer, cream the butter and sugar together till light, fluffy and pale coffee coloured.

Put the bananas in a bowl and mash them with a fork. The mixture should be lumpy rather than crushed to a purée. Stir in the vanilla extract. Beat the eggs lightly with a fork then beat them into the butter and sugar mixture. Introduce a spoonful of flour at any sign of curdling.

Chop the chocolate into small pieces – about the size of fine gravel – and fold them and the bananas into the butter and sugar mixture. Gently fold in the flour and baking powder. Scrape the mixture into the lined baking tin then bake for about fifty minutes. Check the cake is ready by inserting a metal skewer into the centre. If the skewer comes out moist but clean then the cake is done. If there is any sign of wet cake mixture, return the cake to the oven for a few more minutes and cover the surface with foil.

Leave the cake in its tin to settle for fifteen minutes or so, then loosen the sides with a palette knife and carefully lift out of its tin. Leave to cool a little longer then carefully peel off the paper. Serve cool, in thick slices.

## MARCH 16

## Getting the most from a roast

Love the roast, the salad you can put together from the leftovers and the soup you can knock up from its bones, but the ultimate use for any leftover Sunday lunch has to be the sandwiches you can rustle up for days afterwards. Sometimes, those gorgeous, frugal little snacks involve no more than slamming some cold cuts on a piece of bread slathered in mayo. But this weekend my cold roast pork buns got a bit more of my time, with a handmade dressing of shredded carrots and galangal (I could have used ginger), lime juice and coriander leaves. Cool little chaps, they became as much of a treat as the initial roast.

Had I roasted my pork shoulder with garlic, thyme and lemon, I could have used some of the leftovers for a lentil soup with other compatible flavourings – such as red onions, Marsala and spinach, and then maybe made a ciabatta sandwich with the scraps and a salsa verde or garlic mayonnaise. Had I taken an Indian route, cooking it after a short marinade in oil and spices, then I could have put the rest in a sandwich with a spice-paste mayonnaise, or even in a soup finished with yoghurt and garam masala. But my piece of pork had been almost pot-roasted, a piece of loose kitchen foil in lieu of a lid to keep it moist. No crackling. I saved the skin and fat for later. The seasoning of anise, ginger and black peppercorns set the tone for the soup and sandwiches that followed. A broth enriched with the treasure from the roasting tin and trimmings of meat from the joint, then made into something light, fresh and vital with masses of Chinese greens. The broth satisfied, the inclusion of last night's meat felt like a spot of good housekeeping, while the addition of green peppercorns gave it a deep, marrow-warming heat.

The best bit was the sandwiches that followed. Yes, I went to a spot of trouble, making a sort of slaw with a spicy mayonnaise slashed with lime juice and using herbs instead of lettuce, but that bit of effort made each one a sandwich to remember. I see no reason why we shouldn't go to just as much trouble over a butty as we do over a bowl of soup.

The sandwiches that follow Sunday lunch have the benefit of the accompaniments that might also be holed up in the fridge. Stuffing, horse-radish, cranberry or bread sauces, some cold greens for heating up in a frying pan, and maybe even some of the fat from the roasting tin, all present opportunities for gilding the lily of a plain cold-cut sarnie. My favourite of these is probably the one where we have slices of rare beef, some creamed horseradish, plus some leftover Brussels sprouts cut in half and fried in a little butter. Roast duck bits with pickled cabbage or fruity chutney come a close second.

The bread – its quality and most of all its freshness – is crucial. I like soft, doorstop-style bread for a leftover sandwich, with some sort of green leaves in the form of watercress or sprouted seeds (beanshoots can be surprisingly good between two pieces of bread), but a wholemeal-style bun, maybe with nuts and seeds, can be more fulfilling. Mine came from the E5 Bakehouse in London's East End, a tarted-up railway arch full of young, artisan bakers and typical of the adventurous, independent bakeries opening up all over the country. Nothing good will come from stuffing your leftover into a less than decent loaf.

## Pork shoulder with ginger and anise

a boned and rolled shoulder of
   pork, about 1.3kg (ask the
   butcher to score the skin)
stock (vegetable or whatever is
   to hand): 400ml

fresh ginger: 6 round slices, about
   the thickness of a pound coin
star anise: 3
black peppercorns: 8
steamed greens, to serve

Set the oven at 150°C/Gas 2. Put the piece of pork, fat-side up, in a roasting tin. Pour the stock around it and add the ginger, star anise and peppercorns.

Cover the tin loosely with foil, then put it into the oven and leave for three hours. This is the minimum time in which it will be done, but you can leave it for longer if you want meat that falls from the bone. Remove the foil for the last thirty minutes.

Remove the skin and fat from the pork and set them aside to make the crackling for the baps. Reserve a good 100ml of the broth from around the roast for tomorrow's soup. Slice half the meat, divide it between four plates and spoon over the juices. Serve with steamed greens.

Enough for 4, with leftovers

## A main-course soup

### Pork broth with pepper and green leaves

stock (vegetable is best): 800ml
broth from the roasting tin
  on page 121: 100ml
fresh or brined green peppercorns:
  1 tablespoon
whole Szechuan pepper:
  1 teaspoon

small, hot chillies: 6–8
pork from the recipe on page 121:
  150g
soft, tender greens, such as pak
  choy or spinach

Pour the stock into a deep saucepan with the reserved broth from the roasting tin. Bring to the boil, then add the peppercorns, Szechuan pepper and whole chillies. Lower the heat to a simmer and let the soup bubble gently for about fifteen minutes.

Shred the pork into small, bite-sized pieces and divide them between four warm soup bowls. Rinse the leaves and shake them dry, then drop them into the soup bowls. Season with salt if necessary; you are unlikely to need pepper. Ladle the soup into bowls, fishing the chillies out as you go, and serve.

Enough for 4

## A memorable sandwich

There is that sublime moment, usually late at night when you are a little bit pissed, when you come across something delicious hiding in the fridge. A morsel of gorgeousness that you weren't expecting to find. The pork I find in the fridge tonight was fully expected, almost planned. These are sandwiches I have been thinking about all day.

## Pulled pork baps with carrot and galangal slaw

leftover roast pork: 180g
carrots: 180g
galangal or ginger: a large lump (to give 4 teaspoons when grated)
mayonnaise: 150ml

half a lime
the reserved fat and skin from the roast on page 121
floury or seedy baps or soft rolls: 4
coriander leaves (optional)

Using two forks, tear the pork into thin shreds and then put them in a mixing bowl. Grate the carrots coarsely into thick, string-like shreds, as you might for a remoulade (the coarse grater blade of a food processor attachment is good for this). Add them to the pork. Peel the galangal or ginger and grate it very finely, almost to a purée, then add it to the carrots and pork. Spoon in the mayonnaise and mix gently with a fork (it will help to keep the grated carrot from forming clumps). Season generously with black pepper and the juice of the lime.

Put the skin and fat from the pork on a foil-lined baking sheet and place under a hot grill for five minutes or so, until the skin has crisped up. Turn it over and cook the other side, then remove from the heat and leave to cool on a piece of kitchen paper. Slice into thin strips with a heavy knife.

Split the baps, put a small handful of coriander leaves, if using, on the bottom half of each one and spoon on the carrot slaw. Place a few strips of crackling on top. Close and eat immediately.

Enough for 4

## MARCH 20

# Remembering the pierogi

The world is full of tiny edible parcels. The dim sum of Chinatown's rattling trolleys, Japan's neatly puckered gyoza, Cornwall's pasties and even the little mince pie. If I'm honest, I hadn't expected much of Poland's pierogi, the steamed or fried pastry parcels of cabbage, mushroom and pork. I thought it would be a sort of Cornish pasty without the swede. There for the film festival at which *Toast* was headlining, I looked for them only halfheartedly.

Warsaw's pierogi turned out to be delicious little bundles of cabbage, blue cheese, mushrooms or pork, and came not just steamed and fried but baked too, and served with a flowered china boat of soured cream and dill sauce. Yes, tiny dumplings somewhere in size between a gyoza and a pasty. The baked version is not so easy to find but is the easiest to make at home. Today I make a batch, filling them with a mixture of mushroom and very finely shredded cabbage. They vanish in minutes.

## Sauerkraut and mushroom pierogi

Pierogi can be baked, fried or boiled. Recipes for the soft and silky boiled versions are easy to find. This baked version is more unusual, like a sort of mouth-sized Cornish pasty.

*For the pastry:*
plain flour: 500g
butter: 200g, cut into small dice
ice-cold water
an egg, lightly beaten

*For the filling:*
onions: 2 medium
butter: 30g

small mushrooms: 300g
garlic: 2 small cloves
sauerkraut: 350g

*For the soured cream and dill sauce:*
soured cream: 300g
a small bunch of dill (about 15g)
a little wine vinegar

Make the pastry: sift the flour into a bowl, add the butter and rub it into the flour until the mixture has a coarse breadcrumb texture. Add enough cold water to bring the dough to a firm but still pliable ball. Knead very gently for a couple of minutes, then wrap in greaseproof paper or cling film and refrigerate for twenty to thirty minutes.

Peel the onions, cut them in half and slice them very finely. Melt the butter in a large pan and add the onions, letting them soften but not colour.

Chop the mushrooms very finely, peel and slice the garlic and add both to the onions. Continue cooking for five minutes or so. Drain the sauerkraut and rinse briefly in a colander under cold running water, then shake or pat dry. Add the sauerkraut to the onion and mushrooms and mix well. Season generously with black pepper and set aside.

Set the oven at 200°C/Gas 6. Roll out the pastry thinly (I find it easiest to do this a half at a time). Using a round cookie cutter or the top of a wine glass, cut 16 discs of pastry approximately 9–10cm in diameter. Place a generous

spoonful of the sauerkraut mixture on each pastry disc. Brush the edge of the pastry with a little of the beaten egg, then fold in half and press firmly to seal the edges. Place the pastries on a baking sheet, not quite touching one another, and brush with more beaten egg. Cut a tiny slit or two in the top of each and bake for twenty minutes, till the pastry is crisp and golden.

To make the sauce, put the soured cream into a small bowl. Finely chop the dill fronds and the most tender part of the stems. Stir the chopped dill into the soured cream, then add a little salt and black pepper and a few drops of wine vinegar. Serve with the hot pierogi.

Makes 16 small pastries

## MARCH 23

# A luscious pie for a cool day

One of those bracing March days that feels as if there should be frost on the ground. A cupboard cooking day, rather than one for browsing round the food shops. If I am honest, I value these days. They make you realise that treasure is lurking in the cupboard. The packets of lentils and bits of root vegetables, the onions, bay leaves and potatoes that can form an economical, warming meal, but only if they do not fall victim to our blind spot as we cast around for something to cook. This time I use up the large jar of lentils in water that has been in the cupboard seemingly for ever. I usually cook mine from scratch, but actually find the bottled variety perfect for this, cutting down on the not inconsiderable preparation time.

One of the more interesting things to arise from years of hand-to-mouth living when I first came to London – pot washer, coffee maker (before they became baristas), store man, barman (before they became mixologists), waiter (before they became cool), and, dear reader, I loved every minute – was developing an ability to make big, cheap suppers in quantities that would last for a few days. I still cook like that to this day, not only because it makes sound economical sense but because it is such good stuff.

# Lentil and spinach pie

onions: 2 medium to large
carrots: 2
celery: a small stick
olive or rapeseed oil: a tablespoon
large, dark mushrooms: 350g
garlic: 3 cloves
bay leaves: 2
thyme: 3 or 4 short sprigs
a 500g jar of lentils
vegetable stock: 500ml

balsamic vinegar: about
    2 teaspoons
spinach: 500g

*For the potato crust:*
large, floury potatoes: 1kg
butter: 75g (or 3 tablespoons
    olive oil)

Finely dice the onions, carrots and celery, then cook in the olive or rapeseed oil in a deep casserole over a moderate flame for ten minutes or so, till the onions are golden and almost tender. Finely chop the mushrooms and add to the casserole. Peel and finely slice the garlic and stir it in. Add the bay leaves and thyme, then the lentils, together with their bottling liquid, and stir briefly. Pour in the stock, bring to the boil, then turn the heat down and leave the mixture to simmer for a good twenty minutes. Season with salt, black pepper and balsamic vinegar to taste.

Peel the potatoes, cut them into pieces and boil in salted water till thoroughly tender. Drain well, then mash with the butter or oil, using a potato masher, food mixer or fork. Beat hard with a wooden spoon till light and fluffy.

Set the oven at 200°C/Gas 6. Wash the spinach and, if the leaves are very big, tear them into large pieces. Whilst they are still wet, pile 450g of them into a pan with a lid and let them steam, with an occasional stir, over a high heat for a couple of minutes till they start to collapse and darken in colour. Cool them under the cold tap, then wring them out and stir them into the lentils. A word here: don't be tempted to add the spinach raw to the lentils. It will produce a lot of water as it cooks and you will be left with lentil soup. Fold the remaining spinach into the mashed potato.

Spoon the lentils into a baking dish and top with the potato in large, rough spoonfuls. It will want to sink into the lentils, but try to prevent it. Bake for an hour, till the edges are bubbling.

Enough for 6

Sometimes I go to a great deal of trouble with a stir-fry, making a spice paste, neatly chopping vegetables into the smallest imaginable pieces, maybe even par-cooking some of them before throwing them into the wok. Tonight I have no such values and do the quickest lazy-boy stir-fry imaginable. Hot and satisfyingly savoury, it does the trick. It fills a hole.

## A stir-fry of greens and mushrooms

shallots: 3
garlic: 4 cloves
hot red chillies: 2
small closed-cup mushrooms: 150g
spring greens: 2 heads
rapeseed or other flavourless oil:
  3 tablespoons

grated fresh ginger: 2 teaspoons
fish sauce: 2 tablespoons
caster sugar: a teaspoon
a little dark soy sauce
roughly torn coriander leaves:
  a handful

Peel and finely shred the shallots. Peel the garlic and slice it finely. Halve the chillies, discard the seeds and cut the flesh into thin shreds. Cut the mushrooms in half. Shred the greens finely. This is easiest when the leaves are piled on top of one another and rolled up like a cigar.

Get a wok or large, thin-bottomed pan really hot. Pour in the oil and then, just as it starts to smoke, add the shallots, garlic, chillies and ginger. Stir-fry them for thirty seconds or so, till they are fragrant and just beginning to colour. Add the mushrooms and let them colour appetisingly, moving them and the aromatics around the pan regularly. Add the shredded greens and continue cooking till they have softened but are still bright and vibrant in colour – a matter of two or three minutes. Add the fish sauce, caster sugar and soy. Wait till everything is sizzling, then throw in the coriander, toss and stir, and eat immediately.

Enough for 2

## A sweet-sharp duck and an ice cream for a cold day

For someone who is not fond of the colour orange, there is an awful lot of it in my kitchen at the moment: chubby little navels, heavy with juice; tiny blood oranges with ruby and tangerine flesh; knobbly, late-season Sevilles (they normally disappear around the end of February), the fruit for marmalade and *caneton à l'orange*. There are pink grapefruits and the classic white-fleshed ones I prefer, and some rounded Bergamot lemons whose fragrance has a mysterious, spicy edge to it.

I squeeze the occasional orange, mostly one of the blood variety, and swig its juice on a Sunday morning (I go for half orange, half pomegranate for a real wake-up call) but most citrus fruits in my kitchen end up grated, sliced, stuffed inside a roast duck or a chicken hotpot, simmered into marmalade or peeled, sliced and served in a salad. Few are ever eaten as they come, or sliced in half and turned inside out the way my brother used to eat them. I value the fruit for its sharpness, that smack of acidity that it gives, and find its peel useful in lamb stews where it adds a hint of Provence if you include rosemary, red wine and garlic too.

Orange juice squeezed from the fruit can be thin and metallic or sweet-sharp and vibrant, depending on your oranges. The oranges around at the moment are wonderful – heavy for their size, small and firm, and impossible to peel without leaking juice all over the place. I use them tonight in a sort of upside-down tart, where the juice soaked delightfully through the pastry but which I am not happy enough with to include here, and a main course involving pieces of duck cooked with slices of orange and lemon, to which I introduce a bit of seasonal warmth with preserved ginger. I used both legs and breasts but, rather than cook them as they were, I marinated them with salt and ginger syrup before adding them to the pot. That way they stay incredibly juicy and succulent, not something you can always say about this particular meat.

# Duck with ginger and citrus

I have suggested eating this with rice, and in particular nutty brown basmati, but brown lentils could be suitable too. Depending on what is to follow, I would accompany it with some steamed greens, such as bok choy, choi sum or maybe even sprouting broccoli. A watercress salad would be good, too.

duck legs: 2
duck breasts: 2
preserved ginger in syrup:
  6 knobs, sliced into thick coins
syrup from the ginger jar:
  6 tablespoons

sea salt flakes: 2 teaspoons
an orange
a lemon
a little caster sugar (optional)
steamed brown rice, to serve

Make four or five slashes, about a finger's width apart, through the skin of the duck legs and breasts. Put them in a plastic bag with 4 tablespoons of the ginger syrup, 3 tablespoons of warm water and the sea salt. Seal the bag, then set aside in the fridge or a very cool place for a couple of hours.

Remove the duck from the bag, reserving the marinade. Put a large, heavy-based pan over a moderate to high heat, place the duck in it skin-side down (no oil or extra fat is required) and brown lightly, then turn and brown the other side. Tip off any excess fat from the pan (you need to leave a little). Thinly slice the orange and lemon, without peeling them, then add them to the pan, together with the marinade from the duck. Adjust the heat so that the liquid simmers gently, season with black pepper and cover with a lid.

Leave to simmer for about twenty minutes, keeping the heat fairly low and checking regularly to make sure the fruit is not sticking to the pan. Pour in the remaining ginger syrup, then add the knobs of preserved ginger. Check the pan juices; they should be nicely sweet, sharp and slightly spicy from the ginger. Adjust them to taste with salt, orange juice and, if you wish, a little sugar.

Serve the duck, citrus fruits and cooking juices with the rice.
Enough for 4

I have always rather liked eating ice cream on a winter's day. The surprise of an icy chill on a tongue that was probably expecting a sip of hot chocolate. Just as plum sorbet (see July) and damson ice cream (see *Tender Volume II*) are fruitily cooling for mid to late summer, there are flavours that seem particularly suited to cooler days. Vanilla, of course, dark chocolate, liquorice, lemon, orange and cinnamon have a note of warm spice or a bite of citrus that seems right when the sun isn't shining (the scent of lemon blossom on a winter's day in Amalfi is exhilarating).

The ice-cream flavour that interests me now is coffee. Not a creamy, latte-style ice or a wenge-coloured granita but a dark, espresso-flavoured ice, creamy but also pungent with slightly bitter beans. I make my usual espresso, but add it to a quick custard to give an ice suitable for a cold day.

### Espresso and dark chocolate ice cream

milk: 500ml
double cream: 500ml
coffee beans ground for
    espresso: 50g

egg yolks: 4
caster sugar: 150g
dark chocolate: 100g

Put the milk and cream into a saucepan, add the ground coffee and bring to the boil. As it comes up to boiling point, turn off the heat and leave to infuse for twenty-five minutes.

Beat the egg yolks and sugar with a wooden spoon in a non-stick saucepan till they are light in colour. Pour the milk and coffee mixture through a fine sieve on to the egg yolk and sugar mixture and stir throughly. Place over a low to moderate heat and stir until the custard starts to thicken slightly. If you take it too far it will curdle, so it is best to remove it from the heat the second it starts to thicken enough to coat the back of the spoon.

Pour into a jug and chill thoroughly. Transfer to an ice-cream machine and churn till almost frozen. Chop the chocolate into small, rough pieces, stir them into the ice cream and spoon into a freezer box. Freeze for a minimum of five hours.

Enough for 6

April

## APRIL 2

# A dish of olives

The legend that we learned how to eat olives after one was rescued from the sea, nicely brined by the Mediterranean, is one that I am happy to go with. The story suits the simplicity of the olive itself, born on a tree as old as time, bent and gnarled, picked and pickled, then offered in a little dish.

A favourite in this house has always been a sourdough loaf, some cold, pale butter, a few olives and a rugged-looking salami. It's a lunch, snack or midnight feast I come back to time and time again, at lunchtime with a leaf salad to follow, often just lettuce with a grain-mustard-freckled dressing.

There is often more than one type of olive in my kitchen. Tiny, purple-grey niçoise olives from Provence; the salty, black Kalamata from Greece and, perhaps my favourite of all, the glossy green olives that have been marinated in olive oil and lemon from a local deli. All except the stuffed ones are likely to get a look in, but they are increasingly difficult to find in their unadulterated state. Anchovies, peppers, chillies, almonds and pretty much everything else finds its way into an olive nowadays. All I want is the stone to suck.

The silver-grey leaves of the olive tree always seem out of place here. Yes, they will grow in a pot on the balcony of a new-build apartment or in the kitchen garden of an oh-so-English country house, but they will never look as if they belong. The olive is a symbol of peace and of wisdom but also holds some magic for me. The older trees are amongst the most beautiful of all, especially when the branches are twisted, their grey bark peeling.

It is rare I find an olive I don't like. Only those that are tossed in garlic, stuffed with anchovy or red pepper or marinated with chilli get spat out. The less someone has done to an olive, generally the more I appreciate it. From time to time I use them in the kitchen too – scattered over a thin onion tart, chopped and tossed with pasta, preserved artichokes and lemon, or maybe mashed into a paste with olive oil and garlic and spread on discs of toasted baguette. Generally, I keep olives out of my cooking, as they have a tendency to lose all their subtlety and end up as little salt bombs (in France I once had a sorbet made from them that left me gasping for water for days).

Just occasionally, they make it on to the hob or oven, usually, like tonight, in conjunction with their friends, garlic, lemon and chicken.

# Chicken, olives and lemon

chicken thighs, bone in, skin on: 6
olive oil
onions: 2
a lemon
saffron strands: a good pinch
green olives: a handful
coriander leaves: a handful,
   roughly torn

*For the spice paste:*
garlic: 3 large cloves
smoked paprika: a few pinches
ground turmeric: a tablespoon
cumin seeds: a teaspoon
olive oil

Make the spice paste: peel the garlic cloves and crush them with a good pinch of sea salt using a pestle and mortar. Add the smoked paprika, turmeric and cumin seeds and grind to a paste, then mix in just enough olive oil to make the paste thick enough to coat the chicken. A couple of tablespoons or so should do it.

Place the chicken thighs in a bowl, add the spice paste and toss to coat. Cover with cling film and leave to marinate, at room temperature or in the fridge, for a good hour, overnight if possible.

Heat a little olive oil in a large, shallow pan. Peel and chop the onions and add to the pan. When they have softened a little, introduce the chicken thighs to the pan and cook until coloured lightly on both sides.

Thinly slice the lemon and add to the pan with enough water to come halfway up the chicken pieces. Stir in the saffron, then season well with salt and black pepper, cover with a lid and simmer for about twenty-five minutes, until the chicken is cooked through. Toss in the olives and roughly torn coriander and serve.

Enough for 3

# His dark materials

By most enthusiastic cooks' standards, my cupboards are bare. Whilst being inquisitive about new ingredients, the everyday larder fillers from other country's kitchens, I have always resisted the temptation to stack my shelves with stuff I don't use.

That said, there is a small cluster of jars with dark Bakelite lids that hold ingredients I value but use rarely. Precious things like Italian candied peel, crystallised violets and sugared French rose petals. They live on the same shelf as the stickily dark vanilla pods, fine, flaking cinnamon sticks and green cardamom pods. Materials that bring with them the scent of a magical, fragrant world. I am amazed at how a coating of sugar can preserve a violet or rose petal's perfume, their heart and soul trapped in a sugar frosting. These jars rarely see light of day. I would not want their contents to become familiar. They must continue to retain a sense of magic, mystery and preciousness.

## Dark chocolate discs with rose petals

dark chocolate: 100g
flaked almonds: 2 handfuls
caster sugar: a big pinch
shelled pistachios: a handful,
   chopped

sea salt flakes: a few hefty pinches
crystallised rose petals or
   candied peel

Line a baking tray with waxed or greaseproof paper. Snap the chocolate into small pieces and melt it in a bowl set over simmering water. Avoid the temptation to stir. When the chocolate is half melted, turn the heat off and nudge the solid parts into the melted parts, letting it continue to melt in the residual heat.

Toast the flaked almonds with the sugar in a non-stick pan over a low to moderate heat until the sugar starts to melt and the nuts colour lightly. Make discs of melted chocolate on the paper and scatter each one with chopped pistachios, sugared almonds, sea salt flakes and rose petals or candied peel. Leave in a cool place or the fridge to set.

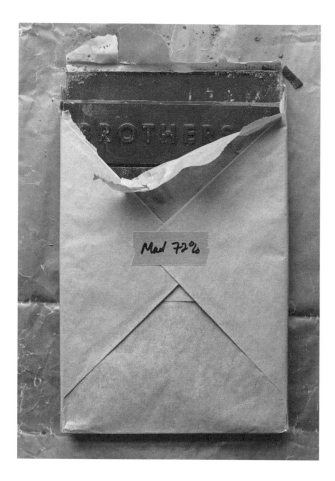

# APRIL 4

I have never been the most experimental of cooks, and stand accused of playing it safe. So I embarked on an episode of *Simple Cooking* (BBC1, 2011) called 'Weird and Wonderful' with more than a tinge of discomfort. My two favourite dishes from the episode involved simple, yet surprisingly controversial twists on classic recipes. Those intrepid enough to try them wrote in singing their praise, and the way my crew hoovered them up was a pleasure to see.

The idea to make a savoury apple crumble was mine and mine alone, but it had its roots in the happy marriage of pork, apple and cheese. I used sharp apples, grated Parmesan instead of sugar, and a little lemon thyme to season. Eaten alongside a pork roast and herb-flecked sausages, it has proved a great success, with even the most sceptical eaters convinced.

## Savoury apple crumble

*For the filling:*
sharp apples: 6 medium-sized
butter: 50g
Madeira: 4 tablespoons

*For the crumble:*
plain flour: 250g
butter: 250g, diced
grated Parmesan: 100g
fresh white breadcrumbs: 100g
lemon thyme: a few sprigs

Set the oven at 200°C/Gas 6. Peel and core the apples and chop them into large chunks. Put them in a deep casserole with the butter, cover with a lid and place over a low heat to cook down for about ten minutes. Uncover the pan, pour in the Madeira, let it almost bubble away, then turn off the heat.

Make the crumble: rub the flour and butter together with your fingertips, as you might for any crumble, to form crumbs. Stir in 80g of the grated Parmesan, plus the breadcrumbs and thyme leaves. Tip the crumble over the apples (or transfer them to a baking dish if you prefer), scatter the remaining Parmesan, then bake for twenty-five minutes.

Enough for 4–6

## A new sausage roll

The second of the tweaked classics involved a more polarising ingredient altogether, yet the recipe caused a gratifying wave of appreciation in my inbox. Black pudding is loved and hated in equal measure, so I include a recipe for its many fans, of which I am one, especially when the puddings are of the soft variety, like some of the boudin noir and Spanish morcilla that are available here now.

### Black pudding in pastry with mustard sauce

A properly made sausage roll is a fine thing if you can find one, with good, coarse, herby sausage meat and a pastry that falls to flakes as you eat it. I took the idea and used it with black pudding, having one per piece for supper with shredded cabbage and a little mustard sauce.

I can't pretend always to make my own puff pastry, there's enough good stuff out there not to bother. If soft, hand-made black pudding escapes you, then find a boudin noir, the French version, which has the necessary open texture and generous seasoning. Many delis and specialist sausage shops have them.

onions: 2
a little olive oil
thyme: 2 sprigs
a bay leaf
puff pastry: 375g
morcilla black puddings:
   4, each about 75g
an egg, beaten

*For the mustard sauce:*
double cream: 150ml
thyme sprigs: 2
grain mustard: 2 teaspoons

Heat the oven to 200°C/Gas 6. Peel the onions and slice them thinly. Pour the oil into a shallow pan, warm over a moderate heat, add the sliced onions, then season with the thyme leaves, pulled from their stalks, and a little black pepper. Add the bay leaf and let the onions cook, with the

occasional stir, until they are completely soft and a pale gold. They should be soft enough for you to crush them between your fingers.

Cut the pastry into four. Roll each piece into a rectangle large enough to wrap the pudding. Divide the onions between the pastry. Place a pudding on each, then brush the edges of the pastry with some of the beaten egg and fold over to make a parcel. Crimp the edges to seal the pastry, then transfer to a baking sheet.

Brush with a little beaten egg, make three small holes in the top to let the steam out and bake for approximately thirty minutes, till golden.

For the mustard sauce, put the cream, thyme and mustard in a small saucepan and heat until thoroughly hot but not boiling. Season carefully and serve with the black pudding sausage rolls.

Enough for 4

# APRIL 7

## The treasure in the pan. And a nannying pudding

I regard the juices left in the pan or roasting tin as nothing less than treasure. Containing the caramelised meat juices, crusty pan-stickings and reduced cooking liquids, these are indeed the essence of the food. I think of them as its heart and soul. Not just revered, for me they are verging on sacred.

Of course, some juices are more interesting than others. Those where there has been time for flavours to marry and develop are often the best of all, but that doesn't mean those left behind from quick cooking are not worth utilising. Tonight, an impromptu supper of big rustic flavours, food that is big and butch with not even a nod towards elegance, has produced pan juices so good that I upend the plate straight into my mouth. The flavours, porky, salty, sweet and hot from paprika, are only for those who appreciate the depth of savour that comes from the marriage of meat and fish, an advancement on the bacon-wrapped salmon or scallop. Unrefined, big-hearted cooking at its best.

### Chorizo, cabbage and crayfish tails

Prick four plump chorizo sausages (about 80g each) with a fork, then place them in a non-stick frying pan over a moderate heat. Leave them to cook till deep rust red and brown on the outside, then remove from the pan, leaving all their delicious, paprika-scented oil behind. Slice the sausages diagonally in half, then return them to the pan for the cut edges to brown. Add six dark green cabbage leaves, whole or shredded, and let them soften and darken slightly in the oil. Lastly toss in 225g cooked prawns, shrimps or, my favourite, crayfish tails, strained from their brine. Leave to heat through, then season with salt and black pepper. Serve immediately with the pan juices. A beer, cold and frothy, works splendidly here.

Enough for 2

# Bread and butter

I love that oh-so-rare moment when a restaurant gets bread and butter right. Rolls so floury, crisp and dark that they are on the verge of being burnt; butter sweet and unsalted and very, very cold. The right knife to spread the butter, the right amount of butter on the crispest shard of bread. It's a simple, perfect moment. And yes, oh so rare.

When I was little, bread and butter came with every meal. A plate of white sliced, each slice cut in half diagonally. I don't remember eating it. Nowadays bread tends to come with a dish of olive oil and some sea salt. I eat less bread and butter than I would like to. Recently, there has probably been as much of it consumed in pudding form as with a meal, which is partly to do with satisfying friends who expect a pudding and partly to do with using up bread and baked goods. I have made several bread and butter puddings over the years, this week's being made with leftover hot cross buns (there is another next month). You can never have too many bread and butter puddings.

The warming, nanny-knows-best pudding is preceded by a somewhat thrown-together and slightly inappropriate main course of broccoli and Savoy cabbage, shredded and tossed in a pan with garlic, ginger, chopped chillies and very finely shredded lemongrass. A last-minute seasoning of Vietnamese fish sauce, a pinch of sugar and a few shakes of dark soy sauce amplify the glossy and slightly sticky quality of what is a deeply impromptu supper.

# Hot cross bread and butter pudding

Any spiced bun or teacake is probably suitable for this. Which reminds me, whatever happened to the toasted teacake?

| | |
|---|---|
| hot cross buns: 420g | golden caster sugar: 50g |
| a little soft butter | chopped candied peel: |
| egg yolks: 4 | a small handful |
| milk: 400ml | sultanas: 50g |
| double cream: 300ml | a pinch of ground cinnamon |
| a drop or two of vanilla extract | |

Set the oven at 160°C/Gas 3. Slice the buns into three and butter them lightly on one side. Beat the egg yolks gently in a bowl and then add the milk, cream, vanilla extract and sugar.

Lightly butter a medium-sized baking dish. Place the slices of bun hugger-mugger in the dish, scattering the candied peel and sultanas among them as you go. Pour over the egg custard and then finally add a mild dusting of cinnamon over the surface.

Lower the dish into a roasting tin and pour enough hot water into the tin to come half way up the sides of the dish. Carefully place in the oven. Bake for forty-five to fifty minutes, till the custard has set and the bread is golden. Take great care removing the tin and its hot water from the oven. Leave the pudding to settle down before eating.

Enough for 6

## Goat's milk cheese

The fresh, clean, slightly piquant notes of goat's and sheep's milk cheeses have a particular appeal for me. I will often choose them over anything else. Goat's milk cheeses are made throughout the year, but their character, always young, mild, often chalk white, seems particularly appropriate in the spring.

The virginal whiteness of Ragstone, Golden Cross or Childwickbury – its surface furrowed like a newly ploughed field – is rarely found in cow's milk cheese, their fragility charming, their scent freshly lactic. My week is not complete without a wedge of chalk-white Ticklemore. Other names to look out for are Golden Cross, Perroche and Tymsboro, or the ash-crusted Dorstone and Sleightlet. These are the fruits of small farms, sold almost exclusively at specialist cheesemonger's and cheese stalls and sometimes by post. I don't expect this sort of cheese to be on every street corner, it is something I am happy to search for.

As it's my birthday, I make a sweet onion and goat's cheese tart, for no other reason than that is what I fancy for supper (it's my party and I'll cook what I want to). I could have used cheaper, supermarket goat's cheese for this, but I am happy to support the small, artisan craftsmen and women who produce the cheeses I love, even if it makes for a more expensive tart. Use whatever you have.

### A goat's cheese and onion tart

*For the pastry:*
plain flour: 200g
butter: 100g, cut into small pieces
an egg yolk
milk: 2–3 tablespoons

*For the filling:*
onions: 400g
butter: 25g
thyme leaves: 2 teaspoons
eggs: 2
crème fraîche: 200ml
full-cream milk: 200ml
a moist, crumbly goat's
  cheese: 180g

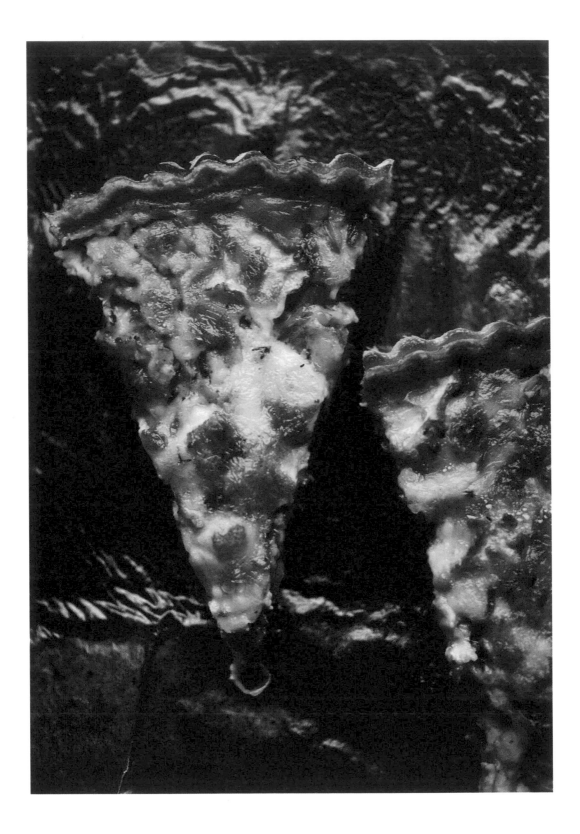

Put the flour and butter into a food processor, add a pinch of salt and blitz to fine crumbs (if you prefer, rub the butter into the flour with your finger-tips, in a bowl). Add the egg yolk and enough milk to bring the dough together into a firm ball. The less milk you add the better, as too much will cause your pastry case to shrink in the oven.

Pat the pastry into a flat round on a floured surface, then roll it out into a circle large enough to line a 22cm loose-bottomed tart tin, at least 3.5cm deep. Lightly butter the tin, dust it with a small amount of flour and shake off any surplus, then lower in the pastry. Push it right into the corner where the rim joins the base, without stretching it. Make certain there are no holes or tears. Trim the overhanging pastry and place the pastry case in the fridge for twenty minutes. Set the oven at 200°C/Gas 6 and put a baking sheet in it to heat up.

Line the pastry case with foil, fill with baking beans and slide it on to the hot baking sheet. Bake for twenty minutes, then remove from the oven and carefully lift the beans and foil out. Return the pastry case to the oven for five minutes or so, until the surface is dry to the touch. Remove from the oven and set aside. Turn the oven down to 180°C/ Gas 4.

Make the filling. Peel the onions and slice them thinly. Melt the butter in a shallow pan, add the onions and leave them to cook over a low heat for a good twenty minutes. When they show signs of softening, add the thyme. An occasional stir with a wooden spoon will stop them sticking or burning. The onions are ready when they are sweet, gold and soft enough to crush between your fingers and thumb.

Crack the eggs into a bowl and beat with a small whisk or fork to mix. Beat in the crème fraîche and milk, then season with salt and black pepper. Spoon the onions into the cooked pastry case and crumble in the goat's cheese. Pour most of the egg mixture over the onions, then transfer the tart to the hot baking sheet in the oven. Pour in the remaining custard mixture and carefully slide the tray into the oven. Bake for forty minutes, till lightly risen. The centre should quiver when the tart is gently shaken.

Eat in the traditional style of a quiche, not hot nor cold but warm.

Enough for 6

## Grasping the nettle

It is a fact that nettles do not sting once they are cooked. Yet I swear I detect a faint, pleasing prickle in a soup in which this common or garden plant has been featured. But that is probably because I know it's there.

I don't think of the nettle as a weed, with its saw-edged, arrow-shaped leaves, white, cream and sometimes pink flowers and the ease with which you can tug the open web of roots from the ground. I have used the youngest leaves once or twice in the kitchen (a soup, a button mushroom stir-fry) almost for a dare, then spent the rest of lunchtime wondering why they are not more popular.

The sting's the thing. Even with Marigolds or gardening gloves on, I usually manage to give myself a jolt. Both the stems and leaves contain the stinging hairs. Rubbing the bite marks with a dock leaf has never worked for me, though I like the idea that the broad-leaved variety was once called butter dock because the leaves were used to wrap and preserve butter. Left in a plastic bag in the fridge, the small, tender leaves at the top of the nettle plant will stay fresh for several days, but their sting will stay with them till they are cooked.

Treat nettles like spinach. Use to make a chilled soup, a tart, something green to mix with cheese sauce and stuff a pancake rather than put them on the compost heap. Their hairy leaves go further than the silky spinach and the flavour is not dissimilar, but only the first few centimetres of the growing tips are of interest in the kitchen. The lower leaves and stems can be tough even for blitzing into soup. Bitter, too.

It is not just the frugality of cooking with wild leaves that appeals to me, although that does come into it. It is more the idea of exploiting something that would otherwise be considered of little use (nettles make excellent compost too). And every time I sting myself picking them, I placate myself with the knowledge that the offending sprigs will soon be in the pot with onions, stock and seasoning and blitzed into soup. Grated nutmeg goes well with anything nettle based. I have learned to go easy on the pepper.

# A nettle rabbit

I am not getting into the rarebit versus rabbit argument. Whatever you call it, it is still cheese on toast. Mustard replaces the missing sting.

Of course, this is hardly supper. But I had lunch out and wanted very little in the evening.

nettle tops: 60g
a little oil
crème fraîche: 100ml
grain mustard: 2 teaspoons

Caerphilly cheese: 80g, grated
sourdough, wholemeal or
  granary bread: 2 large slices

Put your Marigolds on. Wash the leaves thoroughly in cold water – insects tend to treat nettles as a safe home – then drain them in a colander. Put the oil in a small pan and warm it over a moderate heat, then add the nettle tops and cook for a couple of minutes, turning them over occasionally with kitchen tongs, until they have wilted.

Remove the nettle tops from the pan and roughly chop them, then mix with the crème fraîche, mustard, a little black pepper and half the grated Caerphilly.

Toast the bread lightly on both sides. Spread the nettle filling over each piece, then scatter the remaining cheese on top. Cook under an overhead grill till the cheese is hot and pale golden brown in patches. Eat immediately.

Enough for 2

# A fistful of garlic leaves

Walking in the country, you tend to smell the leaves of wild garlic, *Allium ursinum*, before you see them. Each leaf crushed underfoot will send up an instantly recognisable puff of the sweet, fresh young herb, more subtle than even the first spring heads of 'wet' garlic.

'Widespread' is how the foraging books refer to the presence of wild garlic. That may be, but not in my neck of the woods (though friends insist they have come across it on Hampstead Heath). The long leaves, wide and tapering to a fine point, are difficult to miss, the unmistakable smell wafting up from either side of the path as you walk. As with any wild plant, we need to pick thoughtfully, leaving plenty in situ, so there will be some for others and for next year too.

My wild garlic leaves tend to arrive from kind and generous friends whose habitats are less urban than my own – the leaves thrive in cool shade – and it is possible to find them in tied bunches at farmers' markets (usually on the garlic stalls). You can grow the leaves in the garden or on an allotment. I have tried to get a prolific patch going, in much the same way as I have with sorrel. But some things seem to resent being told where to grow, and I find wild garlic one of them. I guess the clue is in the 'wild'.

Spring garlic leaves and bulbs have a meekness in comparison to the chopped mature cloves, gentler and often acceptable to those for whom the older stuff is too potent. They have a politeness to them, and won't overpower anything they are cooked with (*pace* the lamb recipe in early May). That said, I always seal my packet of leaves tightly in the fridge, as even the smallest bundle will send unwanted Gallic notes through your milk and yoghurt. Fine if the yoghurt is for making a raita for your curry, less so if it is intended for breakfast.

These slim, matte-green leaves have turned out to be most successful for wrapping lamb prior to roasting, and this week I mashed them into a verdant butter for basting a long, slender fillet. We ate the rose-pink, allium-scented meat in thick slices, with barely a trickle of the roasting juices on each plate.

I also cook wild garlic – ramsons – as a green vegetable. The sweet leaves and young white stems are piled into a pot with a couple of tablespoons of water and a thick slice of butter. A tight-fitting lid enables them to steam

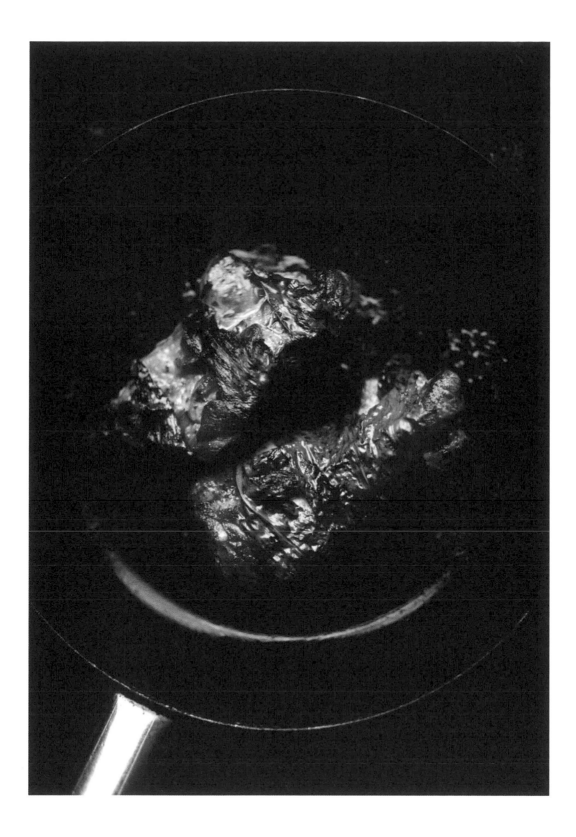

rather than fry, which is the cooking method such infant shoots need. A shot of lemon juice is their only seasoning.

### Roast lamb with garlic leaf butter

We ate a simple lettuce salad with this, the leaves hand torn rather than cut with a knife, dressed with a basic lemon oil vinaigrette.

spring onions: 2
garlic leaves: 30g
butter: 80g, at room temperature

a little mild-flavoured oil
large lamb fillets: 2

Set the oven at 220°C/Gas 7. Chop the spring onions and most of the garlic leaves quite finely, then mash them into the butter with a fork, grinding in a little salt and black pepper as you go.

Warm a film of oil in a roasting tin and lightly brown the lamb fillets in it over a moderate heat. Remove the fillets from the tin, let them cool for a minute or two, then spread the garlic leaf butter over them on both sides. Place the reserved garlic leaves around and over the lamb.

Roast in the preheated oven for twenty-five minutes. Leave to rest, covered with foil, for ten minutes, then carve into thick pieces and serve with any juices from the pan.

To follow, a tray of little white cheeses, so fresh they are barely set, each one carried home in a tiny white paper case, like a muffin.

## APRIL 17

## The lemon zester

Sometimes the kitchen can smell so damn good. The sweet sting that hovers over a day spent making marmalade; the timeless bonhomie of a tray of warm oatcakes being taken from the oven; the intoxicating, almost hallucinogenic hit you get from grinding cardamom for Danish pastries or a curry. These are days that linger in the memory as much for the scent they bring into our lives as for anything else. And so it is with lemon curd, a smell both piercingly clean and rich that fills this kitchen just once a year.

Lemon curd has the extraordinary quality of not only smelling bitingly fresh and soothingly buttery at the same time, but of tasting it too. It is on the knife-edge of sweet and sour, like a slice of passion fruit pavlova or a dish of gooseberries and custard or, I suppose, a good laksa. But unlike a soup or a dessert, where we can fine tune levels of sweet and sharp as we go, this particular balancing act needs a trusted recipe from the outset.

You will need a good sharp grater, one that allows you to use just enough pressure to remove only the lemons' outermost zest. (It is amazing how sharp we keep our knives, only to have a grater in the drawer that won't even draw blood.) Anything below the first fine layer of zest will be bitter rather than pleasantly sour and take your curd well beyond lip puckering. The zest should be so fine as to be indefinable in the finished preserve – this isn't marmalade.

There are three graters in this house, despite my hatred of gadgets. One is a coarse microplane, good for Parmesan but capable of turning young vegetables to mush; another a finer version, good for lemons and limes. The third is a Japanese ginger grater, whose exaggeratedly sharp teeth I have taken to using for lemons, too, being careful not to rub too firmly and expose the bitter white pith underneath.

If there was ever a moment to spend money on fine ingredients, then this is it. The most fragrant lemons, the sweetest farmhouse butter and the freshest organic eggs will make a preserve that is head and shoulders above ones made with lesser ingredients. And that is just what I have done. The lemons are so fresh that their leaves are still glossy. Their skin is ridged and knobbly, and if you pierce it with a thumbnail the spray that spritzes into the air is sweet-sour, without that bitter stickiness you so often find in cheap supermarket lemons. The butter is pale and new. The eggs came from the hens of a friend, who collected them yesterday.

I warm the lemons a little first. They seem to produce more juice that way. I wash the jars by pouring boiling water on to them in the sink, then dry them with a soft, clean tea towel. I choose the wooden spoon that I keep for custard and other sweet things – the one that doesn't smell of garlic. But then I remember the texture is lighter with a whisk. Talk about 'stirring in the love'.

Despite the delights to be had from a warm tartlet of lemon curd and sweet pastry, or a slice of sponge cake filled with the lemony ointment, I often eat it just as it comes, on thick, perfectly fresh white bread. But it is worth mentioning that you can make any number of quick desserts with it too. On a summer's day I fold it into softly whipped double cream and freeze it for an instant ice. The canary-coloured paste is heavenly in a pancake, or as a filling for an éclair, for slathering expensively on roughly torn toasted teacakes or for breakfast on a Sunday morning, spread on a thin, crackling baguette or floury white loaf. But it may also end up held between two meringues or stirred into whipped cream as an instant lemon syllabub.

Expensive, yes. But then, there are only four ingredients and this is probably the day in the kitchen I enjoy above all others.

## A couple of pots of lemon curd

The ratio of eggs, lemons, butter and sugar is crucial if we are to achieve a good balance of astringency and sweetness, set and texture. It is a recipe I have worked on year on year. Most lemon curd recipes instruct you to stir the mixture with a wooden spoon. I find that stirring gently with a whisk introduces just a little more lightness into the curd, making it slightly less solid and more wobbly.

the finely grated zest and juice of  butter: 100g, cut into cubes
  4 unwaxed lemons    eggs: 3, plus 1 egg yolk
caster sugar: 200g

Put the lemon zest and juice, sugar and butter into a heatproof bowl set over a pan of simmering water, making sure that the bottom of the bowl doesn't touch the water. Stir with a whisk from time to time until the butter has melted.

Mix the eggs lightly with a fork, then stir them into the lemon mixture. Let the curd cook, stirring regularly, for about ten minutes, until it is thick and custard like. It should feel heavy on the whisk.

Remove from the heat and stir occasionally as it cools. Pour into spotlessly clean jars and seal. It will keep for a couple of weeks in the refrigerator.

Makes 2 small jam jars (but the recipe doubles or trebles nicely)

# A heavenly parfait of orange and lemon

The ideal here is homemade meringues with a crisp outside and a chewy centre. Failing that, store-bought meringues will do, but the texture of the finished ice will be slightly less interesting. I find it exceptionally useful that it never seems to freeze rock hard, as other homemade ice-cream desserts often do.

whipping or double cream: 500ml

meringues: 180g

lemon curd: 8 heaped tablespoons (about 300g)

the grated zest of an orange

You will need a cake tin or plastic freezer box approximately 24cm x 12cm x 7cm deep, lined loosely with cling film or waxed paper.

Pour the cream into a chilled mixing bowl and whisk till soft and thick. I always stop just short of it forming stiff peaks, so that it can just about hold its own shape.

Crumble the meringues into the cream. I think the texture of the finished parfait will be more interesting if the pieces range in size from coarse gravel to that of a piece of fudge. Add the lemon curd, then grate in the orange zest, taking care not to include any white pith. Stir gently to incorporate the meringue, curd and zest into the cream. Try not to overmix.

Tip the mixture into the lined container, cover with a piece of cling film and put in the freezer till set. Depending on the temperature of your freezer, this will take about 4 hours. You can keep it frozen for several days, but you should remove it from the freezer a good thirty minutes before serving.

To serve, unmould the parfait and cut it into thick, crumbly slices.
Enough for 6–8

## APRIL 20

## Eating bunny

There is a piece in the paper this morning about the damage rabbits are doing to farmers and their crops. If ever there was good reason to kill something to eat, then the rabbit is it. Yet they are the cutest of all the animals we eat, the most likely to have been kept as a fluffy toy or a childhood pet. Generally one doesn't eat one's pets.

The flesh of the wild rabbit can be tender or a little tough, depending on its age and habitat. Farmed rabbits are almost always tender, but one would have to be very careful to buy only rabbits with a decent provenance, and I am not sure that is possible. The wild meat is often a tad more interesting from a flavour point of view, having munched wild flowers and herbs, not to mention a few things they shouldn't along the way.

Roasting a rabbit is living dangerously. Their little limbs work hard and the meat sometimes needs moisture – wine or stock – to help it towards tenderness. None of this means it can't be roasted with just a rub of olive oil and some lemon and garlic, but it's quite a big ask of a traditionally difficult meat. I have sautéed some rabbit joints in a shallow pan with oil, garlic and bacon and they turned out better than I could have hoped. A pleasingly small amount of cream turned the pan juices into a sauce.

Tarragon is always the first herb up. It's just as lovely with rabbit as it is with chicken. I have another recipe, a little more gutsy, with Marsala and pancetta (it's in *Tender Volume I*, if you are interested). The tarragon is gentler and a good introduction to the 'other' white meat.

There is always the fear that rabbit will be dry or tough, a reasonable worry considering its lack of fat and all that bouncing about. I have been working on a way of getting a moist and tender rabbit that involves simmering the bunny bits in stock with onions and fennel, then finishing it with tarragon cream. You could try it with chicken pieces if bunny is too cute for you.

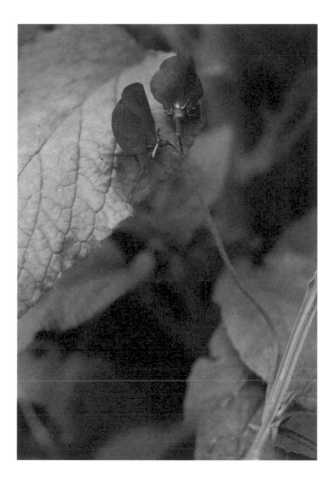

# Rabbit with tarragon

Some new potatoes are called for here, steamed in their skins, no butter. The radish salad below would be good too. Something Mr McGregor about this.

| | |
|---|---|
| onions: 2 | wild rabbit portions: 600g |
| butter: 60g | rabbit, chicken or vegetable |
| fennel: 80g |    stock: 300ml |
| plain flour: 3 tablespoons | tarragon: 15g |
| white wine or white vermouth: | double cream: 100ml |
|   125ml | |

Peel the onions and chop them roughly. Melt half the butter in a casserole and add the onions. Leave them to cook on a low to moderate heat until soft but not coloured. They will need a stir now and again.

Slice the fennel thinly, reserving the fronds, and add to the onions. Put the flour in a plastic bag, season with salt and pepper, then add the rabbit pieces. Shake the bag gently to coat the rabbit in the seasoned flour. Melt the remaining butter in a shallow pan, add the rabbit and leave to colour lightly on both sides.

Transfer the rabbit to the onions and fennel. Pour the wine or vermouth into the pan in which you have fried the rabbit, bring to the boil and stir to dissolve any remains from the rabbit on the base of the pan. Tip into the casserole with the stock.

Remove the leaves from the tarragon and chop half of them. Stir into the casserole, then partially cover with a lid and leave to simmer gently for an hour over a low to moderate heat, stirring occasionally.

When the rabbit is tender – it should come away from the bone with a good tug – stir in the cream and the remaining tarragon. Check the seasoning, adding more salt as you think fit, then serve.

Enough for 3

# A salad of radishes and spring onions

I sometimes add cucumber to this salad, increasing its refreshing quality. A small cucumber, peeled, halved and its seeds removed with a teaspoon, is enough for the quantity below. Radish seedlings are just one of the forms of sprouted seed available from supermarkets and wholefood stores.

radishes: a bunch
lemon juice: 2 tablespoons, plus a
  little more
slim spring onions: 6
fennel: 100g
olive oil: 4 tablespoons

capers, rinsed: a teaspoon
mint leaves: 8, torn into small
  pieces
sprouted radish seeds or mung
  beans: 2 handfuls

Trim the radishes, discarding the green top and long tails. Slice the radishes finely and put them in a mixing bowl. Squeeze over a little lemon juice.

Remove and discard the toughest of the green shoots from the spring onions, then finely slice the rest and add to the radishes. Thinly slice the fennel, reserving its fronds, and add it to the radishes.

Make the dressing. Put a large pinch of salt into a small bowl, then add the 2 tablespoons of lemon juice. Stir in the olive oil, the reserved fennel fronds, capers and mint leaves. Toss gently with the salad and scatter the radish seedlings or sprouting mung beans on top. Serve with the rabbit, above.

Enough for 3

# The salad spinner

It is rare there isn't some form of salad on the table at some point in the day. More often than not, this is a couple of double handfuls of assorted salad leaves bought from the farmers' market and dropped into a bowl, then dressed with olive oil and either lemon juice or vinegar. Uncomplicated and deliberately designed to show each leaf (mizuna, mustard leaf, cress, claytonia, oak leaf, trevise, young chard, etc.) for what it is.

There might be a dressing proper, seasoned with mustard or balsamic vinegar, or there could be a few snippets of bread fried in a pan till they crunch, but generally it is a case of less rather than more. I see little point in buying interesting leaves and then masking them with a highly flavoured or complex dressing. It is not an overstatement to say that I regard the making of the daily salad as one of the quiet pleasures of the kitchen.

You can shake a salad dry after rinsing it in water, in a colander or in a sieve or you can tenderly pat it dry in a tea towel. And if you don't, surely it doesn't matter that much anyway. What's a little clean water to a bowl of salad?

And then, of course, you get a salad spinner. A present from a friend to the cook who has everything, or a mad purchase online, or perhaps you find one in someone else's kitchen when you offer to help them prepare lunch. You put the wet leaves in and push the plonker or pull the cord depending on the model, and the leaves spin round and round and the water flies off into the stainless steel drum. It's fun, like our first chance to play with a humming top since we were four. It's daft, unnecessary. Then you see the leaves in the inner basket, perfectly washed and yes, almost dry. No water to drip over everything, to make the leaves soggy, or to soak the tea towel. More importantly, no water to dilute your dressing. This is the real reason for introducing a salad spinner into your kitchen. The oil and lemon juice or whatever you have so thoughtfully made adhere nicely to the leaves without slipping off or turning watery. A watery dressing is unattractive and difficult to eat. As you gently toss the leaves, you suddenly see the point of the salad spinner and why people who love their salad swear by them. I know I would hate to be without mine.

# Five-spice chicken and pea shoot salad

Sometimes you can find raw diced chicken at the butcher's or supermarket, but if not, then a mixture of thigh and breast, coarsely diced, is fine too. Thinking about it, rabbit would also be an option.

*For the salad:*
pea shoots: 2–3 large handfuls
young, small salad leaves
  (a mixed bag will do)
sprouted seeds or cress: a couple
  of handfuls

*For the chicken:*
fresh ginger: about 40g
a small red chilli

Chinese five-spice powder:
  2 teaspoons
garlic: 2 cloves
groundnut oil: 2 tablespoons
raw chicken meat: 400g, diced
caster or palm sugar: half a
  teaspoon
juice of a lime

Prepare the salad: wash the pea shoots and salad leaves and spin or shake them dry.

Peel the ginger and grate it to a pulp, scraping every bit from the grater into a mixing bowl. Finely slice the chilli, add it to the ginger, then stir in the five-spice powder. Peel and crush the garlic and add to the ginger. Pour in the oil and mix thoroughly. Add the chicken and toss the ingredients together.

Get a wok or frying pan really hot. Add the diced chicken and its dressing to the pan and fry over a high heat for six or seven minutes, stirring from time to time, until it is cooked through (a lid will help the chicken to cook right through). Add the sugar, stir-fry for a minute longer, then add the lime juice and season generously with salt.

Add the pea shoots and salad leaves to the wok, toss for a few seconds till they have started to wilt and darken, then tip everything into bowls. Scatter with the sprouted seeds or cress and serve immediately.

Enough for 2

## APRIL 23

## Needs must

Tonight I have a fancy, or more truthfully a need, for a plate of creamy pasta. I am not one of the world's greatest pasta eaters, and rarely marry the ribbons, shells or twists of dough with a cream-based dressing, but right now this is what is called for. A pot of cream aside, there is very little in the kitchen with which to dress a plate of pasta, so I make a version of Alfredo, the creamiest pasta dish of all.

| | |
|---|---|
| fettuccine: 250g | nutmeg |
| double cream: 250ml | grated Parmesan: 100g |
| butter: a thick slice | |

Boil the fettuccine in deep, heavily salted water till al dente. Put the cream in a saucepan with the butter and warm over a gentle heat. Grate in a little nutmeg. Stir in most of the grated Parmesan and a generous amount of black pepper, then toss in the lightly drained pasta. Toss gently and serve with the remaining Parmesan.

Enough for 2

## APRIL 24

## Salad for free

The cracks between the grey flagstones outside the kitchen doors are a constant source of dandelions. An irritation to many, and yes, most people would have cemented between them, but I am happy to treat the gaps as a source of free salad. When the leaves are no bigger than my middle finger they are sweet enough to use in a salad. Any larger and they are tinged with a bitter streak. They are particularly suited to being tossed with hot bacon. Unlike rocket and some of the more fragile lettuces, they don't dissolve when they come into contact with the hot rashers. You get crunchy, milky-sapped leaves and sizzling bacon.

I had no idea you could eat the yellow flowers too, until I spotted Alys Fowler making them into tiny pancakes on BBC2's 'The Edible Garden'. I have always pounced on them before they turn to clocks and float over the nearby gardens, but now I will pounce on them with the frying pan in hand.

Small, peppery or spicy spring leaves work well with lamb, and especially so when they are tossed with a lemon-scented dressing. Rocket leaves, young dandelions, bitter frisée or watercress are good here. The dressing, which utilises the flavour left behind in the pan after the lamb has been cooked, should be tossed with the leaves at the very last minute.

## A salad of spring lamb, lemon and olives

noisettes of lamb: 4
a little olive oil
mixed salad leaves: 4 handfuls

*For the dressing:*
rosemary: 3 bushy sprigs
garlic: 2 cloves
a small lemon
stoned green olives: 70g
olive oil: 4 tablespoons

Season the lamb on both sides with salt and pepper and moisten with a little olive oil.

For the dressing, remove the needles from the rosemary and chop them finely. Flatten the garlic cloves with the side of a large knife or using a pestle. No need to peel, just squash them lightly. You want only a subtle hint of garlic in the dressing. Remove six short strips of peel from the lemon. Roughly chop the olives.

Place a non-stick frying pan over a moderate heat, then, as soon as it is hot, put the oiled and seasoned lamb into the pan and let it sizzle for a couple of minutes, until it is light walnut brown on the underside. Turn the meat over and cook the other side for three or four minutes. Check the meat is cooked to your liking, then lift it out and leave to rest on a warm plate, covered with foil, while you quickly make the dressing.

Discard any fat from the pan but leave the sticky golden sediment in it; it will form the base of the dressing. Put the pan back on the heat, pour in the 4 tablespoons of olive oil, then add the rosemary needles and the flattened garlic cloves. Add the lemon peel to the pan, squeezing each piece as you go to release the lemon oil. Leave the aromatics to flavour the oil for two or three minutes.

Put the salad leaves in a mixing bowl. Add the olives to the pan; they need only to warm through. Squeeze in the juice of the lemon and add a grinding of black pepper and salt. Stir the pan briefly with a wooden spatula, scraping any undissolved pan-stickings from the lamb into the dressing, then tip it over the salad leaves.

Immediately divide the salad and its warm dressing between two plates, place the noisettes on top and serve.

Enough for 2

## APRIL 26

# Another crab cake

There are two sorts of crab cake in this kitchen, one seasoned with chillies, lemongrass, lime leaves, coriander and ginger, the other a more American-style cake with breadcrumbs and mayonnaise. This is the version I do when there isn't much in the fridge in the way of Southeast Asian ingredients, like today, a milder, simpler version.

These little cakes are fragile. I slide them into the hot pan with the help of a wide palette knife or fish slice, depending on how large I have made them, then leave them to form a crust before turning them over, swiftly and surely, to cook on the underside.

## Crab and coriander cakes

| | |
|---|---|
| brown crabmeat: 200g | a medium-sized, moderately hot |
| white crabmeat: 200g | red chilli |
| white bread, crusts removed: 80g | coriander leaves: a large handful |
| a lime | mayonnaise: 2 tablespoons |
| | a little groundnut or vegetable oil |

Put the crabmeat into a large mixing bowl. Reduce the bread to crumbs in a food processor, then add to the crab. Grate the lime zest finely into the bowl and add the juice.

Halve, seed and finely chop the chilli. Chop the coriander leaves. Add the chilli and coriander to the crab, then add the mayonnaise. Season with just a little salt and some black pepper and mix thoroughly.

Taking 2 tablespoons of the mixture at a time, make it into small patties, about the size of a digestive biscuit. Set them aside.

Heat a shallow film (no more) of oil in a non-stick pan. Using a palette knife or fish slice, gently slide the fishcakes into the hot oil – they should sizzle immediately – then leave them to form a crust on the underside. When it is golden, gently flip them over on to the other side. Cook for three or four minutes, then lift out carefully.

Enough for 4

## APRIL 27

# A gravy for spring

There is a moment, as you lift the roast, still sizzling, from its tin and set it aside to rest, when you get to have free range with the pan juices. For any cook, it's a thoughtful moment. Should you pour in a glass of white wine in which to dissolve the pan-stickings with their baked-on caramelised sugar and umami, their nuggets of golden fat and skin, or should you use stock and, if so, what sort? Should you add the dregs of yesterday's wine or today's vegetable cooking water? Would Madeira or Marsala produce a gravy too sweet and rich for a spring day? The choice is ours.

### Spring chicken with young garlic leaves

Putting garlic leaves inside the chicken sends a subtle, aromatic note through the roasting bird but its real point is to add flavour to the gravy. Oh, and you can eat the leaves too, like spinach.

a large free-range chicken
garlic leaves: 2 large handfuls
butter: 80g
a lemon, cut in half

a large head of new-season pink
  garlic
white wine, white vermouth or
  stock: 2 small glasses

Set the oven at 200°C/Gas 6. Put the chicken in a roasting tin. Rinse the garlic leaves, then stuff them inside the chicken with half the butter and the halved lemon. Rub the remaining butter over the outside of the chicken and season it with salt and black pepper.

Break the head of garlic into individual cloves, then squash them lightly with the flat of a knife, just enough to break them open. Scatter them round the outside of the chicken.

Turn the bird breast-side down and roast in the preheated oven for thirty minutes. Turn it the right way up and continue to roast till its juices run clear when the thickest part of its flesh is pierced with a skewer (just over an hour in total, depending on the size of your chicken).

Lift the chicken on to a heated plate and keep warm. Pour any excess fat from the roasting tin, leaving the darker juices and sediment behind, put the tin over a moderate heat and pour in the wine or stock. Bring to the boil, scraping at the crusty bits on the tin and letting them dissolve, and mashing the garlic cloves into the liquid with a fork. Season with salt and pepper. Strain through a sieve (or pour into a warm jug, holding the crushed garlic back with a fork).

Carve the chicken and serve with the garlicky pan juices.

Enough for 4


## APRIL 29

## Freshwater mussels and a neat chowder

A quick trip on the sleeper to Inverness, where we emerge, after a meal of haggis and neeps and a night of being rocked gently to sleep by the motion of the train, into brilliant Highland sunshine.

We have a long day of filming ahead (I am not one of the world's great drinkers and cannot imagine how two of us got through four bottles of Rioja last night, I only know that we did). Some television cookery is thoroughly planned, other dishes are somewhat impromptu and, way north of Inverness, we spot mussels for sale that will form the backbone of a some-what thrown-together but utterly delicious fish chowder. Its comforting qualities do much to restore and revive.

Rather than the usual saltwater variety I use at home, our booty is actually the rare freshwater mussels, the sort I have only read about, never tasted. Despite over half the global population of freshwater mussels being in this part of the world, they are almost never seen for sale because of their protected status. Very occasionally, for environmental reasons, a licence will be given to sell these freshwater or 'pearl' mussels, and this is what we buy. I have honestly never tasted anything quite like them, their flesh soft, almost

jelly like, and tasting of the very essence of mussel, probably because they were from the river bed rather than the saline waters of the coast. We cook them for seconds, till their shells open, and sigh at the sheer unadulterated sweetness of their flesh. I feel honoured to have eaten them.

Back at home, we retest the recipe with the usual mussels and it becomes a firm favourite in my stable of comfort suppers.

## Smoked haddock, mussel and leek chowder

| | |
|---|---|
| smoked haddock: 2 fillets | butter: a thick slice |
| a few peppercorns | a small swede (about 200g) |
| milk: 500ml | a small cauliflower or half a |
| a leek | large one |
| spring onions: 6 | mussels: 10 |
| thin smoked streaky bacon: | rapeseed or olive oil: a tablespoon |
| 4 rashers | |

Place the smoked haddock, peppercorns and milk in a pan, bring to the boil, then put a lid on and turn the heat off. Leave to infuse for ten minutes.

Finely slice and thoroughly wash the leek. Chop the spring onions and cut the bacon into postage-stamp-sized pieces. Melt the butter in a large pan, add the leek, spring onions and bacon and cook for a few minutes to soften. Peel and roughly chop the swede and break the cauliflower into large florets, then add them to the pan.

Strain the milk from the fish into the vegetables, holding the fish back. Simmer for fifteen minutes.

Cook the cleaned mussels in the oil in a pan with a lid on for two to three minutes, till they all open up, discarding any that refuse to open. Add the mussels to the soup, along with any cooking liquor that has appeared in the pan, then add the smoked haddock, broken into large chunks. Allow the broth to bubble for a further minute or so and then serve.

Enough to serve 2 generously

## Taming the sweetness of the beetroot

Beetroot's unrepentantly earthy flavours need something bright and acidic to bring harmony and balance to a recipe. And that is what it usually gets, in the form of vinegar and pickling spice, soured cream dressings, yoghurt and goat's cheeses. A current favourite of mine is to fold thin threads of grated beetroot into yoghurt for serving with grilled pork steaks or, as I have once, a lentil curry.

A little beetroot goes a long way. I like to bake them whole in a roasting tin, under a sheet of foil, then slip off their skins, slice and dress them, still warm, with a fruit vinegar. Raspberry is good. If the leaves are bright, bushy and not frostbitten, I steam them, stems and all, chop them a little and dress with olive oil, lemon and a showering of chopped dill.

I took the dill route today, with a mustard seed dressing for a batch of beetroot fritters. This root likes oily fish – pickled, it is splendid with grilled mackerel – and so I teamed my little fritters up with a few slices of shop-bought gravlax, the salmon that has been cured with salt and dill. The dressing sat happily with both the vegetable and the salmon. I'm not a canapé kind of guy, but a friend pounced on the idea as being just as suitable for posh nibbles as for a light lunch. Either way, they are sweet, earthy, crisp and delicious.

To think that ten years ago, beetroot was almost a goner. Available only in pickles or occasionally in vacuum packs of four cooked and preserved globes, it is firmly in the spotlight now. It is almost impossible to find a menu that doesn't acknowledge its new-found popularity. At Bibendum restaurant it comes with cured herrings and warm potato salad; St John serves it with boiled egg and anchovies; while at any of the River Cottage delis you might find it in a sandwich with goat's cheese and thyme. Vivid pink gratins are splattered over the tablecloths of many a restaurant and café from one end of the country to the other. It is as if beets have finally come of age.

In many ways, goat's cheese – something young, slightly sharp and fresh – is an almost perfect partner for the sweet notes of the burgundy-coloured root. That pleasing hit of sourness is just what you need. Balance is nigh on essential in any dish, but especially when one of the ingredients is particularly sweet, which is why so many recipes for the more sugary roots, such as carrots, beets and parsnips, contain something lemony, vinegary or lactic. It's a simple enough strategy, but one that might continue beetroot's rise to lasting acceptance.

## Beetroot fritters with gravlax

| | |
|---|---|
| red or golden beetroots: 350g | *For the dressing:* |
| an onion | grain mustard: a tablespoon |
| plain flour: 2 tablespoons | smooth Dijon mustard: |
| an egg, beaten |   a tablespoon |
| oil for shallow-frying | chopped dill: 2 tablespoons |
| gravlax or smoked salmon: | rapeseed oil: 5 tablespoons |
|   300–400g | water: a tablespoon |

Make the dressing: gently whisk together (or shake in a tightly lidded jar) the mustards, chopped dill, oil and water. Set aside.

Scrub the beetroots thoroughly, then grate them coarsely. You may find the medium grater attachment of a food processor best for this (grating by hand tends to produce smaller, rather wet pieces, which often won't form a cake; thin, long shreds are what you need). Peel the onion and slice it very finely, stirring it into the beetroot. Season with salt, plus a little pepper perhaps, then stir in the flour and beaten egg.

Warm a shallow film of oil in a non-stick frying pan. Carefully drop generous spoonfuls of the mixture into the oil, flattening them with the back of the spoon as you go. Leave them to cook over a moderate heat for a couple of minutes, till just starting to crisp a little, then use a palette knife or fish slice to turn them over quickly and cook the other side. Remove from the pan and drain on kitchen paper.

Cut the gravlax or smoked salmon into large slices and divide amongst the fritters. Spoon over some of the dill dressing.

Makes 6, enough for 2 or 3

May

# Turning a flatbread into lunch

Once upon a time, there was only the pitta pocket, a flat slipper of pale dough to split and stuff or toast and tear to shovel up your tarama. It came from any corner shop in a plastic bag with a yellow twist of wire to seal it.

Now there are a few more varieties of flatbread around, the ancient, unyeasted bread traditionally baked in the low embers of an open fire, available to anyone who cares to look beyond the corner shop. Lebanese and other Middle Eastern grocers' are good hunting places, as are some of the supermarkets. I have made my own on many occasions, but have no problem with commandeering a plastic bag of the soft, plate-sized breads from the shops either.

These simple breads can be improved immeasurably by warming (use the grill if the oven isn't on), then stuffing them with whatever takes your fancy. Tonight I go to town, frying some lamb mince and punching it up with mint and chillies. It gets some textural interest, too, with the long, thin pine kernels from Italy (better, I think, than the short, fat and rather cheaper teardrop-shaped ones from China).

The world is full of bread-based meals like this, from the open sandwiches of Norway and Sweden, with their prawn mayonnaise and dill, to the great British sandwich. The Scandinavians provide you with a knife and fork, in the Mediterranean and Middle East they tend to roll theirs, as do the Californians with their wraps of cilantro and crab. You could roll the recipe below, but only if you are sure you can get it to your mouth time and again without spilling a floor-staining pomegranate seed or a toasted pine kernel. I can't.

# Lamb and mushroom flatbreads

Deliciously messy flatbreads to roll up or eat on a plate.

| | |
|---|---|
| groundnut oil: 3 tablespoons | yoghurt: 4 heaped tablespoons |
| small mushrooms: 100g | pine kernels: 2 tablespoons |
| garlic: 2 cloves | flatbreads: 2 large |
| red chillies: 2, small and hot | salad leaves: 2 handfuls |
| minced lamb: 300g | pomegranate seeds: 2 tablespoons |
| mint leaves: a small palmful | green olives, stoned: 12 |

Warm the oil in a wide, shallow pan over a moderate heat. Cut the mushrooms in half and add them to the pan. Cook, stirring them occasionally, till they colour. Peel and finely chop the garlic. Stir it into the mushrooms and leave it to brown nicely for a few minutes. Halve each chilli lengthways, removing the seeds and finely chopping the flesh, before adding to the pan. Cook for a minute, then tip in the minced lamb, stir it into the mushrooms and allow to colour for five minutes or so with only the occasional stir, so that it browns nicely.

Chop the mint leaves and stir them into the yoghurt with some salt and pepper. Chop the pine kernels and stir them into the lamb with a generous grinding of salt and pepper.

Warm the flatbreads and lay them on a chopping board or work surface. Divide the salad leaves between them and tip over the hot lamb and mushrooms. Scatter the pomegranate seeds and stoned olives over the lamb, then trickle over the yoghurt. Roll loosely and eat.

Enough for 2

# Wrong pan, right job

The garden has erupted in an energetic fizz. Gooseberry leaves as acidic as the fruit that will come later, soft clouds of cherry and crab apple blossom, sharp, pointed tulips the colour of a swan's neck, and the unfurling leaves of strawberry plants so sharp they look like origami. A bunch of spring onions as thin as pencils catches my eye in the greengrocer's. Might make a nice omelette.

I'm not sure my omelette pan is any such thing. A pan worthy of the name should probably be non-stick, with a totally smooth surface and gently curving sides. The pan in which I make mine is black steel, only non-stick because of the years of service it has given, regularly being wiped with kitchen roll rather than taking a ride in the dishwater, being used not only for omelettes and the odd frittata, but for frying onions, sautéing the occasional piece of chicken or frying some fingerling-sized strips of bacon to add to a winter salad of chicory, shredded celery and roasted walnut halves. It's as non-stick as Teflon.

Large enough to hold a chop, but only just, this is also a pan that regularly goes in the oven. A pot or pan whose handle won't withstand 200°C has no place in my kitchen. I'm not sure how long it has lived here, but I can't remember a time when this small black pan wasn't around.

An omelette is one of the few egg dishes I can enjoy. It does, however, have to be stacked up with a good few flavourings. One of my favourite additions to the lightly beaten eggs is a spoonful or two of ricotta or similar soft, fresh cheese. This makes the finished omelette more substantial, yet keeps its quivering texture. To that, the additions can be as sparse as a few coriander or tarragon leaves, some rather finely hashed spring onions or maybe a little parsley (a plain parsley omelette served with a few slices of coppa or San Daniele can be a beautiful thing). Or we can get more complicated.

I have recently taken to making small omelettes the diameter of an espresso saucer, serving two or sometimes three per person. Rather than filling the pan in the normal way, I drop a small ladleful into the sizzling butter and let them form their own, often quite wacky shapes. What you end up with is tiny, free-form omelettes to eat as they are or with whatever you fancy. A favourite addition of mine is spicy sausage – chorizo will do nicely – chopped and fried with spring onion, some chilli flakes, garlic and a little soy. Another is chopped mushrooms fried in butter with a sliver of garlic and a few splashes of sherry vinegar. I keep the topping warm in its little frying pan, then spoon it over the omelettes once they are done. Of course, I could make a larger version, spoon on the accompaniments, then fold it over in the traditional style. But that way you lose the look of the filling, which is glossy with sherry vinegar or soy and, with a few shreds of spring onion on top, very appetising.

The more I cook, the more I realise that if a piece of kitchen equipment works it doesn't matter whether it's the correct one or not. Who is to say that a particular knife or pan is right for a certain job? What matters is that it works for us, that we are comfortable working with it, and that it works for the food too. The crucial point is that we end up with something good to eat, and it really doesn't matter how we get there.

## Little spring onion omelettes

Tiny, freeform omelettes the size of a large biscuit. Let them form their own shape in the pan. Eat them as they are, or with the simple dressing below.

ricotta cheese: 250g          coriander leaves: a handful
eggs: 4                       butter: 20g
spring onions: 3

Mash the ricotta with a fork. Lightly beat the eggs and stir into the ricotta. Finely chop the spring onions, then mix with the coriander leaves. Fold them into the ricotta and egg mixture with a generous seasoning of salt and a little black pepper.

Melt the butter in a frying pan. When it starts to sizzle gently, pour a spoonful of the mixture in and let it settle into a small pancake, about 6cm in diameter. Add as many others as you can comfortably fit in the pan. Let them cook for a couple of minutes till lightly coloured on the underside, then flip gently over and cook the other side for a minute.

Lift the omelettes out on to warm plates and serve immediately.

Makes 6, serves 3

A very simple dressing for the omelettes can be made by mixing a tablespoon each of fish sauce, lime juice and soft brown sugar with a little chopped red chilli and grated ginger to taste.

## Soup in the blender

My blender is used pretty much every morning, fizzing up a mixture of frozen berries, apple juice and yoghurt. I can't imagine living without its 8am buzz (it calms me down after my first couple of rocket-fuel espressos). Yes, I could cope with only a food processor, but for liquids, the electric jug blender is best. By which I mean less trouble, easier to clean, more pleasing to use and, let's be honest, more handsome.

The blender is soup producer, salsa verde maker and smoothie master. Its thick glass jug is the place where lumpy soups are turned into velvet-textured purées, where basil, parsley, anchovies and olive oil become a dressing for simmering pots of chicken and root vegetables and where cheat's hollandaise is made in minutes. You can correct a lumpy sauce, providing you know when to stop, and even make praline with nuts and caramel. It has thick glass, an efficient pouring spout and useful measurements up the side. None of which my food processor can offer. And it comes out of the dishwasher without holding water in its nooks and crannies.

Of course, I could do it all by hand. The texture of a carrot or lentil soup is often more interesting if you push it through a sieve with a wooden 'mushroom' or the back of a spoon. A mouli-légumes, the metal sieve on short legs with a handle for turning your vegetables, beans or pulses to a rough, rather thick mixture, probably produces the best texture of all, without whipping everything up into a froth or rendering it into slop. Bugger to clean though.

I'm having a go at a blended cauliflower soup. It has always been my belief that the cauliflower's beautiful, pale curds could make an interesting soup if we put some thought into it. I have had a go many times but have only been truly convinced once, when I threw cheese and mustard at it. This time I started with bacon – it can never fail with members of the brassica family – an onion, a tad of garlic and plenty of silent partners like bay leaves, black pepper and good stock. The trick is, I suppose, to find a balance, where the flavour of the cauliflower is allowed to shine against a good, strong backbone of aromatics. It was a case of try, try and try again, but I do believe this time I have sussed it. It appears the problem all along has been cream, the knee-jerk ingredient that finds its way into recipe after recipe for this vegetable. As soon as that is out of the equation, the little *chou-fleur* stands a chance.

# Cauliflower soup, toasted hazelnuts

smoked streaky bacon: 3 rashers
an onion, roughly chopped
garlic: 2 small cloves
cauliflowers: 2 medium

stock: 1.2 litres
bay leaves: 2
skinned hazelnuts: 100g
a little groundnut or rapeseed oil

Cut the bacon into small pieces, about the size of a stamp, then fry in a deep pan till the fat is golden. Peel and finely chop the onion, add it to the bacon and let it cook without taking on any colour. Peel and slice the garlic, then add to the onion. A regular stir as it softens will help prevent the onion browning. Break the cauliflowers into florets, add to the onion mixture with the stock and bay leaves and bring to the boil. Simmer till the cauliflower is tender; it should be quite soft.

Toast the hazelnuts in a non-stick pan until they darken a little. As soon as the nuts are pale brown, pour in a few drops of oil – just enough to moisten – then add a generous grinding of sea salt and toss gently.

Remove the soup from the heat, discard the bay leaves and blitz in a blender or food processor, till smooth, holding back a few of the cauliflower florets. Pour the soup back into the pan, bring back to the boil and season to taste.

Ladle into bowls, add the toasted salted hazelnuts and reserved cauliflower and serve.

Enough for 4–6

# A warm tart of crab and tarragon

It seems a bit of a pain, making pastry in summer. But you can do it in the food processor and it will be ready in seconds. The trick is not to over-mix it and to rest it in the fridge afterwards. Given the sort of glorious weather we have had this last couple of days, I use a tart such as this as the centre of a meal, offering a herb salad with matchsticks of cucumber in it on the side.

eggs: 3
double cream: 300ml
French mustard: 2 teaspoons
tarragon leaves: a heaped
   tablespoon (about 35–40 leaves)
crabmeat: 500g
grated Parmesan: 2 tablespoons

*For the pastry:*
butter: 175g, cold and in small
   chunks
plain flour: 200g
an egg yolk
ice-cold water: 2 tablespoons

Make the pastry: rub the butter into the flour, either with your fingertips or in a food processor. Mix in the egg yolk, water and a good pinch of salt. Push into a smooth ball and roll it on the table till it is slightly cylindrical – it will slice better in that shape. Wrap in cling film and then put in the fridge to rest for about half an hour.

Set the oven at 200°C/Gas 6. Slice the chilled pastry into thin rounds and put them into a 23–24cm tart tin, pressing the pastry with your knuckles and fingertips to cover the base and up the sides, making certain there are no holes. Prick the bottom with a fork to stop it bubbling during cooking and then chill in the fridge or freezer for fifteen minutes. Bake for fifteen minutes, until it is dry to the touch.

Separate the eggs. Mix the yolks with the cream, add salt, pepper and the mustard, then chop the tarragon and add it. Stir in the crabmeat. Beat the egg whites until they will stand in peaks, then fold then into the crab custard with a large metal spoon. Pour the frothy custard into the baked pastry case and sprinkle the top with the Parmesan.

Turn the oven down to 190°C/Gas 5 and bake the tart for thirty to thirty-five minutes, until it is puffed and golden but still very slightly wobbly in the centre. Remove the tart from the oven and let it cool a little before cutting. It should be set at the edges and soft, almost runny, in the centre.

Enough for 6

# A head of new garlic

You can smell that summer has arrived. I brought the first of the new season's pearl-white garlic home this morning, its waxy skin flashed with paintbrush streaks of green. Two fat heads still on their long, flexible stalks. These youthful bulbs have a subtle, fleeting charm that is destined to disappear as they age. Light, fresh, uplifting, the mild scent of the allicin in these young heads has none of the rasping heat of dry-skinned winter garlic, giving it an affinity with the gentle tastes of May and June – spring lamb and new potatoes, pale broad beans and the first peas, globe artichokes and chicken.

This 'wet' garlic will be around till July if we are lucky. As summer reaches its height, the skin starts to crisp and the flesh of the individual cloves dries out a little, its flavour concentrating and becoming more assertive. Its stems, plaited together whilst young and elastic, tighten and hold the bunches safe throughout the winter.

Last night I used some of the fat, new cloves with greens. To be specific, those long-stemmed shoots of broccoli that are all too easy to buy and eat. The effect was very different from the finely chopped 'stir-fry' treatment that you might give the larger heads of broccoli, or shredded cabbage perhaps, with finely chopped 'winter' garlic. The heat and big flavours were replaced by something altogether more beguiling; a soft, garlicky shadow lurking in the dappled shade.

This is the only garlic to use with mild spring lamb. I have just made a marinade with crushed white garlic, rosemary, olive oil, mild mustard (barely a teaspoon) and a little red wine vinegar, spreading it on to the surface of four neat lamb steaks. Unlike cubed meat cut for a stew, these finger-thick steaks don't need to be in bed with their aromatics for long, and a couple of hours in a cool place will do. I poured the small amount of marinade left after the lamb was removed into the hot pan, sending swooshes of summer garlic and rosemary into the air (and with the doors now almost permanently open, into the garden too), then trickled it over a dish of crushed, golden-crusted Jersey Royals to go with the lamb.

Early garlic's quiet presence in our cooking doesn't extend to the fridge, and anyone hoping to keep their bulbs fresh by storing them there might like to think again. Wrap them in newspaper and keep them somewhere cool and airy is the soundest advice, but also the most infuriatingly difficult place to locate in a modern home. The fridge is often the only suitable spot. I find a loose shrouding of cling film helps, but it will still need using within a week or so of purchase if it isn't to show freckles of mould from the humidity of the fridge.

This is the sort of garlic cooks mean when we are told to wipe a halved clove round the inside of the salad bowl. A hint, a ghost, a mere shadow. Garlic as fresh and sweet as a baby's breath.

## Spring lamb steaks, minted potatoes

Interesting to see how different this is from the lamb with garlic leaves recipe in April.

rosemary: 2 bushy stems
young, sweet garlic: 4 plump cloves
smooth Dijon mustard: a teaspoon
red wine vinegar: 2 teaspoons
olive oil: 3 tablespoons
lamb steaks: 4, about 110g each
new potatoes: 350–400g
mint: a couple of sprigs

*For the mint butter:*
mint: a couple of sprigs
butter: a thick slice, about 20g

Remove the leaves from the sprigs of rosemary (you should get about 2 tablespoons) and chop them finely, then crush to a coarse, intensely fragrant mixture with a couple of good pinches of sea salt flakes using a pestle and mortar (or the end of a rolling pin). Peel the garlic – its skins will be white and soft – then add to the rosemary. Pound to a coarse purée. Add a brief grinding of black pepper, the mustard and then the vinegar. Pour in the olive oil, mixing to a sloppy dressing, then transfer to a shallow dish large enough to take the pieces of lamb.

Put the lamb steaks in the dish with the marinade, turning them over so that both sides are glossy and well coated. Set aside in a cool place (the fridge will do if there is nowhere else suitable), covered with cling film, for a couple of hours.

Put a pan of deep water on to boil for the potatoes. Scrape or wipe the potatoes as you wish (I remove only the flakiest of the skin). Salt the water when it comes to the boil and add the potatoes, and, if you like, a couple of sprigs of mint. Leave to cook for about fifteen minutes, till tender, the exact time depending on their size.

To make the mint butter, finely chop the mint leaves, discarding the stems, then place in a bowl large enough to take the potatoes and add the butter. Drain and lightly crush each potato (a potato masher, applied with light pressure, will do nicely here), then toss with the mint and butter. Tip the potatoes and their butter into a non-stick frying or sauté pan set over a moderate heat. Lightly fry till the broken edges of the potatoes start to crisp up a little. Remove and keep warm.

Give the pan a quick wipe with a piece of kitchen roll, then place it back on the heat. Add the lamb and let it cook for three or four minutes on each side till done to your liking, ideally keeping the inside of the meat pink and juicy. Place on warm plates. If there is any marinade left in the dish, scrape it into the frying pan, let it sizzle briefly, then trickle it over the lamb. Serve with the potatoes.

Enough for 2

## The best sandwich. Ever

My friend Caroline has sent me a padded envelope full of wild garlic leaves, the last of the season. James and I mash them in the Magimix with butter and black pepper to give a green-flecked butter (see April, page 158). We cut a baguette into four, split each piece open, cook a couple of boneless lamb steaks till they are brown and lightly charred, then slice them thickly. A little garlic leaf butter is melted in a pan and poured over the pieces of split baguette, then grill till crisp round the edges. We then spread on a generous slather of mayonnaise and some slices of Taleggio, place the slices of hot lamb steak on top, then a little more garlic butter. The baguette pieces are closed and we tuck in, the melted garlic butter, mayonnaise and meat juices dribbling out of the crusty bread as we eat. We decide later that it is probably the best sandwich we have ever eaten.

## Early herbs

The first herbs in the garden are the most precious and welcome. An early taste of flavours to come. Today is a spirit-lifting day, when the garden is still a froth of blossom, the paths and hedges covered with fallen petals, browning in the early spring sun. The tarragon is up, as is the parsley, and there is surprisingly good hothouse basil from the Italian deli.

Most of the early herbs are exceptionally tender, their leaves having had little sun, their flavours mild rather than full of the pungency that can come from weeks in the scorching summer heat. They end up in a salad, such as the cold salmon with tarragon and lemon mayonnaise I intend to do tomorrow. If I cook with them at all, it is more a question of warming them briefly (such as stirring the leaves into a last-minute pasta sauce), than long slow cooking, or their delicate new growth risks being lost.

With this in mind, I cook some fat fillets of salmon, a surprising bargain, in a shallow pan with tarragon, parsley and basil, plus a little oil to stop them sticking and to keep the herbs from drying. The heat is kept relatively low so none of the leaves brown. The flavours are given a lift with a final squeeze of lime. The quickest of kitchen suppers for a spring day.

### Herbed salmon

I keep the heat fairly low when cooking the salmon here, so the crust doesn't overcook.

tarragon, chopped: a couple of heaped tablespoons
parsley, chopped: 3 heaped tablespoons
basil, chopped: a couple of heaped tablespoons
olive oil: 3 tablespoons, plus a little for cooking
the juice and grated zest of a large lime
salmon fillet: 2 large pieces
limes and a little salad, to serve

Mix the herbs, olive oil and the juice and zest of the lime together in a shallow bowl. Slide in the pieces of salmon and roll them in the herbs and oil. Leave in a cool place for a couple of hours.

Cook the salmon in a little oil in a shallow, non-stick pan over a low to moderate heat for four to five minutes, covered with a lid. Watch carefully to check the heat isn't so high that the herb crust burns.

Serve with salad and fresh limes to squeeze over.

Enough for 2


# MAY 14

## Sucking lemons

I use lemon too much. Its presence, a spritz of zest, a curl of peel or a squirt of juice, turns up in my cooking second only to salt. Some will see its over-appearance as a flaw, I simply see it as a signature. What garlic, cream or chilli does for others, the bright flash of citrus does for me.

Working inwards, the zest is what I add to the ricotta or mozzarella at the soft heart of a summer salad or it can be used as the backbone of a sweet-sharp curd for spreading on toasted muffins. A long strip of the thick, yellow peel is something to add to a slow-cooked casserole of pork or rabbit, sending a clean-tasting warmth through to its soul. The juice is what I add to brighten a dish's flavour, to put a spring in the step of anything that feels too rich or sluggish, or to introduce an edge to my knee-jerk snack of wavy rye crisp-breads and smoked salmon.

Rarely do I use the lemon flesh. Acid flavours bring excitement and vitality to the kitchen, but I have always thought the flesh of the lemon a step too far. Even the heart of the salty pickled lemon is scraped away before use. But I have been missing out. Today I added tiny cubes of flesh to a fresh herb sauce for some steamed spears of asparagus and found it to be both intriguing and successful. I often put a butter and lemon sauce, or just a squirt of juice, on my spears, and have served them before now with a herb béarnaise, so this sharp, cool dressing wasn't the long jump it might sound. Cut exceptionally fine and used with suitably mild ingredients, raw lemon flesh is a far more desirable introduction to a dish than I originally thought.

## Asparagus with lemon and herb sauce

a lemon
olive oil: 4 tablespoons
lemon juice: 1 tablespoon
cherry tomatoes: 8

chives: 6 thin ones
basil: 8 leaves
tarragon: 1 tablespoon
asparagus: 250g

Slice the skin from the lemon, then go over it carefully, removing every little bit of the bitter white pith that lies underneath. I find this easiest with a small, very sharp paring knife.

Remove the sections of flesh and cut them into tiny pieces, discarding any pips as you go. Put them into a mixing bowl, then pour in the olive oil and lemon juice.

Slice the cherry tomatoes in half and add them to the lemon. Finely snip or chop the chives, shred the basil and chop the tarragon, then add them to the lemon and tomato. Season gently, with a little black pepper and sea salt. A few chive flowers would be an appropriate, though far from essential, addition. Set aside in a cool place for the flavours to marry.

Trim the asparagus, removing any tough ends, then steam or cook in boiling water as you wish. When it is tender, after eight or nine minutes or so, drain and divide between two plates. Spoon over the lemon dressing and serve.

Enough for 2

# MAY 16

# Fiddly cooking

Seriously, do I want to be fiddle-arsing around making little parcels of food for supper? Tiny, dollhouse-sized dumplings of minced vegetables and pork to be eaten with chopsticks and dipped into a sauce that I have also made from scratch? My normal answer would be no, I would much rather wash some salad leaves, toss them in dressing, then pile them on a plate with a fillet of grilled fish. I would be happier layering flavours in a vegetable curry, building up textures in a potato-topped pie or chucking meat and vegetables into a wok than snipping, cutting, filling, shaping and baking little parcels.

But then, just as sometimes I buy ready-made pastry and other times relish the tactile pleasure of making my own, there are days when I am happy to stand at the kitchen counter, fiddling with tatters of dough or wielding a pastry brush, crimping and primping and cooking for the sheer joy of the feel of food in my hands. Whilst I refuse to buy into the idea that everything we eat has to be made from scratch, I also refuse to accept that all cooking should be about simply getting something on the table with as little effort as possible. Sometimes, I cook for fun.

Today I make gyoza, the plump dumplings that normally arrive on a bike with a man in a crash helmet from my local Japanese takeaway. The joy comes from pressing the discs of snow-white dough together and crimping the fat little half-moons of pastry with my fingertips. I even put the finished parcels in neat rows on a baking sheet. A Zen cooking moment if ever there was one.

## Japanese pork and cabbage dumplings

The delicious little Japanese dumpling, with its filling of pork, chicken or vegetables, has been politely waiting for its moment of glory. Originating in China, they have been slowly increasing in popularity and I suspect they won't have to wait for much longer. The wrappers are available from Japanese food shops, usually in the frozen section. Use the top, green bit of the Chinese cabbage in the stuffing, not the firm white stalks.

Chinese cabbage: 2 handfuls
spring onions: 6
sesame oil: 2 teaspoons
garlic: 3 cloves
· fresh ginger: 2 teaspoons,
   finely grated
white pepper
minced pork: 250g
a pinch of sugar
Chinese chives: 2 teaspoons,
   finely chopped

a little light soy sauce
dumpling wrappers: 20
a little oil for cooking
water: 100ml

*For the dip:*
sesame oil: 1 tablespoon
rice wine vinegar: 100ml
sweet chilli sauce: 2 teaspoons
dark soy sauce: 2 tablespoons
sugar: 2 teaspoons

Put the ingredients for the dip into a small saucepan and bring to the boil. Simmer for two or three minutes, then leave to cool. It should be sweet, sharp and salty.

Shred the cabbage very finely, then put it in a colander, place on a plate, sprinkle heavily with salt and leave for twenty minutes. This will help it to soften. Rinse briefly, then squeeze out the moisture with your fist.

Finely chop the spring onions, put them in a frying pan with the sesame oil and let them soften over a low to moderate heat. Peel and finely crush the garlic and add to the pan together with the grated ginger and some ground white pepper. It is worth remembering that white pepper is hotter than black.

Add the minced pork to the mixture, turn the heat up slightly and fry till the meat is pale gold, a matter of three or four minutes. Add the sugar, chives and three or four drops of soy sauce. Let the mixture cool.

Place a dumpling wrapper on the work surface and put 2 teaspoons of the pork mixture in the centre of it. Dampen the edge of the wrapper with water, then fold the bundle in half to give a semi circle and press firmly to seal, crimping the dough as you go with your finger and thumb. Set aside and repeat with the remaining wrappers and filling.

Warm a thin layer of oil over a low to moderate heat in a shallow pan to which you have a lid. Place the dumplings in the pan so their crimped edge stands uppermost. Let the bottoms colour lightly; they should be pale amber. Pour in the water, cover the pan with a lid and leave for five minutes. Remove the lid and let the water boil for a minute or two, till it has evaporated. Serve the gyoza with the dip.

Makes about 20, enough for 4

MAY 17

## A sweet-sharp sauce for rhubarb

Most of my recipes are fairly impromptu. They depend on what I have found in the shops, what is in the cupboard or who is likely to be at the table. I cook on a whim, a fancy and, it has to be said, sometimes out of desperation, in a sort of 'what the hell can I make for dinner tonight?' mood. Planning doesn't really come into the equation.

Television doesn't often work like that. The team needs to know what I am up to, and for once I have to think weeks, sometimes months, ahead. Planning the 'Sweet and Sour' programme of *Simple Cooking* for BBC1 continues this morning with a new take on rhubarb and custard. I am after a sauce to sweeten poached or baked rhubarb that doesn't involve making custard yet retains something of its nannying vanilla sweetness. A few weeks ago I made a sauce using the sharp rhubarb baking juices with cream and muscovado sugar that I was rather pleased with, and I repeat it today. It results in a sauce whose first notes are of butterscotch with an underlying one of rhubarb. In many ways it is exactly what I am trying to communicate in the programme. A recipe of certain harmony.

## Rhubarb with butterscotch sauce

| | |
|---|---|
| rhubarb: 400g | *For the sauce:* |
| caster sugar: 2 tablespoons | light muscovado sugar: 50g |
| water: 6 tablespoons | double cream: 125ml |
| | a few drops of vanilla extract |

Chop the rhubarb into pieces the length of a wine cork, removing any strings as you go. Tip into a saucepan, add the sugar and water and bring to the boil. Lower the heat so that the rhubarb simmers gently, then cover and cook for about eight minutes, till it is tender to the point of a knife. Lift the rhubarb out of its syrup with a draining spoon, set aside and return the syrup to the heat.

Turn up the heat so the syrup starts to reduce and thicken very slightly. Add the muscovado sugar, continue boiling till it dissolves, then stir in the cream and vanilla extract. Lower the heat and let it simmer for two minutes, then leave to cool a little.

Divide the rhubarb between four plates or shallow dishes and spoon over some of the sauce.

Enough for 4

Our main course, while not the highlight of the day's cooking, is a perfectly decent spring frittata, which we eat with a salad of pea shoots and new potatoes.

I will be out for dinner tonight so the main meal is lunch. It needs to be quick, cheap and simple.

## Frittata of peas and spring herbs

A light lunch dish, rather good with a few folds of ham or smoked salmon at its side.

| | |
|---|---|
| peas: 200g | dill: 2 heaped tablespoons |
| Parmesan: 50g | tarragon or chervil: 2 tablespoons |
| eggs: 3 | butter: a large knob |

Cook the peas briefly in boiling salted water, then drain them. Finely grate the Parmesan. Break the eggs into a small bowl and mix them lightly with a fork. Finely chop the herbs. Stir them into the eggs with the grated Parmesan and add the peas. Heat an overhead grill.

Melt the butter in a shallow pan, about 20cm in diameter. When it starts to froth, pour in the egg and pea mixture. Let it cook over a relatively low heat till the bottom has formed a golden crust. The centre will probably still be wobbly. Lift the pan from the heat and put it under the grill till the eggs have set and the top is lightly coloured.

Cut into wedges, like a cake.

Enough for 2

## MAY 18

# Lettuce salad and a spiced pudding

The delight of bread and butter pudding is its bread, crisp and chewy on top and soggy underneath; the custard that surrounds it is usually sweet and lightly set but rarely anything more than that.

Over the years, I have used almost every imaginable type of bread, from white sliced to hot cross buns, sourdough loaves to panettone. A pudding made with malt loaf came with warm waves of nostalgia (though mostly for its heavily waxed wrapper); a pudding with brioche was pure Marie Antoinette; a version using stale pain au chocolat proved over the top. A 'lite' version with holey ciabatta rang nobody's bells.

There is an interesting form of bread and butter pudding in India that includes ground spices in the egg custard. I first came across this exceptionally sweet and aromatic adaptation in the lush hills around Thekkady in Kerala, where its arrival at the table almost made up for our hotel's failure to warn us that we were booking into a 'dry' establishment. Staying at a teetotal oasis wouldn't bother me now, but twenty years ago the lack of alcohol came as a jaw-dropping disappointment after our long, dusty and dangerous drive from hell. If ever there was proof that pudding heals the soul, their bread and butter pudding, with its air of cinnamon and cardamom, was it.

Over the years, I have tinkered with the recipe and its curious balance of sugar and spice. Thinner than the norm, with warm notes of butterscotch, vanilla and cinnamon, it is now my favourite interpretation of this particular nursery pudding. Today I brought it to the table as part of a light lunch of salad leaves with smoked bacon and mustard dressing.

## Soft lettuce and hot bacon salad

mixed salad leaves: 4 handfuls
smoked streaky bacon: 8 rashers

*For the dressing:*
Dijon mustard: 1 tablespoon
the juice of half a lemon
basil leaves: 12 large
egg yolks: 2
olive oil: 4 tablespoons

To make the dressing, put the mustard, lemon juice, basil leaves and egg yolks in a blender and blitz for a few seconds. Slowly add the oil until the dressing has the consistency of double cream. Season to taste.

Gently rinse the salad leaves in cold water, checking them carefully as you go, then drain them and dry in a salad spinner.

Grill or fry the bacon rashers till crisp. Drain briefly on kitchen paper to remove any excess fat, then snip into short pieces.

Put the leaves into a salad bowl and add the bacon and dressing. Toss the ingredients gently together and eat immediately.

Enough for 4

# Spiced bread and butter pudding, fried bananas

coconut milk: a 400ml can
milk: 400ml
cardamom pods: 6
light muscovado sugar: 80g
ground cinnamon: a knife point
a vanilla pod
eggs: 2
egg yolks: 2
butter

bread: 12 small slices (about 250g)
a little demerara sugar

*For the bananas:*
bananas: 4
butter: 50g
golden caster sugar: 2 tablespoons
a small orange

Pour the milks into a mixing bowl and whisk briefly till smooth (there will inevitably be a little coconut cream that stays in small lumps, but no matter). Crack the cardamom pods open and remove the black seeds, then crush them to a coarse powder with a heavy weight or grind them with a pestle and mortar. Add them to the milks with the sugar and cinnamon.

Set the oven at 160°C/Gas 3. Slice the vanilla pod in half lengthways and scrape out the sticky black seeds. Stir them into the milk mixture, then beat in the eggs and yolks. Set aside.

Butter a dish about 22cm in diameter. Butter the bread generously, remove the crusts, then cut each piece into triangles. Lay the slices of bread, slightly overlapping, in the buttered baking dish. Pour over the milk mixture and tuck in the halved vanilla pod. Sprinkle over the demerara sugar.

Bake for about twenty-five to thirty minutes, until the custard is just set. It should quiver when the tin is gently shaken. Remove and leave to cool a little.

Peel the bananas and slice them into thick rounds. Melt the butter in a frying pan, add the bananas and fry for a couple of minutes, till they start to soften and take on a little colour. Add the sugar and continue cooking till it starts to caramelise and the bananas, given the occasional gentle stir, become golden and sticky. Finely grate on the zest of the orange. Serve with the pudding.

Enough for 4–6

## The endlessly useful aubergine

A pie teases us, with only a hint of what is to come under its golden crust (chicken and leek, steak and mushroom, maybe cod and a few mussels). A tart, on the other hand, has everything on show. Rarely is anything left to the imagination. I rather like the French *jalousie*, named after the slatted blinds, whose slashed crust permits the shopper a sneaky peek inside but no more.

Today, with an almost midsummer warmth in the air, I make a tart whose filling of baked aubergine, feta cheese and thyme is there for all to see, but holds something back. Namely a layer of smoky baked aubergine cream hiding underneath. We eat it at the garden table, with a tomato salad (surprisingly sweet and herbal for this early in the season) dressed with olive oil and basil leaves. The olive oil, bright and peppery, also gets trickled over the top of the tart.

I am constantly asked about the habit of salting aubergines, and although I went through it in *Tender Volume I*, I will mention it briefly again. Some strains of aubergine are bitter, and leaving their cut edges sprinkled with salt for half an hour can help to draw out the bitter juices. However, they are few and far between, I can barely remember the last one, and most aubergines we buy have had that bitterness bred out of them. The habit of salting aubergines cut into slices or cubes is still valid though, as it makes the fruit much less likely to sponge up your precious olive oil. But then, sometimes I want an aubergine to drink up the oil. It renders the texture soft and silky and has an affinity with the flesh that is both ancient and magical. It is my belief that without olive oil, an aubergine has little to say.

### Aubergine, thyme and feta tart

aubergines: 3 medium
puff pastry: a 320g sheet
a little beaten egg and milk
garlic: 2 large cloves

olive oil
thyme: 10 small sprigs
feta cheese: 200g

Set the oven at 180°C/Gas 4. Score two of the aubergines down their length in four places. Place on a baking sheet and bake for twenty-five minutes or until soft. Remove from the oven and set aside. Turn the oven up to 200°C/Gas 6.

Roll the pastry out a little so that it measures approximately 27cm x 37cm. Place the pastry on a baking sheet and score a line along each side about 3cm in from the edge. Don't cut right through the pastry. Brush the rim of the pastry with egg and milk without letting any drip over the edge (it will stop the pastry rising). Bake for fifteen minutes, until the pastry is pale gold. Remove from the oven and gently push the central rectangle of pastry down with your hand or the back of a spoon so that it leaves a shallow, upstanding border all the way round.

Crush the cooked aubergine flesh with a fork. Peel and finely slice the garlic, then fry it in 2 tablespoons of olive oil in a shallow pan for a couple of minutes, till pale gold. Remove with a draining spoon and add to the creamed aubergine, then season lightly with salt and black pepper.

Slice the remaining aubergine into rounds approximately the thickness of a two-pound coin. Heat more oil, about 4 or 5 tablespoons, in the pan, then add the slices of aubergine, seasoning them as you go with black pepper, a very small amount of salt and the sprigs of thyme. When the aubergine is golden and tender, turn the slices over and cook the other side. Remove with a draining spoon to kitchen paper.

Fill the inner rectangle of the pastry with the aubergine cream, then place the fried aubergine and thyme leaves on top. Crumble the feta over the aubergines. Return the tart to the oven for fifteen minutes, until the cheese starts to soften. Trickle over a little olive oil as it comes from the oven and serve warm rather than hot or cold.

Enough for 6

# MAY 21

## A crisp treatment for lamb

There is a well-known stir-up of breadcrumbs and aromatics traditionally used by Sicilians as a stuffing for sardines. Called *beccafico*, it is principally anchovies, raisins, pine kernels and breadcrumbs, given a lift with orange zest. As much as the filling appeals in theory, I am not the sort of cook to stuff a sardine.

The full mixture of ingredients – olive oil, sweet raisins, crisp crumbs, finely chopped parsley and anchovies – must surely lend itself to other possibilities. It occurs to me this morning that they all have an affinity with lamb. A leg of lamb pierced with anchovy and rosemary is one of my favourite Sunday roasts; I often dunk strips of orange peel into a lamb and rosemary casserole; lamb and garlic is a legendary and ancient pairing. So today I make the stuffing, crisping the breadcrumbs in a shallow pan, then scatter the result over lamb cutlets (I could have grilled them but I am anxious to save washing up).

The experiment, if you could call it that, turns out to be a surprisingly good dish, the tiny cutlets piled on the garden table in their hot frying pan, served with a bowl of lettuce hearts tossed with chopped green olives and their oil. The recipe's utter deliciousness makes up for the times when other 'good ideas' turn out not to be worth recording.

## Lamb cutlets, crumbs and anchovy

white bread: 175g
olive oil: 60ml
anchovy fillets: 8
sultanas or small raisins: 60g

parsley: 6 heaped tablespoons
a small orange
lamb cutlets: 12 small

Grate the bread into large crumbs, or, quicker and easier, blitz it in a food processor. Warm 40ml of the olive oil in a wide, shallow pan and cook the crumbs in it over a sprightly heat, tossing and stirring till they are a pale, toasted gold. This always takes slightly longer than I expect, a good eight or ten minutes or so. Rinse or wipe the anchovy fillets and chop them. Remove the pan from the heat and stir in the chopped anchovies and the sultanas.

Remove the leaves from the parsley and roughly chop them, then stir them into the breadcrumbs. Grate in the zest from the orange. Add its juice and some salt and black pepper, then tip into a bowl.

Heat the remaining 20ml (just over a tablespoon) of olive oil in the empty pan, season the lamb cutlets generously on both sides with salt and pepper, then fry them quickly over a high heat, turning as necessary. They should take no more than a couple of minutes on each side.

Scatter the seasoned crumbs over the cutlets and continue cooking for a minute or two, till the crumbs are warm. Serve immediately.

Enough for 4

# A bunch of carrots

Every Saturday morning I head off to a tiny street market in Bermondsey. It's not far, as the crow flies, and the journey takes me through the city at its most calm and empty. Without its scurrying suits, the city's architecture becomes the star, the monolithic office blocks, their windows shining black in the early summer sunshine, the dark, whiffy alleyways and the rows of thoughtfully restored silk weavers' houses that now house artists, authors and bankers. It is my favourite part of London, and one I often dream of living in.

My first call at the market, before picking up coffee, yoghurt, cheese or bread, is for vegetables. Today there are bunches of carrots so young you can almost see through them. Pale and long tailed, these immature root vegetables will collapse in a stew. They have no earthiness to bring to the party. No sweet, fudgy quality to add to a stew. But what they lack in substance, they make up for in vitality, freshness and sweetness. Their youth makes long, slow cooking pointless. These are the carrots to steam briefly, then toss in melted butter and lemon zest; olive oil and grated orange; butter and fresh mint. They are the carrots that you cannot grate – their tender flesh would turn to mush – but are best cooked whole, turned in warmed crème fraîche or cream and snipped herbs. Young tarragon, mint or chervil perhaps.

Dinner is cold ham today. Bought ready sliced from the market, huge margins of white fat framing its almost maroon flesh. Carrots will be good here, but they need some interest in the way of a sauce. Dill is very flattering to carrots, though a rare choice, as is basil. I tear them up and add them to warm crème fraîche, then brighten the mood with a squeeze of lemon juice.

## Spring carrots, herb sauce

| | |
|---|---|
| slim, young carrots: 2 bunches | dill: 8 sprigs |
| a medium shallot | crème fraîche: 200ml |
| basil: a small bunch | lemon juice: a good squeeze |
| parsley: 6 bushy sprigs | |

Wipe or rinse the carrots, but don't peel them. Place them in a steamer basket or colander set over a pan of boiling water and steam for seven to ten minutes, till tender but not soft. If you prefer to boil them in lightly salted water, then do that, and drain them.

Peel and very finely chop the shallot. Remove the leaves from the basil and parsley and discard the stems, then chop them quite finely, together with the dill fronds. You should have a couple of good handfuls of chopped herbs. Put the crème fraîche into a saucepan large enough to take the carrots in a single layer, add the shallot, herbs and lemon juice and bring to the boil. Season with black pepper and a little salt, then add the drained whole carrots. Leave to simmer for a couple of minutes or so, with the occasional gentle stir, taking care not to break the carrots up. Serve immediately.

Enough for 4 as a side dish

## MAY 25

# Cooking steak

My perfect steak is usually that cooked by someone else. I say this because I like my steak with béarnaise sauce and chips and I rarely, if ever, fancy doing battle with a chip pan at home.

Sometimes, it just has to be steak. A nicely glistening, rare to medium-rare sirloin, rump or preferably rib-eye, with a road map of fat through its flesh, must be near the top of my 'last-supper' dishes. Grilled over hot charcoal outdoors; fried in shallow butter; flash fried in olive oil; cooked under an overhead grill; given plausibly authentic diagonal stripes with the help of a cast-iron griddle – I have tried every way to cook the perfect steak at home.

I have recently taken to cooking my steaks in a dry, arm-wrenchingly heavy cast iron pan. The only oil is on the meat, a light, almost invisible film, scattered with sea salt and black pepper (I don't agree with the notion that a steak should never be salted before cooking, though of course it's up to you). The pan is heated slowly and thoroughly before the meat is added, first on its edge, to cook the fat, then on one side till the surface has lightly browned, then on the other. I like to turn it regularly during cooking too. At the final turn, a thin slice of butter is slipped under the meat, resulting in a steak whose surface is nicely and patchily charred, with translucent gilt-edged fat.

Today I have two pieces of sirloin, an expensive and a rare treat. In order to feed four, I slice the cooked steaks and serve them with steamed Chinese greens and a homemade chilli sauce, the seed-mottled, orange-red style you find in Vietnamese and Chinese kitchens. Sweet, sticky and hot, it is a startling contrast to my usual primrose butter-and-egg-rich béarnaise, but it is an accompaniment whose fire fuels my steak lust as successfully as béarnaise quenches it.

## Grilled sirloin with sweet chilli dipping sauce and Chinese greens

sirloin steaks: 2, about 200g each
a little oil
bok choy: 200g

*For the sweet chilli dipping sauce:*
small hot chillies: 4
garlic: 3 cloves

golden caster sugar: 2 tablespoons
water: 4 tablespoons
groundnut oil: 1 tablespoon
fish sauce (nam pla): 1 tablespoon
lime juice: 2 tablespoons
chopped herbs (Thai basil,
    mint, etc.): a handful

First make the dipping sauce. Remove the stalks from the chillies and chop the chillies finely. Peel the garlic, chop or mince finely and add to the chillies. Put the sugar and water into a small saucepan and bring to the boil. A good stir should dissolve the sugar before the water boils. Cook for a couple of minutes, till the syrup starts to thicken. It will barely colour. Remove from the heat and allow to cool. Stir in the oil, fish sauce, lime juice, chopped herbs, chillies and garlic and set aside.

Lightly oil the steaks and season them with ground black pepper. Grill, or cook in a shallow pan, turning regularly, till nicely done on both sides. The inside should be rose pink. Leave to rest in a warm place for a full five minutes.

Break the bok choy into separate leaves and steam them very briefly, then drain. Slice the steak diagonally into pieces approximately the width of your little finger, dropping them into a warm bowl. Add the steamed greens and a little of the chilli sauce, then toss gently to mix. Transfer to a warm plate or serving dish, spooning over a little more of the chilli sauce. Serve with the remaining sauce.

Enough for 2–3

## Another wonderful sandwich

I spend pretty much the whole day writing and recipe testing. There is no particular place reserved for this, and today I am holed up in the basement at the kitchen table, its raw oak surface warm and rough to the touch. As the evening draws in, I put a match to the lanterns in the fireplace and write by their flickering amber light.

I have few rules as to what and when I eat. Today has been a picking day. Breakfast was a blueberry smoothie but everything else has been bits and pieces eaten from a batch of recipes that I am testing with James, who is helping me in the kitchen. This sporadic, unplanned eating continues into the evening.

After a long day of typing, cooking and eating, I am done. One of the things we have been working on is a sandwich, which James suddenly produces as the day ends. As someone who loves nothing more than hands-on cooking, I always find it a treat to eat something made by someone else. He slices a sourdough loaf, piles it with fried mushrooms and grated cheese, then cooks it in a shallow pan, the crusts turning crisp and deep gold, the cheese between oozing and peeping at the edges. Finally, it goes on to a small, wooden board and is sliced into six fingers. A perfect thing.

| | |
|---|---|
| small mushrooms: 100g | sourdough bread: 2 thin slices |
| olive oil: 2 tablespoons | grated cheese: 4 tablespoons |

Slice the mushrooms thinly, almost like paper. Warm the olive oil in a frying pan and add the mushrooms, seasoning with salt and pepper. Let them cook over a moderate heat for ten minutes or so, till soft. Using a draining spoon, pile them on to one of the slices of bread. Scatter over the grated cheese. Place the second piece of bread on top and press down gently. Wipe the pan out lightly with kitchen roll – you need a film of oil in which to fry the sandwich – then place the sandwich in the pan, letting it cook for a few minutes till the bread is golden and the cheese is starting to melt. Using a fish slice, turn the sandwich over and cook the other side. Perfection is when the bread is lightly crisp, the mushrooms soft and the cheese oozing at the edges.

I'm not sure that everything we eat has to be remarkable, memorable or a classic. It doesn't have to be the greatest, the world's best or even anything to write home about. No, sometimes I simply want something to eat. Food to fill that doesn't cost the earth and that doesn't mean I have to spend the entire evening chopping and stirring. You know, just nice, understated, hand-made food. The spiced lentil recipe I put together tonight is exactly that. It's fine.

## Spiced lentils, mint labne

Adding creamed labne, the Middle Eastern strained yoghurt, to what is virtually a curry, will upset the purists and pedants. (Like I care.) Brown rice would make a nutritious accompaniment, but I am not sure it is entirely necessary. We scooped ours up with warm flatbreads.

large green or brown lentils: 250g
fresh ginger or galangal: 60g
garlic: 4 cloves
cumin seeds: a teaspoon
ground coriander: a teaspoon
garam masala: 3 heaped teaspoons
red chillies: 2 small
ground turmeric: a heaped
  teaspoon

rapeseed oil
a medium onion
chopped tomatoes: a 400g can

*For the mint labne:*
fresh mint leaves: a small handful
labne or strained yoghurt: 400g
dried mint: half a teaspoon
a little olive oil

Bring the lentils to the boil in a pan of deep, unsalted water, then let them simmer for twenty to twenty-five minutes, until they are quite soft.

Peel the ginger or galangal, roughly chop it, then purée in a food processor with the peeled garlic, cumin seeds, ground coriander, garam masala, red chillies, ground turmeric and enough oil to make a soft but not runny paste.

Peel and finely slice the onion. Warm a tablespoon or two of oil in a medium, heavy-based casserole over a moderate heat. Add the onion and let it colour, stirring from time to time so it doesn't burn. Add the spice paste. When it is fragrant, golden and almost soft, pour in the chopped tomatoes and a can of water, add the drained, cooked lentils and some salt and leave to simmer for half an hour or so. The lentils should be soft but still retaining a little of their texture; the sauce should be thick.

Remove a third of the mixture and blitz to a khaki-coloured slop in a blender or food processor. Stir it back into the lentils, then check the seasoning.

To make the mint labne, simply chop the fresh mint leaves and stir them into the labne or yoghurt with the dried mint. Trickle over a little olive oil and serve with the spiced lentils.

Enough for 4

## MAY 28

I need to make a little bit of cheese and ham go a long way. The cheese is a small lump of Anne Wigmore's Spenwood, a firm ewe's milk cheese I tend to eat in short curls cut with a cheese parer. It has something of an aged pecorino about it, and I often use it grated too, like Parmesan. The ham, some fine and dark slices from an English animal, is from the sort of well-cared-for pig that probably had a Christian name.

Always preferring a small amount of something special to a surfeit of something mediocre, I often find myself in this situation, with hand-crafted ingredients of perfect pedigree, but too small in quantity to eat as they are. A salad is a possibility, the cheese and ham cut in small pieces and tossed with celery, apple, watercress and a creamy vinaigrette-type dressing, but I use the bits instead to add interest to some savoury muffins. The quantity of the flavourings is small, but their impact is extraordinary, making the little buns really special.

### Cheese, ham and apple muffins

plain flour: 275g
caster sugar: a tablespoon
baking powder: 2 teaspoons
eggs: 3
yoghurt: 175ml

cooked ham: 200g, chopped
a small apple, grated
firm, mature cheese such
    as Spenwood: 75g

Line 12 bun tins with muffin cases. Set the oven at 200°C/Gas 6. Put the flour, sugar, baking powder and a pinch of salt in a bowl, mixing together

thoroughly. In a separate bowl, lightly beat the eggs together, then stir in the yoghurt, chopped ham and grated apple. Grate the cheese and stir it into the yoghurt mixture, then lightly mix with the dry ingredients.

Divide the mixture between the muffin cases, grate over a little extra cheese, then bake for twenty-five minutes, till risen and pale gold. Allow to cool down a little before eating, but eat on the same day.

Makes 11–12

# MAY 29

## A bit of a hash

A cook collects kit, an assortment of pots, pans, knives, bowls and other bits and pieces that form the tools with which they make themselves something to eat. I am sure some collections, the *batterie de cuisine*, are carefully thought out and possibly matching, the best money can buy and the correct tool for the job, but my own collection is more of a hotchpotch.

I prefer to work with as little kit as possible. A drawer full of gadgets and cupboards full of equipment I don't use is my idea of kitchen hell. Whether it's an exquisitely handcrafted copper casserole brought back from Japan or a vegetable peeler that cost less than a cup of coffee, I carry a fondness for most of my cookware. Each piece has proved its usefulness time and again. It feels good in the hand, has a true purpose and is a thing of simple beauty. Cookware, a pan, a knife, a plate or a pot, should be a pleasure to use and should carry reminders of good times had both cooking and eating. I have never understood why even a washing-up brush cannot be beautiful. Its role is crucial, and it should be a pleasing thing to touch and to look at.

My frying pan weighs a ton. At least, it feels that way as I lift it from hob to trivet. Its cast iron surface is not non-stick, though the pan is now so old it has developed a patina to which nothing will adhere. Cast iron needs caring for.

What makes the pan so heavy is the thickness of the iron. The point of this is that the heat moves gradually through the pan, creating a lasting, even heat, unlike the thinner frying pans I own whose purpose is to cook, wok-like, at high speed. Gradual heat is better for foods that not only need to brown appetisingly on the outside but need to cook inside too, such as slices of potato or a piece of chicken.

The pan's black, slightly pitted surface has seen steaks, chicken, potatoes and many a burger or fritter. I rarely use it for fish, which responds better to an altogether quicker, more direct treatment. Tonight I use the pan to make a quick, cheap supper for friends, though the fry-up of grated potato, onion, sausage and egg could just as well have been a Sunday breakfast dish.

### Sausage and egg hash

potatoes: 2 medium
a medium to large onion
large, Cumberland-type
    sausages: 275g (or 4 large
    butcher's sausages)

a little oil, such as rapeseed
large eggs: 2

Grate the potatoes coarsely, without peeling them. I find the sort of long, thin shreds you get from a food processor better for this dish than the short ones from a microplane or box grater. Peel the onion, then slice it very finely. Mix the potato and onion together and season with salt and a little black pepper.

Warm a thin film of oil in a shallow, heavy-based pan. It should be really quite hot. Put the onion and potatoes in and let them colour on the underside, then turn them over. Remove the skin from the sausages, break them into short, thick chunks and add to the pan. As they turn golden, flip them over to cook the other side, then tip off any excess fat.

Break the eggs into the pan and let them cook for a couple of minutes, till the whites have set but the yolks are still runny. Now stir the eggs into the potatoes and onion and serve immediately.

Enough for 2

# MAY 30

## Baked chicken with wheat and dill

A recipe to soothe.

whole wheat: 250g
butter: 30g
rapeseed oil: a tablespoon
a chicken, jointed into
    8 pieces

hot chicken stock: 400ml
a lemon
dill: a small bunch

Put a saucepan of water on to boil. Rinse the wheat in a sieve under running water, tip into the saucepan of boiling water, turn down to a rolling boil and leave till the wheat is almost soft. It should be tender, with a bit of bite left in it, al dente if you like. This will take anything from twenty-five to forty minutes. Drain and set aside.

Set the oven at 200°C/Gas 6. Warm the butter and oil in a deep casserole. Season the chicken with salt and pepper and add to the pan, letting it cook over a moderate heat till the skin is golden. Turn and colour the other side, then add the drained wheat, the hot stock and the juice and squeezed shells of the lemon. Place the dish in the oven, covered, and bake for about an hour, till the chicken is truly tender. About 15 minutes before the end of cooking, chop the dill and stir it into the stock. Adjust the seasoning with a little salt and pepper if necessary before serving.

Enough for 4

June

# A bunch of asparagus

In money terms, asparagus is no longer quite the luxury it used to be. Mid-season, you can pick up a bunch for the price of a packet of frozen peas. Perhaps it's my background, but no matter how cheap they get, those long, soft-green spears always feel like a luxury. The thin ones, barely the thickness of a pencil, are often the most flavoursome of all, and a good price too. That is what I pick up today, laying them on top of my bag like a fragile bunch of flowers.

I have always liked to eat asparagus with pastry, the spears laid out in a quivering quiche like spokes in a wheel; the tips wrapped up in puff pastry and served with a classic hollandaise; or even just the vegetable laid on a round of pastry with a trickle of melted butter. Whichever way you play it, the combination of silky spears and crisp pastry is a fine one to have on your fork.

Tonight I make a rather neat little puff pastry tart, long and thin like a pencil case, the asparagus coated in a soft blanket of cream and grated Parmesan.

## Asparagus tarts with lemon and crème fraîche

Short of homemade, the best pastry for these is one of the ready-rolled sheets of all-butter puff pastry.

asparagus spears: 10
puff pastry sheet: 375g
double cream: 100ml

grated Parmesan: 50g
flat-leaf parsley: a few sprigs
a lemon

Boil the asparagus spears, or steam them if you prefer, till tender. They will take anything from five to nine minutes, depending on their thickness. They are ready when you can easily slide the point of a knife into the stem. Drain the asparagus and set aside.

Set the oven at 200°C/Gas 6. Lay the puff pastry out on a lightly floured work surface, longest edge facing you, then cut it into five long rectangles. Place these on a baking sheet. Use a knife to score a narrow rim, roughly

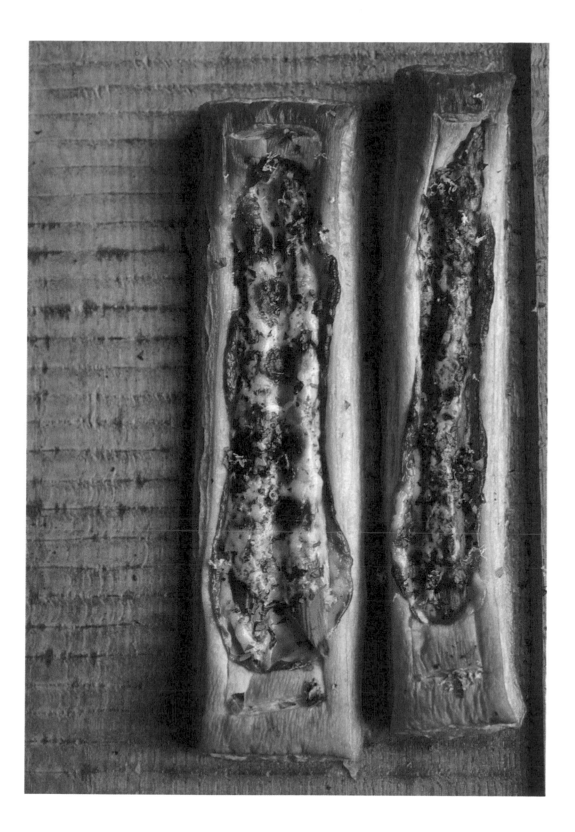

1.5cm in from the edge. Don't score so deeply that you cut right through to the baking sheet.

Warm the double cream and grated Parmesan together and grind in a little black pepper. Divide half of this mixture between the centre of each tart. Place two asparagus spears on each one, then spoon the remaining cream and cheese mixture on top. Bake in the preheated oven for fifteen to twenty minutes, till the filling is just starting to turn golden brown in patches.

While the tarts are baking, finely chop the parsley leaves, finely grate the lemon zest and mix them together. Remove the tarts from the oven and scatter over the lemon and parsley. Serve immediately, while the tarts are still hot and crisp.

Makes 5 long, slim tarts

## JUNE 3

# Making a strawberry sing

Strawberry plants are survivors, putting up with rich or poor soil, drought or deluge, neglect or well-meant smothering. My plants, Garrigue, Florence and Chelsea Pensioner, arrived from the nursery frozen, their tightly pleated leaves and snow-white roots curled up like a row of sleeping children. Apparently they travel more safely that way. Some have spent their lives in a pot outside the scullery door, others in the sunniest bed in the vegetable patch, tucked around the roots of the currant bushes. One particularly tenacious root survives through scorching sun and long frosts in a crack in the paving stones.

And yet for all its determination to bring us sweet, scarlet fruit, the strawberry family is prone to virus attack that can wipe out an entire variety over a number of years and is the main reason why some of the most ancient, such as Black Prince and Keen's Seedling, are no longer with us.

The fraise de bois, the wild berry of wood and country lane, is still around, its charming, diminutive fruit intensely flavoured and with a pleasing crunch. It has more seeds than flesh. A gift from a friend, the wild strawberry has long been a weed in my garden, establishing itself anywhere its tentacle-like runners care to put down a root (snip the runner off once it has rooted and you will have a new plant). It is a weed I am grateful for, the berries so tempting they rarely make it to the table.

The last couple of years have seen some of the best berries I have ever grown: small, dark and deeply flavoured. But all too often the strawberries I find in my shopping basket can disappoint and need some help in the kitchen to be truly delicious. Slicing the fruit, tossing it with caster sugar and leaving it for an hour to gather its thoughts certainly helps, as does eating it slightly warm from an hour left on a sunny windowsill. Marriages that will tease out its qualities are those involving pistachios, red wine and the meanest grinding of black pepper.

Curiously, a dash of raspberry juice will work wonders, bringing richness to even the dullest strawberry. A luscious presentation might involve crushing a handful of raspberries with a cup of softly whipped cream, then folding in the whole strawberries. This week I came up with a simpler way to make a strawberry shine – dressing it with a raspberry sugar.

### A mint and raspberry sugar for strawberries

strawberries: 400g          mint leaves: 8
caster sugar: 100g          raspberries: 4

Remove the green hulls from the strawberries, then slice each fruit into three or four. Put the sugar into a food processor, add the mint leaves and pulse till the mint appears as tiny green flecks. Drop in the raspberries and blitz till the sugar has turned pale pink. Scatter a spoonful of the sugar over the sliced berries, toss very gently, then set aside for about twenty minutes.

Serve in bowls, scattered with the remaining raspberry mint sugar.
Enough for 4

Even more interesting, I think, and less sweet, is a version using just raspberries. Put the strawberries in a bowl. Reduce an equal amount of raspberries to a purée with a little lemon juice and sugar. Cut a few more raspberries in half and toss them with the purée. Spoon it over the strawberries and serve.

Someone placed five cream crackers in a row on the pavement outside the house during the night. I spend much of the day wondering/worrying about their significance.

It is only when I go to the shops that I see bits of rubbish dotted all the way up the road. The dustmen have been again.

Arriving home tired and ravenous, I mix half a cup of hoisin sauce with a tablespoon each of Vietnamese chilli sauce, grated ginger, light soy sauce and lime juice, plus a teaspoon of five-spice powder and a crushed clove of garlic. I toss four chicken thighs in it, then tip the lot into a roasting tin and bake for half an hour. What emerges is 'cuisine approximate' – a rough copy of something I remember eating long ago, sticky and dark, not quite Chinese, not quite Vietnamese, but nevertheless utterly delicious. I haven't the energy to cook rice, so I wipe my plate with bread.

## JUNE 5

## A cake for coffee

I have always been rather taken with the mitteleuropean ritual of stopping for mid-morning coffee and cake. The apfelstrudel at the Café Einstein in Berlin, the cheesecake at Gerbaud in Budapest, and the chocolate cake at the glittering jewel that is Demel in Vienna are all places of pilgrimage for me. Each location, be it grand café or local konditorei, has its speciality (I once found a delectably moist apricot slice at a tiny, cushions-and-curtains café in a side street in Stockholm).

The streusel cakes with their pebble-textured crusts particularly interest me. The pleasure is not solely in their sugar-encrusted top but in the contrast between that and the layer of fruit and sponge cake underneath. Often served in square slices, they sit nicely with a cup of dark, slightly bitter coffee around ten-thirty in the morning and are useful for dessert too, with chilled whipped cream.

The base of these sweet crusts is flour, butter and sugar, rubbed to a crumble, then scattered over the sponge and fruit as the cake is about to go in the oven. It is a recipe I have worked on over the years until I feel, now at

last, I have got it right. A fruit with a sharp bite, such as blackcurrant or cherry, sandwiched between the sponge and the crumble is more successful than something bland and sweet such as apple. The lingonberries I brought back from Finland in a Tupperware box produced the most dramatic result, and the gooseberry version was a close second.

## Gooseberry crumble cake

gooseberries: 300g
butter, softened: 180g
golden caster sugar: 90g
light muscovado sugar: 90g
eggs: 2
ground almonds: 80g
self-raising flour: 150g
vanilla extract: a few drops

*For the crumble:*
plain flour: 110g
butter: 80g
caster sugar: 2 tablespoons

Preheat the oven to 180°C/Gas 4. Line the base of a 22cm round cake tin with baking parchment. Top and tail the gooseberries and set aside. Make the cake: beat the butter, caster and muscovado sugars in a food mixer for a good eight to ten minutes, till pale and fluffy. Break the eggs, beat them gently with a fork – just to mix the yolks and whites together – then gradually introduce them to the mixture with the beater on slow.

Fold in the ground almonds and flour, then add the vanilla extract. Transfer the mixture to the prepared tin and smooth it flat. Scatter the gooseberries on top.

Make the crumble topping: blitz the flour and butter to crumbs in a food processor. Add the sugar and mix lightly. Remove the bowl from the stand and add a few drops of water. Shake the bowl a little – or run a fork through the mixture – so that some of the crumbs stick together like small pebbles. This will give a more interesting mix of textures. Scatter this loosely over the gooseberries.

Bake for about an hour, checking for doneness with a skewer. Remove the cake from the oven and set aside. Leave to cool before cutting.

Enough for 8

## Savouring the apricot. Stoning the cherry

There is something of the kid-in-a-sweetshop about this morning's shopping trip. Cherries in a woven birch-twig basket, a nest of apricots like speckled eggs, green cardboard punnets of strawberries, and small, flat 'Saturn' peaches vie for attention in the way humbugs, sherbet lemons and Bluebird toffees did when I was a kid. I bring a few of each home, unsure as to where they will lead.

Whereas each day of summer seems to bring another drippingly ripe peach, you could count the number of perfect apricots I encounter on the fingers of one hand. Elusive, capricious and frustrating, the apricot can infuriate more often than it delights, leaving us wondering why anyone would bother with its pale-orange, cotton-wool flesh.

The occasional, ambrosial fruit aside, the apricot is probably best taken to the kitchen, where we can use a few cook's tricks to tease out its magic. Sugar, in surprisingly large quantities, is the apricot's good Samaritan. Even the most disappointing specimens that refuse to ripen can be transformed into something worth eating when you scatter-dust them thickly with golden caster and bake them in a slow oven. Generosity with the sugar bag will win over the meanest little fruit.

Other cards to have up your sleeve are vanilla (use it in the apricot's presence whenever you can), orange zest and juice (wonderful as a marinade with sugar), honey (trickle it over the raw fruit prior to baking) and elderflower cordial, which can be used as a marinade for ripe but tasteless fruit or added to its poaching syrup.

In a savoury sense, the apricot seems to work best when it is dried, and that is the sort I use in Indian and Middle Eastern recipes, where the fruits slowly swell during cooking, soaking up the spices and juices in the dish. Until today, I have only ever cooked fresh apricots in sweet applications. Those in *Tender Volume II* – a lamb casserole with rosemary, a guinea fowl and Szechuan pepper dish and a stuffing for roast pork – were all made with dried.

# Chicken with apricots and coconut milk

Apricots, flushed with vermilion and freckled with deepest ruby, tempt me almost more than any other fruit. Those I bring back from the shop today are disappointing, so I take my purchase to the kitchen, tucking them almost absent-mindedly into a chicken curry. Rather than the sweetness overkill I feared, the apricots bring a welcome tang to the coconut-scented sauce and produce a partnership with the chicken that deserves investigating further (think stuffing with apricots and pistachios, maybe). What's more, the hot, creamy, salty sauce studded with a few luscious apricots on the point of collapse is a triumph.

lemongrass: 3 short, plump stalks
fresh ginger: 50g
hot red chillies: 2 small
garlic: 2 cloves
coriander: a bunch
limes: 2
groundnut oil: 1 tablespoon, plus
   a little more for the paste

tomatoes: 200g, roughly chopped
fish sauce (nam pla): a tablespoon
dark soy sauce: 2 tablespoons
chicken: 8 thighs
apricots: 8
coconut milk: a 400ml can

Peel and discard the outer leaves of the lemongrass to reveal the softer inner leaves. Cut into short lengths and put in a food processor. Peel the ginger, slice into thin pieces and add to the lemongrass. Chop the chillies, discarding their stems, and add to the ginger with the peeled garlic cloves and the roughly chopped stems and half the leaves of the coriander. Grate the zest of the limes into the food processor, then turn the machine on and let it chop everything to a coarse paste, adding a little oil. Add the tomatoes, fish sauce and dark soy and continue whizzing.

Warm the oil in a deep pan over a moderate to high heat and use it to brown the chicken pieces lightly, turning them so they colour nicely on both sides. Meanwhile, halve and stone the apricots and set aside. Lift the chicken out and pour anything more than a tablespoon of oil away. Add half the spice paste and let it fry over a low to moderate heat for two minutes, till fragrant, then return the chicken to the pan. Pour in the coconut milk, stir, cover and leave to simmer gently over a low heat for ten minutes. (The remaining spice paste can be kept in the fridge, covered with a little oil and a lid, for about a week.) Slide the apricots into the sauce and cook for ten minutes, until soft. Test the chicken and fruit for doneness, then add the juice of the limes and the remaining coriander leaves, roughly chopped. Correct the seasoning with a little salt if necessary. Serve with rice or bread.

Enough for 4

As a rule, I don't mess with cherries, feeling they are probably best eaten from the bag. But I don't always want to suck and spit, so I patiently stone a bag of cherries one by one to serve as dessert. Eating cherries without constantly having to remove a stone from my mouth is a rare pleasure, and the repetitive action of stoning the fruit into a bowl turns out to be less of a chore than I expect, even mildly relaxing. The inclusion of elderflower cordial adds a certain spritz and the two flavours are surprisingly happy together.

## A sweet cherry salad

ripe cherries: 400g
elderflower cordial: 100ml

caster sugar: 2 tablespoons
(optional)

Stalk and stone the cherries, dropping the fruit into a stainless steel or glass bowl. Pour over the elderflower cordial, adding the sugar if you like your desserts particularly sweet. Toss the cherries gently so they are soaked with the cordial, then set aside for half an hour or so.

This is good served with cream, but expect some curdling.

Enough for 4

## JUNE 11

# Getting tarragon right

Garden plants need support. Being buffeted by the wind makes them rock back and forth, unsettling their roots, some of which are fine, hair-like and easily damaged. I spend a good hour before lunch tying up the Butterfly and Marmande tomatoes, the sweet peas and purple climbing beans that had such a hard time in yesterday's pummelling showers. No job in the vegetable patch feels quite so nurturing as tying the delicate stem of a plant to a stick.

Struggling (or enjoying, depending on your outlook) with the second-driest spring since 1910, and with rainfall barely 8.8mm for the spring quarter, the last few days' steady rain has been truly a gift from heaven. While half of me wants to run naked into the garden and stand in the blissful rain, arms held up in thanks, the downside is that slugs and snails come out in force to bask in the raindrops and munch on my lettuces and beans. They have had the new shoots from the dahlias too.

The tarragon, grown in a pot rather than in the rose bed like the oregano, fennel and lemon verbena, is lapping up the water. Herbs need a regular clipping if they are not to get too tall and topple over. I once watched a young gardener at Sissinghurst trimming the creeping thyme with what were clearly nail scissors, visibly obeying the textbook rules of removing anything longer than two leaves on each stem.

The tarragon gets a good trim and back in the kitchen I strip the leaves from the cut stems. This is French tarragon, the one whose aniseed notes perfume *poulet à l'estragon*, rather than the bushier but less fragrant Russian type. It's a like-it-or-loathe-it herb, but for me one of the essential scents of summer.

## The whisk

Anyone who cooks regularly will have their favourite piece of kit. The single piece of equipment they would hate to lose above all others, the piece that turns a job into a joy. It may be a thing of quiet beauty or just an especially efficient tool. Whatever else it may be, your favourite bit of kit will make your task easier, it will feel right in the hand and, above all, this much used tool will be a pleasure to exploit.

As someone who takes the aesthetics of cooking equipment a little too seriously (it's only a potato peeler, for heaven's sake), I guard my kit carefully, taking great care with much loved tools whenever they accompany me on a trip or when someone else uses them. I still wince over losing the 'perfect' bottle opener.

To pick one favourite is almost impossible, like choosing your favourite pet or child, partly because its use is so specific. I do, however, have a particular soft spot for my whisk. Apart from its ability to turn limpid egg whites into a proud pavlova, egg yolks and olive oil into wobbling mayonnaise or beat the lumps out of a cheese sauce, my whisk is a thing of beauty. The handle is rolled copper, the head has fine spokes of great flexibility and the whole thing has a perfect weight and balance. The generous size of the balloon of spokes seems

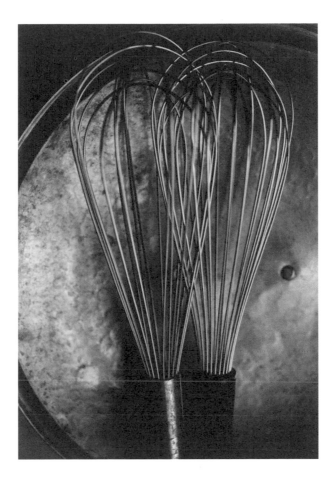

to get air into a mixture better than any other whisk I have used. And that, of course, is its sole purpose. The most basic of kitchen equipment made perfect by careful design, and presumably by someone who knows what a cook needs a whisk to do. Oh, and did I mention it is a thing of almost aching beauty too?

## Chicken tarragon mayonnaise

If you don't fancy making your mayonnaise, use a mild proprietary brand.

| | |
|---|---|
| chicken breasts: 2 | *For the mayonnaise:* |
| olive oil | egg yolks: 2 |
| a squeeze of lemon | groundnut oil: 125ml |
| a cucumber | olive oil: 125ml |
| pea shoots: 4 handfuls | Pernod: a few drops, to taste |
| | tarragon: 8 sprigs |
| | flat-leaf parsley: a small handful |

Heat an overhead grill. Put the chicken breasts skin-side up in a shallow baking dish, brush them with a little oil, then season with pepper, salt (a generous amount) and lemon juice. Grill for fifteen minutes or so, till the skin is crisp and blistered. Turn and cook the other side briefly, then check for doneness with a skewer. Leave the chicken to rest for ten minutes.

Make the mayonnaise by putting the egg yolks into a mixing bowl and beating in the oils with a balloon whisk, drop by drop at first, gradually increasing the flow as the mayonnaise thickens. Stir in the Pernod and then the chopped leaves of the tarragon and parsley, discarding the branches. Season with salt and pepper.

Peel the cucumber, cut it in half lengthways and scrape out and discard the seeds. Cut the cucumber into thick chunks and fold them into the mayonnaise.

Slice the chicken into thick pieces and fold them into the cucumber and tarragon mayonnaise. Rinse and dry the pea shoots in a salad spinner. Put them into a serving bowl and add the chicken mayonnaise.

Enough for 2–3

## Cherry almond crumble

It is not often I cook a cherry, but this summer crumble is a good reason to.

| | |
|---|---|
| sweet cherries: 750g | *For the almond crumble:* |
| water: 4 tablespoons | plain flour: 120g |
| sugar: 4 tablespoons | butter: 85g, cut into cubes |
| cornflour: 1 teaspoon | golden caster sugar: 4 tablespoons |
| the juice of half a lemon | ground almonds: 4 tablespoons |
| cream, to serve | flaked almonds: 1 tablespoon |

Set the oven at 180°C/Gas 4. Rinse, stalk and stone the cherries, then put them in a pan with the water and sugar. Bring to the boil, lower the heat and simmer for ten minutes. Put the cornflour in a small cup or bowl and stir in 2 tablespoons of the juice from the simmering cherries. When the cornflour has dissolved, stir the mixture into the hot cherries. As soon as the syrup starts to thicken a little, remove from the heat, stir in the lemon juice and transfer to a baking dish.

Whiz the flour and butter in a food processor until the mixture resembles fine fresh breadcrumbs. Add the sugar and ground almonds. Scatter loosely on top of the fruit, add the flaked almonds and bake for thirty-five to forty minutes, till the fruit is bubbling under the pale golden crumble. Serve with cream.

Enough for 4

## JUNE 12

# A new crab salad

Dark-shelled crabs of a deep, rusty orange have always delighted me more than lobsters or crayfish. Both the sweet white meat and the more savoury brown interest me, especially when used in a sandwich with fluffy white bread. Despite crab feeling right in summer – it literally smells of the beach – late June and July are not the best time to eat it, as this is when they are busy breeding. That red, wax-like substance you sometimes find tucked away in a hen crab is the eggs and, although edible, is hardly a delicacy. But find me anything that tastes more perfect on a summer day than a crab and cucumber sandwich.

My fishmonger sells whole cooked crabs and also nicely prepared dressed crab in its shell. Or perhaps that should be in 'a' shell. My guess is that, rather like a chicken's gizzards, a crab shell rarely contains the meat that belongs to it. Something I have always found faintly disquieting.

Which I buy will depend on whether I feel like smashing the claws open and teasing out the white flesh with a knitting needle or whether I am prepared to forgo the spanking freshness of a newly cooked crustacean for the ease of one where all the work has been done for me. Much depends on my mood.

I used to live in St Ives, where we bought crabs directly from the fishermen's blue boats and boiled them in a deep pot full of very salty water. A tablespoon of salt to a litre is about right. They took approximately fifteen minutes and emerged sweet, fresh and snowy-fleshed. The scent of crab boiling on the stove is one that stays with you, like your Gran's pea and ham soup or Mum's mince pies.

Today I return with a fresh cooked crab, crack its fat claws and pick its flesh. I make two small, untidy piles of meat, with, weight-wise, about twice as much brown as white. It needs to go a long way, so I fold it very tenderly into a salad of avocado and cucumber and dress it with a sweet-sharp mixture of fish sauce, coriander and lime juice. Sweet, invigorating and refreshing, it is worth every bit of trouble and crab-flecked kitchen.

## A salad of crab, avocado and lime

A rather luxurious salad here, one for a special occasion. I sometimes use this as a first course instead of a light lunch, in which case it will serve three, rather elegantly. In a perfect world you could use your own home-cooked crab, but I often use ready-dressed crab from the fishmonger's.

a small, red chilli
thin spring onions: 2
cucumber: a 10cm piece
avocados: 2 small
mixed crabmeat: 300g

*For the dressing:*
palm sugar, or golden caster
   sugar: 1 heaped teaspoon

fish sauce (nam pla): 1 tablespoon
lime juice: 3 tablespoons
coriander leaves: a handful

*To serve:*
ciabatta: 4 slices
half a lime
a little olive oil

Seed and very finely chop the chilli. Cut the spring onions into very fine slices and add to the chilli. Peel the cucumber, halve it, scrape out the seeds with a teaspoon, then dice the flesh into tiny cubes. Remove the flesh from the avocados and dice it finely. Toss the cucumber and avocado with the spring onions and chilli.

Put the sugar in a small mixing bowl, add the fish sauce and lime juice and stir till the sugar is dissolved. Chop the coriander leaves and stir into the dressing. No further seasoning is necessary.

Toast the slices of bread till crisp, rub with the cut side of the lime to release a little of the juice, then trickle over enough olive oil to saturate each one.

Put the crabmeat in a mixing bowl with the cucumber and avocado mixture, pour over the dressing and toss very gently, using a fork to mix. Pile on to plates and serve with the lime toasts.

Enough for 2

## JUNE 15

## A new kitchen table

A train journey through Berkshire to choose wood for my kitchen table. I leave the train to fine pine-needle rain prickling my face.

I can eat anywhere, standing up if I have to. That said, I have always loved the idea of a kitchen table around which people can gather. Having spent a good year or more scouring the internet, antique shops and reclamation yards for something that works for me, I finally decided to have one made. The idea had never crossed my mind until I saw, quite by chance, a barn piled high with thick oak planks, each one with its own notches and splits, ridges and undulations.

My preference is for a simple, unpolished, everyday table that will show the timber in all its natural beauty. A table that will get better for a few wine rings, oil spots and maybe even the odd burn from a hot casserole. Scars can hold a great beauty.

The idea of a precious, polished piece doesn't appeal in the slightest. I long ago decided on English oak, but this is oak with a story. Oaks that had suffered flooding in the Cambridgeshire fens around 4,000 years ago, resulting in the trees lying hidden in the sodden ground till they were found by a farmer and his plough. In cookery terms the tree had been marinating, not in olive oil and herbs but in the cool, dark waters of the fens, slowly darkening in colour from the outside in, like a piece of gravadlax. Hence its name, bog oak.

The timber is fragile and has been dried, wrapped in hessian, and sprayed in ever-decreasing amounts for up to five years. It now lies stacked, with air circulating around it, in a Berkshire barn, waiting to live again. We discuss planing, carving, polishing the wood but I decided the moment I saw it that we would do as little as possible to it. As I rub my hand along the chocolate-coloured planks, I faintly wonder what will be its first meal.

Tonight I peeled and roughly chopped a couple of ripe avocados, dressed them with lime juice, a chopped spring onion and a squeeze of wasabi paste from a tube, then piled them on to pieces of sourdough toast trickled with olive oil whilst it was still hot. Pudding was slices of chocolate and Nutella sponge from the cake shop.

JUNE 21

# Roses

Midsummer night and the roses are damp with raindrops and heavy with scent. The heads of the burgundy *Francis Dubrueil* are hanging heavily, their faces turned towards the dark loam below. *Direktor Benschop*, the single white that climbs the garden boards, has, like a cloud of white butterflies, gone. The crimson, magenta and apricot *Mutabilis Chinensis* has stopped to catch its breath before the next cluster of buds opens. Most loaded with fragrance is the pair of *Tradescant* in their moss-stained terracotta pots on the kitchen steps. A good feed of rose food and regular batches of used tealeaves keep the pot-bound bushes well nourished.

The coolest of the garden beds is home not only to a *Mutabilis* and an inky black-red Louis XIV but to a creamy rose called *White Gold* and a new one named in memory of Natasha Richardson and given to me by her mother, Vanessa Redgrave. An open rose, with a soft arrangement of large, pink petals and a sweet, delicate perfume that is somehow cool, like a flowing brook. Any of the roses may end up in a glass jar on the kitchen table, but some might be used in the food too.

You would need barrow loads of roses to make your own rosewater. Gulab jamun, balls of dough made notably in Pakistan and Sri Lanka – though I only have first-hand experience of them in India – from buffalo-milk solids and steeped in rose- and cardamom-scented syrup, are probably

the ultimate use, but I will leave these to those who know what they are doing. Deep fried and served in sugar syrup. Sounds so very wrong, but in reality is so very, very right.

I am not someone who really likes flowers with food that much, aside from the odd nasturtium flower in a salad. But why should a leaf be so workaday and a flower seem so prissy and flippant? There is certainly flavour, albeit subtle, in many edible flowers – from the cucumber-like charms of borage to the spiciness of an old-fashioned garden pink. This morning I pick rose petals by the fistful, morning being when they are at their most fragrant, then lay them out to dry a little before crystallising them. They should keep for weeks in a screw-top jar, and will end their days being scattered over vanilla or strawberry ice cream or to decorate tiny cupcakes.

## Crystallised rose petals

Pick full-blown, unsprayed garden roses and break them gently into separate petals. Lay them on a tray, then brush each one with a little lightly beaten egg white. Dust with caster sugar and leave to dry in a cool, very dry place. They will darken and crisp up. Store in a screw-top jar till needed.

## A warm jam of gooseberries and strawberries

I do make the traditional long-life summer jams from time to time but more fun, I think, are the ones for instant consumption. The jams that you serve freshly made to trickle over warm scones or for dipping fingers of toast or warm madeleines into. The advantage of these is that they contain less than half the sugar you need for a preserve that has to keep till winter. The immediacy of their consumption and the short cooking time mean a fresher flavour. My inclusion of gooseberries makes everything really sing.

strawberries: 400g
gooseberries: 150g

granulated sugar: 250g
lemon juice: 2 tablespoons

Rinse and hull the strawberries but don't dry them. Top and tail the gooseberries. Pile the fruits into a stainless steel or enamel pan with the sugar and lemon juice. Crush the fruit with your hands or a potato masher, then place the pan over a low to medium heat. Cook, stirring occasionally, for fifteen to twenty minutes, spooning off the pink froth as you go. The jam

should be thick enough to fall slowly from the spoon, like syrup, but nowhere near thick enough to set.

Pour into a bowl and serve with scones (where it will drip down your fingers) or slices cut from a sponge cake, or spoon over goat's yoghurt, or stir into a mess of whipped cream and crumbled meringue. Just don't expect it to set or to keep for very long.

Makes a couple of jars, will keep in the fridge for several days

## JUNE 23

## A new risotto

### A risotto of spelt and pea shoots

There is a nubbly quality to a risotto made with pearled spelt. Now easily available from supermarkets and grocer's, this ancient grain has an extraordinary comforting quality. It seems to handle vegetable stock more successfully than rice does, restoring some of the silky texture that is often missing in a traditional risotto when made with vegetable stock (the unctuous quality of a good risotto is dictated as much by the stock used as by the rice).

Pea shoots are available in bags from the major supermarkets but easily grown at home too. I plant trays of them on shallow compost.

pearled spelt: 250g
a small onion
butter: 40g, plus a large knob of
   butter to finish

hot vegetable stock: a litre
pea shoots: 80g
grated Parmesan: a handful

Put the spelt in a bowl, cover with cold water and leave for ten minutes. This is not strictly necessary, but will give a softer and more sumptuous result than if you use it straight from the pack. Peel the onion and chop it finely. Melt the butter in a saucepan, add the onion and cook until it is softened but not coloured.

Drain the spelt and add it to the onion, then pour in about a third of the hot stock. Let the liquid come to the boil, then lower the heat to a simmer and cook for eight to ten minutes, stirring regularly. Add half the remaining liquid, cook for five or six minutes, then stir in the remainder. Continue cooking for seven minutes or so, checking the texture of the spelt as you go. It should be soft, with a very slight bite to it.

Rinse the pea shoots and stir them into the risotto. As soon as they have wilted, but before they darken, stir in the knob of butter and the grated cheese. Check the seasoning, adding salt and ground black pepper as you need. Serve with a little more cheese, if you wish.

Enough for 4

JUNE 25

## Sorting the wheat

Wholegrain, farro, cracked wheat, bulgur. The sort of wheat available is extraordinary and all have their uses. Farro and wholegrain wheat add sustenance to a winter stew, used as you might pearl or pot barley to thicken the cooking liquor. The whole grains are exactly that, the complete grain, sometimes with its husk attached. These take longer to cook but you can shorten the time by soaking them for a good hour or so first. The chicken with whole wheat on page 227 is an example of just how sustaining a dish can be once we include a whole grain.

Bulgur, burghul, pourgouri or, as it also known, cracked wheat is different in that it is cooked wheat that has cracked open and needs little more than rehydrating for twenty minutes in water, then squeezing dry before use. This is the one to use for tabbouleh in equal amounts with chopped parsley, or for adding to minced meat for meatballs. In its Middle Eastern home, there are grades of cracked wheat that we never see, including one as fine as dust that is used for binding small patties.

As much as I like the penny-pinching notion of using wheat to bolster my winter suppers, thickening broths and stews, rather than turning the heating up, I also feel grains are too good to keep for cold weather alone. As a base for a salad, they can act as a way to 'balance the books' with more expensive ingredients such as tropical fruits or seafood. The mangoes around at the moment make a refreshing, if rather dear, side salad for prawns off the grill or even lamb cutlets. Add some wheat and you have something deeply satisfying to scoop up by the forkful.

# Wheat with mint and Alphonso mango

Although I tend to serve this as a side dish, it is good as a main-course salad too.

cracked wheat: 100g
spring onions: 6 slim ones
very ripe mangoes: about 500g
a small, hot red chilli
mint: 8 bushy sprigs, to give
   4 heaped tablespoons

flat-leaf parsley: a 60g bunch
   (weighed with thick stalks)
half a small cucumber
radishes: 8-10
juice of a lemon
olive oil: a couple of tablespoons

Tip the cracked wheat into a bowl and pour over enough boiling water just to cover, then set aside.

Finely slice the spring onions, discarding the toughest of their green leaves, then put them into a mixing bowl. Peel the mangoes, cut the flesh from the stone in large slices, then cut it into small dice and add to the onions.

Seed and finely chop the chilli, then roughly chop the mint and parsley leaves, discarding the stalks, and add to the onions. It will seem like a lot of parsley, but it is essential: it is the main ingredient rather than the wheat. Peel, seed and finely dice the cucumber, slice the radishes and toss both with the other ingredients. Add the lemon juice, olive oil and a generous seasoning of both salt and black pepper.

Rough the soaked wheat up with a fork, draining it if it has not absorbed all the water. Crumble into the bowl with the other ingredients, fork through gently and serve.

Enough for 4–6 as a side dish

# JUNE 26

# A bit of pastry work

There are days when my heart sinks at the thought of making a tart, lining the tart tin with pastry, weighting it down with beans and partially baking it, carefully removing the baking beans and returning it to the oven until it is dry enough to fill. There is the filling itself to be made, which may or may not involve peeling, slicing and cooking onions, the savoury egg custard to make and pour over, and then the oh-so-careful carrying of the tart to the oven, filled to the brim with liquid cream and egg.

Then comes the day when I decide to have a go. The day when I remember the pleasure of rubbing butter into flour with my fingertips; rolling the dough out on a floured board with my little beech rolling pin (I find rolling pastry with a skinny pasta pin easier than with a great heavy one) and then peacefully pushing the pastry into the corners of the tin so it doesn't shrink, trimming its edges with my little cook's knife and carefully filling it with paper and the now honey-coloured haricot beans I use to weigh it down. I remember the sweet smell of onions softening in the old black frying pan, the gentle breaking of eggs into a china bowl and the slow, deliberate beating in of the cream. Then there is the lovely little moment when you grate, very finely, a little nutmeg on top of the custard and carry it gently to the oven as if it were a peacefully sleeping baby you do not wish to wake.

I am not sure whether we should be proud of our own cooking, but I do think there is something deeply satisfying about taking a huge, golden tart to the table. A tart we have made ourselves. A tart we can give to others knowing it will give as much pleasure to them as making it did to us. Sometimes.

## A salmon and spinach tart

salmon fillet: 400g
a little butter or groundnut oil
large-leafed spinach: 2 large
   handfuls
eggs: 4
double cream: 400ml

*For the pastry:*
plain flour: 200g
butter: 100g, cut into small pieces
an egg yolk

Make the pastry: put the flour and butter into a food processor, add a pinch of salt and blitz to fine crumbs. (If you prefer, rub the butter into the flour in a bowl with your fingertips.) Add the egg yolk and enough water to bring the dough into a firm ball; you will probably need 2–3 tablespoons. The less water you add the better, as too much will cause your pastry case to shrink in the oven.

Pat the pastry into a flat round on a floured surface, then roll out to a circle large enough to line a 24cm loose-bottomed tart tin. Lightly butter the tin, dust it with a small amount of flour and shake off any surplus, then lower in the round of pastry. Without stretching the pastry, push it right into the corner where the rim joins the base. Make certain there are no holes or tears. Trim the overhanging pastry and place the pastry case in the fridge for twenty minutes.

Set the oven at 200°C/Gas 6. Put a baking sheet in the oven to heat up. Line the pastry case with kitchen foil, fill it with baking beans and slide it on to the hot baking sheet. Bake for fifteen minutes, then remove from the oven and carefully lift the beans and foil out. Return the pastry case to the oven for five minutes or so, until the surface is dry to the touch. Remove from the oven and set aside. Turn the oven down to 180°C/Gas 4.

Place the salmon in a baking dish, brush with butter or oil, season lightly with salt and pepper and bake for fifteen minutes, till the flakes will part easily. Remove from the oven and leave to cool a little before breaking it into large pieces. Place the fish in the tart case.

Wash the spinach leaves and remove and discard the thickest of the stems. Put the still-wet leaves into a saucepan, cover tightly with a lid and place over a high heat. Cook for a couple of minutes or until the leaves wilt a little. They should keep their colour. Turn the spinach over once with tongs, let it steam a further few seconds, then remove from the heat, cool under cold running water and squeeze dry.

Tuck the spinach into the tart case in between the salmon. Whisk the eggs and cream together, season, and pour them over the salmon and spinach. Bake for twenty-five minutes, till just set. Serve warm.

Enough for 6

JUNE 27

# Summer

I am happiest in winter, worshipping its festivals and folklore, adoring its crisp, clean air and gentle grey skies. Not for me the coarse harshness of summer's bright colours as seen in piercing, ugly light. The only part of summer I truly enjoy is shade and shadow, and the notion of the mythical meadow with its buttercups, babbling brook and overhanging branches. But the food is another thing, and even I can melt at the thought of salmon, a little dill and the cool scent of sliced cucumber. Today I do a riff on the traditional, much loved marriage of salmon and cucumber, making crisp, pink patties and serving them with a cucumber and yoghurt sauce as cool as that mythical babbling brook.

# Salmon and dill patties

salmon steaks: 500g, skinned
fresh white breadcrumbs:
   2 generous handfuls
dill fronds: 3 tablespoons
capers: 2 teaspoons
a little butter and oil

*For the cucumber sauce:*
cucumber: a 4cm piece
yoghurt: 8 tablespoons
a little dill, chopped
white wine vinegar: a few drops

Cut the salmon steaks into pieces, removing the bones, and chop finely in a food processor. Take it easy, pulsing gently until the mixture is very finely chopped but not quite a paste. Tip the salmon into a bowl and add the breadcrumbs. Chop the dill fronds, rinse and dry the capers, then add them to the salmon with a little black pepper. Shape the mixture into small, slightly flattened balls, about 3cm in diameter.

To make the sauce, halve the cucumber lengthways and remove and discard the seeds from the middle with a teaspoon. Slice the cucumber into matchsticks. Stir them into the yoghurt, then add the dill, vinegar and a light seasoning of salt and black pepper.

Warm a little butter in a shallow pan – you want just a light film on the bottom – then add the oil. When it starts to bubble lightly, slide in the salmon patties and let them colour underneath. This will take about two minutes. Now flip them over and cook the other side. When they are cooked in the middle (a matter of three or four minutes), serve them with the cucumber yoghurt.

Enough for 4

# JUNE 28

There is a small bundle of asparagus in the fridge. It is not enough for two, and whilst a plate of asparagus can be eaten as a lone, sybaritic feast, I am going to stretch my bounty so it will feed two.

There is leftover chicken in the fridge from the weekend as well. Again, hardly enough for two. Rice, so useful for stretching things – I once saw the tiniest amount of turmeric-yellow mangold wurzel stew stretched to feed about twelve workers in a rice paddy by the cook mounding up the rice beneath – is my first port of call. The dish is more interesting than expected, and turns out to be an excellent way of using up a quantity of cold roast meat from the weekend. Cold lamb or beef would have been good too, though I would probably swap the gentle aniseed charms of chervil for the more punchy notes of tarragon. This time I added small leaves of sorrel because I happened to have some, but they should be considered a treat rather than being essential to the recipe.

### Roast chicken, herb and asparagus rice

asparagus: 250g
brown basmati rice: 120g
butter: 30g
bay leaves: 2
whole black peppercorns
thyme: leaves from a couple of
   sprigs
leftover roast chicken: 250g
spring onions: 4 thin ones
parsley: 3 or 4 sprigs
mint: 4 bushy sprigs

sorrel (optional): 4 or 5 leaves
chervil: a few sprigs
lemon olive oil: 3 tablespoons

*For the yoghurt sauce:*
mint, chopped: 2 tablespoons
olive oil: 2 tablespoons
thick, but not strained,
   yoghurt: 200ml
a small garlic clove, crushed
   (optional)

Trim the asparagus and cut it into short lengths. Boil or steam for four or five minutes, till almost tender. Drain and cool quickly under running water.

Wash the rice three times in cold water, moving the grains around in the water with your fingers. Warm the butter in a small- to medium-sized saucepan, add the bay leaves, peppercorns and thyme leaves and stir them round in the butter for a minute or two, until the fragrance wafts up. Drain the rice and tip it into the warm herbs. Cover with a couple of centimetres' depth of water and bring to the boil. Season with salt, cover with a lid and turn the heat down to a simmer. Leave to cook till the rice is tender but has some bite left in it, about fifteen minutes or so. Set aside with the lid on but the heat off.

Tear the chicken into large, jagged pieces and put them into a large mixing bowl. Trim and finely slice the spring onions. Chop the parsley and mint. If you are using sorrel, shred it finely. Pick the leaves from the chervil and add to the chicken with all the other herbs. Fluff the rice up with a fork. Tip the warm rice into the herbs and chicken, add the steamed asparagus and toss gently with the lemon oil. Correct the seasoning to taste with salt and pepper. The mixture should be light, green and fresh.

Stir the ingredients for the yoghurt sauce together and season with a little salt. Spoon it over the pilau at the table.

Enough for 2 as a main dish

# Food that fits

I have worked pretty much non-stop since I left school at sixteen. Over a decade ago, I bought a house that I have slowly been restoring, repairing and generally tarting up in the way that so many of us do now, a gradual process, doing bits and pieces as and when I can afford it. Perhaps oddly, the kitchen has been one of the last rooms I have worked on, partly because it was the most expensive part of the project and partly because I had to do it with the blessing of the local planning department.

My kitchen – that is, my home kitchen, not the television studio that many people think is my own kitchen – is often described by visitors as having a monastic air. The white, uneven walls, deep, open fireplaces (an exciting find under years of plasterboard and delightful woodchip wallpaper) and the smell of smoking candles no doubt have much to do with that. My kitchen is in a basement, and the low ceilings and sound of shoes on the old stone flags do create a cloister-like echo. The light comes in from both east and west, and even at the height of midsummer the room is shadowy and cool.

Of course, that is how it was meant to be. The house was built before refrigeration was part of every home and it was essential that there were cool cupboards for storing food. What was the pantry is now where I keep pots and pans, mixing bowls and cake tins, and the larder (a pretentious name for what is essentially a converted broom cupboard) is just outside the kitchen itself, in the unheated part of the basement.

This space had previously been two bedrooms and a shower room, a separate flat really, formed from the basement kitchen, parlour and scullery of the old house. I like the fact that it is now returned to its original use. It feels right and somehow respectful to the building. But the room still holds its mysteries too. The tiny fireplace in a cupboard whose walls show signs of ancient shelves and hooks makes me wonder if the family once smoked their own ham and fish. The truth is probably rather less romantic. I expect it was somewhere to dry the laundry in winter.

The style of the kitchen has much in common with my cooking, especially the mixture of the old with the new. The modern fridge and oven blend happily enough with the old stone flags and sooty fireplaces in much the same way as treacle sponge or steak and kidney pie appear on my table as often as, say, sashimi, wasabi mayonnaise or the stock I made yesterday with mirin, sake and a chicken carcass.

## JUNE 30

## A new sauce for dried pasta

The pasta I like best is one capable of holding a sauce – those that come with nooks, crannies, pockets and hollows in which a dribble of cream or a morsel of sauce can safely hide till it gets in your mouth. It's the shells, tubes and spirals that get my vote over the ribbons and strings every time.

Of course, this could be pure greed – there is something much more satisfying about biting into a bit of pasta that oozes cheesy, herby sauce into your mouth than one that feels like a piece of oily string.

The more interesting pasta shapes, such as the shell-shaped conchiglie or the ear-like orecchiette, didn't just happen. You know that someone once put a great deal of thought into the stuff we now treat as the ultimate no-brain supper. It took nothing short of a genius to come up with the classic shapes of pasta. Those clever twists and curls and flowing lines are much more drawing board than chopping board. Although as a sauce hound, I would suggest that Frank Gehry would probably make a better pasta designer than the late Mies van der Rohe.

I'm not quite sure when I kicked my pasta habit. One minute it was three times a week, the next thing it was down to twice a month. There was no deliberate attempt at cutting the carbs or trying to clamber my way out of the knee-jerk pasta supper option. It just happened. The upside is that I now treat those bags of pillows and knots with a lot more respect. I guess I think about them more and, crucially, their suitability to the sauce.

## Orecchiette with aubergine, basil and lemon

It is worth noting that my starting point for this recipe contained toasted pine kernels and fettuccine. I should have known that wouldn't work, the carefully toasted kernels falling off the ribbons of pasta. Then I proceeded to trofie, the squiggly pasta, but that didn't look good on the plate. I have

ended up with ear-shaped pasta and no pine kernels. You will need some Parmesan to pass around.

dried pasta such as orecchiette: 300g

*For the sauce:*
aubergines: 2 large
olive oil
onions: 2 large
basil leaves: a large handful
half a lemon

Set the oven at 200°C/Gas 6. Slice each aubergine in half lengthways, make shallow cuts almost down to the skin in a criss-cross fashion, then brush with olive oil. Bake for thirty minutes or until the skin is black, preferably a little charred, and soft to the touch. (Alternatively, prick the whole aubergines all over with a fork, then grill till the skin darkens and the inside is soft.)

Meanwhile, peel and very finely slice the onions. Let them cook over a moderate heat in a little olive oil till very soft, deep bronze in colour and lightly caramelised here and there.

Scrape the flesh out of the aubergine skins into a mixing bowl. Beating constantly, pour in the olive oil a little at a time – you will need about eight tablespoons, but stop as soon as you have a smooth sauce that is just thick enough to coat the pasta.

Shred the basil and fold it into the aubergine sauce with a seasoning of salt, plenty of pepper and a shot of lemon juice to make it sing.

Cook the pasta in plenty of boiling, heavily salted water until al dente. Drain the pasta and toss gently with the aubergine sauce. Divide between 4 warm bowls, and top with the cooked onions and a few more torn basil leaves.

Enough for 4

July

My spirits have been exceptionally high of late. The series we have just started filming is looking good (I am enjoying it more than ever before), the new kitchen at home is coming on in leaps and bounds and I am having a lot of fun. I can't remember a time when I was happier. In short, I am in a good place.

I have to laugh when television viewers tweet or blog that I always seem to eat on my own. As if there is no camera in the kitchen (there are two), no sound and lighting engineers, director, producer, series producer, executive producer and assorted runners present. I am, indeed, surrounded. The idea that the viewer is peering through a hole in the wall and watching me cook and eat at home is about as far from the truth as anyone can imagine. Television is a fantasy. Far from being alone, the way the crew, myself included, descends on the food once the cameras are switched off means I am usually cooking for ten or more. Perhaps I should bring in the rent-a-crowd that suddenly appears in so many television cookery shows to hoover up the food.

Yet much of what I do for the cameras is just as it would be at home. Ingredients often grown in my own little garden, a relaxed pace, simple, unchallenging recipes, and a certain thoughtfulness that brings about a slower pace at the stove is very much the way things really are. The kitchen may be a conceit (just try wedging an entire television crew into a home kitchen), the walls may be moveable and the weather occasionally contrived (if it stops raining on a 'second take', we have to stand there aiming hosepipes at the windows so it matches the first take), yet the spirit of my television cookery perfectly echoes the way I cook at home. Simple, calm, uncontrived and non-showy. It's real, even when it isn't.

## Iberico ham, broad beans

Perhaps my favourite salads of all are those that are seasonal and simple. A classic in my own kitchen has always been a bean and ham salad. At first, it involved fine French beans and thinly sliced Bayonne ham, then a white bean salad with strips of San Daniele or Parma. Lately, I have been much taken by the Spanish hams, particularly the dark Iberico hams with their sweet fat. As so often with a premium ingredient, it is something I like to present as a star

in its own right, in this case served in thin snippets with a salad of early-summer broad beans and a classically straightforward dressing.

I included a version of this salad in *Tender Volume I* but, as so often happens, a recipe gets tweaked a little here and there. This time, the ham is incorporated into the dressing rather than sitting on the side like a wallflower; instead of chopping the parsley finely, I have torn it into small pieces so it is an ingredient in its own right; I have ditched the mustard from the dressing so that the flavour of the ham is left to speak for itself. I like the new version. It is simpler and less cluttered. It is ham and beans in all their summer glory.

broad beans in their pods: 1kg
flat-leaf parsley: a small bunch
air-dried ham such as Iberico: 100g

*For the dressing:*
sherry vinegar: a tablespoon
olive oil: 3 tablespoons

Pod the beans and cook them in lightly salted boiling water till tender – about six to ten minutes, depending on your beans. Drain them and cool under running water. Pop the beans out of their skins by pressing them between your thumb and finger. If the beans are very small and tender, or you particularly like the skins, you may not need to do this.

Make the dressing by adding a small pinch of salt to the sherry vinegar, stirring to dissolve, then whisking the olive oil in with a fork. Tear the parsley leaves and add them to the dressing with the broad beans and a little ground black pepper.

Shred or tear the ham into small pieces and toss gently with the broad beans.

Enough for 4

## JULY 3

## Finger-licking chicken

Friends are coming tomorrow who I know appreciate hot and spicy food. More to the point, they tend to get wound up by anything too self-consciously 'foodie'. Mention a farmers' market, an artisan-made cheese or a heritage tomato and they will raise their eyes to the ceiling. Fine, I'll give them chicken thighs, roasted till the skin has crisped, with a hot, deeply savoury sauce to spoon over. That should keep us all happy.

# Chicken wings and hot sauce

I have baked this mildly spiced chicken dish, but you could also cook it on the grill. Just make sure the heat is low enough for the meat to cook right through to the bone.

chicken thighs: 8–12, depending on their size

*For the marinade:*
vegetable oil: a tablespoon
light soy sauce: a tablespoon
lime juice: a tablespoon
fish sauce: a tablespoon
a clove of garlic
a stalk of lemongrass
sugar: a level teaspoon

*For the dipping sauce:*
fish sauce (nam pla): 3 tablespoons
water: 6 tablespoons
rice vinegar: 3 tablespoons
caster sugar: 6 tablespoons
fresh ginger: a thumb-sized lump
hot chillies: 2 large
the juice of 2 limes
light soy sauce: a teaspoon

Make the marinade: put the oil, soy sauce, lime juice and fish sauce in a small, screw-top jar. Peel and crush the garlic, thinly slice the lemongrass (removing any tough outer layers as you go) and add to the jar with the sugar. Cover and shake thoroughly, then pour into a shallow bowl. Add the chicken pieces and set aside for at least an hour. Overnight won't hurt.

For the dipping sauce, put the fish sauce, water, rice vinegar and sugar in a small saucepan and bring to the boil. Peel the ginger and chop it finely with a heavy knife, then crush it to a pulp with the flat of the blade. Add the ginger to the pan and let the mixture boil till it has started to thicken slightly. Leave to cool. Remove the stems from the chillies, halve the flesh and chop it finely. Don't discard the seeds; you need their heat for this. Stir them into the sauce with the lime juice and soy.

Set the oven at 200°C/Gas 6. Place the marinated chicken pieces in a roasting tin or baking dish and roast for twenty-five to thirty minutes, till their skin has become lightly golden and their flesh is cooked through.

Serve with the chilli dipping sauce, spooning it over the sizzling chicken.
Enough for 4

# JULY 8

## A pot of basil

Even now, basil seems as if it doesn't belong here. Its notes of pepper, clove and aniseed and the fact that it cannot give us its soul without having first had a dose of searing sunshine make it seem like a visitor. A traveller from another culture, bringing with it tales of thick green olive oil, purple olives, gnarled sun-scorched tomatoes and meals taken outdoors. It sings of terraces too hot to walk on, red wines served chilled and the sound of cicadas.

But I'm getting carried away (basil does that). You can get it at the supermarket.

The basil plants we can buy from the shops have been pampered, overwatered and overfed, making them flabby tasting, more like peppery lettuce leaves than a true flavour-of-the-Mediterranean herb. But they are better than no basil at all, and can be rescued by transferring them to a terracotta pot, pushing them carefully (their roots are very tender) into rich garden soil and putting them in a sunny spot outside. Once their surroundings start to approach that of their homeland, their oils will concentrate, their leaves will toughen and they will give us their best. And their best is wonderful. I am having more success with herbs since I stopped digging quite so much compost and manure into my garden. What started out as impenetrable London clay needed breaking down and enriching, which I did over the course of six years. But then I made it too rich for herbs, or at least for those that are happier growing in light, dry soil, like thyme, oregano and rosemary. But basil does best in ordinary potting compost, with a dose of tomato feed every two weeks.

The leaves of the basil plant are possibly the most tender of all herbs, even more so than the fine lacework of chervil or the fragile stems of coriander. A bunch of basil bruises easily. A clumsy shopper like myself can end up with pesto by the time they get home. Crushed, the scent wafts up in little clouds of clove and grass. Unlike thyme or oregano, this is the herb that will turn black at anything lower than 3°C, which is the temperature I keep my fridge at.

Once picked, the leaves will keep in a plastic bag in the fridge for a good few days without coming to much grief. The trick with shop-bought leaves, I find, is to remove the bunch from its thin cellophane bag and slide it into a roomy plastic one, the heavy sort that seals when you press the edges together. A quick spray of water before you close the bag will help your bunch stay perky for a good five days or more.

I don't have a great deal of interest in basil unless the sun is shining. It is the herb most associated with high summer, feeling strangely out of sorts in the winter. Basil is the tomato herb, the mozzarella herb, the one that takes you to the Med in a haze of pepper, clove and cinnamon. It is perhaps the herb whose smell is most spice like.

Yes, it loves warmth but it hates to be cooked for more than a few minutes. You can sneak it into a pair of roasting peppers or tomatoes but it needs to be covered in oil if the leaves are to keep any flavour. Even then it will lose its top notes. In other words there is no point in putting it on the surface of a pizza (tough old oregano is the one for that). But warmth will make it come to life, a heaven-sent experience that can be tested by simply pressing hard on a large leaf between your hands, then inhaling. It is the warmth from a bowl of freshly cooked fettuccine that makes the pesto so fragrant and brings us to the table.

## Mussel soup with tomato and basil

This soup can be made more substantial by placing a slice of toasted bread – sourdough, perhaps, or ciabatta – in the bowl before you ladle in the soup.

| | |
|---|---|
| an onion | *For the basil sauce:* |
| olive oil | basil leaves and their stems: 20g |
| garlic: 2 cloves | olive oil: 75ml |
| tomatoes: 400g | a little lemon juice (optional) |
| mussels: 450g | |
| parsley: a few sprigs | |

Peel and finely chop the onion. Let it soften in a little olive oil in a deep, heavy-based pan over a moderate heat. Try not to let the onion colour, so stir it regularly; you want it to be pale and soft enough to crush easily between your fingers and thumb. Peel and crush the garlic cloves and add them to the onion. Roughly chop the tomatoes and add to the pan. Let them cook for ten to fifteen minutes, crushing them with a spoon as they cook to a bright-red slush.

While the tomatoes are cooking, scrub the mussels and check them thoroughly for broken shells or any that are obviously dead. Tip them into a deep, heavy-based pan, cover tightly with a lid and cook over a high heat for a couple of minutes, till their shells open and there is much steam in the pan. Tip them into a colander set over a bowl to catch the juices that have appeared in the pan. Sieve the juices to remove any grit. This isn't a detail to skip, as even the tiniest amount will ruin a soup. Add 400ml of the mussel cooking juices to the tomato and onion (in the event of there not being that much liquid, make up the amount with water). Simmer for five minutes or so, then season lightly with black pepper, chopped parsley and possibly a little salt. Pull the mussels from their shells and drop them into the soup.

Make the basil sauce. Put the basil into a blender and slowly pour in the olive oil. Taste and add a little lemon juice, if you like, and ground pepper. You are unlikely to need salt. Stir the basil sauce into the soup, but not too thoroughly. The point is to have a thick thread of fragrant green sauce running through each bowl of soup.

Enough for 3

## JULY 9

## Sweet and sour

I am working on a television programme about the marriage of sweet and sour. My starting point is the classic Sunday lunch of roast pork and apple sauce, where a sharp, acidic apple purée is used to slice through the fat and accentuate the sweetness of the meat. (The infamous sweet 'n' sour chicken of the too-drunk-to-care takeaway remains the elephant in the room throughout the entire programme.)

We are going on a thirty-minute journey through sour (lemon juice, lime zest, tamarind, vinegar, pomegranate, bitter orange, verjuice) and sweet (honey, coconut milk, maple syrup, sugars from muscovado to caster). It is a prime-time, recipe-led cookery programme and first off is a piece of meringue that I dip into a pot of lemon curd. A quick fix for when pancakes with sugar and lemon seem too much trouble. But that is where my love of this particular marriage started, the grittiness of the sugar and the lip-puckering lemon. Or maybe even earlier than that, sitting on the back step with a cooking apple and a bag of sugar.

The best dish of the programme is my friend Jeremy Pang's sea bass and tamarind curry (see page 516), but the one I have found the most useful is a simple idea of matching a pork chop with a handful of gooseberries, the

berries baking down into an impromptu sauce that slices like a knife edge through the quivering fat of the chop.

## Pork chops and gooseberry sauce

butter: a thick slice
pork chops: 2 large
dry vermouth or cider: a good
   splash or two
gooseberries: 250g, topped
   and tailed

a little light muscovado sugar,
   to taste
oregano: a few sprigs

Melt the butter over a moderate heat in an ovenproof pan just large enough to take the chops. Add the chops, seasoning them with salt and black pepper, and fry on both sides for a few minutes, till the meat and fat are pale gold.

Add a splash or two of vermouth or cider, plus the gooseberries, a teaspoon or less of sugar and the sprigs of oregano. Cover and cook for fifteen minutes or so. The gooseberries will collapse somewhat and make their own sauce.

Check the sauce for seasoning; it should be acidic but not rasping. I like to have the same sourness as apple sauce. Add a little sugar if it is too sharp for you. Serve alongside the chops.

Enough for 2

As I'm taking four duck legs out of their wrapper for dinner, it strikes me that whilst we cook duck with orange, we rarely do it with lemon. I have a go, not completely forgoing the orange, with both lemon thyme and a lemon. The skin refuses to crisp at first, then I turn up the heat and nuke it till it crackles lightly. Plenty of black pepper and salt, together with the sharpness of the lemon, make this worth another go, maybe next time with some rice on the side. I am very taken by the mixture of rice and warm duck fat.

## Grating Parmesan

Grating Parmesan, like making breadcrumbs, is something I do en masse, then dip into as necessary. If it is likely to be used within the next few days, I put it in the fridge in a plastic tub with a tight-fitting lid. If not, then it goes in the freezer, where it will keep for weeks and can be used, unless it is going into a salad dressing, straight from the freezer.

Different graters give subtly differing results. Depending on which one you use, your Parmesan can end up like dust, tiny grains or even fluffy. There is also one blade that makes it looks like shredded cellophane. Even specialist Parmesan graters will produce different grades, depending on how their teeth have been cut. The only way to tell is to get stuck in and have a go. I can't imagine any shop will welcome you turning up with a lump of Reggiano in your pocket and having a quick rub on each and every grater in the shop. So it's a question of trial and error till you find the one that suits you.

None of this would matter if Parmesan was always melted, but often it simply colours in the oven, keeping the same shape, like cheese-flavoured breadcrumbs. Whether you have sand or grit or gravel-textured Parmesan is suddenly rather important. One of my favourite ways to use it is to coat a fillet of plaice with a mixture of finely grated cheese and fine fresh breadcrumbs.

But Parmesan doesn't always end up as a crust on something, it is occasionally used as a melting cheese, such as when we fold it into warm, freshly drained pasta. Tonight I make one of those pasta recipes that many Italians would shudder at, yet it is fast, cheap and delicious and I love it.

### Pasta, peas and Parmesan

| | |
|---|---|
| shelled peas: 250g | butter: 50g |
| small dried pasta such as orecchiette: 250g | snow peas or mangetout: 200g |
| | pea shoots: a couple of handfuls |
| Parmesan: 35g | large, peppery basil leaves: 12 |

Put a deep pan of water on to boil. Lightly salt the water, add the peas and boil for a few minutes until tender. Drain and set aside.

Bring a large pan of water to the boil, add the pasta and cook for about nine minutes, till firm but tender. Meanwhile, grate the Parmesan on to a plate.

Place a non-stick frying pan over a moderate heat and add the butter. Leave to melt, then add the snow peas or mangetout. Cook for a couple of minutes, then add the pea shoots. As soon as they start to wilt, add the basil leaves. Add the cooked peas to the pan, then add the drained pasta, followed by the Parmesan cheese. Toss gently, then serve immediately.

Enough for 2

## JULY 12

# Le crunch

Risotto for lunch, gooseberry fool for dessert. I could kill for something with a bit of a crunch to it. Something that crackles on the tongue or snaps between the teeth rather than slithers down in silence.

A good crunch is essential in a meal. A baguette is what makes breakfast in France bearable. It is what makes the velvety, the silky and the smooth acceptable in quantity. That little sugar-coated biscuit with a strawberry fool; the crystallised rose petals or toasted nuts on the soft custard and cream layers of a trifle; the crust on the lemon tart and the filling it carries; the crumbled meringue in a bowl of Eton mess. The success lies in the harmony of the crisp with the soft.

I am on record as saying I am not fond of pasta salads. The softness of cold pasta, especially ribbons (tagliatelle and her fatter sister, pappardelle) and tubes (penne, rigatoni), has never floated my boat. I feel I am missing out, so tonight I set out in an attempt to put matters right, introducing a selection of crunchy textures to a bowl of cold noodles. I start with cucumber and shredded ripe peppers, then add raw peas and cashews, each one contributing another layer of crunchy texture to the slithery noodles.

The resulting salad works and solves a riddle too. It works because I have got the ratio of soft to crisp right. In other words, more crisp than soft.

# A cold noodle and tomato salad

A summer jumble of crunchy textures and fresh, bright flavours.

rice noodles: 60g
sprouted seeds: a large handful
a medium-hot red chilli
a red or orange pepper
half a cucumber
shelled peas: 100g
cherry tomatoes: 125g
salted roasted cashews: 100g

coriander: a small bunch, roughly
    chopped
mint: 4 sprigs

*For the dressing:*
lime juice: 3 tablespoons
fish sauce (nam pla): 3 tablespoons
caster sugar: 1 teaspoon

Put the noodles into a heatproof bowl, pour boiling water from the kettle over them and leave for two minutes (or whatever it says on the packet). Drain the noodles and let them cool in a colander under cold running water. Drain again thoroughly.

Rinse the sprouted seeds under cold running water, drain them, then tip into a mixing bowl. Finely chop the chilli and thinly slice the pepper, then add them to the sprouted seeds. Peel and core the cucumber, cut it into small dice, then add to the seeds with the raw peas. Halve the cherry tomatoes and add them to the bowl with the salted cashews, roughly chopped coriander and mint leaves.

Mix together all the ingredients for the dressing. Add them to the noodles and all the other ingredients and toss well. Chill for a good half hour before serving.

Enough for 4

Spotted some exquisite wild mushrooms in a posh food hall today. Hideously expensive and a bit of a treat. Tonight, I scattered them in a shallow pan of melted butter with the tiniest amount of garlic (barely half a clove) and a palmful of chopped parsley. They were cooked until they had darkened a little and were sizzling in their butter. I gave them a squeeze of lemon.

## JULY 13

I knock up a great little salad tonight of rose-edged 'rabbit-ears' chicory from the greengrocer's with segments of pink grapefruit and toasted pine kernels. The dressing is little more than the juice from the grapefruit with some olive oil and a little salt. Refreshing, crisp, luscious.

## JULY 19

A piece of bread destined for bruschetta should be cooked quickly, otherwise it dries out in the centre. Get the grill heat up high before you start cooking, so the bread colours in seconds rather than minutes and the crusts blacken enticingly. Charred crusts, golden bread that is crisp outside and moistly steamy in the centre, with sweet-sour roast tomatoes is a wonderful combination.

### Tomato and basil bruschetta

olive oil: 6 tablespoons
basil: 20g
cherry tomatoes on the vine,
   ripe and juicy: 4 sprigs

crusty white bread: 4 small slices
marinated artichokes: 4 small

Get an overhead grill hot. Pour the oil into a blender. Tear up the basil and add it to the oil, then blitz to a smooth green purée. Place the sprigs of tomatoes, still on the vine if you wish, on a baking sheet and grill till the skins just start to blacken and burst here and there. Place the slices of bread on the baking sheet and pour over the basil oil. Season with salt and black pepper, then place under the grill for a couple of minutes, till the edges are crisp.

Place a sprig of cooked tomatoes on each and tuck in the artichokes, halved or sliced. Serve immediately, while the toast is still hot and crisp.

Makes 4 small toasts

## Brown rice and pedantry

I am no kitchen pedant. But I suspect that I am not the only one whose heart sinks just a little when presented, in a restaurant, with someone's oh-so-original take on a classic.

Take risotto. If I order a risotto, then I want a plate of warm, slowly oozing short grain rice that has been continuously stirred with stock and enriched with butter and Parmesan till the grains are swollen and creamy. I do not want something that can stand up in a castle shape or be presented as a round patty. I don't want it as a smear on the plate, as if someone has been careless with the rice pudding, or cut into a cake. It may be perfectly nice to eat, but you cannot call it after the classic dish because it has totally the wrong consistency.

All of which is to say that the little dish I made for supper tonight might look like a risotto but it isn't. Yes, the recipe involved lovingly stirring short grain rice with stock until the grains were creamy, and it happily took more than a fistful of grated Parmesan and plenty of butter into its plump little belly. At a glance it may even have resembled a vegetable-speckled version of the classic risotto milanese.

But no, my supper is something of a hybrid, with a texture that is nuttier, chewier and rather more interesting than the classic recipe. Made with short grain brown rice, sold in wholefood stores as brown risotto rice, it was stirred for a good forty-five minutes with a wooden spoon and served in a pool of savoury, herb-flecked sauce. Utterly, fabulously delicious, cheap and extremely nourishing. But not, absolutely not, a risotto.

### A dish of brown rice, courgettes and mint

courgettes: 300g
broad beans: 400g
  (120g podded weight)
hot vegetable stock: 1 litre
medium shallots or a small onion: 2
butter: 60g
brown short grain rice: 250g

white vermouth or white wine:
  a medium glass
mint leaves, chopped: 3 heaped
  tablespoons
courgette flowers: 2–4 (optional)
Parmesan: a large handful, plus
  extra to serve

Wipe the courgettes, then shred them using a coarse-toothed grater. Put them in a colander in the sink, generously grind salt over them and leave for at least twenty minutes.

Pod the beans, cook them for seven to ten minutes in very lightly salted boiling water, then drain. If the beans are large and you have the inclination, pop them out of their skins. Heat the stock in a saucepan and keep warm over a low heat.

Peel the shallots or onion and chop finely. Cook in 40g of the butter till soft but not coloured, stirring regularly so they don't brown. Add the rice, stir to coat the grains in the butter, then pour in the vermouth or wine. Let it almost evaporate, then start to add the hot stock a ladleful at a time, stirring almost continuously. You will find that the rice will take a good forty minutes to cook to tenderness – that is, considerably longer than white risotto rice.

As the rice approaches tenderness (at least thirty-five minutes into cooking), squeeze the grated courgette dry in your hands and stir it in. Continue cooking then, as the rice is almost cooked, add the beans, chopped mint and, if you are using them, the courgette flowers. Check the seasoning, adding black pepper and a little salt (you may not need any salt at all), then stir in the remaining butter and the grated Parmesan.

Serve in warm shallow bowls, with a little more cheese if you wish.

Enough for 2

## JULY 23

## The tart tin

I have two tart tins, both round and made of steel, one 20cm in diameter, the other 22cm. One has sides high enough to allow a cheesecake filling the depth to quiver, the other is shallow enough to give the impression of the sort of tart you might find in the window of a Parisian pâtisserie. Between them, they have held fillings both substantial and frivolous, from the classic quiche Lorraine – that's the one without cheese – to the economical housewife's treacle and breadcrumbs. They have witnessed pastry so fine it shatters like ice and fillings so soft and tender they shake perilously as you slice. Each one has supported pastry crusts shortened with butter, lard and cream cheese and fillings of everything from plums and almond frangipane to lemon and cheese curds pocked with golden sultanas and grated lemon zest.

They have seen their (or perhaps I should say 'my') fair share of failure: fillings that overflow, pastry sides that shrink and now and again those that glue themselves to the rim. But on a good day they will hold a tender crust and a soft, barely set filling of the sort dreams are made of.

Each tin has a loose bottom so you can release the cooked tart in its pristine entirety more easily than you could from one with a fixed base; the first rule when shopping for a new one. The trick to removing the tart is to slowly, tenderly, prise the crust away from the edges of the tin with the point of a knife, then place the tin on top of a can or a bowl and tease the side of the tin downwards, leaving the tart and its metal base in place on top of the can or bowl.

You can serve your tart on its metal base or slide it off with the help of a palette knife. The downside of the loose base is that if you absent-mindedly pick up the tart from underneath rather than by holding its sides, the bottom will spring up, sending your tart flying into the air. A pantomime tart. A mistake that reads like pure slapstick on paper but can happen all too easily in the adrenaline-soaked panic of a busy kitchen. The other point is that a particularly juicy or liquid filling can leak out on to the floor of the oven.

When you finally decide to make a tart, place a flat metal baking sheet in the oven to heat up first. Place your tart on it and it will help to crisp the base as it cooks.

A good tart tin ages well. The colour softens from gleaming silver to the dull grey of a rainy sky. Stains from a particularly potent blueberry tart or burned-on treacle may appear on its surface like a road map. It will take on a homely, much-used look. Can there be a more welcoming piece of kitchen equipment than a much used tart tin? Well, yes, there can. That much used tin with a freshly baked tart in it. Oh, and a bone-handled knife at its side.

## Plum (or greengage) and almond tart

The frangipane-filled tart, studded with figs, apricots, blueberries or peaches, is a classic of the French kitchen. Recipes can vary from the dry to the sticky and back again, and many seem mean when you spread them into the pastry case. This one, something I have developed over the years, works a treat. Use any fruit you like, from tiny Mirabelle plums to blackcurrants.

*For the pastry:*
plain flour: 200g
butter: 100g, cut into small pieces
an egg yolk
milk: 2–3 tablespoons

*For the filling:*
butter: 100g
caster sugar: 125g
eggs: 2
ground almonds: 125g
plain flour: 60g
greengages or small plums: 400g

For the pastry, put the flour and butter into a food processor, add a pinch of salt and blitz to fine crumbs (or, if you prefer, rub the butter into the flour in a bowl, using your fingertips). Add the egg yolk and enough milk to bring the dough together into a firm ball. The less milk you add the better, as too much will cause the pastry case to shrink in the oven.

Pat the pastry into a flat round on a floured surface, then roll it out till it is large enough to line a 22cm loose-bottomed tart tin, at least 3.5cm deep. Lightly butter the tin, dust it with a small amount of flour and shake off any surplus, then lower in the round of pastry. Push the dough right into the corner where the rim joins the base, without stretching the pastry. Make certain there are no holes or tears. Trim the overhanging pastry and then place in the fridge for twenty minutes.

Set the oven at 200°C/Gas 6. Put a baking sheet in the oven to heat up. Line the pastry case with kitchen foil or baking parchment, fill with baking beans and then slide it on to the hot baking sheet. Bake for twenty minutes, then remove from the oven and carefully lift the beans and paper out. Return the pastry case to the oven for five minutes or so, until the surface is dry to the touch. Remove from the oven and set aside. Turn the oven down to 160°C/Gas 3, and return the baking sheet to the oven.

Make the filling. Cream the butter and sugar together with an electric beater till pale and fluffy. Lower the speed, then mix in the eggs a little at a time. Slowly fold in the ground almonds and flour. Spoon the almond filling into the cooked pastry case, smoothing it lightly with the back of the spoon.

Cut the greengages or plums in half and remove their stones. Place the fruit on top of the almond filling, neatly or at random, as the mood takes you. Slide the tart on to the hot baking sheet and bake for forty minutes, till the filling is well risen and golden brown. Remove the tart from the oven and allow to cool slightly before serving.

Enough for 8

# JULY 24

Each year I set off to Japan. It's a private holiday and I rarely write about it. It is exactly that, my holiday. That said, it is an essential part of my year and no matter how hard I try not to (it is a holiday, after all), I always spot something I want to recreate when I get home. Pickled ginger, the sort you get in your pack of sushi but juicier, is one of my favourite ingredients. It is not a particularly easy ingredient to introduce into recipes, but it does lend itself quite easily to inclusion in a salad. Anyone who eats sushi regularly will know how good it is with cucumber, a hit of hot and cold in one pinch of the chopsticks. Add a few other sushi-friendly ingredients – carrots, lime and tuna – and you have a neat little salad. Startling but also strangely familiar. This is light, fresh and bright tasting. A light lunch, perhaps.

## Tuna, pickled ginger and cucumber salad

fresh tuna steak: 500g
limes: 4
mild oil, such as groundnut or
    rapeseed: 1 tablespoon
rice vinegar: a tablespoon
pickled ginger: 20 small pieces

liquor from the pickled ginger:
    2 tablespoons
caster sugar: a teaspoon
cucumber: 100g
carrots: 400g
sprouted seeds: a handful

Cut the tuna into large dice, place them in a shallow bowl and pour over the juice of the limes and the oil. Set aside for about thirty minutes. A little longer will not hurt but don't leave it overnight or it will get 'woolly'.

Make the dressing by stirring the rice vinegar into the liquid from the pickled ginger, then adding the sugar and a pinch of salt. Mix until the salt has dissolved.

Lightly peel the cucumber (a little dark green is attractive in a salad), then peel off full-length strips with the vegetable peeler and drop them into a bowl. Peel the carrots and grate coarsely. The sort of setting you would use for a celeriac remoulade is perfect.

Put the bits of pickled ginger in with the cucumber, then add the carrot and the sprouts. Cut the tuna pieces in half to expose their semi-raw centre, add them to the salad and then add the dressing. Toss gently.

## JULY 26

## A celebration of hot and cold

Still filming, I have spent the week recording a television programme about the pleasure to be had in eating something hot with something cold: that moment when a blisteringly hot sauce meets an icy dessert and vice versa. A ball of vanilla ice cream with a stinging-hot espresso; a fried fish straight from the pan with a fridge-cold dressing of lime juice and ginger (*The Kitchen Diaries* volume I) and a soup-stew of beans with a last-minute spoonful of cold, spiced yoghurt (September).

The joy of hot and cold is still on my mind at the weekend, when I go to the market in Bermondsey and come across baskets of great Herefordshire-grown plums. I bring them back, leaves and all, their skins mottled amber and blood red. A good third of them disappears in the half hour it takes me to unpack the shopping and tidy the fridge; the others are made into a rose-pink sorbet studded with pieces of golden fruit and, later, a metal dish of eye-wateringly hot plums whose skins have caramelised in the oven. It is probably my favourite pudding of late summer.

### A plum water ice

| | |
|---|---|
| dark, ripe plums: 500g | *For the sugar syrup:* |
| caster sugar: 1 tablespoon | caster sugar: 200g |
| juice of a lemon | water: 200ml |

Make the sugar syrup: bring the sugar and water to the boil in a small saucepan, switch off the heat and leave to cool, then chill thoroughly.

Set the oven at 200°C/Gas 6. Wipe the plums, remove their stalks and put the fruit in a baking dish or roasting tin with the caster sugar. Bake for about thirty minutes, until they are soft, the skins have burst and the juices are starting to escape. Remove from the oven, leave to cool and then take out the stones. Roughly mash the plums and their skins with a fork. I prefer a slightly lumpy mash to give a more textured ice, but you could remove the skins if you prefer. Stir in 200ml of the sugar syrup (there may be a little over), then add the lemon juice. Pour into an ice-cream machine and churn

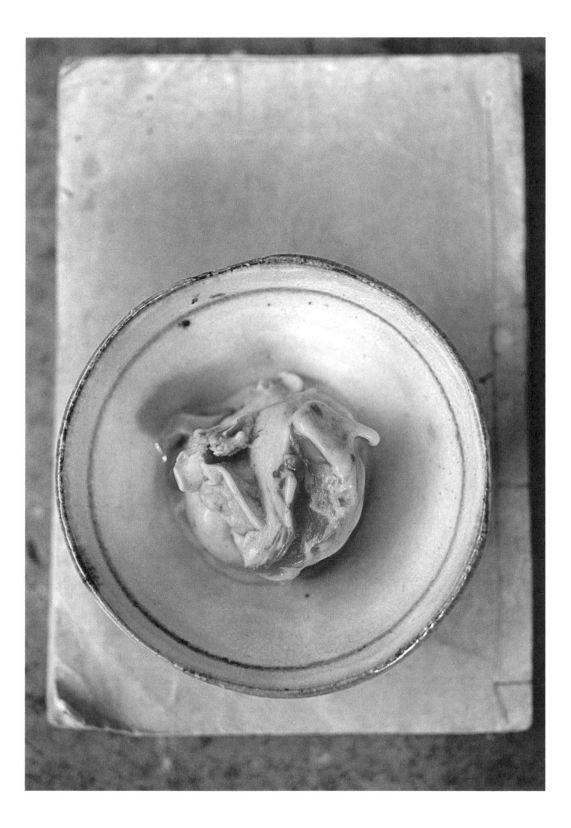

till almost frozen – or freeze by hand, by pouring the mixture into a plastic freezer box and freezing for about four hours, stirring it every hour.

Enough for 6

## Roast plums, gin and juniper

| | |
|---|---|
| butter: 40g | juniper berries: 6 large, squashed |
| caster sugar: 4 tablespoons | plums: 1kg |
| gin: 2 tablespoons | double cream, to serve |

Set the oven at 180°C/Gas 4. Melt the butter and sugar in a non-stick pan, avoiding the temptation to stir more than once or twice, then add the gin and juniper berries. Wipe the plums, put them in a baking dish and pour over the butter and sugar mixture.

Bake for fifty to sixty minutes, till the plums have burst their skins and are soft and slightly caramelised. Serve with a jug of double cream.

Enough for 6

## JULY 29

## Alone at last

Tonight I am having a rare quiet meal alone. To be honest, I have been waiting for this all week. I splash out on a sirloin steak (it wasn't that expensive) and cut it into strips about as thick as my little finger. I rub a little of the fat over a ridged griddle pan, then grill the strips two or three at a time. Just as they are sizzling and starting to colour on each side, I dip them first into a little sesame oil and then into the barbecue sauce below.

My chuck-it-in-a-bowl barbecue sauce is a stir-up of rice wine, dark soy and runny honey. Put a tablespoon of sugar in a bowl with a couple of finely chopped spring onions and a crushed garlic clove. Then stir in 3 tablespoons of dark soy sauce and the same of rice wine, a tablespoon of runny honey and a drop or two of sesame oil. I also find a pot of sesame seeds lurking behind the soy, a handful of which goes in too. A good stir, so that the sugar dissolves, is all it gets. I jig around with the soy and honey a bit till it tastes right – sweet, nutty, slightly salty.

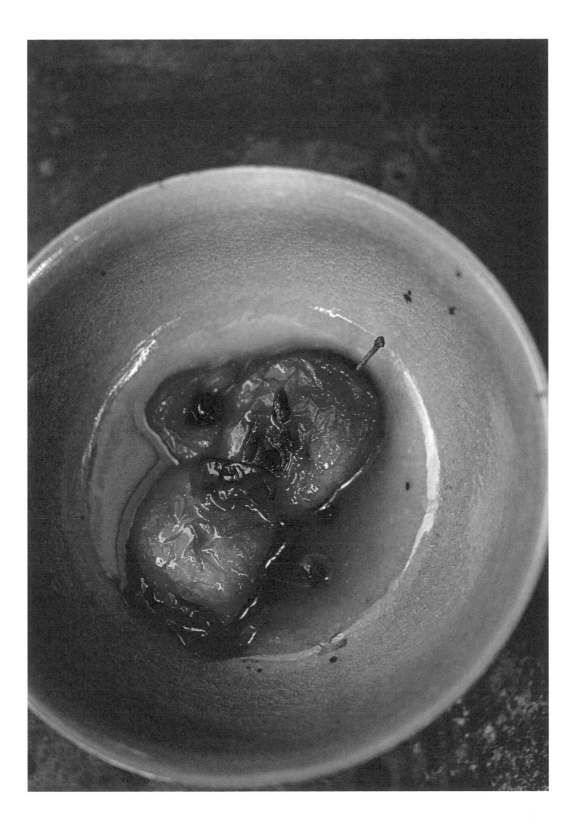

August

## AUGUST 6

## Picking plums

Friends have abandoned this summer's persistent rain for a fortnight in France, leaving behind a key and a generous invitation to raid their heavily laden plum tree. I brave the battle that is other-people's-front-door-locks to find a five-year-old plum tree humming with wasps. The branches, so heavily fruited that the leaves of the lowest five are brushing the lawn, contain a mixture of ripe, not so ripe and past-it plums that are filling their back garden with the scent of warm jam.

Picking plums needs to be done with respect for the tree's brittle, lichen-dusted branches, which can snap more easily than those of apple or pear. I take my time, picking for half an hour, maybe longer, then gratefully retreat with my bowls of yellow, amber and carmine fruit.

Even with tacit permission, helping yourself to someone else's crop feels like stealing, and I walk away in a daze of greed and guilt. I plan to make jam to give them, a handful of jars in a row on their kitchen table when they return.

The quantity of ripe fruit, the odd one falling from the bowl as I walk home, would make too much jam, so I put a small mountain of fruit to one side, then make the rest into a shallow, juice-soaked plum pie.

## A latticework pie of plums and raspberries

For a traditional plate pie such as this, I much prefer a simple butter short-crust to a highly sweetened, egg-rich pastry.

plums: 750g
caster sugar: 60g
raspberries or loganberries: 150g
a jug of cream, to serve

*For the pastry:*
plain flour: 200g
butter: 120g, cut into small pieces
caster sugar: 1 tablespoon
ground cinnamon: a pinch
chilled water: about 3 tablespoons
a little milk, to glaze

Lightly brush a 24cm pie plate (measured across the base) with butter.

Cut the plums into quarters and drop them into a bowl, discarding the stones and stalks as you go. Scatter the plums with the sugar and leave them for forty minutes.

Set the oven at 180°C/Gas 4. Place a metal baking sheet in the oven.

Make the pastry: tip the flour into a mixing bowl, add the butter and rub it into the flour with your fingertips until the mixture is the texture of coarse fresh breadcrumbs. Stir in the caster sugar and ground cinnamon, then mix in as much of the chilled water as you need to produce a nice, soft, manageable dough. It shouldn't be dry or sticky. Pat the dough into a flattened ball, wrap in kitchen paper and place in the fridge to rest for twenty minutes.

Cut off roughly two-thirds of the pastry and roll it out on a floured board to measure a little larger than your pie plate. Line the plate with the pastry, taking care to repair any cracks or tears as you go. Roll out the smaller piece of pastry to roughly the same size, then cut it into strips about 2cm wide, rather like pappardelle.

Remove the plums with a draining spoon, leaving the juice behind in the bowl. Put the plums into the lined tart case, then scatter the raspberries or loganberries amongst them. Brush the edge of the pastry with a little milk then lay the cut strips of pastry in a lattice fashion across the plums. Brush lightly with milk, place on the hot baking sheet and bake for about forty-five minutes, till the pastry is golden and the fruit is bubbling. Remove from the oven, brush with some of the reserved juice, then return to the oven for five minutes. Serve with cream.

Enough for 6

## AUGUST 7

### Smoked salmon and cucumber spread

I generally spend much of August filming, often leaving the house at sparrow's fart and returning, exhausted and numb, late in the evening. After eight hours of standing cooking in front of the cameras, I rarely want to come home and start cooking all over again (though, in truth, I often do). As a result, most of my home cooking this month is done at the weekends. Even then, I tend to want to play (cakes, tarts, jams and the like) rather than make everyday meals. Couple this with the August heat and it is not

surprising that most of the month's main dishes are those that can be thrown together in minutes.

The teasingly piquant spread below has saved my life several times during the last few Augusts – the cucumber and smoked salmon being a perfect cargo for over-tired, late-night feasts of crispbread or rounds of sourdough toast and late-night bottles of something very cold.

half a small, ridged cucumber
cornichons: 2 or 3
capers: a teaspoon
mayonnaise: 100g
soured cream, cottage cheese or
  crème fraîche: 100g

smooth Dijon mustard: half a
  teaspoon
lemon juice: a teaspoon
dill: a small bunch
smoked salmon : 150g

Peel the cucumber, halve it and remove the seeds with a teaspoon. Cut the flesh into thick, match-like strips and put them into a colander or sieve over a bowl. Sprinkle with salt and leave for twenty minutes, during which much of the water will drain from the cucumber. Pat dry with kitchen paper.

Cut the cornichons into small dice. Rinse the capers, dry them and add to the chopped cornichons, then stir in the mayonnaise, soured cream, cottage cheese or crème fraîche, mustard, lemon juice and a little black pepper. Finely chop the dill fronds and fold them in.

Shred the salmon into thin strips, then fold into the mixture with the drained cucumber. Chill briefly before serving on discs of rye crispbread, such as my favourite, Peter's Yard.


## AUGUST 9

There is a load of green vegetables in the fridge that need using. Some green beans – the skinny French sort with pointy tails – some tenderstem broccoli and some asparagus that I probably shouldn't have bought. They are all tipped into boiling water, simmered for five minutes, then drained (the broccoli ends up a little crunchy but no matter). I peel and slice an onion, cut it first in half and then into thin strips and soften it in a pan with a little oil, I then add the cooked green vegetables, followed by 3 teaspoons of thick chilli paste and stir over a fairly high heat with one hand for long enough to awkwardly uncork last night's wine and pour a glass of wine with the other.

# A marinade in minutes

Marinating, the idea of keeping a piece of meat, fish or vegetable in some sort of seasoned liquid, paste or powder before cooking, is something I have only recently taken to, having assumed, wrongly as it turns out, that I have to be organised and know what I will be eating tomorrow.

The concentration of the marinade matters. A highly spiced, intensely flavoured paste will do the job in less than an hour. A thick paste will also produce an interesting crust as the meat or fish cooks. It is rather different from the long, slow, oil-heavy marinades that can be so good for roasting joints or cubes of meat to be cooked in a casserole (I like grilling marinated food but find the smoke produced too much).

Marinating is half cooking, half magic. We can assemble the ingredients ourselves, but the transference of flavour seems to be something between the food and its marinade. I love the fact that ingredients sometimes get on with things themselves and we are only a small part of the equation. I don't see why we always have to be in control of everything that happens in a kitchen. The science behind what happens when we cook is interesting, but please leave me some magic and surprise too.

# Grilled lamb with lemon harissa

Tonight I marinated the lamb in its spice paste for a couple of hours and it worked just as well as when marinated overnight. Just go with whatever is most convenient. Some hummus on the side would be pretty much perfect.

4 lamb steaks
roughly chopped mint leaves and very finely grated lemon zest, to serve

*For the harissa paste:*
coriander seeds: a teaspoon
cumin seeds: a teaspoon
caraway seeds: a teaspoon
garlic: 3 cloves
a roasted and peeled red pepper (bottled is fine)

tomato purée: half a tablespoon
red wine vinegar: 1 tablespoon
long, medium-hot fresh red chillies: 2
a small preserved lemon
smoked paprika: a teaspoon
olive oil: 2 tablespoons

*For the yoghurt mint sauce:*
natural yoghurt: 200ml
mint, chopped: 2 tablespoons
cumin seeds: a teaspoon

Put the coriander, cumin and caraway seeds into a small frying pan and toast them till their scent starts to rise. They will smell warm and nutty. Grind them to a fine powder.

Peel the garlic, put it into a food processor and add the ground spices – don't try to add them whole, as they won't grind to a fine enough powder. Add the red pepper, tomato purée, vinegar and chillies and blitz.

Wash the preserved lemon, discard the soft innards and add the remaining outer shell to the other ingredients with the paprika and olive oil and blitz briefly. Stir in a couple of generous pinches of sea salt.

Put the lamb steaks in a shallow dish or roasting tin, pour over the spice paste and toss gently so that each piece is lightly coated. Cover tightly with cling film and set aside for at least a couple of hours. Overnight will not hurt.

For the yoghurt sauce, put the yoghurt in a bowl and stir in the mint. Put the cumin seeds in a small pan and toast over a low heat for a minute or two, till fragrant. Crush slightly with a pestle and mortar and scatter over the top of the yoghurt.

Get an overhead grill or griddle pan hot. Cook the lamb till nicely browned on each side, turning it once during cooking. Check the steaks are pink in the middle. Put the lamb on four plates and finish with roughly chopped mint leaves, very finely grated lemon zest and the yoghurt sauce.

Enough for 4

## AUGUST 13

# More plums

There is a heavy, unbearable sadness at the sight of a fruit tree whose crop has been left to rot at its feet. With this in mind, I make a second trip to my friends' loaded plum tree. Those fruits that were too shaded by leaves to ripen are now ready, their tips pierced with a single bead of nectar the colour of honey. I return home with another bowl of scrumped fruit.

I have a theory that the plum and its stone are one, and should be cooked together, just as a piece of beef should be cooked on its bone. I leave a few in a batch of jam, though not enough to annoy anyone at breakfast, and often leave a few stones in a bowl of plums and custard. The dose of pectin in the stone may aid the set of jam, though I suspect there is deeper magic at work. The only time I stone them is for a tart, which I make today with a classic almond filling, like a Bakewell pudding.

The tart turns out pitch perfect (see July), the ground almonds echoing the nutty note of the missing plum stones, and the feel is distinctly French, in spite of being made with English butter, flour and eggs. Even the plums are named after the grumpiest of our royals. It follows a soft and crunchy supper of buffalo mozzarella, roughly torn and scattered with toasted Parmesan crumbs, that looks like a salad and tastes like a pizza.

## Mozzarella salad with tomato crumbs

All the elements that make pizza such an everlasting success – the softness of melted cheese against a crisp crust; the tang of tomato and Parmesan; the peppery note of basil – but without the weight of a bread dough base. A dish I made earlier in the week for a television programme about recipes that

work because of their ability to balance the satisfying crisp with the lusciously soft. It is so successful and so simple, I go on to make it all summer.

buffalo mozzarella: 2 balls
basil: a 15g bunch
parsley leaves: a 20g bunch
olive oil: 3 tablespoons
assorted salami and prosciutto,
  thinly sliced: 50g

*For the tomato dressing:*
tomatoes: 4 large
basil leaves: 8 medium, taken
  from the above
Parmesan: 60g
olive oil: a tablespoon
breadcrumbs: 50g

Tear the mozzarella into pieces and place, slightly overlapping, in a serving dish. Finely chop the basil and parsley leaves, then add a few twists of black pepper and the olive oil. Pour this herb dressing over the slices of mozzarella, cover with cling film and refrigerate for up to four hours.

Set the oven at 200°C/Gas 6. Cut the tomatoes in half, scoop out and discard the seeds, dice the flesh into small pieces, then transfer to a mixing bowl. Tear or shred the basil leaves and finely grate the Parmesan, then add to the tomatoes with the olive oil. Toss together gently with the breadcrumbs, then tip into a baking dish and bake for fifteen minutes or until the mixture has crisped lightly on top.

Divide the slices of salami and prosciutto between 4 plates. Remove the mozzarella from the fridge, scatter the tomato dressing over, then slide, using a fish slice, on to the plates.

Enough for 2–4 as a light main dish

AUGUST 15

## Sweet and sticky, and as good cold as hot

### Thyme and garlic chicken wings

thyme: about 12 bushy stems
garlic: 2 cloves
thick honey: 4 tablespoons
dried chilli: a couple of good
  pinches

a large, juicy lemon, plus a lemon
  to serve
chicken wings: 1kg

Pull the leaves and any flowers from the thyme branches, measure 2 lightly heaped tablespoons of them and put them into a food processor. (If you are making the marinade by hand, put the thyme into a mortar.) Retain any extra leaves and discard the stems.

Peel the garlic and add the cloves to the thyme, together with a generous grinding of black pepper, the honey and dried chilli. Grate the zest of the large lemon into the mixture, then squeeze in all of the juice. Blitz for a few seconds, till the ingredients become a sloppy paste or, if you are doing it by hand, pound with the pestle instead.

Transfer the paste to a non-stick roasting tin and add the chicken wings and the reserved thyme, turning the wings over in the marinade so they are thoroughly coated. Cover and refrigerate for at least four hours, or even overnight if that is convenient. Turn them from time to time, so the wings stay in contact with the marinade.

Set the oven at 200°C/Gas 6. Season the wings with salt, then roast them for forty minutes or until they are deep, golden brown and the marinade has turned dark golden brown. If there is a lot of liquid in the tin, cook for a few minutes longer, until dark and sticky. Cut the lemon in thick segments and squeeze it over the chicken wings as you eat.

Enough for 3–4, depending on the size of your wings

# AUGUST 16

## A new shop and a tub of cockles

It is a brave man who opens a new fish shop in this day and age. But that is exactly what has happened in my neck of the woods. (All we need now is for the betting shop to be replaced by a decent bakery and the sub-McDonald's fast food joint to become a Southeast Asian grocer's. Fat chance.) The arrival of the fish shop is a delight (I should add that I haven't deserted my beloved Steve Hatt, still visiting when I am shopping that way). I have everything from razor clams to sushi-grade tuna on my doorstep, which is more than anyone has the right to ask.

My interest in seafood is matched, almost, by my wish to eat ethically. It's a tricky balance, and one that I am occasionally guilty of getting wrong. I do my best to eat thoughtfully but refuse to beat myself up over it. The best news is probably that many of our less popular seafoods are in fact pretty safe from an ethical point of view. Their supply is plentiful, their habitat not endangered, their consumption safe and healthy – in particular, many of the shellfish that come from our own shores.

At the fishmonger's this morning, we spot cockles in brine. I have wheedled these tiny, juicy little molluscs from their shells before now but have never bought them ready prepared. They turn out to be bursting with salty, fishy piquancy, need no cooking and end up in, of all places, a carrot soup. It is a revelation. The salty seafood and the sweet vegetable form a natural bond and we have a soup that is both unusual and interesting. A last-minute addition of spinach leaves brings with it a pleasing hit of chlorophyll.

This whole soup was another of James's ideas. The original intention was to put sorrel in it, for its lemony note, despite the fact that even when lightly cooked, the leaves have the colour and texture of something dropped by a passing seagull. The sorrel proves elusive, and we settle for young spinach instead. A great bowl of soup.

## Carrot and cockle soup

carrots: 650g
bay leaves: 2
shelled cockles in brine: 250g

young spinach leaves: a large handful
a little lemon juice

Scrub the carrots, cut them into short lengths and bring them to the boil in lightly salted water with the bay leaves. Turn the heat down to a simmer and cook for about twenty minutes, till tender enough to crush. Drain the carrots, reserving 600ml of the cooking water. Remove and discard the bay leaves.

Put the carrots and the reserved cooking water into a blender or food processor and blitz till smooth, then return to the pan. Add the cockles, drained of their liquid, then shred the spinach leaves and stir them in. Bring briefly to the boil until the spinach has softened. Correct the seasoning with salt, pepper and, if you wish, a little lemon juice. Ladle into bowls and serve.

Enough for 4–6

Deep in the throes of filming, for lunch, which we are eating in the garden amongst the marigolds and nasturtiums that seem to have taken over the vegetable patch (seriously, there is nothing but flowers, chard and a few blight-crisped tomatoes), I make a hot, spicy chicken dish.

I get the oven up to 200°C/Gas 6. Stir together 4 heaped tablespoons of oyster sauce, 2 of brown sugar and 1 of chilli sauce (the thick red sort with a few seeds in). The sauce gets tossed with 6 chicken thighs, then they go into an oven dish skin-side up to bake for about forty minutes.

We eat the ridiculously sweet, spicy chicken with a salad of ice-cold iceberg lettuce leaves and whole leaves of fresh mint. We drink beer so cold it has ice crystals in it, then make a mad dash to the shops for vanilla ice cream.

# AUGUST 18

## Rolling pastry

Peach pie. Whisper the words. Luscious fruit under a crust that must, surely, be as soft and crumbly as the most buttery shortcake. It must sparkle with sugar and break tenderly under the fork. A crust that sighs rather than snaps.

Handling a butter-rich pastry needs to be done with more care than rolling a factory-made puff pastry or a simple home-made shortcrust. The high ratio of butter to flour dictates a necessity to keep the pastry, the surroundings and your hands cool, lest the butter starts to melt and it becomes unworkable. I have cold hands, but still run them under the cold tap before I start. I have even put the rolling pin in the fridge on particularly humid days. If there is water in the recipe, then chill that too.

Once you have brought the ingredients together to form a soft dough, tip it out on to a generously floured board or work surface. Pat the dough into a rough ball and knead it very lightly against the work surface with the heel of your hand for a minute or two (some cooks say you should never knead pastry but I disagree, as long it is done briefly and with love, not anger). Once the pastry has no cracks and feels smooth to the touch, shape it into a short, fat log, wrap it in cling film or greaseproof paper and let it rest in the fridge for thirty minutes. I cannot emphasise enough the effect this short snooze will have on the workability of your dough.

The pastry is short (i.e. short on flour, high on butter). It wants to crumble and split when it is cooked, so is unlikely to be easy to handle. If rolling pastry is the reason you don't bake, then you might like to try this 'pastry for dummies' method of lining your tart tin (I use it all the time): place the pastry on the work surface and unwrap it, then slice the log into rounds as if you were cutting a loaf of bread. The slices should be a little thicker than a two-pound coin. Place the slices in the base and up the sides of your tart tin, just touching or slightly overlapping one another. Press them into shape with your knuckles or fingertips, making sure there are no cracks or gaps. Return the tin and pastry to the fridge for fifteen minutes, then bake.

If you are determined to roll even the shortest of crusts, then placing the dough between two pieces of greaseproof paper and rolling as usual is worth trying.

## A peach pie with lemon pastry

A pie of gentle seductiveness on a hot, still afternoon when there is little else to do. This is a dessert whose name alone wins you over by its unapologetic softness and deep scent of summer. The idea that you might have enough of the ripe fruit to put under a crust must mean that we have reached high summer. The fruits, and their sisters the apricot and the nectarine, won't get any better than they are now, and the price is reasonable enough to bring them into the kitchen.

A grating of orange zest in the filling, and lemon in the pastry crust, lift this home-style pie away from the risk of cloying. A jug of cream may be welcome.

*For the pastry:*
butter: 150g
golden caster sugar: 150g
an egg
the grated zest of a small lemon
plain flour: 250g
baking powder: 1 teaspoon
a little milk and sugar, to finish

*For the filling:*
ripe peaches: 6
caster sugar: 2 tablespoons
the grated zest of a small to
    medium orange
cornflour: a heaped tablespoon

317

Cream the butter and sugar together till light and fluffy. Mix in the egg, continue creaming, then add the grated lemon zest. Sift together the flour and baking powder and fold them tenderly into the butter and sugar mixture. Form the dough into a ball and place on a floured work surface. Knead very lightly for a minute or so, then cut in half. Wrap in cling film and rest in the fridge for half an hour. Use one half of the dough to line a lightly buttered 24cm (18cm across the base) metal pie plate. Place this, and the remaining half, in the fridge.

Set the oven at 180°C/Gas 4. Halve the peaches and remove their stones. Cut each peach half into large pieces and put in a bowl with the sugar, orange zest and cornflour. Toss together gently, then spoon into the lined pie plate. Roll out the reserved pastry to fit the top of the pie generously. Brush the rim of the pastry in the pie plate with a little milk, then lower the second piece of pastry on top. Press the edges to seal, pressing or pinching them together as you wish, then brush the pie lightly with milk and dust with sugar. Pierce a small hole or cut in the centre of the crust to let the steam out.

Bake for forty minutes or so, till the crust is pale gold. Leave to settle for a good ten to fifteen minutes, or more, before serving.

Enough for 6

## AUGUST 20

## To the coast, and a bunch of thyme

There is the smell: parched ground, sea breeze, warm and resinous. And then there is the taste: aromatic, medicinal, with evocations of charcoal grills. I hadn't noticed the leaves or even the purple flowers as I trudged up the path that winds its way through the undulating towans, but only when I sat to take a breather did I spot the thyme, and stare out at the Atlantic with its silvery heat haze. It is easy to forget that thyme grows wild on our Cornish coastline just as it does on that of Greece or Provence.

Anyone who leafs through my recipes will see that thyme is a favourite pot-herb, just as coriander and mint find their way with unapologetic frequency into my salads. And just as mint brings gusts of clean, fresh air, thyme adds deep notes of summer warmth and a faint but pleasing bitterness.

This is the herb that I leave to simmer in the deep gravy of a lamb stew with its lifelong mate, rosemary, and wide strips of orange peel. These are the tufts of leaves I tuck inside the cavity of a roasting chicken or guinea fowl and scatter over the surface of roasted peppers and tomatoes for a high-summer lunch. Thyme is the holiday herb, the flavour of lunches eaten barefoot on baked earth; of red meat on the grill and tingling, salt-encrusted lips. The hotter the weather, the more the essential oils have to offer. Whilst chervil falls in a dead faint and coriander bolts into white-lace parasols, thyme just gets better, stronger and more pungent as the season progresses.

I have taken to crushing my leaves of thyme with salt and a heavy weight. A pestle and mortar is perfect for pounding the tough leaves with coarse sea salt. A jam jar and wooden board will do. Drop a few whole black peppercorns in there too. The sharp edges of the salt break the surface of the leaves, then soak up the resinous oils.

Thyme is my knee-jerk marinating herb. The one that celebrates in the company of olive oil and squashed garlic cloves as a basting liquor for lamb that will be roasted or grilled. Once those ingredients hit the bars of the grill, the garden will smell as old as time, almost biblical. In the depths of winter, the tough, woody stalks and their oval leaves bring a shaft of sunlight into our cooking.

Common thyme aside, the most used of the family in my kitchen is the lemon thyme that has survived for four years now in pots outside the back door, despite having thinner stems and more tender leaves than the usual broad-leaved *Thymus vulgaris*. The lemon notes work with pork (crumbled on a chop; included in the stuffing for a rolled garlicky loin) and I tuck them into a marinade for cubes of hake (olive oil, a bay leaf, peppercorns, no garlic) destined for the grill too.

The idea of slipping them into my usual lemon cake recipe (*The Kitchen Diaries* volume 1) came after a successful attempt to include them in a classic shortbread. I have a fancy for a lemon thyme sorbet too, but have yet to get it right. Frozen cough mixture is as close I am right now.

The orange variety is something to run your fingers through as you drink that once-a-year glass of Campari, or use in a garlic-spiked braise of young lamb. Sicilian thyme has celery-scented leaves that I suspect might be good in cream cheese on rye bread, and a caraway-scented version calls out for crispbread or to be included in the sticky dough of a loaf.

The tough branches with crisp, brittle stems have the strongest flavour. They are from second or even third year's growth and will have had the opportunity to bake in the sun. As with basil, the sun gives this herb more clout. Mature thyme leaves can have a bitter quality if eaten raw. Save them for your stew. The floppy type with stems as fine as fishing wire has a less shouty presence, as you might expect from such infant growth. It may well have been brought up in a greenhouse and packed for a supermarket.

Despite this herb's toughness – you can walk on it without it coming to much harm – few green herbs survive the unflinching heat from a charcoal grill. Thyme copes better than most, especially if it has a chance to get a look-in at the food early. An hour spent in the company of a fillet of lamb before you lower it over the coals should do it. Or try the younger leaves – chew one; is it soft enough to eat raw or not? – in with goat's cheese to melt over roasted tomatoes. And if you know a place where it grows wild, leave it be, so others can sit on it and inhale the deep soul of summer.

## Roast tomatoes, thyme and goat's cheese

Another arrangement of tomatoes and cheese, this time with a wild, rustic feel.

| | |
|---|---|
| large, ripe (but not beefsteak) tomatoes: 4 | olive oil |
| garlic: 6 cloves | small soft goat's cheeses: 4 |
| thyme: 7 bushy sprigs | a few thyme flowers |

Set the oven at 200°C/Gas 6. Wipe the tomatoes, remove their stalks and cut them in half. Place them cut-side up, snugly, in a baking dish or roasting tin. Season them with salt and coarsely ground black pepper, then tuck the unpeeled garlic cloves and four of the thyme sprigs in amongst them. Trickle over just enough olive oil to wet their surface and bake for thirty minutes or so, till the garlic cloves are soft inside. Remove the garlic and return the tomatoes to the oven.

Pop the soft centres from the garlic into a mixing bowl by squeezing them between your thumb and finger. Add the leaves from the remaining thyme sprigs and a little coarse salt and pound the mixture together with a pestle or the back of a spoon. Spread a little on each tomato. Cut the cheeses in half and put a half on each tomato. Return to the oven, letting the cheese partially melt before putting the dish on the table. Scatter over a few thyme flowers. Eat with large chunks of roughly torn bread.

Enough for 4 as a first course, 2 as a light main course

## A thyme and lemon cake

butter: 200g
caster sugar: 200g
plain flour: 100g
baking powder: half a teaspoon
ground almonds: 100g
large eggs: 4
a lemon
thyme leaves: a teaspoon

*For the top:*
caster sugar: 4 tablespoons
lemons: 2 large
water: 2 tablespoons
thyme leaves: half a teaspoon

You will also need a 20cm loaf tin, lined with baking parchment.

Set the oven at 160°C/Gas 3. Cream the butter with the sugar in an electric mixer till pale and fluffy. Sift together the flour and baking powder and mix with the almonds. Lightly beat the eggs, then add them to the butter and sugar mixture in two or three sessions, beating them in thoroughly each time. If the mixture looks as if it is about to curdle, stir in some of the flour.

Grate the zest from the lemon and mix it with the thyme leaves. Pound the two together with a pestle or some other heavy weight. Fold into the cake mixture with the flour, baking powder and almonds.

Spoon into the lined tin and bake for forty-five minutes. While the cake bakes, dissolve the sugar in the juice of the lemons and the water over a moderate heat and stir in the thyme leaves (a few flowers would be good here, too). As the cake comes from the oven, spike the surface with a skewer and spoon over the syrup. Leave to cool and then serve in slices, with thick yoghurt.

Enough for 8

## AUGUST 22

# Another quick chicken dinner

By mid afternoon the day is warm, a little muggy. Fine needles of rain at dawn have left the soil damp. Each leaf you touch leaves your hand wet. I walk round the garden taking stock. The Reine Claude plums, in shades of absinthe flashed with rose, are ready to pick.

The wild plum, of whose heritage I know nothing, has fruits along its branches as sweet as sugared almonds. The elderberries hang heavy, ravaged here and there by the pigeons, who have left purple splatters over the seats.

The pears, bulbous and without blemish, appear barely days from ripening (it turns out later they need another three or four weeks). The last of the redcurrants hang forlornly. The Discovery apple, cheeky as a robin, needs to be picked. Pity this fruit does not keep. There are no more flowers on the runner beans, and the plants are heavy with long, rough pods. A row of chard, pink, scarlet and yellow, is better for the rain it got today. Everywhere there are marigolds in full flower. The radishes too, tiny white flowers like sweet rocket but without the scent. The pumpkin is in hiding under a mass of sodden leaves.

The rain that has cooled this month's fierce sun has taken its toll on the tomatoes. Without exception, tomato plants prefer dry heat to ripen and like to be watered from below rather than on top. The plants are starting to show signs of blight, a condition that thrives in humid summers like this one. I pick what I can, ripe or not, and use them in an effortless supper of baked chicken thighs and black olives.

## Baked chicken with tomatoes and olives

Using up the last of the tomatoes, both the ripe and the green ones, is immensely satisfying, but the green ones do need quite a bit of cooking if they are to be worth eating. Slowly baked with the juices from the chicken, they take on the sweetness of their riper cousins. For this recipe, I use about one-third green tomatoes to two-thirds ripe ones.

| | |
|---|---|
| chicken thighs: 8 large | tomatoes: 350g |
| black olives: 12 | garlic: 6 plump cloves |
| the juice of a lemon | thyme: 3 large sprigs |
| olive oil: 2 tablespoons, plus a little extra for frying | |

Set the oven at 180°C/Gas 4. Rub the chicken pieces all over with salt and black pepper. Put them snugly in a roasting tin.

Stone and halve the olives. Pour the lemon juice and the 2 tablespoons of olive oil into a mixing bowl, then add the olives. Cut the tomatoes into quarters, unless they are very small, when you can simply halve them. Add

them to the bowl. Peel the garlic and squash each clove with the flat of a knife, but keep them whole. Pull the leaves off the thyme sprigs and add to the tomatoes with the garlic, a generous seasoning of black pepper and a little salt.

Colour the chicken lightly on both sides in a little oil in a roasting tin over a moderate heat. The skin should be pale gold. Tip the tomato mixture over the top and bake for forty to forty-five minutes, until the tomatoes are soft and have produced plenty of juice and the chicken's juices run clear when you pierce the flesh with a skewer.

Serve with rice, couscous or crusty bread to soak up the tomatoey-chickeny juices.

Enough for 4

## AUGUST 23

# Elderberries and an early-autumn breakfast

I wake at 5.30 to the sound of rain on the bedroom window ledge. Warm and steady, this is the sort of rain farmers and gardeners have been praying for. The trees and bushes hang heavy now, as if bowing their heads in thanks. But the wet instantly creates a problem too. As the rain slows to a proper drizzle, the air is left warm and humid and anything remotely ripe will need to be picked urgently to stop it rotting. Wet fruit keeps much less well than dry.

The elderberries that overhang the garden are almost touching the ground now, their tiny jet berries perilously close to the muddy paths. There is nothing in their growth or manner to remind us that they are part of the honeysuckle family. I pick as many of the purple-black berries as I can reach, getting soaked to the skin as I go. I leave the unripe green ones for another day. (Elderberry vinegar maybe, or a pot or two of sticky jam? Or perhaps I should try Jekka McVicar's soup recipe made with grape juice and nutmeg.) Rather than picking off individual berries, pigeon style, it is easier to snip away entire clusters with a pair of secateurs.

Once inside, I change my shirt and strip the berries quickly, and surprisingly nimbly, from their stems. I am left with a pile of denuded umbels that look, appropriately, like the spokes of a broken umbrella. As soon as the rain subsides, they will go on the compost. And I haven't even had breakfast yet.

The elder tree exists, as so many of them do, because my neighbours have decided to let it be. Few are ever planted deliberately, the seeds being sown, probably, by passing birds. Unlike the sloe and the rowan, the elderberry is a kitchen fruit that will grow anywhere. For once, something even the most ardent townie can forage for. The berries, incidentally, are a rich source of vitamin C and have been used as a tonic for centuries. Modern research shows that those patients taking elderberry juice recovered more quickly from a cold than those who didn't.

## Elderberries and apples for breakfast

There has been a temptation to stir a handful of blackberries into the chilled stewed apple I have been eating for breakfast. Made on a Sunday, just over a kilo of apples will usually see me through most of the week. I keep the cooked apple in the fridge, then eat it by the small bowlful with a dollop of goat's or sheep's yoghurt. This week I tossed in a handful of elderberries, which brought a clean, sharp fruitiness and looked beautiful: the white yoghurt against the glowing purple-gold of the fruit. The late gardening writer Christopher Lloyd took stewed apple for breakfast for most of his long life. There are worse ways to start your day.

> sharp apples: 1.2kg        elderberries: 4 heaped tablespoons
> caster sugar: 80g

Peel the apples, core them and chop into small pieces. Put them in a heavy-based pan with the sugar (if you put even a couple of tablespoons of water in, you will end up with too sloppy a texture). Leave to simmer over a low to moderate heat, stirring occasionally so they do not stick, until the apples have collapsed. Stir in the elderberries and leave to cook, with the occasional stir, for a minute or two, till the mixture is soft and fluffy. Try not to stir too much, otherwise you will crush the elderberries.

Serve warm or thoroughly chilled.

Enough for 6, with yoghurt

# AUGUST 24

The mixture of apples and elderberries I made yesterday is proving more versatile than I expected and has been both a hot pudding with vanilla custard and a filling for these pancakes. They take about an hour to prepare from scratch but are simple enough if you can make a half-decent pancake.

## Elderberry and apple pancakes

butter: 30g, plus a little extra melted butter for cooking
plain flour: 100g
caster sugar: a level tablespoon

a large egg and an extra egg yolk
milk: 350ml
the stewed apple and elderberry recipe on page 326, for the filling

To make the pancakes, melt the butter in a small pan, remove from the heat and leave to cool. Sift the flour, along with a pinch of salt, into a large bowl. Mix in the sugar, make a well in the centre and add the egg and egg yolk, plus the cooled melted butter. Stir, drawing in the flour and gradually adding the milk, to give a smooth batter. Leave to rest for half an hour.

Brush a 20–22cm non-stick frying pan or crêpe pan with melted butter, or wipe it over with buttered kitchen roll. When the butter starts to sizzle, stir the batter, then pour in enough for a wafer-thin layer, tipping the pan round so the batter just covers the base very thinly (a small ladleful should be enough for each pancake). Cook for a minute or so, until the underside is golden in patches. Loosen the pancake all the way round with a palette knife, then, sliding the knife carefully underneath, turn the pancake to cook the other side. When the second side is brown in blotches, lift it out and set aside, then continue with the rest of the batter. You should end up with about six pancakes, allowing for the first couple to be less than perfect.

Set the oven at 180°C/Gas 4. Place a pancake on the work surface, spread generously with elderberry and apple filling, then either roll up or fold into a triangle as you wish. Place in a shallow baking dish. Follow with the rest. You may have a little filling left over for breakfast, depending on how generous you are feeling. Warm for fifteen minutes in the hot oven.

Enough for 6

# Chickpeas, chard and a new spoon

A recent introduction to this kitchen has been a couple of wooden spoons. My kitchen equipment is so old and loved that any newcomer is treated with interest and a little suspicion, like a new kid joining school half way through term. The spoons intrigue because of their distinctive and unusual bent shape and their short handles. The shortness of the stem, and possibly its shallow curve like that of an almond tuile, is pleasing in the hand. I feel as if I have more control over what I am stirring than with a long-handled spoon.

One of the spoons gets its inaugural outing. Barely the length of my palm, half bowl, half handle, I like it immediately. Japanese, it is in fact a rice spoon, but I see no reason to restrict its fun. The gentle curves – a great deal of thought has gone into its shape – the dark, almost black wood, the lightness of feel make me suspect this will be a piece of kit that will become a good friend in no time at all.

Perhaps the spoon should have had a meaningful introduction to the kitchen but it starts its life stirring an impromptu chickpea supper. I heat a rather generous splash of olive oil in a frying pan, add a peeled and diced parsnip and fry till it starts to soften and colour a little. I stir in a few chard stalks, chopped into small dice, and, after three or four minutes, when they are softening, I throw in a handful each of chopped mint and parsley leaves. I stir in a drained can of chickpeas, a hefty squeeze of lemon juice, a flick of salt and a grinding of black pepper and let everything warm through whilst I mix a small tub of yoghurt, a spoonful of olive oil and some more chopped mint together.

The chickpeas and chard stalks go into a bowl, and the mint yoghurt goes on top with more olive oil. It's the sweetness of the parsnip together with the earthy chard stalks that makes this dish work for me. It won't win supper of the year, but then neither do I need it to.

# Crushing garlic

Sometimes, you want to reduce garlic to a pulp that will dissolve as it cooks rather than stay in slices or nuggets. Perhaps to stir into a dressing, add to butter or season mayonnaise.

I own a garlic press. There, I've said it. What is more, I use it too (cue Elizabeth David turning in grave). Derided by many cooks or, more truthfully, chefs and home-cooks-who-think-they-are-chefs, who argue that the ultra-fine holes in the metal press smash the cell walls of the garlic so finely that the resulting purée is often bitter and pungent.

I have tested this theory and have to say I agree with them if the garlic is old and dried or the metal press is made from aluminium, as so many are. They are the presses that go grey and mottled with age. Anything remotely acidic will produce a pungent, metallic flavour when it rubs shoulders with aluminium. The acrid results that cause people to dismiss this piece of kitchen equipment usually come from garlic cloves that are sprouting and contain the bitter green shoot of next year's growth.

But … put fresh, young garlic through a stainless steel garlic press and the resulting purée is light in texture, sweet and mild. It emerges from the holes as a soft, airy paste that will almost dissolve when you rub it between finger and thumb. As someone who likes their garlic on the delicate side, I find pressed garlic works better for me than very finely chopped. What is more, you don't end up with garlic-scented fingers. (Anyone who has ever dated a chef will know where I'm coming from.)

The oldest way of crushing garlic is probably to mash it with a pestle and mortar and this remains my favourite method. The weight used may be heavy but the process is smooth rather than violent. You crush and spread the paste rather than slam and bash the clove to death. The scent this method produces is often more subtle than when the cloves are chopped finely. Barely worth the washing up for one or two cloves, this is nevertheless the method I use most. Unlike when using a metal press, you need to skin the cloves first, and then remove the root and, in dried garlic, the central core with the point of a knife. A pinch of salt flakes will stop the cloves shooting out of the mortar as you push the pestle down.

Today I am crushing roasted garlic cloves using a pestle and mortar. The smell is sweet, a blend of garlic and caramel. Soft too, with a honeyed warmth that shows you just how subtle this allium can be.

## Grilled aubergine, roast garlic cream

| | |
|---|---|
| whole garlic bulbs: 2 | a little milk |
| olive oil, a rich fruity one | aubergines: 2 large |
| thyme sprigs: 2 | capers: a teaspoon |
| mayonnaise: 6 tablespoons | basil leaves: 6 or so |

Set the oven at 200°C/Gas 6. Loosely wrap the garlic bulbs in kitchen foil, adding a trickle of olive oil and the thyme sprigs as you do so. Roast for forty-five to fifty minutes, until the cloves are soft enough to squeeze. Remove from the oven, unwrap and set aside till cool enough to handle.

Squeeze the garlic out of its skin, breaking off single cloves and pressing each one between thumb and finger till the soft, ivory-coloured paste comes out. Stir into the mayonnaise, then add enough milk to bring the paste to a consistency where it will fall easily from the spoon.

Score the skin of the aubergines, cutting down from stalk to base, just deep enough to cut through the skin but not the flesh. Lightly oil the aubergines and grill under a hot overhead grill, turning every five minutes or so, until the flesh feels soft and the skin is a dark brown-black. Once the aubergines are cool enough to handle, peel away the dark skin and split the naked aubergine down the middle to form two halves. Trickle with olive oil, season and return to the grill to cook through. Spoon the garlic mayonnaise over the grilled aubergine, then add the capers and the basil leaves, torn or shredded finely.

Enough for 2

# AUGUST 26

# A new mushrooms on toast

A scent of autumn crosses the garden, ghost like, this morning, as if someone had lit a fire under damp leaves. A favourite time of year approaches and, in me at least, there is a stirring of new energy. I celebrate with a substantial version of mushrooms on toast.

## Chicken livers, chestnut mushrooms and toast

smoked streaky bacon: 100g    chicken livers: 250g
small mushrooms: 200g    Marsala: 75ml
butter: 30g    hot, buttered toast: 2 large rounds

Cut the bacon into small pieces. Halve or quarter the mushrooms. Melt the butter in a shallow pan. As it starts to froth, add the bacon and leave to sizzle for a minute or two, then add the mushrooms. Cook for a good ten minutes, making certain that you don't move the ingredients around too much. Ideally, you want a sticky, savoury residue to build up on the surface of the pan. It is what will give the flavour to the pan juices.

Push the mushrooms and bacon to one side of the pan and add the chicken livers to the other. Let them sizzle for two minutes or so, till they are golden around the edges, then stir them into the mushrooms and bacon. Season with salt and some coarse black pepper. Turn up the heat briefly, then pour in the Marsala. Bubble for a minute, no longer, then tip everything on to the buttered toast.

Enough for 2 as a light but substantial main course

## AUGUST 27

# Sugar plums

It has stopped raining. The colours in the garden – mostly dark greens, ochres and reds – are suddenly brighter, like dusty jewels washed in soapy water. Dahlias shine against the wet black-green of the hedges. Nasturtiums too. The candy-pink chard seems to have grown six inches since I last looked at it. For the first time in two days I step out into the garden. Sodden, glowing, somehow richer, it is evident something has changed. We have, in the space of twenty-four hours, entered the third quarter. Autumn is here.

I walk round the vegetable patch picking up fallen fruit. Plums mostly, the odd apple, a pear on the twig. The biggest haul is the Reine Claude gages, twenty of them. They had a basket of these at the market on Saturday too. It is their time.

The French Reine Claude is thought to have originated in Armenia, and from there on to Greece and Italy, where it was known as Verdocchia. The name, Reine Claude, comes from the wife of François I, in whose reign the fruit first appeared in France.

This is the member of the plum family I look forward to almost more than any other. Rounder and smaller than the Victoria type, green, yellow and occasionally flushed with red, the gages are exceptionally sugary. This week they have also turned up at the greengrocer's and were on the menu at Le Café Anglais, the brasserie in the old Whiteleys in Queensway, which was London's first department store. Without any trace of the larger plum's inherent acidity, could these, rather than the candied fruits of Christmas, be the true sugar plums of fairytales and Tchaikovsky's *Nutcracker*?

Not a fruit to use in savoury recipes, too precious to hide in a cake, too fragile to stew, the ripe gage is a fruit to enjoy raw. But fallen, bruised fruit needs using quickly if it is not to spoil, so I bake most of my catch (like their owner, they are a little tatty) in a shallow dish with white wine and sugar. They swell, the flesh fluffs up, but best of all the wine, sugar and juice from the greengages makes a warm, straw-coloured syrup that is the very essence of early autumn. I add flaked almonds caramelised with a little sugar as a textural contrast.

## Baked greengages, sugar-crusted almonds

greengages or small plums: 12
caster sugar: 3 tablespoons
white wine: 4 tablespoons

*For the sugar-crusted almonds:*
a little groundnut or rapeseed oil
flaked almonds: 40g
caster sugar: a lightly heaped
  tablespoon

Set the oven at 200°C/Gas 6. Wipe the fruits and remove their stalks. Halve them, discard the stones and place the fruit cut-side up in a baking dish. They should sit snugly against one another.

Scatter the caster sugar over the fruit, then pour over the white wine. Bake for twenty-five to thirty minutes, until the greengages are very soft and sweet.

Oil a baking sheet with a little groundnut or rapeseed oil and put the almonds on it. Sprinkle the sugar over them and cook under an overhead grill till lightly crisp. Scatter them over the cooked plums.

Enough for 3

## The first damsons and a new chocolate cake

Golden day. Walking round the vegetable patch this morning, I could pick myself a potful of runner beans, six different varieties of tomato, from the tiniest yellow plum to a Marmande as knobbly as a clenched fist, greengages, maroon-black plums, overripe redcurrants, a giant cucumber, red and golden raspberries, purple gooseberries and half a dozen or more courgettes. I don't. Someone is coming to photograph the patch tomorrow, so everything must hang, glorious and bountiful, for another day. As a gardener, I'm proud; as a cook, frustrated.

Behind the compost, where the photographer's lens is unlikely to peer, lies my damson tree with its brittle twigs and dusky fruits. You could measure my life, or at least my autumns, in the fruit of the damson tree. Flicking back through my books, there have been crumbles and crisps, fools and compotes, a soft-set jam and a spicy pickle. More recently, I have made a sauce for duck and another for gammon, a soft-crumbed sponge and a glossy-topped cheesecake. Trifle as well, and two ice creams, one made with custard, the other with cream and yoghurt. Not to mention a glowing gin, my favourite frosty-day tipple.

The damson has something in common with the Morello cherry. They both share a mouth-puckering smack of fruit and acidity that remains intense even when they have been cooked with sugar. It occurs to me that if the Morello has an affinity with dark chocolate, then why not the damson? I am briefly reminded of the wonderful chocolate-coated prunes – the dried plums – they sell in wicker boxes in Italian delis at Christmas. It is worth a try.

Ideas come and are gently tossed aside: a tray of damson brownies (too claggy); a chocolate mousse with a layer of damson purée in which to sink your teaspoon (too cheffy); a hot chocolate pudding with damson sauce (probably too rich). I end up reworking my own brownie recipe, folding cooked damsons in at the end, just before baking. Dark, sumptuous, intense, faintly reminiscent of the best sort of *Schwarzwälder Kirschtorte* but without the cream, it is a full afternoon's work. I eat slices of it in the shade of the robinia tree, at the end of the garden, the first golden leaves of autumn falling as I eat.

# Chocolate damson cake

dark chocolate: 250g
butter: 250g
eggs: 3
light muscovado sugar: 125g
golden caster sugar: 125g
self-raising flour: 60g
unsweetened dark cocoa powder:
   2 tablespoons

*For the damsons:*
damsons: 400g
water: 4 tablespoons
caster sugar: 100g

Put the damsons in a heavy-based saucepan with the water and sugar. Bring to the boil, then lower the heat and simmer, with the occasional stir, until the damsons are soft and on the verge of bursting. A matter of ten to fifteen minutes. Remove from the heat. The damsons need to cool. To do this quickly, I half fill the sink with cold water, tip the cooked damsons into a cold bowl and lower it into the water. Stir to let some of the steam out.

When the damsons are cool enough to handle, lift them from the syrup with a draining spoon into another bowl. Sort through the fruit, discarding the stones as you go. This is boring, but it is essential you remove the stones. Even one would be a nasty surprise in a cake. As you pop each stone out, try as much as possible not to crush the fruit (inevitably, this is bound to happen to a certain extent, but try not to crush them to a purée).

Set the oven at 180°C/Gas 4. Line the base of a 22cm square non-stick cake tin with a sheet of baking parchment.

Put a heatproof bowl over a pan of simmering water, making sure the base is not touching the water, then break the chocolate into it. As the chocolate starts to melt, turn off the heat, but leave the bowl over the water, then add the butter, cut into small dice. As the butter melts, stir very gently to mix.

Meanwhile, separate the eggs, putting the whites into a large bowl and the yolks into the bowl of a food mixer. Add the sugars to the yolks and beat till pale and fluffy. Add the melted chocolate and butter, stirring gently but thoroughly. Carefully add the flour and cocoa powder to the egg yolks and sugar.

Working quickly, whisk the egg whites till they stand in soft peaks, then fold, using a large metal spoon, into the cake mix, taking great care not to over-mix. Scrape the mixture into the cake tin, using a rubber spatula. Spoon in the damsons and gently swirl them through the chocolate mixture with a spoon. Take care not to over mix. You want ripples of fruit throughout the cake. Bake for forty-five to fifty minutes. The cake should be very slightly soft in the centre and almost mousse like. Remove from the oven and allow to cool completely before removing it from its tin and cutting into rectangles.

Enough for 8

As the oven is hot, it makes sense to find something for supper that will roast. I settle for tomatoes stuffed with butter beans and some of the basil, whose leaves are now the size of bay leaves.

# A stuffed tomato

Tomatoes are dotted through this month's cooking like cherries in a fruit cake. There have been lamb cutlets, the odd grilled steak and a chicken wing dinner that missed out, but the love apple has been by far the most used ingredient in the kitchen of late. It will stop of course, as soon as the first frost hits and I am left with supermarket tomatoes.

Today I stuff them with meaty butter beans and let them bake till their skins wrinkle and juices form in the pan. Like the stuffed tomatoes you see displayed in Greek tavernas.

## Butter bean tomatoes

olive oil
a medium onion
carrots: 2 medium
garlic: 3 cloves
a bay leaf
beefsteak tomatoes: 4

chopped canned tomatoes: 400g
butter beans: a 400g can
red wine vinegar: a tablespoon
sugar: 2 teaspoons, or to taste
basil leaves: 8 large

Warm a couple of glugs of olive oil in a medium saucepan. Peel and finely chop the onion and cook in the olive oil for ten minutes or so, till soft and pale. Scrub and finely dice the carrots, then add to the pan. Peel and finely slice the garlic, add to the pan with the bay leaf and continue cooking for five minutes or so, till all is fragrant.

Slice the tops off the beef tomatoes to form lids. Using a teaspoon, scoop the insides of the tomatoes out without tearing the skins. Put the empty tomato shells on a baking sheet. Chop the insides of the tomato and add to the onion mixture, together with the canned tomatoes and their juice. Season generously with salt and pepper, then simmer for fifteen minutes. Set the oven at 200°C/Gas 6.

Stir the butter beans, drained of their liquid, into the mixture. Add the red wine vinegar, sugar and the basil leaves, torn or shredded. Spoon the mixture into the tomatoes; you will have too much, so spoon it around them as well. Top with their lids and bake for forty minutes, till the tomatoes are on the verge of collapse.

Enough for 4 as a main dish

## AUGUST 30

## A pot of chutney

When, I wonder, did I become the sort of guy who makes his own chutney? The kind of cook who is not content with just throwing something hand-made in the oven for supper but now tenderly stirs bubbling pots of dark sugar, fruit, vegetables and spices until they are thick and sour-sweet.

Looking back through faded, butter-blotted notebooks, it seems that the chutney habit (tomato, runner bean, onion and now fig) entered my kitchen a decade after I started making my own ice cream and baking my own bread. Probably around the same time I took up growing some of my own vegetables in earnest. My glowing jars came not out of the need to preserve a glut or to make ribbon-decked gifts for my friends but from a desire to have a spoonful or two of home-made relish to go with a piece of cheese and a wodge of bread.

Chutney was originally a way of preserving a harvest of vegetables or fruits for the winter. Onions, shallots, cauliflower, tomato, apples and plums spoil quickly, and a savoury preserve was an alternative to storing the vegetables in vinegar or salt or the fruit in sweet syrup – a delicious treat born out of frugality. I rarely end up with too much veg but the figs in my garden ripen in quick succession, hanging maroon and purple on the tree till they are so heavy they fall, leaving wine-coloured splats on the lichen-pocked stone below. The blackbirds dive in to feast, which somewhat assuages my guilt at not catching the fruit before it falls, but better for my own peace of mind would be to find a way of keeping them. A man can only eat so many figs.

Dark chutneys are easy to make. You simply simmer the fruits or vegetables with onions, vinegar, allspice, the darker sugars, dried fruits, coriander seeds and peppercorns. The basic recipe is straightforward; the details of acidity, sweetness and spicing are more personal and can be tinkered with to your heart's content.

Today I pick every fig I can (frustratingly, many are left out of reach), get out my deepest pan and begin the process of chopping and stirring. It's a Radio 4 kind of afternoon, the weather seesawing from rain to brilliant golden sunshine, the air in the kitchen running the gamut from jam to sinus-piercing vinegar. As the glossy mahogany goo cools, it seems a reasonable balance of sweet and sour, but what interests me is how it will mellow over the next couple of weeks.

## A dark and sticky fruit chutney

soft brown sugar: 250g
figs: 8 large (about 1kg)
malt vinegar: 150ml
cider vinegar: 150ml
onions: 250g, chopped
sultanas: 250g

salt: 1 teaspoon
allspice: 1 teaspoon
black peppercorns: half a
   teaspoon, cracked
coriander seeds: 1 teaspoon

Warm the sugar in a bowl in a low oven. Roughly chop the figs, removing any tough stalks as you go, then put them into a large, stainless steel or enamelled saucepan. Add the vinegars, onions, sultanas, salt, allspice, cracked peppercorns and coriander seeds, then bring to the boil. Simmer for thirty minutes, until the onions and fruit are soft.

Stir in the sugar. Bring slowly to the boil, then turn the heat right down so that the chutney bubbles gently. Cook for ten to fifteen minutes, with the occasional stir to stop it sticking on the bottom, until the mixture is thick and jam like. Bottle whilst hot and seal.

Makes a couple of jars

September

# The heart of it all

Breaking through a pastry crust, watching it shatter and crumble beneath the spoon, is one of those moments when every second spent cooking seems worthwhile. You dig deep into the filling, the heart of the pie, the sauce pools in the spoon and you just make it to the plate. You hand it over and dig in once more.

Handing round plates of homemade pie, steaming, juicy, crisp and soft, is one of those things that remind me why I bother. Yes, it's about feeding, nurturing and making people happy, but more than that, it's about saying you care enough about everyone to go to the trouble of chopping, frying (gently, not too much colour), making a sauce, rolling pastry (or even making it from scratch). Even more, it is about sharing something. As cute as an individual pie can be, there is something insular and hands off about them. The way I see it, an individual pie says 'mine', whereas a big pie says 'ours'.

And that is it really. 'Ours.' A huge, pastry-topped pie to share. You will need a big dish. My pie dish, at least the one I use for a chicken pie, is deep enough to enable you to sink the bowl of the biggest kitchen spoon into it, large enough that there will be the right ratio of filling to crust (there can never, never be quite enough pastry for me). I like the old ivory-coloured pie dishes made by Mason Cash. The designs have hardly changed in years. Sophie Conran's ridged pie dishes are a pleasure to use too. These are dishes that get better for use. Try to find ones that are happy to go in the freezer, dishwasher and microwave. A wide rim is useful for that extra bit of pastry and for securing the crust with a little beaten egg and milk. It will be helpful too for those occasions when you want to make a fancy crust, crimping and pinching the edge of the pastry between thumb and index finger. Mine show on their faces that they have had a life, a bit like me. The odd crack and even, dare I say it, a chip, make a dish feel like an old friend. A friend you have shared a few good times with.

# Chicken, leek and parsley pie

A big, informal pie for a family gathering. Use cooked roast chicken if you wish, but this is something worth roasting your chicken pieces for. By all means crimp and primp your pastry, but I prefer the simpler approach of laying a ready-made pastry sheet over the top, brushing it with seasoned egg and milk for a good shine.

chicken pieces: 800g, on the bone
leeks: 4
butter: a thick slice
plain flour: 3 heaped tablespoons
hot stock: 650ml
bay leaves: 3
parsley: a small handful
all-butter puff pastry: a 375g sheet
beaten egg and milk, seasoned,
    for brushing

Set the oven at 200°C/Gas 6. Put the chicken pieces in a roasting tin and bake for thirty minutes, till golden. Remove from the oven, leave to cool a little, then remove the flesh from the bones in large, bite-sized pieces and set aside.

Thinly slice the leeks, wash them thoroughly, then cook them with the butter and about 100ml of water till soft and brightly coloured. It is essential not to let them colour, so keep a lid on and don't have the heat too high. When they are soft, stir in the flour, leave to cook for a few minutes, then gradually pour in the hot stock, stirring as you go. Continue to cook, letting the leek mixture simmer for ten minutes or so, till you have a thickish sauce. Add the cooked chicken, bay leaves, chopped parsley and some salt and pepper and continue cooking for a good five minutes. Try not to let the chicken break up too much.

Spoon the chicken and leek filling into a pie dish. Unroll the pastry and place it over the top of the dish, letting it overhang the sides. Brush the pastry with the seasoned beaten egg and milk, cut 3 small slits in the top to let out the steam and bake for twenty-five minutes or until the pastry is crisp and golden.

Enough for 6

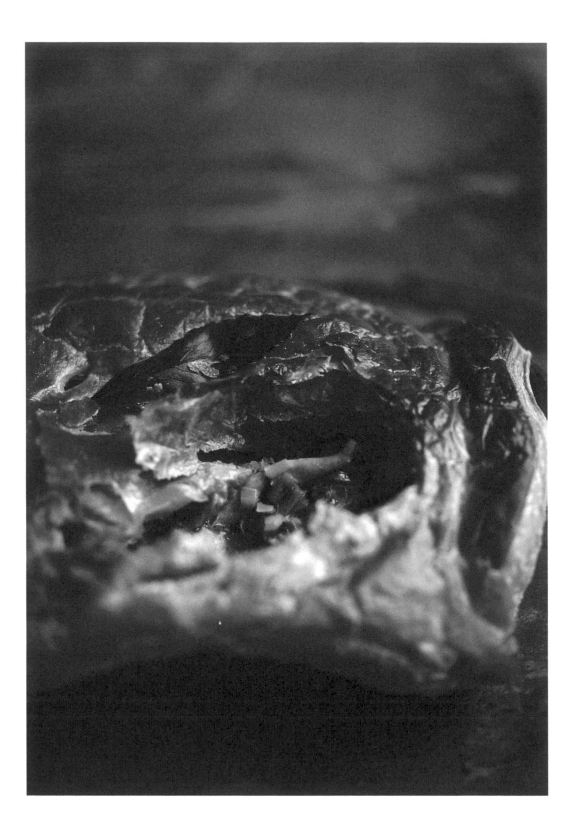

## A new couscous

The smell of food, its fragrance, seems somehow stronger in the autumn. Yes, 'tis the season of mellow fruitfulness, and the honeyed, sweet scent of overripe fruit, mushrooms and sweet vegetables will be more evident in the market on a sultry autumn day than will the gentle scents of spring on an April morning, but it also has something to do with the type of food we probably want to eat.

Rice, pasta, potatoes and 'something on toast' are very much the food of the season. Vegetables and meat bolstered with the satisfying quality of carbohydrate. This is the food that fills the kitchen with a warm, homely note, the smell of comfort. Add to this list couscous. It is not something I eat in quantity or even very often, but the day is a little chilly round the edges and I have been in the garden working. I need a comfort blanket.

I find the smell of warm starches – pasta, potatoes, porridge, rice and toast – the most reassuring of all. Fairly new to me is the beaded starch known as giant couscous. The large pearls have a curiously familiar note to them. It took a while to click that they have a sticky quality similar to gnocchi.

Disappointingly, mograbia, this giant form of couscous, is not especially easy to track down. I get it from Middle Eastern stores, two bags at a time. It keeps for ages. I am not entirely sure why I decide, on this early-autumn evening, to marry mograbia with apricots and a spicy dressing, but the ingredients sit comfortably together in a not quite Middle Eastern kind of way. The result is a dish of supreme comfort and originality.

### Apricot couscous

onions: 2
butter: a thick slice
green cardamom pods: 5, lightly crushed
a clove of garlic
the finely grated zest of a lemon
ripe apricots: 250g

*For the couscous:*
hot vegetable stock (or water, at a push): about 300ml
giant couscous: 150g
olive oil: 2 tablespoons, plus a little extra
lemon juice: a tablespoon
harissa paste: 2 teaspoons
a small bunch of parsley

To prepare the couscous, bring the stock to the boil in a good-sized saucepan, then pour in the couscous. Bring back to the boil and salt the liquid generously, as you might for pasta. Simmer for nine to ten minutes, until the couscous is tender but still with a bit of bite. Drain in a colander and run cold water through it to cool it quickly. Tip into a bowl and toss gently with a few drops of olive oil to stop it sticking together.

While the couscous is cooking, make the apricot seasoning. Peel the onions, dice them finely and cook in the butter, with the lightly crushed-cardamom pods, till soft and pale. Peel and slice the garlic and stir into the onions. Add the lemon zest. Halve and stone the apricots, add to the onions and set aside.

Stir the warm onion and apricot mixture into the cooling couscous, then stir in the lemon juice. Put the harissa paste in a small bowl, stir in the 2 tablespoons of olive oil then fold gently into the apricots and couscous. Remove the leaves from the parsley, roughly chop them and stir into the couscous.

Enough for 4


## SEPTEMBER 4

## A smoked chicken and dill sandwich

Tonight I recreate a favourite sandwich. Two pieces of sourdough bread (they use something lighter altogether), toasted almost without colour, then used to hold a filling of thick pieces of smoked chicken, finely sliced cooked asparagus and iceberg lettuce bound together with a mayonnaise flavoured with very finely chopped rosemary needles (weird, I know, but use only a little and chop them very finely), dill (be generous) and basil. A few pine kernels, toasted in a pan, tend to make a bid for freedom as you pick up your sandwich but add a pleasing, waxy crunch. I don't toast the bread more than very lightly – the idea being that it should only just be warm to the touch rather than my usual 'charred round the edges' look.

If ever there was a sign that I am a cook, not a chef, it is the inclusion of a traybake in this book (perhaps we can now, finally, put the whole matter to rest). I include it because it is a delicious, straightforward piece of baking, great for a crowd or packed lunches, cheap and cheerful and endlessly useful. It is a good recipe for anyone new to baking, as it is difficult to know

how you could fail with it. The inclusion of raspberries, straight from the freezer, adds much in the way of damp, heavily scented fruitiness. It smells wonderful as it comes from the oven.

## Victoria traybake

unsalted butter: 225g, at room temperature
golden caster sugar: 225g
eggs: 4
self-raising flour: 150g

ground almonds: 75g
raspberries: 200g (frozen are fine)
flaked almonds: 3 tablespoons
a little demerara sugar

Set the oven at 180°C/Gas 4. Line a 30cm x 22cm x 4cm deep baking tray with baking parchment.

Put the butter into a food mixer with the sugar and beat till light and fluffy. Break the eggs and beat them lightly, then add, a little at a time, to the butter and sugar mixture.

Remove the bowl from the machine and add the flour and ground almonds, stirring gently with a large metal spoon until no flour is visible. Fold in the raspberries.

Spoon into the baking tin, gently smooth flat and then scatter the top with the flaked almonds. Bake for forty minutes, then test for doneness with a skewer; there should be no uncooked mixture on the skewer. Add a light dusting of demerara sugar as the traybake leaves the oven.

Enough for 9–12

SEPTEMBER 5

# Bright peppers for darker days

How many times have I read of someone's sadness at the shortening days? Yet these nights hold no fear for me. At last. Cooler nights, gentler light, less oppressive air. This point in the year is when I feel I can breathe again. But summer doesn't want to let go, and there is still plenty of warmth in the sun, masses of tomatoes, home-grown aubergines and summer squash at the farmers' market. The peppers today were an extraordinary sight, blood red and curling like Aladdin's slippers.

These are not the peppers you would usually choose to stuff. They fall over and their dips and furrows make removing the skins more of a task. But they are more intriguing than the usual fat bell pepper, and I pick them up nevertheless. The time-honoured way of removing the skins from peppers is to grill or bake them, then put them in a plastic bag so the skin steams and become easier to remove. A piece of cling film stretched over the top of a bowl containing the warm peppers works best for me. It has to be said, the plumper the pepper, the easier it is to get the skin off. My stuffed-pepper plan for dinner goes out of the window, but I am rewarded by a warm pepper salad with a vivid green basil sauce that I can only describe as summer's last gasp.

## Baked peppers, summer sauce

large peppers: 4
olive oil

*For the basil dressing:*
basil leaves: a couple of good
   handfuls

oregano leaves: a small handful
mint leaves: a small handful
a plump clove of garlic, peeled
extra virgin olive oil: about 150ml

Set the oven at 180°C/Gas 4. Cut the peppers in half, tug out the seeds and cores and lay the peppers cut-side up in a baking tin. Trickle a little olive oil over them, then bake until the skins have blackened. Remove from the oven and cover with a tea towel or cling film (the steam this creates will make it easier to remove the skin).

Put the basil leaves into a blender or food processor with the oregano and mint, the peeled clove of garlic and the olive oil. Add a good pinch of sea salt and mix till almost smooth.

Peel off the skins from the peppers and put the peppers on a plate. Trickle the herb sauce around them and serve warm.

Enough for 2–4 as a side dish

## A mirabelle feast

No matter how careful you are, small, translucent plums can come cascading down as you endeavour to pull them, one at a time, from the branch. I get round this by holding a bowl in the other hand, waiting to catch any that fall. It feels awkward, a bit like juggling, but it saves the precious fruit from getting damaged. Even landing on soft, damp soil, a ripe plum can bruise.

I pick what is probably the last of the Reine Claude, gold with pink mottled shoulders; tiny greengages the size of sweets; some wild gages and several deep-yellow mirabelles with carmine freckles. I pinch a couple of next door's temptingly ripe Victorias whilst I'm at it (look, they are away, okay).There is a sense of disbelief at how beautiful the box of assorted tiny plums is. Even more so at the fact that I planted them all save the wild greengage, which sort of planted itself. The larger varieties will ripen later.

It seems absurd to throw all the fruit in together, losing the chance to enjoy each variety for what it is. So today's pickings go nowhere near the cooker. Instead, they are piled precariously on an oval plate and passed round the table after the Sunday roast. Whilst everyone goes along with the generosity of the gesture and seems enchanted by their glowing colours, I can't help but detect a slight air of disappointment that my precious collection of fruits didn't become a crumble.

# Waxed paper, greaseproof and other kitchen papers

I will admit to a slight obsession with paper. Not the coloured writing paper of designer stationery shops but simple, useful paper, functional but nevertheless beautifully made. There is a recycled baking paper, a pale shade of bamboo, you can find in some wholefood stores that is excellent for lining cake tins and baking sheets. I keep a roll in the house at all times. Another, rather beautiful non-stick brown paper is something I can never be without. Standard supermarket stock, it is endlessly useful (wrapping sandwiches, lining the base of a cake tin, for making praline or setting chocolate on, as well as for lining cookie sheets). Matt to the touch, a pale walnut colour, it is one of those things that manage to be both useful and beautiful.

More difficult to find nowadays is old-fashioned waxed paper. Just the thing for wrapping sandwiches, it is also what I use at home for enclosing jagged blocks of Parmesan, maturing gingerbread (a day or three under wraps will give homemade ginger cake a moister texture) and lining the enamelled boxes I keep bacon and cheese in. I love the heavy feel of it, and the way it crackles as you unwrap it.

This is the paper that is perfect for keeping air-dried hams fresh. You could use cling film but it often causes the ham to sweat, and is rather wasteful. I have also reached the age where I can no longer find the end of the roll. Ditto Sellotape. Ditto bloody everything. Many delicatessens and food halls wrap their carved hams, prosciutto and sliced salami in some sort of waxed paper, and this is fine for storing them for a couple of days, maybe longer. But if they come in other paper or film, and this is often the case, then it is best to transfer them to a piece of classic waxed paper.

I find greaseproof paper as good as useless, but it is fine for short-term wrapping of dry food, such as a sandwich in a lunchbox. But get it even slightly wet and it will stick to your food. You will find yourself peeling it off.

Like Parmesan and mineral water, there is usually a stash of some sort of cured or air-dried meat in the fridge. A few slices of moist, crumbly fennel-freckled salami; some wavy, fat-rimmed slices of Parma ham; a few curls of salami. This week I picked up some coppa, with its dark red and white marbling, which needs using. It works as well in a salad as it does with chunks of bread and a few cornichons.

# A salad of plums, lentils and coppa

I think there is a genuine need for interesting main-course salads that will keep for at least twenty-four hours in reasonable condition, making them ideal for use in a lunchbox. I made twice the quantity below: half was eaten on the day, the rest tucked into a plastic box for the following day.

| | |
|---|---|
| small green lentils | coriander: 35g |
| (such as Puy): 2 cups | spring onions: 2 |
| olive oil | plums: 200g |
| mint: 35g | the juice of a large lemon |
| flat-leaf parsley: 70g | coppa, speck or firm air-dried ham |

Rinse the lentils briefly and cook them in vigorously boiling water (no salt) for fifteen to twenty minutes, till they are tender but retain a little nuttiness (the only way to tell is to lift a couple out and try them). Drain them, then cool quickly in a sieve or fine colander under cold running water. Tip them into a mixing bowl and trickle a little olive oil over them. Just enough to make them shine. This will stop them drying out.

Pull the mint, parsley and coriander leaves from their stems and chop them roughly. Add them to the lentils. Finely slice the spring onions and add them too.

Halve each plum, discard the stone, then slice the fruit into four or more pieces, depending on its size. I tend to cut each half into no more than four. Toss these gently with the lentils, lemon juice and a little more olive oil, say a couple of tablespoons. Then tip the mixture on to a serving dish and serve with slices of coppa.

Enough for 2 as a main course

## SEPTEMBER 9

Partridges are neither cheap nor filling, but a pair of them makes a lean, light dinner for two and they have just come into season. I split mine in half down the backbone with a knife and a pair of scissors and opened each one out like a book. I rubbed them with a mixture of salt, crushed red chillies and olive oil, then put them on one side for an hour whilst I tried to knock a hole in the endless, endless pile of emails. The overhead grill hot, the flattened birds went underneath, with the occasional turn, till they were nicely crisped around the edges and still quite pink and bloody within. About twenty-five minutes. Halves of lemon were put on the table too, and more salt. To fill us up, we ate them with thick toast rubbed with garlic and moistened with rather a lot of olive oil.

## SEPTEMBER 11

# A celebratory soup-stew for a special day

The thick wall that divides the warren-like basement of this old house is no more. Well, almost. The builders knocked a hole in it today big enough to drive a car through (I told you this book is not chronologically correct). Dust swirls in the air, ghostly, like fine gauze, covering every available surface on every floor of the house. You can feel it in your hair, taste it on your lips. Unexpected golden light suddenly pours into what was a dark and useless space, the room that will, in the coming weeks, become my new kitchen. Or more accurately, the old kitchen, as this project is being done in order to return the house to its original 1820s floor plan, restoring the basement kitchen with its York stone floors, two fireplaces and deep fireside cupboards. For the first time, I can actually see the space where I will soon be cooking my daily food. The place in this house where food was always meant to be cooked.

Golden days like these – seeing the first chink of light appear on a project you thought would never happen, and that of creating a useful space where there wasn't one – demand a suitable celebration. A bottle or two of cider and a big, bolstering dish, tied as always to the season, seem appropriate. Golden flesh to celebrate a golden day.

# A lentil and pumpkin soup-stew

a medium onion
rapeseed or olive oil: 2 tablespoons
  (or a thick slice of butter)
a large carrot
garlic: 2 large cloves
a bushy sprig of rosemary
small green or blue lentils,
  such as Puy: 250g
vegetable stock: 1.25 litres
a couple of bay leaves

pumpkin or butternut squash:
  1.5kg (weight before peeling)
red wine vinegar: 2 tablespoons
roughly chopped parsley:
  a handful

*To finish:*
crème fraîche or labne:
  4–6 tablespoons
extra virgin olive oil

Peel the onion, cut it in half from root to tip, then into thick slices. Warm the oil or butter in a large casserole, add the onion and cook over a low to moderate heat for fifteen minutes or so, till soft and pale gold. Meanwhile, scrub the carrot and cut it into small dice. Stir it into the onion.

Peel the garlic and slice it thinly. Pull the leaves from the rosemary stems and chop roughly, then add to the softening vegetables with the sliced garlic. When all is soft, sweet and lightly coloured, tip in the lentils and a litre of the stock. Drop in the bay leaves. Bring the mixture to the boil, then lower the heat so that the lentils simmer gently and cook for forty-five minutes.

Meanwhile, peel and deseed the pumpkin and cut the flesh into large, meaty chunks. I make these large enough that you will have to cut them to put them in your mouth; any smaller and you may find they dissolve into the soup. Add to the lentils and leave to simmer till the squash is thoroughly tender – about fifteen minutes. This is also the point to add the seasoning. It will need salt, black pepper and the red wine vinegar. Stir in the chopped parsley.

Remove 2 large ladlefuls of the stew and blitz to a purée in a blender or food processor with the remaining 250ml of stock (you can beat it to a pulp with a potato masher, if you prefer). Return the puréed mixture to the pan and stir gently.

To serve, pile into wide bowls or deep plates. Drop a heaped tablespoon of crème fraîche or labne on to each portion, then pour a little extra virgin olive oil over the top.

Enough for 4–6

# Broad bean, feta and spinach pie

broad beans: 250g (shelled
  weight)
spinach: 500g
feta cheese: 400g

filo pastry: 6 sheets, about 270g
melted butter, for brushing
sesame seeds: a teaspoon

Set the oven at 200°C/Gas 6. Put a saucepan of water on to boil. Tip in the broad beans and leave to cook for seven to ten minutes, till tender. Drain, then squeeze the beans out of their grey skins and set aside. If you cool them quickly in a colander under a cold tap, they will retain their bright colour.

Wash the spinach very thoroughly to remove every little bit of sand and grit. Whilst the leaves are still holding some of their water, put them into a large, deep pan over a low to moderate heat, without any further liquid. Cover with a tight lid and cook for a few minutes, turning occasionally with kitchen tongs, till they are wilted and dark emerald green. Drain in a colander or sieve, then cool under cold running water. Squeeze the spinach almost dry with your hands. There is no more effective way to do it. Leave some moisture in there, but it should not be soggy. Place in a bowl, then add the broad beans, a generous seasoning of black pepper and a little salt. Crumble the feta into the bowl and fold it in.

Place a sheet of filo pastry on a baking sheet and brush it with melted butter. Place a second sheet on top, brush with butter, then continue till all six sheets have been used. Pile the broad bean, spinach and feta filling on one half of the pastry, shaping it into a rough rectangle. Fold the edges over, book-style, and press loosely to seal.

Brush with butter, cut a small slit or two in the top, then scatter lightly with the sesame seeds. Bake for fifteen to twenty minutes, till golden.

Enough for 4–6

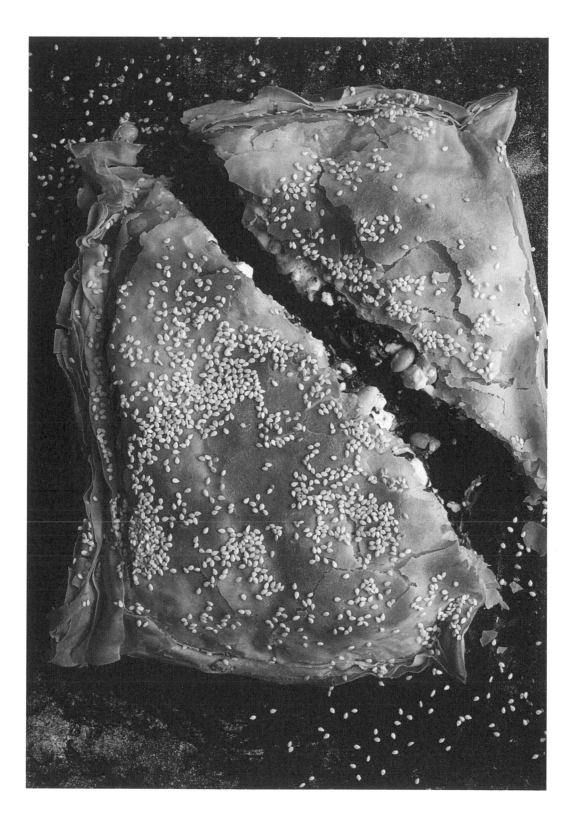

SEPTEMBER 12

# A new everyday tomato sauce

I return from Haringey allotments, where we have been filming, with a bag of San Marzano tomatoes, the long, thin, pointed variety that occasionally has a streak of yellow to its shoulders. The San Marzano is the one that is rumoured to have come to Italy in 1770 as a gift from the kingdom of Peru, and thrived on the volcanic soil around Mount Vesuvius. There is a distinct lack of seeds to this slim, sweet tomato. I have grown them, but not with what you could call success. It is often said they make the richest tomato sauce of all, but obviously much depends on the ripeness of your tomatoes and, I would venture to suggest, on whether they were grown in Italy.

These came from a friend with a glut and are exceedingly ripe, with much flesh and few seeds. The ones to avoid are those that feel light in the hand, as they can be dry. These are heavy and deepest scarlet. My promise to make batches of sauce to freeze or bottle is never kept. Over the years, I have made both raw tomato sauces and cooked ones. I have grilled the fruit before making them into a sauce; given them sweetness with sugar; a kick with red wine vinegar; and depth with a drop or two of balsamic. I have sieved my sauces and left them chunky, lent them warmth with basil and ruined them with cream. I once spent half a day making a long-simmered version only to end up with something indistinguishable from Heinz tomato soup.

Finding a bowl of tomato sauce in the fridge (or the freezer or cupboard for the more organised) is like finding an almost endless pot of opportunities: sauce for pasta, for lasagne, for meatballs and gnocchi. Sauce for grilled polenta, for grilled chicken, for baked peppers or sausages. It is like finding a pot of gold.

# Baked squid with chilli tomato sauce

Get your fishmonger to do the preparation of the squid. There is no reason to do it yourself.

cleaned squid: 4

*For the stuffing:*
fresh white breadcrumbs: 150g
anchovy fillets: 6
the grated zest of a lemon
flat-leaf parsley: 20g, chopped
olive oil: 6 tablespoons
tomato: a moderately large one

*For the sauce:*
a medium onion
olive oil: 2 tablespoons
a red chilli
tomatoes: 3 large (not beefsteak)
a red pepper
vegetable stock: 200ml

Put the breadcrumbs in a mixing bowl. Chop the anchovy fillets and add them to the crumbs with the lemon zest, parsley, olive oil and a seasoning of salt and black pepper. Roughly chop the tomato into small dice and mix into the stuffing.

Place the squid bodies on a chopping board and stuff them using a teaspoon. Push the stuffing along the body with your fingers, getting as much as you can in there without splitting the skin. Place the stuffed squid in a baking dish. If there is any leftover stuffing, scatter it over the squid. Drop the tentacles into the dish.

Set the oven at 180°C/Gas 4. Make the sauce: peel and roughly chop the onion and let it soften in the olive oil in a deep casserole. Halve, seed and finely chop the chilli and add to the onion. Roughly chop the tomatoes and thinly slice the pepper, discarding the core and seeds of the pepper as you go, then stir them into the softening onion. Continue cooking for ten to fifteen minutes, with the occasional stir, until all is soft. Pour in the stock, season with salt and pepper and cook for a few minutes longer. Spoon the sauce over the squid and bake for forty-five minutes, until piping hot.

Enough for 4

There has been a bag of peas in the freezer for a few weeks now. I'm rather a fan of frozen peas, partly because I have room to grow only enough for a couple of meals and partly because they are so damn useful. I pour the whole bag into a large pan with some vegetable stock made up from a tub of powder and boiling water, add a few spring onions, chopped up, 4 sprigs of mint and a little salt, then bring them to the boil. Cooked at a rolling boil (there is something very jolly about peas boiling), poured into a blender with a little cream and a few sprigs of mint, blitzed and poured into bowls. We eat the warming, vivid-green soup with rye crackers and smoked salmon.

## SEPTEMBER 16

# The last of the runner beans

Back from three days away to a noticeable change in the vegetable patch. The leaves of the redcurrant bushes have turned a translucent, russet yellow; tomatoes lie squashed across the back steps; the cucumber plant appears to have dissolved. The sun is still warm on your back and the raspberry canes continue to be dotted with both ripe and unripe berries, but there is a bracing chill at seven in the morning and again at seven at night. The heating thermostat has a come-hither look to it. Instead, I reach for my fleece jacket, unsure if the accompanying glow is that of the environmentally friendly homeowner or plain parsimony.

At the little vegetable stall in Bermondsey this morning, I spot a tray of runner beans that seems out of step with the autumn's Buttercup pumpkins and still-green quinces. A foot long and with a matchbox roughness to their skins, they nevertheless have the crisp, clean snap of a young summer bean. It seems late to find them as good as this.

Back home, I discover mine, too, are still there, hanging long and heavy, a piercing green amongst the slowly browning stems. I break one in half to find it, even now, virtually stringless (and if there were strings, I would simply pull them off with a small knife, taking the stalk as I go). These middle days of September were when my family would salt their beans for the winter, pressing the finely shredded pods into large sweetie jars, each layer covered with a snowfall of coarse salt to keep them in good condition till the spring. The process worked, despite the vegetables getting softer as the winter wore on and the aluminium lid turning an unappetising black from exposure to the salt. Our squirrel store of beans was edible even in February if you remembered to rinse them thoroughly before cooking and not to salt the water in which they boiled. I like the intelligence involved in preserving one season's excess for another, less abundant day, but I am not sure of the point of salting beans since the advent of the freezer.

The thoughtful cook will always find ways to use up the last of the tomatoes from the greenhouse; the beans going cheap at the market; that culinary end-of season bargain. The essence of the summer vegetable garden, but hardly the most versatile of crops, runner beans leave me a little weary by late September. The sliced and steamed beans have been passed around the table for two months now, in deep green bowls with olive oil and lemon juice, or tossed in softened butter and finely chopped shallots. They have snuggled up to roast lamb at Sunday lunchtime and cheered up a plate of pickle-spiked cold cuts on Monday. I have presented them in a tomato and lemon zest sauce (*Tender Volume I*) and added them, too soon for their own good, to a late-summer soup. I am besieged by them, yet disinclined to waste any either.

But the runner bean will make a rousing pickle if treated in the same way as cauliflower, simmered in a thick sauce with vinegar, ground turmeric and mustard seeds and packed into jars for the winter. I use a recipe that is based on a true piccalilli, ochre yellow and sharp with malt vinegar, the texture softened with a spoonful of cornflour.

A creamy, bright-ochre chutney with enough sharpness to wake up a roast beef sandwich. Salt figures here not only as a seasoning but, along with the sugar and vinegar, as a preservative. It is meant for later, but we nevertheless tuck into the scrapings from the pan, stuffing them into soft baps with a grilled patty of beef.

# An autumn-coloured bean chutney

Makes 1 large and 1 smaller Kilner jar

medium onions: 2
malt vinegar: 150ml
allspice berries: 8
coriander seed: 1 teaspoon
yellow mustard seed: 1 teaspoon
runner beans: 750g
English mustard powder:
  a tablespoon

grain mustard: 2 teaspoons
turmeric: 2 teaspoons
granulated sugar: 200g
salt: a heaped teaspoon
cider vinegar: 150ml
tomatoes: 250g
cornflour: 28g

Peel and finely chop the onions and put them into a medium-sized saucepan with the malt vinegar, allspice, coriander and mustard seeds. Bring to the boil, then lower the heat and simmer for ten minutes.

String the beans, removing the stalks as you go. Thinly slice each bean, cutting diagonally to give fine shreds about 4–5 cm long. Bring a pan of water to the boil, add the beans and let them cook for a full minute. Drain and set aside.

Mix the mustards, turmeric, sugar, salt and half the cider vinegar in a small basin.

Chop the tomatoes into small dice, then add to the vinegar and onions. Stir in the beans and the mustard mixture, followed by the remaining cider vinegar. Bring to the boil, turn the heat down and simmer for fifteen minutes, stirring regularly. The beans should be tender, but still bright in colour.

Remove 2 or 3 tablespoons of liquid and use it to mix the cornflour to a paste. Stir gently back into the beans. Leave to simmer for a minute or two, until the mixture has thickened slightly. Ladle into warm, sterilised preserving jars and seal.

# Using up the leeks

The French and the Flemish have more ways to use the humble leek than the Inuit have words for snow or the Lapps have for reindeer (one hundred). The pallid and elegant vichysoisse; a savoury open tart; as a sweetener in a pot-au-feu; or cut into wine-cork-sized pieces and gently simmered in red wine. If there are leeks to use up, I prefer the more robust notes of our own leek and potato soup, where more of the blue-green leaves are used than in the virginal French vichysoisse. It's a more common soup – you rarely see it on menus now – and seems rough and masculine when served alongside the version from over the Channel.

Today, a neighbour gave me the excess leek thinnings from her vegetable patch. Removed in order to give the rest of the crop a chance to fatten up (heartbreaking but wise), the pencil-thin roots were handed over in a damp newspaper parcel to keep them fresh. There are already a few fat leeks in my fridge looking hopefully for a supper to be part of. Leek soup is probably better suited to frosty weather but today is a rainy day, and the wind is howling round the trees in the garden. What I call a pastry day. I decide on making some sort of tart.

There are two ways to use this lengthy allium in a pastry case. Softened in butter and cooked with diced bacon, it will make the filling for an open tart, a quiche that will show off the leek's affinity with eggs. It is superb as a filling for an omelette. Another way is to bind the softened leeks with cheese and bake inside a double crust – a pasty capable of feeding the family. I use a milky cheese such as Taleggio for this. Leeks have a delicate nature that can be smothered by something stronger, such as Camembert.

Later, as we tuck into the steaming pie with its puff pastry and sweet, mild filling, it occurs to me that the precious leeks my neighbour had grown from seed were actually meant for my garden.

# Tarts of leeks and cheese

leeks: 500g
butter: 50g
puff pastry: 375g

an egg, beaten with a little milk
Taleggio cheese: 100g

Remove the roots and tough dark green stalks from the leeks. Thinly slice the white and pale green parts and rinse very thoroughly. Grit tends to get trapped in their layers.

Melt the butter in a heavy-based pan. Add the leeks, still wet from their rinsing, and cover them with a piece of greaseproof paper and a lid. Let them cook over a moderate to low heat for ten to fifteen minutes, until they are soft and pale. They should not colour at all, so keep an eye on them. When they are done, remove from the heat.

Set the oven at 180°C/Gas 4 and put a baking sheet in to get hot. Roll out the pastry, cut out twelve 8cm discs and place half of them on a baking sheet. Brush the edges with beaten egg. Cut the cheese into small cubes and toss it into the leeks together with a grinding of salt and black pepper.

Divide the filling between six of the discs, then place a second disc on top of each. There is no need to press down to seal the edges, though you can if you want. Bake for about twenty-five minutes, till golden and crisp.

*To make a large pie:*
Use a 375g sheet of pastry. Cut the sheet in half, roll one half out to half its original thickness and transfer to a baking sheet. Spoon the leek and cheese filling on to it, leaving a narrow rim. Brush the edges of the pastry with the egg and milk. Roll out the second half and use it to cover the top of the pie, pressing down the edges against the overlapping pastry to seal them (I sometimes do this with a fork or by pinching them together with my finger and thumb). Brush the top with egg and milk, then pierce a hole in the centre of the pastry to let the steam out during cooking.

Place the tart on the hot baking sheet and cook for fifty minutes or till the top is golden.

Enough for 4

# Blackberrying

Blackberrying, picking fruit for a pie, comes laden with nostalgia, guilt (we are stealing; hedges inevitably belong to 'someone') and the heart-racing delight of finding food for free.

I have always been a 'blackberrier'. I collected them on my way home from school, from a vast, cloud-like thicket in a field complete with the menace of a ring-nosed Hereford bull. Almost at the top of Ankerdine Hill, just off a road leading from Martley to Knightwick in rural Worcestershire, it was the largest blackberry bush I have ever seen. It is gone now, but there are bramble hedges further up the lane. Later, there were trips through the Lake District, the lanes around Thornbury, and the occasional chance sighting you get when you have no bag in which to put your shiny black booty.

Today, berries hang over my garden wall from next door, vast, glistening skeins of them with artery-threatening thorns. It is not often I reach this point in their year without a dot-dash-dot of dried scabs on the inside of my arm.

Blackberries freeze exceptionally well. Unlike a strawberry, they are made up of lots of tiny berries, druplets, held together to form one larger berry, so they don't collapse when defrosted. I keep some in the freezer for a winter blackberry and apple crumble. The cultivated varieties aren't bad, but are often too large and sweet to remind us of childhood hedgerow feasts. They come far behind the wild berry in terms of flavour, and somehow feel wrong – too plump, too flabby – in an apple pie. Where they are good is in an ice-cream cake, such as the one here, which comes in the form of a loaf, the store-bought vanilla ice studded with biscuit crumbs and fat fruits.

## Blackberry ice-cream cake

blackcurrants (fresh or frozen): 150g
sugar: 1 tablespoon
water: 2 tablespoons

shortbread biscuits: 200g
shelled pistachios: 6 tablespoons
vanilla ice cream: 900ml
blackberries: 250g

You will need a loaf tin or freezer box approximately 22cm long, 12cm wide and 7cm deep, lined with a piece of cling film that overhangs the sides.

Pull the blackcurrants from their stalks and put them in a small saucepan with the sugar and water. Bring to the boil, lower the heat and cook for two or three minutes, till the berries start to burst and the sugar melts. Set aside.

Put the biscuits into a food processor with the pistachios and blitz till the biscuits are reduced to coarse crumbs – this will be just a matter of seconds. Take care not to overprocess; stop while you can still clearly see the pistachios.

Let the ice cream soften slightly, then tip it into a mixing bowl. Add the biscuit and pistachio crumbs and the blackberries and mix gently but firmly, without over mixing; the ingredients should be clearly defined. Transfer a third of the mixture to the prepared loaf tin, pushing it firmly into the corners but without flattening it too much. Spoon in half of the warm blackcurrants and their juice, then add another third of the ice-cream mixture followed by the rest of the blackcurrants. Add the remaining ice-cream mixture. Wrap the overhanging film over the top and freeze for a minimum of 4 hours. Turn out and slice with a warm knife.

Enough for 8

# SEPTEMBER 22

# A glut of courgettes

My courgettes, Striato d'Italia or the golden, slightly softer Gold Rush, are grown in large pots on the kitchen steps. Sometimes grown from seed, sometimes bought as a tiny plug plant, they survive my seesaw treatment of overbearing love and neglect. This year is no exception and they have kept me supplied with fruit from July until now. They don't mind their feet in recycled compost either, as long as you feed them every two weeks with tomato food and lavish them with plenty of water, but not so much that their roots get soggy for long. I give them a bit of gravel or broken brick in the base of the pot, so the water drains away.

Two plants are enough for most families and too much for this kitchen. The plants, whose leaves tend to be smaller when they are pot grown, produce an almost endless supply till the first frost, when they will lie exhausted and squishy stemmed.

I have written much about courgettes, which I like to call zucchini just because it is such a beautiful word to say, in *Tender Volume I*, but I use them less than I would like to. My problem with the courgette is the way it comes at you non-stop. I feel besieged. Another day, another courgette recipe. This summer I have bowed to the Italians and their heritage of deep-frying. First the male flowers, then the fruits themselves. The point is the courgette's ability to turn unremarkable flesh into luscious, juicy flesh once it hits the hot oil (that said, I quite like a newly picked, creamy-fleshed courgette in a salad with lemon and basil). Trap that steaming, deep-fried flesh inside the thinnest and crispest of batter shells and you have something worth eating for the contrasting textures alone. And if anyone tells me they find courgettes taste of very little, and sometimes that is indeed the case, then I serve them with a salty, highly savoury sauce such as the one I made tonight, with the deep southern Mediterranean flavours of rosemary and anchovy. Stopping just short of pungent, it teases out the courgette's delicate flavour rather than masking it.

## Courgette fritters with tomato and rosemary sauce

oil for deep-frying
courgettes: 2 large or 4 small

*For the batter:*
plain flour: 100g
sunflower oil: 2 tablespoons
sparkling mineral water: 175ml
an egg white

*For the dressing:*
anchovy fillets: 6
olive oil: 3 tablespoons
rosemary: a small sprig
a single clove of garlic
cherry tomatoes: 16

Make the batter. Sift the flour into a large basin, then add the oil and water, beating slowly to a thick paste. Set aside for thirty minutes. Don't be tempted to skip the resting time; this is essential for a light batter. Just

before you plan to fry the courgettes, beat the egg white till almost stiff and fold it gently into the batter.

For the dressing, pat the anchovy fillets with kitchen paper to remove the excess (excessively fishy) oil. Chop them finely, then put them with a tablespoon of the olive oil in a shallow pan over a moderate heat. As they cook, remove the needles from the rosemary (you need about a heaped teaspoon) and chop them finely. Add them to the anchovies. Peel and slice the garlic and add it to the pan. Quarter the cherry tomatoes and stir them in, letting them cook for five minutes till soft and squashy. Pour in the remaining olive oil, season with black pepper but no salt and leave to simmer for a further ten to fifteen minutes, till all is soft. Check the seasoning. (You can keep this warm for a while, with a last-minute stir before serving.)

Heat the oil for frying in a deep pan. Wipe the courgettes, cut them into 3cm lengths and then into halves.

Test the oil to make sure it is hot enough – it should send a cube of bread golden in a few seconds – then dip the courgettes into the batter and lower them a few at a time into the hot oil. Hold them under the oil by pushing down with a spatula. Fry for three or four minutes, till the batter is pale gold and crisp, then lift out and set briefly on to a piece of kitchen paper to drain. Eat the fritters with the dressing whilst they are hot and crisp.

Enough for 4


## Courgettes with goat's cheese and toast

While I have the courgettes out, a quick recipe from the archive that I have been meaning to give a more permanent home for a while now. A good kitchen snack for when you are hungry but don't need a full meal.

| | |
|---|---|
| a lemon | a small goat's cheese |
| basil leaves: 8 large | courgettes: 250g |
| olive oil: 4 tablespoons, plus a little for frying | good white bread: 4 thick slices |

Grate the zest from half the lemon into a bowl with a fine grater, then add the juice. Finely shred the basil leaves and drop them in with the lemon, then pour in the olive oil. Add a little salt. Crumble in the goat's cheese in small pieces and stir very gently.

Rinse the courgettes and dry them. Using a vegetable peeler, slice them very thinly all the way down from one end to the other. Warm a little oil in a frying pan, add the courgettes and cook until golden. Drop them into the dressing and toss gently.

Make toast with the slices of bread, then pile on the courgettes and their dressing.

Enough for 2

SEPTEMBER 23

# Sweet juice

## A pudding for autumn

You could measure my life in summer puddings, those bulging, gloriously juicy globes of raspberries and currants held prisoner by slices of bread. I used to make them daily at a café a hundred years ago and can't get out of the habit. The first one of the year is always a traditional raspberry and redcurrant, but then I get into a more contemporary mood and swap the fruits around. In the past it has appeared in my kitchen made with goose-berries (*Tender Volume II*, and so good with thick, yellow unpasteurised cream), or with lots of blackcurrants in with the raspberries (serve with vanilla ice cream) but I have always wondered if damsons – as you probably know, a favourite fruit of mine – would be a worthy addition for when the currant season has finished. With the exception of the slightly fiddly task of removing their stones (and we must), it is a pudding of serious pleasure and inky sour-sweet juice.

damsons: 750g
caster sugar: 100g, or more to taste
water: 250ml
raspberries: 250g

blackberries: 250g
blueberries: 250g
sloe gin: 100ml
white bread: 10 or so slices

You will need a 1.5 litre pudding basin or 6 individual ones.

Put the damsons in a stainless steel or enamelled saucepan with the sugar and water and bring to the boil. You can add a little more sugar if you wish, depending on how sour your fruit is. As soon as the fruit is thoroughly soft,

about fifteen minutes, remove from the heat and leave till it is cool enough to handle. Squeeze the stones from the fruit and discard. This is messy but shouldn't take longer than ten minutes. It is certainly quicker than trying to stone the damsons before cooking. If you skip the stoning process you will, I promise, regret it later. Place the pan back on the heat and tip in the raspberries, blackberries and blueberries. Add the sloe gin and continue cooking, but now at a low simmer, till the fruit has started to burst and the juice in the pan is a good rich colour. About ten minutes.

Cut a disc of bread to fit the bottom and top of the dish, or of each individual dish, then cut the rest into thick, crust-free fingers. The exact measurements will depend on whether you are making one large or six smaller ones. Dipping them briefly into the warm juice as you go, tuck the smaller of the discs in the bottom of the pudding basin. Press the fingers of bread, again briefly dipping them into the juice, all round the sides of the dish, carefully butting them up together so there are no gaps where the juice can leak out. When the basins are lined on the base and sides, fill them with the fruit, spooning the juice right to the top. Place the second disc of bread on top, then cover tightly with cling film. Place on a plate (to catch any stray juice) in the fridge with a heavy weight on top to compress the fruit and bread. Leave overnight.

To serve, turn out on to a serving dish or individual dishes. Running a palette knife around the sides, between bread and basin, then turning it upside down on to a plate and giving it a good hard shake will make it easier to turn the pudding out complete.

Enough for 6


## Chard and feta tart

| | |
|---|---|
| a large onion | crème fraîche: 200ml |
| butter: 25g | grain mustard: 2 teaspoons |
| chard: 700g | feta cheese: 200g |
| tarragon, chopped: 1 tablespoon | puff pastry: 375g |
| plain flour: 1 tablespoon | a small egg, beaten |

Peel the onion and chop it finely. Melt the butter in a large, shallow pan over a moderate heat and add the onion, leaving it to cook with the occasional stir for ten to fifteen minutes.

Separate the chard leaves from the stalks. Cut the stalks into thin slices across their width. Tear the leaves into large pieces, keeping them separate from the stalks. Add the stalks to the onion and continue cooking till both the onion and chard stalks are soft and tender.

Stir in the tarragon and then the flour, letting the mixture cook briefly before stirring in the crème fraîche and mustard. Crumble in the feta, keeping the pieces fairly large, and season with black pepper.

Set the oven at 200°C/Gas 6 and put a baking sheet in to get hot. Wash the chard leaves and, while they are still wet, pile them into a saucepan and cover with a tight lid. Let the leaves steam, turning them once or twice, for a few minutes, till they are dark green and wilted. There will be water to discard in the bottom of the pan. Remove the leaves and drain in a colander. When they are cool enough to handle (you can run cold water through them to speed things up), squeeze the leaves in your hand to remove as much water as possible. Stir the squeezed leaves into the onion and chard stalk mixture.

Cut the pastry in half and roll out one half slightly larger than a 20cm shallow tart tin. Line the tin with the pastry, letting it overhang a little. Add the chard and feta filling, pulling the overhanging pastry edges over the edge of the filling. Brush the edges of the pastry with the egg.

Roll out the second half and use it to cover the top of the pie, pressing the edges against the overlapping pastry to seal them (I tend to pinch them together with my finger and thumb). Brush the top with more beaten egg, then pierce a hole in the centre to let the steam out during cooking.

Place the tart on the hot baking sheet and cook for thirty minutes, till the top is golden. Leave to rest for ten minutes or so before cutting.

Enough for 4

SEPTEMBER 25

# Savoury juice

Once the roast has been lifted from its tin, we have the treasure in the pan to contemplate. I have long regarded the juices left in the pan or roasting tin as nothing short of treasure. Containing the caramelised meat juices, crusty pan-stickings and reduced cooking liquids, they are indeed the essence of the meat. I think of them as its heart and soul. Seeing them thrown away with the washing up (and believe me, I have seen people do this) goes beyond wasteful. I think of them as not just revered but verging on sacred. Dipping a piece of bread into them, or a roast potato, is probably as perfect and simple as eating gets.

You know, we can spend all evening making a sauce, but the juices that come from the dish itself are to my mind unsurpassed by any separately made sauce. It should be said that some are more interesting than others. Those where there has been time for flavours to marry and develop are often the best of all, but that doesn't mean those left behind from a spot of quick cooking are not worth utilising. Last night, an impromptu meal of big rustic flavours, food that is big and butch with not even a nod towards elegance, produced pan juices so good I almost upended the plate straight into my mouth.

## Roast pork and rocket salad with lemon and olives

a small loin of pork, scored, about 500–600g
rosemary: 3 bushy sprigs
garlic: 3 cloves
olive oil: a tablespoon
rocket: 4 handfuls

*For the dressing:*
stoned green olives: 3 tablespoons
lemon juice: 2 tablespoons
olive oil: 4 tablespoons

Set the oven at 220°C/Gas 7. Put the pork in a roasting tin. Finely chop the rosemary needles, discarding the stems as you go. Flatten the garlic cloves with the side of a large knife but don't peel them. Mix the rosemary and garlic cloves with the olive oil, season with salt and black pepper, then spread over the pork, massaging it into the cuts in the skin.

When the oven is up to temperature, roast the pork for twenty minutes, then turn down the heat to 180°C/Gas 4 and cook for twenty minutes longer. Check the meat is done, then remove it from the oven. Let the joint rest on a warm plate while you quickly make the dressing.

Roughly chop the olives and mix with the lemon juice and olive oil. Wash the rocket leaves and dry them.

Discard any fat from the roasting tin but leave any sticky sediment behind – it will form the base of the dressing. Put the pan on the hob, pour in the olive dressing and place over a moderate heat, stirring as you go, until the roasting juices have dissolved into the dressing.

Slice the pork thinly. Divide the rocket between 4 plates, then add the slices of pork. Spoon over the warm olive dressing and serve.

Enough for 4

There is a bowl of cooked lentils in the fridge. Boiled last night and tossed with olive oil to stop them sticking together, they need using. I soften a little onion in some rapeseed oil over a moderate heat, toss in 4 rashers of bacon, cut into short strips, then toss with the lentils and a dressing made from rapeseed oil, Dijon mustard, red wine vinegar and chopped parsley. A cheap and hearty little dinner.

## Another main-course salad

### Roast lamb and tomato salad

| | |
|---|---|
| black peppercorns: a tablespoon | *For the dressing:* |
| sea salt flakes: half a tablespoon | grain mustard: 1 tablespoon |
| lamb fillets: 2 medium | the juice of half a lemon |
| olive oil | mint leaves: about 20, finely |
| tomatoes: 4–6 medium-sized, | chopped |
| perfectly ripe | egg yolks: 2 |
| a lemon, to serve | olive oil: 4–5 tablespoons |

Set the oven at 220°C/Gas 7. Roughly crush the peppercorns using a pestle and mortar and mix them with the salt. Rub the lamb with a little olive oil, then roll it in the seasoning, pressing down so that most of the salt and pepper sticks to the meat.

Warm 2 tablespoons of olive oil in a roasting tin till it starts to sizzle. Brown the meat quickly on all sides, then transfer to the oven and roast for ten minutes only. Remove from the oven and leave to rest for five minutes.

To make the dressing, put the mustard, lemon juice, finely chopped mint and egg yolks in a blender and whiz for a few seconds. Pour in the oil slowly, stopping when you have a dressing the consistency of double cream.

Slice the tomatoes and divide between 4 plates, then slice the lamb quite thinly and place over the tomatoes. Spoon over the dressing and pass round halves of lemon for squeezing.

Enough for 4

## SEPTEMBER 29

# A simple sole

I come home from the shops with four neat fillets of lemon sole. I had no intention of buying sole, they just grabbed me when I tried to walk past the fish shop. Sparkling fresh, slippery as a bar of wet soap. This is the fish that has very slimy, rust-brown skin speckled with pink and coral. I particularly like the sweetness of its white flesh and the fact that it is in relatively good supply. I grate the zest of a small lime into about 50g of butter, mash in the juice (easiest to do when the butter isn't too cold), then fry the fillets in a little oil in a non-stick pan. The fish is turned just once, some of it breaks up a little (this fish is so fragile), then I serve it with the lime butter melted on top. On the side, frozen peas.

## SEPTEMBER 30

A slightly lazy meal tonight, comprising some rice I cooked for lunch, thrown into a pan in which I first softened 4 chopped spring onions in a thin film of oil with a spoonful of shop-bought red curry paste. A head of broccoli, snapped into florets, then a quick fry before chucking in the rice. A seasoning of fish sauce and a scattering of basil leaves and that was it. A one-pan, rice-based broccoli main course.

October

## Oxtail another way

The flesh on an oxtail is sinewy, a delectable road map of bone, cartilage, connective tissue and fat. Slow cooking is the only way to go. Liquid of some sort is essential: red wine, stock or cider is ideal. Water will do. As the oxtail cooks, the fat and gelatine melt, enriching rather than thickening the cooking liquor. The fat is almost the whole point of oxtail to me, and I would never dream of discarding it, but if you prefer not to eat it you can leave the finished dish overnight in the fridge and scrape the solidified fat from the surface the next day. It will peel away easily in large, thin pieces.

You need a good kilo and a half of oxtail for four people, and your tail is most likely to come ready cut, in pieces that descend in size. Those nearer the body will be meatier, but the smaller end pieces have much to contribute to the overall dish, even if they are frustrating and somewhat fruitless to deal with on the plate. Some people find that cooked oxtail can be less than attractive in colour, and the cooking liquid more grey than brown. The way to prevent this is to bring the pieces to the boil in a pan of water, then skim off the fat that rises to the surface, before draining and rinsing. I can't honestly say I have ever had a problem with this, but this may be due to the onions, wine and stock I often cook it with. A plainer dish of tail cooked with water and carrots, especially if the meat is not browned first, may benefit from this treatment.

My early recipes for this cut used onions, bay leaves, red wine and occasionally orange peel, rosemary and garlic. A more recent and highly successful interpretation involved cooking the meat with sliced onions till they were golden and sweet, the juices enriched with grain mustard and cream. This winter, a new version has been simmering away, its juices given a sharp kick up the backside with tamarind. Available at wholefood shops, Indian and Chinese grocer's and many supermarkets, tamarind paste comes either in a solid and sinister-looking block of paste and seeds or as a more user-friendly, slightly tamer paste in a jar. Either way, it adds the sort of welcome sourness that any fatty meat will appreciate.

In step with many of the slower-cooked recipes, anything with an oxtail is better for a night in the fridge. Let it cool thoroughly first (I often speed up the process by leaving the pan half way up to its rim in a sink of cold

water). Then leave it to gather its thoughts in the fridge for a good eight hours. Like a curry eaten the day after it is made, the flavours will be richer, deeper and more intriguing. Some of this is down to the flavourings having time to marry and merge, some of it is sheer magic, and nothing at all to do with the cook.

## Slow-cooked oxtail with five-spice and tamarind

Good though this is on the day it is made, the sauce is even better after a night in the fridge.

A note about the tamarind. I use the block tamarind, complete with seeds. Simply put it in a small bowl, pour over enough boiling water just to cover it, then leave for ten minutes or until cool enough to handle. Pour the mixture through a sieve, pushing the solids through so that only the large seeds remain. Discard them. Stir the resulting liquid into the onions. If you have ready-to-use tamarind paste, then start with 2 tablespoons and increase to taste.

| | |
|---|---|
| large, meaty oxtail: 1kg | star anise: 3 |
| butter: 40g | beef stock: 1 litre |
| onions: 3 | soft brown or palm sugar: |
| rapeseed oil: 2 tablespoons | 1 heaped tablespoon |
| fresh ginger: a thumb-sized lump | dark soy sauce: 25ml |
| garlic: 4 cloves | tamarind paste: about 50g, |
| Chinese five-spice powder: | to taste |
| 1 tablespoon | |

Set the oven at 160°C/Gas 3. Season the oxtail with salt and pepper. Melt the butter in a heavy-based casserole, brown the meat in it on both sides and then remove from the pan. Pour in 250ml water, bring to the boil, then pour into a bowl and reserve. Peel and thickly slice the onions. Heat the rapeseed oil in the casserole, add the onions and let them cook over a low heat. Meanwhile, peel and finely shred the ginger and add to the onions. Peel the garlic, halve each clove lengthways and add to the onions, together with the five-spice powder, whole anise, stock, sugar, soy, tamarind paste and the reserved pan liquid. Bring to the boil.

Add the browned oxtail and any liquid from it (there won't be much, if any), cover with a lid or foil and bake in the preheated oven for a good two and a half hours. Once during cooking, turn the oxtail pieces over in the liquid. Check the tenderness of the meat; it should come easily away from the bone. If not, bake for longer. Adjust the seasoning and serve.

Enough for 3

## Poached pears with cream cheese and ginger sundae

water: 500ml
caster sugar: 100g
vanilla pod: 1
orange zest: a curl or two
cloves: 4
pears: 6
a lemon, halved

*For the sundae:*
full-fat cream cheese: 200g
icing sugar: 2 tablespoons
double cream: 3 tablespoons
vanilla extract: 1 capful
ginger biscuits, soft and crumbly:
   200g
dark chocolate: 50g

Put the water and sugar into a saucepan and bring to the boil. Add the vanilla pod, orange zest and cloves and simmer over a low heat. Meanwhile, peel the pears and rub them with the lemon halves to stop any discoloration. Cut them in half and remove the cores and seeds. Place the pear halves in the syrup, squeeze in the remaining lemon juice and cook for twenty minutes or so, until tender. Leave the pears to cool in the syrup.

Put the cream cheese in a mixing bowl, add the icing sugar and beat lightly, folding in the cream and vanilla as you go. Crush the biscuits lightly and fold them into the cheesecake cream. Take care not to over mix.

Halve or quarter the pears, depending on size, and divide them between 6 dishes. Add dollops of the cream cheese mixture and grate over the chocolate.

Enough for 6

# Tomatoes, spices, coconut
# (shouldn't work but it does)

### Baked tomatoes

If you cannot find small cans of creamed coconut, then break off 100g of coconut cream, crumble it and make up to 160ml with boiling water, stirring to a thick cream.

groundnut oil: 1 tablespoon
mustard seeds: 1 teaspoon
onions: 2, finely chopped
garlic: 3 cloves
fresh ginger: a 3cm piece
chilli: a medium-hot red one

red or orange peppers: 2
ground turmeric: 1 teaspoon
cherry tomatoes: 8, halved
large plum or vine tomatoes: 8
creamed coconut: 160ml

Heat the oil in a pan, add the mustard seeds and cook until they pop. Add the onions and leave to soften and colour while you peel and slice the garlic, peel and finely shred the ginger and chop the chilli. Add the garlic, ginger and chilli to the pan and continue cooking till the onions are pale golden brown. Core and thinly slice the peppers and stir them in. Continue cooking over a moderate heat, with the occasional stir, till the peppers start to soften, then stir in the ground turmeric and the halved cherry tomatoes.

Set the oven at 200°C/Gas 6. Remove a slice from one side of each large tomato (or the top if you are using large vine tomatoes), then scoop out the seeds and core to give a deep hollow. Chop the filling you have removed, discarding any tough cores, and add to the pan. When the mixture has cooked down to a soft, brightly coloured mush, pour in the creamed coconut. Bring to the boil, season with salt, then remove from the heat.

Fill the hollowed-out tomatoes with the mixture, spooning any extra around them. Bake for forty minutes, until the tomatoes are soft and fragrant.

Enough for 4

## OCTOBER 8

## The baking sheet

The baking sheet, a rectangle of black steel that should last a lifetime, has been part of this kitchen for as long as I can remember. Strangely, it is considered more of a chef's thing than a piece of equipment found in a home kitchen, though I am at a loss to know why. From scones to bacon, the flat steel sheet with a fine, shallow rim is as essential as a roasting tin or a colander.

The problem with baking sheets is that they buckle. Even the best will suddenly develop a kink that stops them having a totally flat surface, rendering them almost useless for a quiche or lemon tart, or anything that has a liquid filling that reaches the brim. Other than that, a buckled tray is no less useful than a flat one.

Contemporary versions tend to come with integral handles, though I am not sure why, and often with a non-stick surface. My own preference is for a black steel sheet that has been seasoned. By seasoned, I mean cooked in over a period of months without being scrubbed, so that a patina builds up on the surface. A homemade non-stick coating, if you like.

You can speed up the process by rubbing the surface with olive or rape-seed oil and baking it several times over, till it smokes and stains. The less you wash it the better. A gentle wipe with a damp cloth followed by a dry one is best. Should it find its way into the dishwasher, it will almost certainly rust.

If you store your baking sheets on their side, any liquid left on the surface will slide off and not form rust pools. Of course you can just buy a non-stick sheet, but they have no character, and will eventually scratch, scuff and find their way into landfill. The old baking sheet did its stuff tonight, once again as a base for a simple, gorgeous savoury tart.

## Warm aubergine tarts

You can use puff pastry for these tarts if you wish, scattered with grated Parmesan just before baking, but the handmade pastry – like a very cheesy biscuit – works even better. It doesn't take long to make. If capers aren't your thing, then a few sliced olives – purple or green – might be an interesting substitute.

aubergine: 600g
a large onion
garlic: 2 cloves
olive oil: 10 tablespoons
thyme: 4 sprigs
anchovy fillets: 16
a teaspoon of capers,
    or a few olives

*For the pastry:*
butter: 80g, cut into cubes
self-raising flour: 120g
mature Cheddar, grated: 40g
Parmesan, finely grated: 50g
an egg yolk
milk: 1 tablespoon

Set the oven at 200°C/Gas 6. Cut the aubergine into cubes of roughly 2cm, then place in a large roasting tin or baking dish in a single layer. Peel and finely slice the onion. Remove the skin from the garlic, finely crush the cloves to a paste and add to the aubergine with the onion. Pour over a good 6 tablespoons of the olive oil, then pull the leaves from the thyme sprigs and add them to the aubergine with a generous grinding of salt and pepper. Toss till lightly coated in the oil and seasonings. Bake for an hour or so, tossing once or twice during cooking, until the aubergine is soft enough to crush with a fork.

Whilst the aubergine is baking, make the pastry. Rub the butter into the flour with your fingertips until the mixture resembles fresh breadcrumbs, then add the grated cheeses, egg yolk and milk. Bring the mixture together to form a ball, then knead lightly for a minute – no longer. Wrap in grease-proof paper or cling film and leave in the fridge to rest for twenty minutes.

Cut the pastry into eight equal pieces and roll each into a thin rectangle measuring roughly 12cm x 10cm. Transfer to a baking sheet and bake at 200°C/Gas 6 for about ten minutes, till pale golden and lightly crisp.

Remove the aubergine from the oven as soon as it is tender. Reserve about a quarter of the mixture, then put the rest in a food processor and blend to a stiff paste. Pour in the remaining 4 tablespoons of oil and blend again till smooth and spreadably soft. Spread the puréed aubergine over the pastry, then top with the reserved aubergines and some capers or olives. Criss-cross each tart with 2 anchovies.

Makes 8

# Grilled figs with Marsala

I like this made with small, intensely sweet black figs. If you have any other sort, they may need a little longer under the grill, or may be better baked. The recipe, incidentally, will also work with very ripe plums.

ripe figs: 10  dry Marsala: 125ml
thick honey: 2 tablespoons

Heat an overhead grill. Wipe the figs tenderly and cut them in half. Place them, cut-side up and in a single layer, in a baking dish or roasting tin.

Warm the honey and Marsala in a pan, stirring until the honey has melted, then pour it over the figs. Grill for ten minutes or so, until the figs are dark and soft, basting them from time to time with the juices to keep them moist. Leave the figs to calm down for ten minutes before serving. During this time the juices will thicken very slightly.

Serve the figs, spooning the juices over as you go.

Enough for 4

# Another quick curry

Tonight I knock up the quickest curry ever. Mild, sumptuous, a doddle. Serve with rice or with Indian bread that you have warmed under the grill. Tamarind paste is available in Indian and Southeast Asian shops and in major supermarkets, usually near the fish sauce.

## A mild and fruity curry of salmon

I serve this with a spoon, so as not to waste a drop of the gently spiced juices.

salmon fillet: 500g, skinned
a large onion
groundnut oil: 2 tablespoons
small, hot chillies: 2, finely
  chopped
mustard seeds: half a teaspoon

ground turmeric: half a teaspoon
ground cumin: a teaspoon
ground coriander: a teaspoon
tomatoes: 6 fairly large ones
tamarind paste: a tablespoon
coconut milk: 200ml

Cut the salmon into about 20 thick cubes. Peel the onion and chop it finely, then let it soften in the oil in a deep, non-stick pan. When it has started to colour lightly, add the chillies, mustard seeds, turmeric, cumin and coriander and stir for a minute or so till the spices are warm and fragrant. Chop the tomatoes, add them to the pan and leave to soften for a minute or two. Stir in the tamarind paste.

Bring to the boil, then turn down to a simmer and cook for ten minutes. Add the pieces of salmon and some salt and black pepper. Now leave to cook for ten to fifteen minutes, until the salmon is completely opaque. Pour in the coconut milk and simmer for a further four or five minutes.

Enough for 4

# Light lunch

### Courgette and ricotta tart

| | |
|---|---|
| courgettes: 400g | basil leaves: 15g |
| olive oil: 2 tablespoons | plain flour: 2 heaped tablespoons |
| puff pastry: 375g | eggs: 2, lightly beaten |
| ricotta: 400g | double cream: 150ml |
| garlic: a large clove | Parmesan, finely grated : 75g |

You will need a rectangular baking tin (a Swiss roll tin) measuring approximately 30cm x 20cm.

Cut the courgettes in half lengthways (or in thin slices if you are using large ones). Warm the olive oil in a shallow pan, add the courgettes and leave to soften over a moderate heat. They should be translucent but still firm.

Set the oven at 200°C/Gas 6 and place a baking sheet in it. This will help the pastry to bake crisply. Roll out the puff pastry and line the tin with it. Put the ricotta in a bowl and season with salt and black pepper. Peel and crush the garlic and add it to the ricotta together with the torn-up basil leaves, flour, eggs, cream and most of the grated Parmesan.

Spread the ricotta mixture over the pastry, then place the courgettes on top. Shake over the remaining Parmesan. Bake for thirty minutes or until the pastry is golden and the tart has puffed up.

Enough for 6

## OCTOBER 15

### Five-spice squid

I used small, whole frozen squid for this but you could use larger ones, sliced into manageable pieces. To make the seafood go further, include shredded greens such as long-stemmed broccoli.

small squid: 800g
(prepared weight)
garlic: 2 cloves
small, ripe chillies: 4
Chinese five-spice powder:
4 lightly heaped teaspoons
black peppercorns: 16

sea salt: a lightly heaped teaspoon
groundnut or rapeseed oil:
3 tablespoons
sesame oil: a few drops
coriander: a small bunch
a lime

Check the squid and tentacles, making sure they are completely clean. Peel and finely chop the garlic and put it in a mixing bowl. Halve, seed and finely slice the chillies and add to the garlic. Put the five-spice powder into the bowl, then coarsely crush the peppercorns and add them too, with the salt.

Heat the oil in a wok. Pat the squid dry. When the oil is hot – it should be just starting to shimmer, but not yet smoking – drop the squid first into the spice mixture, patting it on firmly and turning to coat lightly, then into the oil. Fry, tossing almost continuously, for two or three minutes, till the squid is opaque. Shake over a few drops of sesame oil. Chop the coriander leaves and toss briefly with the squid, till the coriander wilts and darkens slightly. Serve immediately, with halves of lime for squeezing.

Enough for 4

## OCTOBER 16

Raking the leaves up from the garden paths, picking the Autumn Bliss raspberries that are still going strong, and tidying up the pots that contain the remains of the courgette plants. A nip in the air and it's a definite carb moment. Supper is baked potatoes, salt-crusted by rolling the damp, freshly rinsed potatoes in sea salt flakes, baked till their skins crisp, then split open and stuffed with smashed smoked mackerel and chopped dill. A dollop of soured cream and that is a quietly splendid evening meal.


## OCTOBER 18

# A favourite pasta

Pasta in all its forms – tubes, ribbons, curls, shells and chubby little gnocchi – has been part of my cooking since I was in my late teens. I was in at the beginning, and have watched how spaghetti, at first in long blue paper, became popular in the 1960s, followed by ravioli, albeit in a can. As each form took its place on the supper stage, nib-shaped penne, ribbons of tagliatelle, then shells and the ridiculous bows that look so absurd in the bowl, I followed.

Pasta recipes have all had their fifteen minutes of fame: first, long noodles in tomato sauce, then tiny curls in claggy cheese sauce, then sheets of green or white lasagne with layers of minced meat and a seasoned white sauce, and penne or fettuccine in pesto. The basil and garlic notes of the latter aside, the usual rule was that the dough came with some form of tomato, either as a creamy sauce, a rough, onion-based mixture or just a ghostly presence, as in a ragu sauce with a helping of cheese.

It took forty years of cooking and eating pasta before it dawned on me that I prefer it without the knee-jerk accompaniment of tomato and the ever-present cheese. Now, still part of my cooking, pasta has a less frequent but more interesting place: broken into pieces in bean-speckled soups, formed into plump cushions tossed with melted butter and crumbled cheese, or twinkling like tiny stars and rice-like grains in clear, shimmering soups. It comes stuffed with shredded meat and minced chicken, with sweet white ricotta, aubergine or spinach, and the ribbons now turn up gently bathed rather than drowned in sauce.

Twenty-first-century pasta, in my kitchen at least, comes in less gut-pounding portions too, with simpler sauces, more imaginative accompaniments, and virtually never with tomato. If I had to put my finger on my favourite, it would be orzo, sometimes called riso, the plump, rice-shaped grains that are as much at home in Greece, where they are known as *krithurárki* or *manéstra*, as they are in Italy. Known, delightfully, as *sehriye* – songbird tongues – in Turkey, they are found in slightly differing sizes, but my own preference is for the plumper ones that resemble melon seeds or flattened pine kernels more than they do grains of rice or barley. Historically made from barley, whose shape it echoes, this is thought of as a soup pasta, but I also like using it to soak up the cooking juices from a roast or braised meat dish, stirred in a pilaf or added to the sauce of a recipe for polpettini or meatballs.

This evening, with a cool wind stirring the remaining leaves of the robinia tree in the garden, I toss my favourite pasta shape with fried courgettes, golden onion and coarsely grated Grana Padano, the mild and nutty cheese that is too often thought of as poor man's Parmesan. It is no such thing.

## Orzo with courgettes and Grana Padano

Here, the grains are held together with grated cheese. I have suggested the mild and nutty Grana Padano for a change. Use Parmesan if you can't track it down.

| | |
|---|---|
| orzo: 300g | white wine: 250ml |
| pancetta, in the piece: 150g | courgettes: 4 medium |
| a large onion | Grana Padano or Parmesan, very |
| olive oil: 2 tablespoons | coarsely grated: 50g |

Bring a deep pan of water to the boil, salt generously, then add the orzo and boil for nine minutes or till it is approaching softness. It should retain a certain bite. Drain.

Cut the pancetta into large dice. Peel and chop the onion. Fry it with the pancetta in the olive oil in a shallow, heavy-based pan over a moderate heat for fifteen minutes, stirring regularly, till the onion is soft and translucent and the fat on the pancetta is pale amber.

Pour in the wine, turn up the heat slightly, then bubble till reduced by half. Cut the courgettes lengthways, then into thick slices, and add to the

pan. Season with salt and black pepper and continue cooking for eight to ten minutes, until the courgettes are tender. Stir in the drained orzo and the Grana Padano or Parmesan. The cheese should melt slightly, bringing the whole dish together.

Enough for 4

## OCTOBER 19

## Making a pizza dough

I like kneading dough, not in an anger-management kind of way but as a moment or two of relative peace and calm. Ten minutes spent deeply connected with my food, feeling the tight mix of flour, yeast, salt and water slowly relax in my hands. I still rate making dough as one of the most pleasing jobs the kitchen has to offer.

That said, I knead pizza dough for less time than I used to. The original fifteen minutes has now become more like ten – by which I probably mean about six or seven. Not out of sloth, but because I find the results much the same no matter how long I roll and fold and push and pull. The more often you knead, the more you realise that the clock has little to do with it. The dough will tell you when it is ready by the way it feels in your hands. It should feel as if something is going on, as if it is coming to life. Which of course it is.

I should probably invest in a proper pizza stone to provide the extra heat the soft dough needs to grow up to be a crisp crust, but the large tile I found in the back garden a few years ago soldiers on, providing a reasonable substitute. Not that cooking dough on a stone is ever going to be as good as baking it in a stone oven but we domestic cooks must do what we can. Of course, you can bake it on a metal sheet but a stone will give a crisper result. It is not just about the extra heat a solid pizza stone is capable of harnessing but also about its porous quality, which helps to ensure your pizza gets a crisp bottom.

This time, I avoided the mixture of tomato and melted cheese that seems to guarantee all pizza toppings taste the same whatever else you choose to add. In fact, there wasn't a tomato in sight until I had a go at calzone on Tuesday night (pizza is a Saturday thing in our house, part of the increasingly laidback lunch). The tomato gloop was replaced by a mixture of traditional mozzarella and decidedly non-traditional crème fraîche. The savoury quotient came from small mushrooms, peeled whole garlic cloves and a little Parmesan.

I have used both fontina and Taleggio on pizza before now and have been happy with the result. The cheese gets so little time in the oven that its qualities remain pretty much intact. I have tried pizza dough at every temperature short of the one on the mega-hot self-cleaning setting and it is always the case of the more the merrier. I now go as high as 250°C/Gas 10 and leave them in for barely ten minutes.

| | |
|---|---|
| *For the dough:* | a pinch of sugar |
| strong white bread flour: 500g | fine sea salt: a teaspoon |
| dried yeast: a 7g sachet | warm water: 325–350ml |

Tip the flour into a large mixing bowl. Pour in the dried yeast, sugar, salt and water and mix to a smooth dough. It should be slightly sticky, so add as much of the water as you need. Tip out on to a floured board and knead until the dough is no longer sticky.

Place the ball of dough in a floured bowl, cover with a clean damp tea towel and leave in a warm place for an hour or until it has risen to twice its size.

Turn the dough out and press it down with your fist. It is now ready to roll out and cover with your toppings.

Enough for 2 very large or 4 medium pizzas

## Mushroom with crème fraîche and mozzarella pizza

| | |
|---|---|
| chestnut mushrooms: 175g | crème fraîche: 2 generously |
| butter: a thick slice | heaped tablespoons |
| garlic: 4 cloves | mozzarella: 100g, cut into cubes |
| thyme: a few small sprigs | grated Parmesan |
| half the quantity of dough above | |

Set the oven at 250°C/Gas 10 and place either a pizza stone or a baking sheet in there to get hot. Wipe the mushrooms and cut each into four or five thickish slices. Melt the butter in a shallow pan, add the mushrooms and let them colour over a moderate heat. Peel the garlic cloves, add them, with a few pinches of thyme leaves, to the mushrooms and cook for a couple of minutes.

Roll out the dough. I tend to make one large pizza because I have only one pizza stone, but this quantity of dough will make two smaller ones if you prefer. Put the cooked mushrooms, garlic and a few sprigs of thyme on top of the dough, leaving a small rim of uncovered dough around the edge. Spoon on the crème fraîche, then dot pieces of mozzarella over that. Shake over a little grated Parmesan (not traditional, but wonderful in this context), then slide the pizza on to the hot pizza stone or baking tray. The easiest way to do this is to slide the base of a removable cake tin under the pizza and lift and slide it on to the baking stone or hot tin. Bake for about ten minutes, until the dough is crisp and risen and the cheese has melted but not coloured. Leave for a minute to settle down, then cut into wedges and eat.

Makes 1 large or 2 smaller pizzas

## OCTOBER 20

## A tin for a sweet tart

Made of aluminium, my tart tin is not a perfect thing. Blueberries leave an indelible stain; rhubarb leaks acidic pink juice through the holes in the base; damsons did it no favours; yet my tart tin has changed the way I bake.

The case is thin, so that when it is placed on a hot oven tray or a baking stone, the base of the tart crisps nicely. The holes drilled into the base help this too. The narrow rim means it is as good for a pie whose edges must be sealed as it is for an open tart. The tart tin is light (I carried it back from New York's Williams-Sonoma in my hand luggage) and the size is perfect for four to six, depending on the filling.

What separates this from the straight-sided French-style tart tin is the homely appearance of everything baked in it. This is the sort of tin the Amish might use for a blueberry tart or a shoo-fly pie. The nearest I have found here are the good old enamel baking tins you can still see in old-fashioned ironmonger's. They have a proper rim for a crusty edge and no holes for the juice to leak through. A wobbly blue line edges the dish, framing a blackberry and apple or blueberry tart.

This is the tin I use for a simple pear tart. No top crust or almond-based filling. No jam or jelly. No crumb crust. Just a pure tart of sweet pastry and chopped pears. The pears are twice cooked and soft as butter. The pastry is crisp at the edges and robust enough to hold a spoonful or two of juice that may escape from the pears as they bake.

# A simple pear tart

*For the pastry:*
butter: 75g
golden caster sugar: 75g
an egg yolk
plain flour: 150g
a little milk

*For the filling:*
small, ripe pears: 1kg
butter: 15g
light muscovado sugar: 3 lightly
    heaped tablespoons

You will need a traditional rimmed pie plate for this, about 18cm across the base, 24cm across the top.

Make the pastry. Cut the butter into small dice and put it into a food mixer. Add the sugar and beat for at least five minutes to give a smooth, thick cream. On a low speed, add the egg yolk, then the plain flour. Bring it to a soft, rollable ball with a couple of tablespoons of milk.

Turn the dough out on to a generously floured board. Knead softly for a minute or two to make it easier to work, then roll it out into a disc large enough to line your pie plate. With the help of a rolling pin, lift the pastry on to the pie plate and press it carefully into shape. Trim the overhanging edges and patch up any holes. Refrigerate for thirty minutes. It is important not to miss this essential resting of the pastry, so don't. Otherwise your tart will shrink in the oven.

Set the oven at 180°C/Gas 4. Place a baking sheet in the oven. It will help to cook the pastry on the bottom of the tart. Cut the pears into quarters, peeling them if their skin is coarse, then remove their cores and slice each piece of pear into 1cm-wide chunks. Melt the butter in a pan and add the pears to it, then the sugar. Leave them to cook for a good ten minutes until the fruit becomes translucent. As a test to see if they are ready, the pears should effortlessly take the point of a knife (if you undercook them, they won't be soft enough in the finished tart).

Use a draining spoon to lift the pears from the pan into the chilled tart shell. Boil any juices remaining in the pan over a fierce heat until you have a few tablespoons left, then spoon them over the pears. Bake for approximately forty minutes, till the pastry crust is golden brown at the edges and the pears have coloured lightly here and there.

Enough for 4

## Some herbs and a rabbit, and a crumble

I have been seriously considering growing more herbs. My problem is that the soil in this little garden is too rich. A decade of breaking down the 'good old London clay' with organic matter has made it a happier place for vegetables to grow but rendered it too rich for most herbs – especially those tough-stemmed varieties such as thyme that need good drainage if they are not to rot from the roots up.

I have a good, hot, sunny bed whose aspect is ideal, but in order to have the fine tilth and good drainage on which herbs thrive, I would need to lift the soil from the entire bed and replace it with something very different, a mixture light and full of grit. A Herculean task. So the herbs remain in pots, mostly of reclaimed terracotta, running down the back steps on to the stone terrace, each with a soil of their own. The downside is that they dry out quickly in hot, windy weather and there is too little protection for their roots during severe frosts. I have lost more thyme, chervil and tarragon than I care to remember. When any of these are planted in the rose bed, which contains a fairly light but dry soil, they get to live another day.

Yes, of course I grow them to use in the kitchen, to perfume and flavour my cooking, but I grow them too for their leaf form, the lace-like fronds of chervil, for the scent of their leaves, the piercing lemon-lime hit of verbena and the weirdly captivating smell of rue. For their flowers, particularly the Ascot hat of the red bergamot and the deep purple and yellow petals of the viola. For their folklore especially.

The garden wouldn't be the same without the cheerful orange of the pot marigold or the tiny, pale-blue flowers of rosemary Sissinghurst. My garden would seem out of kilter with no majestic angelica or diminutive, laughing-faced heartsease. And no garden of mine could ever be without the rambling nasturtium – hardly a herb, but it peppers a salad.

Possibly the main reason for planting herbs in my garden is simply to run my fingers through their leaves as I pass. A midnight walk up the garden path touching the oregano, the thyme, the golden marjoram, the sage, the verveine and the rue. There are herbs I don't grow. The nasty curry plant, the capricious sorrel, the sulky lavender (I long ago gave up on them, managing to kill every plant I have owned). Not to mention the wacky herbs such as mint that smells of pineapple or thyme that tastes of chocolate. What interest me are the herbs that smell the same as they did in medieval times, whose flavours and scents are truly timeless.

At the end of each summer, once the nights start to smell of wood smoke and there is a warning of frost on the weather forecast, I try to use up as many of the soft herbs as I can, those that are unlikely to make it through the winter. A recipe may even include three or four, despite my normal preference for keeping things simple. There is rabbit tonight, a whole one jointed by the butcher into neat pieces. It seems a sensible way to use up the tarragon but also some rosemary prunings. The result is a tasty little casserole that would be rather good with chicken, if you don't fancy rabbit.

### A slow-cooked rabbit with herbs

| | |
|---|---|
| onions: 2 | thyme: 4 sprigs |
| butter: a thick slice | wheat beer: 1 litre |
| rabbit: 500g (1 rabbit, jointed) | double cream: 150ml |
| rosemary: 2 bushy sprigs | tarragon: 4 lush sprigs |

Peel the onions, roughly chop them, then soften them in the butter over a moderate heat till they are translucent and pale gold. Season the pieces of rabbit all over with salt and black pepper. Remove the onions, either to one side of the pan if there is room, or to a bowl if not. Add the rabbit pieces to the pan and let them brown appetisingly for five minutes, turning as necessary. Mix the onions in.

Add the rosemary needles, minus their stems, together with the thyme sprigs, wheat beer and some salt and pepper. Bring to the boil, then lower the heat so the liquid continues cooking at a low simmer and cover partially with a lid. Leave to putter away on the stove for a couple of hours, till the rabbit is tender. The exact timing will depend on the age and provenance of your rabbit, but it is ready to serve when you can remove the flesh from the bones with a decent table knife. The liquid in the pan will still be quite thin and plentiful, so turn up the heat for a few minutes and let it reduce by about half (this is not a thick sauce, and will always be the sort to eat with a spoon).

Pour in the cream and stir in the leaves from the tarragon, chopped if they are very long. Continue simmering for five to ten minutes, then check the seasoning and serve.

Enough for 2

# Pear and chocolate oat crumble

If you prefer, make this in individual dishes.

large, ripe pears: 4
half a lemon
butter: 30g
golden caster sugar: 50g

*For the crumble:*
butter: 85g
plain flour: 80g
demerara sugar: 80g
jumbo oats: 3 tablespoons
dark chocolate (80 per cent
  cocoa solids): 70g

Set the oven at 180°C/Gas 4. Peel the pears, rubbing each one with the lemon half to stop it discolouring, then cut them in half and discard the stalk. Scoop out the core with a teaspoon.

Melt the butter in a shallow pan. As it starts to sizzle, tip in the peeled and halved pears and the sugar and let the fruit colour lightly. As the pears soften, let the sugar caramelise here and there, leaving them patchily golden. Tip the pears and their sweet, buttery juices into a 1.5 litre baking dish.

Make the crumble by rubbing the butter into the flour with your finger-tips or using a food processor. When the mixture looks like fine breadcrumbs, stir in the demerara sugar and jumbo oats. Add a tablespoon of water and shake the crumble mixture till some of it sticks together in gravel-sized lumps. Chop the chocolate into small pieces, about the size of coarse gravel, then fold it through the crumble.

Tip the mixture over the pears, leaving the surface quite rough and making no attempt to pack it down. Bake for forty-five minutes, till lightly coloured.

Enough for 4

## Lamb 'osso buco' with parsley pappardelle

One of those dinners that look as if they've taken forever but are in fact very quick. Ask your butcher for lamb leg steaks with the bone in. If you have no luck, then use a thick chump chop, bone in.

olive oil: 2 tablespoons
leg of lamb steaks, bone in:
    4 (about 1kg in total)
a large onion
celery: 2 ribs
large carrots: 2

Marsala: 250ml
pappardelle: 250g
parsley, finely chopped:
    4 tablespoons
butter: 50g

Heat the olive oil in a large shallow pan, then brown the lamb steaks on both sides. Remove to a plate. Chop the onion, celery and carrots into roughly 1cm cubes and add to the pan in which you browned the meat. Cook over a moderate heat for at least fifteen minutes, stirring occasionally, till they are nicely coloured and approaching softness. Return the lamb to the pan, add the Marsala, season and bring to the boil. Lower the heat and continue cooking, covered with a lid, for thirty to forty minutes, till the lamb is tender.

Cook the pappardelle in plenty of generously salted water till al dente, then drain. Remove the lamb and vegetables from the pan, dividing them between 4 warm plates. Add the pasta and parsley to the lamb cooking pan together with the butter and a grinding of black pepper. Let the pasta warm through in the butter and pan juices, then serve with the lamb steaks and vegetables.

Enough for 4

## OCTOBER 26

# Toasting nuts

In Nishiki market in downtown Kyoto, they have a stall that roasts chestnuts the size of cobbles. An exaggeration, but they are quite the plumpest chestnuts I have ever seen, perhaps more like the size of a baby's clenched fist. The smell wafts through the market, reminiscent of a London street on an October day when one of the last few chestnut roasters is out.

I take shortcuts in the kitchen, though fewer than I might, but some things are worth every moment of our time. Roasting nuts is one of them. The difference in flavour between an almond, hazelnut or chestnut that has been roasted and one that hasn't is extraordinary. The smell alone is probably worth it, but the effect is most noticeable once the nuts are mixed with sugar, as in a praline, or when chocolate becomes involved. If you need to put it to the test, toast a handful of almonds in a shallow pan, no oil required, then bury them in melted chocolate. Now do the same with untoasted nuts and compare.

The most successful way to toast a nut is to put it, shelled and skinned, in a frying pan over a moderately hot flame. Let the nuts toast for five minutes or so, shaking the pan regularly, so they colour evenly. Once they are a pale hazelnut brown, tip them out of the pan so they cool without further cooking. You can grill them if you prefer, letting them colour lightly under an overhead grill.

Nuts burn in a heartbeat. The oil that makes up so much of the nut has a very low smoke point, which is why nut oils such as walnut and hazelnut tend to be used in salads rather than for cooking. Once they are burned, they will turn bitter. A warm honey brown is what we should be after.

With the new season's nuts on their way, I will be popping them into lettuce salads and scattering them over cheese. A current favourite is to shave pieces of Beaufort or other firm handmade cheese and toss them with toasted walnuts, very finely shredded cabbage and sliced pears with their russet skin intact. A dressing of walnut oil, Dijon mustard and a little cream. Some toasted brown croûtons scattered over the top complete the dish.

First, dinner. Basil leaves, a good couple of handfuls, a clove of garlic, a teaspoon of Dijon mustard, a couple of tablespoons of white wine vinegar, a teaspoon of capers, blitzed with enough olive oil to make a thick pouring consistency. Stir in 2 or 3 tablespoons of cream and some salt and pepper, then toss with a bowl of cooked cappelletti. Pine kernels, toasted in a non-stick pan, get chucked over after the pasta and sauce have met.

# Chocolate and toasted nut tart

Rarely is the marriage of toasted nuts and chocolate demonstrated so perfectly as in this shallow tart.

*For the pastry:*
plain flour: 150g
butter: 90g, cut into small pieces
ground hazelnuts: 50g
an egg yolk
caster sugar: a tablespoon

*For the filling:*
hazelnuts: 100g
walnuts: 80g
caster sugar: 75g
fine dark chocolate: 250g
butter: 40g
espresso coffee: 25ml
eggs: 4

For the pastry: put the flour and butter into a food processor, add a pinch of salt and blitz to coarse breadcrumbs (or if you prefer, rub the butter into the flour with your fingertips). Add the ground hazelnuts, egg yolk, sugar and enough water to bring the dough to a firm ball. The less water you add the better, as too much will cause your pastry case to shrink in the oven.

Turn the pastry out on to a heavily floured board and knead very lightly. Pat into a flat round, then roll out to a circle large enough to line a 24cm tart tin that is at least 3.5cm deep. Push the dough right into the corner where the rim joins the base, without stretching it. The pastry is rich and very fragile, so push it into place, patching up any holes as you go. Trim the overhanging pastry and then place in the fridge to chill for twenty minutes.

Set the oven at 200°C/Gas 6. Put a baking sheet in the oven to heat up. Line the pastry case with kitchen foil, fill with baking beans and slide it on to the hot baking sheet. Bake for fifteen minutes, then remove from the oven and carefully lift the beans and foil out. Return the pastry case to the oven for five minutes or so, until the surface is dry to the touch. Remove from the oven and set aside.

Toast the hazelnuts and walnuts in a shallow pan till the skins have darkened. Put them in a tea towel and rub roughly till the skins flake off. Return the nuts to the pan and continue toasting until they are light brown and deeply fragrant. Put the sugar into the pan with the nuts, place it over a moderate heat and leave until the sugar starts to melt. Once the sugar turns golden, tip the mixture on to a lightly oiled baking sheet and leave to cool.

Snap the chocolate into small pieces and put it, with the butter and the coffee, in a mixing bowl. Place over a saucepan of simmering water and leave it to melt. The less you do to the chocolate the better, so avoid the temptation to stir it more than once or twice. Meanwhile, crush the sugared nuts with a knife or in a food processor – they should be a mixture of textures, from fine to coarse gravel.

Remove the melted chocolate from the heat. Separate the eggs, lightly stirring each yolk into the melted chocolate. In a large bowl, beat the whites till they are thick and fluffy. Fold the egg whites into the chocolate. This is easiest done with a large metal spoon. Make sure that you leave no bits of egg white unmixed, at the same time taking care to treat the mixture gently. Tenderly fold in the crushed nuts, trying not to knock the air out in the process.

Scoop the filling into the cooled tart case, then place in the fridge for two or three hours to set. The filling will be at its best at this time. Any further refrigeration may make the pastry damp.

Enough for 6

## OCTOBER 27

A tin of sardines, drained of their oil and dusted lightly in flour. Fried in a little fresh oil (the other stuff is way too fishy) for two minutes, then slapped between two pieces of toasted bread spread with mayonnaise, with thickly sliced cucumber.

## OCTOBER 28

A mid-autumn evening, not quite dusk, the leaves on the horse chestnuts already crisp and brown. This third quarter seems longer now than it did when I was a child, the leaves turning yellow earlier but falling later. A phenomenon that allows us to marvel at the sulphur, crimson and burnt-orange leaves just that bit longer. It may well be my imagination. Either way, my shopping is moving away from the piercing green of courgettes and beans towards brown and gold: a butternut squash, a bag of mushrooms, a dark-green cabbage.

My butcher suggests some bacon chops. I have seen boneless gammon steaks in the supermarket (a quick supper when one is too tired to do more than slap something under the grill and stir some cream and black pepper into a tin of sweetcorn). But a bacon chop with its bone is a rare sight. He has cut them from the loin so they resemble the usual chop in all but colour. I fall for them partly because of the quiet beauty of their madder-rose flesh and creamy fat but also for the idea of eating smoked meat from the bone, which is not something I can remember doing very often. A smoky bone on which to chew feels right for the day.

## Bacon chops, cabbage and apple

| | |
|---|---|
| white cabbage: 650g | thyme leaves: a teaspoon |
| an onion | rapeseed or groundnut oil |
| medium apples: 2 | bacon chops, on or off the bone: 4 |
| juniper berries: 8 | red wine vinegar: 50ml |
| sea salt: half a teaspoon | brown sugar: a tablespoon |
| black peppercorns: 6 | ground mace: a pinch |

Set the oven at 180°C/Gas 4. Shred the cabbage coarsely and rinse it well in cold water. Peel and finely slice the onion. Core the apples and cut them into thick slices.

Crush the juniper berries, salt, peppercorns and thyme leaves using a pestle and mortar. Mix in a tablespoon of oil to make a loose paste. Spread this over the surface of the bacon chops. Warm a little oil in a shallow pan, lower in the chops and let them brown very lightly. As the fat starts to colour, turn and brown the other side. Lift the chops from the pan and set aside.

Add the sliced onion and allow it to soften for a few minutes. Put the apple slices in and let them colour lightly, then add the shredded cabbage. Add the vinegar and bring briefly to the boil, then stir in the sugar and mace. Season very lightly, cover with a lid or some kitchen foil and place in the oven. Cook for twenty to twenty-five minutes or until the cabbage has started to wilt. Return the chops to the pan, tucking them amongst the cabbage and apples. Cover and return to the oven for twenty minutes or till the chops are cooked through.

Serve piping hot, perhaps with beer or cider to drink.

Enough for 4

# OCTOBER 29

A glorious autumn day, despite two heavy showers, working amongst the pots on the back steps. The tomato plants have collapsed, their stems now mostly crisped and brown, and the last few tomatoes are dotted amongst the pots, quietly rotting. I pick up most of them and hurl them into the compost. Others I slip on. Things past redemption – the cucumber, two aubergine plants and some rocket gone to seed – get pulled up, their place taken by wallflower plants the size of my middle finger.

The sun shines through the giant, yellowing fig leaves. Here and there, the strawberry leaves have turned a fiery vermilion. Yet so much is still green. There are even runner beans worth looking at. The last of the damsons are soft enough to eat raw, like plums; a few golden raspberries have escaped the inevitable October mould that happens when the autumn is a damp one; beetroots and carrots are poking their shoulders through the wet soil as if to remind me they are still around. If that wasn't enough, here and there marigolds and golden dahlias are in flower.

On the dot of four-thirty, the sun hanging low in the sky, the occasional, far-off roar of ecstasy from the local football match (we win, two nil), I have had enough. The pots are weeded, cleaned and in some cases put away for the winter. The steps are swept. The last few grapes from around the kitchen door are picked. I leave behind the smart, newly planted wallflowers and enough of a tangle of old tomato plants, sweet pea haulms and bolted marigolds to leave the garden in a state of gentle, romantic chaos.

First thing this morning, I had picked up a small, bright-orange onion squash, a can of haricot beans and a ciabatta loaf. For lunch I peel and seed the squash and steam it in a colander over boiling water. I get some butter hot in a nonstick frying pan, chop up a few rashers of smoked bacon and cook them in the butter. I tip in the squash. As it sizzles, and making sure it doesn't stick too much, I let it cook till lightly golden and starting to break up, then add the rinsed beans. A little vegetable stock, just enough to moisten rather than turn it into a soup (I just used the powdered stuff and some boiling water from the kettle), then a ten-minute simmer before spooning the sweet, smoky mess on to rounds of hot doorstep toast.

# Pork cooked with bay and milk

Some things taste better than they look. The Italian dish where pork is simmered in milk till the liquid curdles into nuggets is a case in point. The curdling comes from the long, slow cooking – barely a shudder – of the pork in its bath of milk and lemon. The flavour – mild, elusive, savoury yet sweet – comes from bay and garlic. The curdled milk forms semi-soft pebbles, which caramelise to the colour of old netsuke. A strange and delicious recipe. Just go with it.

A not too fatty cut is good here. I sometimes use shoulder and remove most, but not all, of the fat.

olive oil: 2 tablespoons
shoulder of pork, rolled and
    tied: 2kg
milk: 1 litre
garlic: 4 large cloves

butter: 40g
sage leaves: 6
bay leaves: 3
a lemon

Warm the oil in a large, deep, heavy-based pan over a moderate to high heat. Season the pork and lower it into the hot oil. Leave it to colour lightly, turning it over several times, until all sides are nicely coloured. Lift out the pork and pour away all the fat from the pan.

Bring the milk to the boil in a saucepan and set aside. Peel the garlic cloves but leave them whole. Put the empty pork pan back over a low to medium heat, add the butter and garlic and cook for a couple of minutes, until the garlic starts to turn pale gold. Add the sage and bay leaves, then place the pork back in the pan and pour over the boiled milk. Remove the zest from the lemon with a vegetable peeler and add to the pan. Bring the milk back to the boil, turn the heat down, partially cover with a lid and allow to simmer very gently for two hours. The milk should have cooked into small, pale-brown, curdled lumps and a little thin sauce. Remove the meat and let it rest for ten minutes. Remove any fat with kitchen paper, then slice the meat finely and serve with trickles of the curdled sauce.

Enough for 6–8

## Apples with maple syrup

Choose the smallest apples you can find for this. If large ones are all that is available, then halve them and remove their cores before baking.

lemons: 3
small apples: 8
maple syrup: 7 tablespoons

cloves: 5
ground cinnamon: 2 teaspoons
a vanilla pod

Set the oven at 200°C/Gas 6. Squeeze the lemons into a mixing bowl. Peel the apples, leaving them whole, and drop them into the lemon juice, moving them round in the bowl to stop them discolouring. Pour in the maple syrup, add the cloves and the ground cinnamon, then tip everything into a baking dish. Tuck in the vanilla pod and bake for fifty minutes to an hour, till the apples are soft and starting to collapse. Serve with crème fraîche.

Enough for 4

## OCTOBER 30

The solid fats – butter, dripping and lard – tend to appear in this kitchen only in autumn and winter. The same goes for my favourite duck fat too. The exception is probably a pork pie for a picnic or the dripping I might use to start a roast. Sadly, the fat with the best flavour is also the most expensive. But duck fat is worth the occasional extravagance, and nowhere does it work better than with potatoes.

You get a good colour with potatoes fried in the fat of the duck. Richness too, and more flavour than you will get with anything else. They won't burn easily either. But the richness needs to have something to sharpen its edge, otherwise the meal will cloy. Today, I use a glass of fruity sloe gin (the Sipsmith brand is good, if you don't make your own) to balance the richness of the fat in a simple supper of griddled duck.

## Duck breasts with damson gin and duck-fat potatoes

*For the duck:*
duck breasts, skin on: 4
brown sugar: 2 tablespoons
sherry vinegar: 4 tablespoons
sloe or damson gin: 4 tablespoons
juniper berries: 8

*For the potatoes:*
medium potatoes: 3
duck fat: 3 tablespoons
a few thyme leaves
garlic: a single clove, finely chopped

Make three or four deep slashes on the skin side of each breast, cutting down into the flesh but not through it. Put them snugly into a china or steel dish.

Put the brown sugar into a mixing bowl with the sherry vinegar, sloe or damson gin and a grinding of salt and black pepper. Mash the juniper berries to coarse, fragrant crumbs and add them to the sugar and vinegar mixture. Pour it over the duck breasts, massaging the liquid into the skin and flesh. Cover with cling film and leave in a cold place such as the fridge to marinate for at least an hour. No less; four hours is even better. Overnight will not harm.

Set the oven at 200°C/Gas 6. Peel the potatoes and slice them as thinly as possible. Melt the duck fat in a heavy, shallow pan, turn off the heat and add the potato slices in one layer, neatly overlapping and seasoning them with salt, black pepper, thyme leaves and a little chopped garlic as you go. Place in the oven and bake for thirty-five to forty minutes, till golden brown.

When the potatoes are ready, get a griddle pan hot. Pat the duck breasts dry with kitchen paper, then place them skin-side down on the hot griddle. Keeping the heat moderately high, leave them to colour on the skin side, brushing them regularly with the marinade left in the dish, then turn them over and cook for a further four or five minutes, till they are golden on the outside and pink in the middle. A good way to test them for doneness is to pierce the centre with a skewer. For a rose-pink centre, you want the beads of juice that seep out to be red, not golden. Let the breasts rest for four or five minutes before serving.

Cut each duck breast diagonally into about 4 thick slices and serve with the roast potatoes.

Enough for 4

# Slow

Hallowe'en, when the dead are supposed to be able to communicate with the living, used to be an evening I looked forward to. The death of summer. Good riddance. All the witches and ghosts, fairies and hobgoblins are abroad. Tragically the ancient and frankly terrifying black-faced mummers who called door to door asking for money have been replaced by pesky kids playing trick or treat, demanding money and some of whose antics barely stop short of vandalism. Such is modern life.

The pumpkin lantern, such a rare sight when I was a kid, is now common, the squash's insides gouged out for a hollow in which to put a nightlight. If you get the face right, with wide teeth and a scary grin, it can bring a suitable shiver to the proceedings. Food at All Hallows is often pork based, this being the season for killing the family pig, and apples usually get a look in too, often baked in the embers of the fire. Those coming to dinner tonight will have a slow, pig-based meal followed by classic baked apples.

Simple doesn't have to mean quick. Simple cooking can also be something that is left to cook for a long time over a low heat, quietly puttering away, filling the kitchen with the scent of welcome.

There's a pan on the stove, on a heat so low that its contents, a carrot-speckled mixture of onions, celery and mushrooms with baby pork ribs peeping up through the surface, are barely moving, just a blip and shudder. The smell that fills the kitchen and wafts up the stairs is ancient, earthy, dark, faintly rank, and yet full of bonhomie. It is a simple smell (barely half a dozen ingredients), yet deep and rich (beef stock, browned pork, sweet carrots) and seasoned, reeking of nostalgia.

The recipe is uncomplicated, its apparent complexity coming from nothing more than a few ingredients thoughtfully combined and left to get to know one another over a low heat. The mixture of pork ribs with beef stock seems odd at first, but as the ingredients slowly become acquainted, it starts to make sense. This recipe was first cooked by James, whose help in this kitchen is invaluable, to celebrate the end of filming the first series of *Simple Cooking*. It has become a favourite. No shortcuts, by the way. If you are pushed for time, make something else. The long, slow simmering is essential.

# Rib ragout with pappardelle

| | |
|---|---|
| onion: a large one | mushrooms: 250g |
| celery: 3 ribs | beef stock: 800ml |
| large carrots: 3 | pappardelle: 250g |
| butter: 50g | a little olive oil |
| baby pork ribs: 1kg, cut into short racks (about 3 bones each) | |

Peel and finely chop the onion, celery and carrots. Melt the butter in a large, deep casserole, add the ribs and brown lightly. Add the vegetables and cook for fifteen minutes, stirring from time to time, till slightly softened. Finely chop the mushrooms, add to the pan and continue cooking for five minutes. Add the stock, bring to the boil, then turn down to a simmer and cook, covered, at a low bubble for a good three hours, stirring from time to time. Take the lid off for the last half hour.

Bring a pan of water to the boil, salt generously and add the pappardelle. Cook until al dente, then drain. Season with a little olive oil and black pepper.

Whilst the pasta cooks, slide the flesh from the ribs – it should come off effortlessly – and stir it through the sauce. Serve with the pappardelle.

Enough for 6

November

# A pan, a pork chop and some pears

There are moments when a certain magic happens in a kitchen. Like tonight, when the sticky sediment left behind in the pan from cooking a pork chop met some cider (actually perry, the pear version) and then some cream and became a sauce so delicious, so right for the season and the hour, that I felt my part in it was as little more than an observer.

For any piece of meat to leave a layer of sticky, umami-rich sediment behind, it needs time to be in contact with the surface of the pan. The heat should be steady and high enough to give the surface of the meat a chance to brown but low enough to prevent it burning. I leave the meat in place so that it colours and forms a light crust, but then turn it regularly rather than just once or twice. Too hot and it will burn and you will be flavouring your sauce with carbon; too cool and you won't get a good colour. You are after sediment under the meat that is deep bronze-gold in colour.

The garden is looking more beautiful than at any time since the blossom was out in May. The leaves on the pear tree are red, the witch hazel's are orange. There are raspberries hidden amongst the yellowing leaves and the wineberries glisten like clusters of garnets on rusty iron supports. The pears, save those on the Winter Nellis, have been picked and need eating. They lose their point in a pie and are too dry for a crumble. Two of them end up in a huge frying pan with four small pork chops, and together with the pan-crustings they flavour a sauce made with perry and cream. A rich dish for a chilly evening and a bit of kitchen magic.

## Pork with pears and cream

| | |
|---|---|
| a little olive or groundnut oil | a thick slice of butter |
| pork chops: 4 | perry or dryish cider: 200ml |
| thyme: 4 bushy sprigs | double cream: 150ml |
| pears: 2 | |

Lightly oil the chops. Strip the thyme leaves from their stems and chop them finely, then use them to season the chops, with some salt and pepper.

Peel the pears, remove the cores and cut the flesh into large dice. Melt the butter in a shallow pan, add the pears and cook till golden and approaching tenderness. Turn them now and again with a spoon, gently, letting them take on an even colour. Lift them out and set aside.

Return the pan to the heat, lower in the chops and leave them to cook over a moderate heat till they are done to your liking and have formed a sticky residue on the surface of the pan (probably about five minutes on either side). Lift them out and keep warm.

Pour the cider or perry into the pan and stir to dissolve the sticky residue. Leave to bubble and reduce till there are just a few tablespoons left – a matter of three or four minutes or so. Pour in the cream, whisk lightly to mix it with the liquid in the pan and let the mixture bubble down for a minute or so. Return the chops and pears to the pan. When all is thoroughly hot, check the seasoning and serve.

Enough for 4

### NOVEMBER 2

# Learning to love the sprout

I have been slowly coming round to the Brussels sprout. Not a Damascene conversion, more a slow warming (I have still to work out the allure of cooked carrots). Fried rather than boiled, partnered with the meat of the pig and slathered in cream, these are the sprouts for me. They never see water in this recipe – only hot butter, cream and bacon. There are almonds too, an inspiration. They were cooked for the last show of my third cookery series, a programme set in Scotland, where they appeared with roast wild venison and potatoes cooked with onions. The recipe is not mine but one of James's. I used purple Brussel sprouts but use whatever you have.

## Brussels sprouts, bacon and almonds

smoked streaky bacon: 100g
an onion
Brussels sprouts: 400g
butter: 50g

whole unskinned salted
  almonds: 100g
double cream: 250ml

Cut the bacon into finger-width strips and let them cook in a large, shallow pan over a moderate heat till the fat runs and colours to a pale gold.

Peel and thinly slice the onion. Trim the sprouts and cut each one in half. Place them cut-side down in a single layer in the pan, add the butter and let them brown very lightly, then add the onion. Continue cooking for about ten minutes, until the sprouts are softening and the onion is translucent. Add the almonds, then the cream. You need no salt, because of the salted almonds and the bacon. Leave to bubble briefly, then serve.

Enough for 4 as a side dish, 2 as a main dish with brown rice


## NOVEMBER 4 AND 5

# The mother of all baked potatoes

I sometimes picture all the fireplaces in this house lit, with the smell of wood smoke drifting through the rooms. Now they are mostly blocked off to stop soot-falls and birds nesting in them. Even now, I wake up to find black powder over the floors after a storm. Once a squawking black crow flew out of one of the bedroom fireplaces, terrifying the occupant. It was their first and last night in the house.

Although I could light a fire in the fireplace in the hallway, I don't. I light one in a massive steel bowl in the garden, lay a grill over it and cook chicken on it. Occasionally I put potatoes wrapped in foil in the embers. Sometimes they emerge dry and overcooked. With luck, if there is enough heat left in the ashes, the potatoes will come out with the much sought-after snow-like centre. This is the one night of winter when much of the country takes its cooking outside and attempts a fire-baked potato. It rarely works, and I tend to bake them in the oven, with salt not foil.

This year I am hollowing the skins out and mashing the insides with butter, very finely chopped rosemary and strands of soft pork rillettes. Dusted with grated Parmesan that forms a crust on top, they are the most humble yet delectable of potatoes. I sometimes think this is my favourite recipe of all. I make the coarse fatty pâté from scratch, but they are also good made with shop-bought rillettes too.

# Rillettes

A coarsely textured pâté that I like with rounds of hot sourdough toast, or maybe very crisp French bread and a pot of pickled cornichons or other crisp gherkins.

| | |
|---|---|
| belly pork: 1kg, skinned and boned | garlic: 3 large cloves, peeled |
| bay leaves: 3 | water: 250ml |
| thyme: 3 large sprigs | |

Set the oven at 160°C/Gas 3. Put the piece of pork in a roasting tin or large shallow pot. Rub a tablespoon of salt all over the meat, then drop in the bay leaves, together with the thyme and the whole garlic cloves. Add the water, cover with tight foil or a lid, then place in the oven and cook for three hours or until the pork is completely tender.

Remove the lid, lift the meat from its juices and tear it into very fine shreds with the aid of two forks. This takes a little while to do thoroughly, but is a rather pleasing task. Pack tightly into a china or earthenware bowl. Pour the liquid in the roasting tin through a sieve over the rillettes and mix lightly. Leave to cool, then refrigerate till the fat has set.

Serve with toast or exceptionally crusty bread and cornichons, or perhaps pickled chillies, or potatoes.

Enough for 8

# Baked potatoes, rillettes and rosemary

Most delicatessens and decent supermarkets can be relied on for a tub of pork rillettes. The coarser the better.

| | |
|---|---|
| baking potatoes: 4, about 350g each | pork rillettes, homemade or deli-bought: 250g |
| rosemary: 2 bushy sprigs | Parmesan, finely grated: 2 tablespoons |

Scrub the potatoes and prick them a few times with a fork. Pat them almost dry, then dust lightly with salt and leave them to dry for a few minutes. Bake them at 200°C/Gas 6 until the skin is crisp and the inside soft and fluffy –

a matter of forty-five minutes to an hour, depending on the variety and size of the potato (I find an hour is about right for a large potato).

Remove the rosemary leaves from their stems and chop them finely. You need about a teaspoonful. Slice the top off the potatoes. Using a tablespoon, scrape out the flesh from the potatoes and their lid into a food mixer. Mix briefly with the flat beater so that the potato no longer has any lumps, but take care not to over mix. Carefully introduce the rillettes and the rosemary. Be mindful that the texture of the pork should still be visible, so avoid mixing for too long. You can of course do this by hand if you prefer.

Pile the mixture back into the skins and place snugly on a baking sheet. Put the lids upside down on the baking sheet too. Scatter the grated Parmesan over each potato and return them to the oven. Bake for ten minutes, till the top of the filling is starting to crisp lightly, then replace the lids and serve.

Makes 4

# Righting a wrong

There is a certain comfort in following a recipe, but there is also much fun to be had in working with a few ingredients ourselves, mixing and matching till we find something that suits us. Most importantly, we need to taste, taste, taste all the way from start to finish. Today I make a sort of teriyaki sauce starting with 150ml dark soy sauce, 4 heaped tablespoons of honey and 100ml sake, then tweak it in a pan over a low heat till it is sweet and salty enough.

Instead of being a marinade for fish or meat, the sauce is destined for mushrooms – a mixture of quartered chestnut mushrooms, sliced flats, halved buttons and whole shiitake, added in that order, then, as a final touch, some girolles (a slightly pointless addition, as it turns out). The mushrooms are quickly sautéed in a little groundnut oil before the teriyaki sauce is added to the pan. The whole lot is left to simmer for about ten minutes, till the mushrooms are soft and the sauce is starting to reduce.

It turns out that I have things slightly wrong. The flavours are altogether too powerful, too salty, sweet, earthy, almost liquorice-like in style. What started as a bit of an experiment must still end up as dinner. I rescue the concentrated flavours of the ebony-coloured mushrooms with a bowl of steamed brown rice, whose effect is to calm. The starch successfully turns down the volume, diverting disaster. Lesson learned.

# A different pumpkin pie

There has been a round winter squash sitting in the kitchen for over a month. Six weeks actually. The pale blue skin hides the sort of dense, orange flesh that doesn't collapse to a slush like that of the summer squashes. Gaining admission might be easier with an axe than the kitchen knife.

The advantages of the hard-skinned squashes over the summer varieties are their long shelf life and their deep saffron-coloured flesh that keeps its shape when cooked. In a curry or bean-based casserole, it is pleasing to find recognisable pieces of pumpkin rather than a golden sludge. The firm texture also means you can use them to fill a pasty or pie, whose shape won't collapse as the pumpkin cooks.

'Big Blue' weighs in at a couple of kilos – nothing for a member of the pumpkin family but about twice that of the average supermarket user-friendly butternut. The older these fruits become, the longer they take to cook. Roasting them increases their sweetness. Steaming gives a faster result. My way is the best of both worlds: a quick steam – in a colander balanced over a pan of boiling water for want of a proper steamer – followed by fifty minutes' roasting, ensures both melting flesh and deep sweetness.

A pumpkin entering my house is likely to end up as soup, stew or curry, or if it is particularly unlucky, a doorstop. Last night was the first time a member of the squash family has ended up as a savoury pie in my kitchen. Steamed, roasted, mashed and wrapped in pastry, the flesh was saved from cloying by a generous pinch of black pepper, cinnamon and sea salt. I dithered about putting finely chopped red chillies in, and half wondered about a few spring onions, but in the end left it more or less unadulterated.

I rarely do battle with homemade puff pastry, its tactile pleasures having so far escaped me. I tend to rely on the bought alternative. Looking beyond the usual brands, you can sometimes find one made with butter and even organic flour. Rather than a solid block, the pastry comes in user-friendly rolls, like parchment. It saves time and sweat, though not money. Ready rolled as it is, I give it a further going over with the rolling pin, leaving it thinner and, once baked, considerably crisper. The pie would have worked with a simple shortcrust too, but the extra-crisp quality of puff pastry is a contrast to the soft, golden filling.

A sauce might be welcome on the side – a slow-cooked tomato one, perhaps with garlic and rosemary. The filling is so moist you probably won't need it, but it will add an extra dimension. The pie works cold, and would slice neatly for a lunchbox, but it is at its best when recently out of the oven.

## A savoury pumpkin pie

A 2kg pumpkin will give about 1.5kg of flesh once it has been peeled and its seeds and fibres removed.

pumpkin: 1.3kg (peeled and seeded weight)
rapeseed or groundnut oil: 4 tablespoons
butter: a thick slice
ground cinnamon: a generous pinch
puff pastry: 375g
an egg, lightly beaten, for brushing

Set the oven at 200°C/Gas 6. Cut the pumpkin flesh into small pieces, roughly 2cm square (the shape is immaterial, as they are going to be crushed later, but an equal size will help them cook evenly). Steam for fifteen to twenty minutes, till the flesh is giving and tender enough for a skewer to slide effortlessly through. Remove from the heat and tip into a roasting tin or baking dish. Pour over the oil and add the butter and cinnamon. Grind over plenty of salt and pepper and toss the pumpkin gently so the pieces are coated with oil. Roast for thirty to forty minutes, until the flesh is soft and lightly golden on all sides. Using a fork or potato masher, crush the cooked pumpkin to a coarse mash.

Cut the pastry in half and roll out each piece into a rectangle measuring roughly 23cm x 35cm. Lay one piece on a baking sheet lined with baking parchment. Pile the filling on top of the pastry. Brush the edges of the pastry with some of the beaten egg. Lay the second piece over the top and press firmly around the edges to seal. You could pinch the pastry together at this point if you wish, or use any trimmings to make some sort of decoration for the top. Make two or three small slits on the surface of the pie. This will prevent the pastry splitting as it cooks.

Brush the pie all over with more of the beaten egg, then bake for twenty-five to thirty minutes, until crisp and golden. Leave for five or ten minutes to settle, then slice and serve.

Enough for 4 as a main course, 6 as part of a light lunch

# Eating Bambi

The sight of a deer in the snow should make your heart melt. Those fragile legs and sweeping eyelashes. You would have a heart of steel to think of the roasting tin. I have seen them in the open, living like lords and ladies on a Scottish farm, feasting on a mixed diet as they do in the wild, pampered and happy.

Killed, skinned and butchered, all meat becomes less challenging, and it is the only way most of us want to deal with it. Venison, like rabbit, is a meat whose popularity has been killed by Walt Disney. Venison is lean and light of flavour. It needs very fast (the chops, fillet and saddle) or very slow cooking (the shoulder and breast). Deer of any sort, wild or farmed, is becoming more affordable and available. Many of the major supermarkets have the farmed variety; enterprising butchers may stock the wild. It is worth bearing in mind that deer is not intensively farmed, and the animals are shot and often butchered on the farm.

Cooked rare, so its flesh is barely warm, and rested for ten minutes, the texture is almost jelly-like, a cross between rare fillet steak and lamb's liver. Seared on the outside, it will develop a light crust, but not one as succulent as beef. Venison lacks fat. I have yet to find a better way to present it than simply fried in a shallow pan in butter. That way you end up with a tender, lean piece of protein with a mild, gamey character.

# Venison with sweet-sour chard

chard stalks: 150g (weight minus leaves)
white wine vinegar: 4 tablespoons
venison haunch steaks: 2, weighing about 180g each

butter: 50g, plus a little extra for frying
balsamic vinegar: 1 tablespoon
a very little caster sugar, to taste

Remove the leaves from the chard and reserve them for another dish. Slice the chard stalks thickly and put them into a bowl with the white wine vinegar. Set aside for at least twenty-five minutes.

Season the venison generously on both sides. Melt a little butter in a non-stick saucepan. Place the venison in the pan and leave, without moving, for a good two to three minutes, until a slight golden crust has appeared on the underside. Turn and continue cooking for two to three minutes. Remove the venison from the pan and set aside to rest in a warm place, such as on a warm plate under an upturned mixing bowl.

Put the chard stalks and their vinegar into the pan and cook over a moderate heat for three to four minutes, until they are tender but still crisp. Remove the chard from the pan, leaving behind any juices, and place on warm serving plates. Melt the 50g butter in the pan and stir to dissolve any tasty pan-stickings. Add the balsamic vinegar and a little sugar – start with a good pinch, then add according to taste. You want the sauce to be nicely balanced between sweet and sharp.

Slice the venison thickly. Place on the warm serving plates with the chard and spoon over the pan juices.

Enough for 2

# Blackberry and hazelnut friands

butter: 180g

plain flour: 50g

icing sugar: 180g

ground hazelnuts: 100g

lemon zest: 1 teaspoon

egg whites: 5

blackberries: 60g

Set the oven at 200°C/Gas 6. Lightly butter 12 shallow bun tins or friand moulds.

Put the butter in a small pan and melt over a moderate heat, then watch it carefully until it becomes a dark, nutty gold. Take great care not to let it burn. Leave it to cool a little.

Sift the flour and sugar into a large mixing bowl and add most of the ground hazelnuts. Grate in the lemon zest. In a separate bowl, beat the egg whites to a soft, rather moist, sloppy foam – they shouldn't be able to stand up.

Make a well in the centre of the dry ingredients and pour in the egg whites, together with the melted butter. Mix lightly but thoroughly, then pour into the buttered tins. Roughly chop the blackberries and drop them into the tins. Scatter the remaining ground hazelnuts over the top.

Bake for ten to fifteen minutes, until risen and pale gold. Remove from the oven and leave to settle before carefully removing from the tins with a palette knife.

Makes 12

## NOVEMBER 14

# Cooking onions

The more slowly you cook an onion, the sweeter it becomes. The instruction to cook chopped onions for five minutes – I see it all the time – doesn't really work, because it shows the cook doesn't understand the onion at all. Cooked briefly, the onion has nothing much to offer. Cooked over a fierce heat, chopped onions will burn and turn bitter. They have a high water content in summer and autumn, less so in winter. That water is why, even when fried for a long time, they sometimes won't brown properly, and steam rather than fry in the pan.

November is when the onion comes back into the kitchen. Dinner needs a backbone in winter and the onion provides it. This evening I peel four the size of pomegranates, halve them from tip to root, then slice them into thick segments, like a chocolate orange. I put butter in a shallow pan, then the sliced onions, and let them cook, with the occasional stir and turn with a wooden spatula. But this is my point. I let them cook for half an hour. Half an hour. They soften, they sweeten, they turn amber, then gold, then nut brown. They take on a honeyed smell. They become so tender you can squish them between thumb and index finger. They almost melt.

At this point your onion is ready to serve with liver, with bacon, with steak. Tonight I season them with mustard seeds, raisins, vinegar and sticky vin cotto, and offer them to a trio of liver lovers.

## NOVEMBER 15

## Something for cheese

Matching cheeses to their starchy accompaniment can be rewarding in the same way as matching a pasta to its sauce. It's a deeply personal thing. Cracker or baguette. Sticky rye bread or toasted sourdough. Doughy white loaf or crispbread. There are no precise rules. Soft cheese, crisp cracker, firm cheese, soft bread is a fair rule of thumb. But such pairings are not just about texture. Flavour comes into it too, as anyone who has ruined their goat's cheese with a slice from a caraway loaf will testify. A nutty loaf for a Caerphilly; a flour-dusted, slightly burnt, pencil-thin baguette for a piece of dripping Brie. A Cheddar so sharp it brings the veins out on the roof of your mouth with a piece of white bread whose edges are charred almost black.

One that got me recently was a fig and fennel loaf for a goat's cheese. Worked like a dream. Here it is.

# Fig and hazelnut loaf for cheese

Part of the joy of these particularly moist loaves is that they will keep for several days in good condition. They freeze well too.

wholemeal spelt flour: 250g
strong white bread flour: 250g
Easy Bake yeast: a 7g sachet
black treacle: 1 tablespoon
salt: 1 gently heaped teaspoon

warm water: 350ml
soft dried figs: 250g
hazelnuts: 70g
fennel seed: 3 large pinches

Put the flours into a large bowl (or the bowl of a food mixer) and stir in the yeast. Add the treacle and salt, then mix in the water with a wooden spoon (or the beater attachment of the food mixer). Keep mixing till all is smooth.

Turn the dough out on to a generously floured surface and knead for three or four minutes. I am never too fussy about my kneading method, and find simply working the dough with my hands until it feels springy and alive, moist but not sticky, does the trick.

Flour the bowl and return the kneaded dough to it. Cover with a clean cloth and leave in a warm place for an hour. It should have risen to almost twice its original size.

Slice the figs finely. Turn the dough out on to the floured surface again and push the figs, whole hazelnuts and fennel seeds into it, kneading lightly as you go. Cut the dough in half and form into balls. Place on a floured baking sheet, cover and leave to prove once again for forty-five minutes, until nicely risen. Set the oven at 220°C/Gas 8.

Bake the loaves for twenty-five to thirty minutes, until the bottom sounds hollow when tapped.

Makes 2 small loaves

# Poached quinces with goat's cheese

I like the sweet fruitiness of the baked quince with the goat's cheese. It is a short step on from the traditional marriage of quince paste and cheese. The baked fruit is good on its own too.

honey: 4 generous tablespoons
water: 500ml
smallish quinces: 4
half a lemon

quince, medlar, apple or
  redcurrant jelly: 6 tablespoons
goat's cheese: 8 slices

Put the honey and water into a saucepan and bring to the boil. Peel and halve the quinces and rub them with the lemon to stop them browning (quinces discolour even quicker than pears). Lower the quinces into the syrup and simmer till tender. They may be ready in twenty-five minutes or may take up to forty, depending on how hard they are. Whatever, they need to be soft and tender, despite the fact that they are going to be cooked again.

Set the oven at 180°C/Gas 4. Lift the quinces out of the syrup and put them in a shallow baking dish or roasting tin. Measure out 100ml of the cooking liquid and add to the quinces. Add the fruit jelly and bake for about thirty minutes, until the fruit is very soft, checking and basting occasionally to make sure the fruit and its jelly are not overcooking – ideally, there will be a little sticky jelly or syrup at the bottom of the dish. Remove from the oven and leave to cool.

Serve the quinces with the slices of goat's cheese and any syrup or jelly from the baking dish.

Enough for 4

## A regression session

I like, from time to time, to eat things that take me back instantly to childhood. Dairylea, the soft cheese spread, milk chocolate buttons and, most of all, banana custard do it every time. Mine was made with Bird's custard powder but we can take it up a notch by using ready-made instant custard. Better still, and without losing its comforting, nannying heart and soul, is to make your own version with eggs, cream and a vanilla pod.

The other food that tunes in to my inner child is trifle. You could almost measure my life in trifle – from those of my childhood, with their white and blue waxed cartons and glacé cherry, through the Swiss-roll based sherry trifles of family Christmases, the berry versions made with syllabub, orange and lemon trifles, and the one with orange curd and mincemeat sponge you will find in the next chapter.

Although I have had bananas in a trifle before now, the effect has been less than successful in terms of colour and texture. This afternoon I make a trifle with a classic vanilla-seed-freckled banana custard at its heart. There's amaretti and bananas, custard, a hint of lemon, the scent of rose petals and the crunch of sesame snaps. It tastes of childhood, which I have always suspected is most trifle lovers' real reason for making them. Less of a dessert, then, more of a culinary regression session.

### Banana trifle

| | |
|---|---|
| bananas: 3 | *For the custard:* |
| amaretti: 125g | double cream: 500ml |
| Limoncello liqueur: 3 tablespoons | a vanilla pod, split lengthways |
| double cream: 250ml | eggs: 2 |
| crystallised rose petals | egg yolks: 2 |
| sesame snaps: 3 or 4 | caster sugar: 3 tablespoons |

For the custard, warm the cream and the split vanilla pod over a gentle heat till almost boiling. Set aside, covered with a lid, for ten minutes for the vanilla to infuse the milk.

Put the eggs and yolks into a mixing bowl with the sugar and whisk for a couple of minutes, till pale and thoroughly mixed. Pour in the warm cream, minus the vanilla pod, and stir to mix. Transfer to the saucepan in which you boiled the cream and place over a moderate heat, stirring regularly as the custard warms. Regular stirring is essential if the custard is not to curdle. As soon as it starts to feel heavy on the spoon, take the pan off the heat and pour the custard into a cold bowl. Stir regularly as it cools.

Chop one of the bananas and stir it into the custard. Put the amaretti in a 1.5 litre dish, then pour over the lemon liqueur, crushing the amaretti a little as you go. Slice the remaining bananas and put them in a layer over the amaretti. Pour the cooled banana custard over and leave to set in the fridge for an hour.

Whip the cream, spoon it over the custard, then decorate with crystallised rose petals and lightly crushed sesame snaps.

Enough for 6

## NOVEMBER 17

# Poor man's potatoes

I sometimes feel I have cornered the market in chuck-it-in-a-pan suppers, having been doing that all my cooking life, and this evening's meal only goes to compound the thought. The Spanish tapas dish of *patatas pobre* was the inspiration for this fry-up of potatoes, onions and peppers. The classic dish uses green peppers, which I like less than almost anything else, and slices the potatoes into rounds. This is a more rustic, hearty version, suitable for a weekday main course.

There are two of us tonight, so I wipe 500g of very small potatoes and halve them. A little olive oil is poured into a shallow pan, then I place the potatoes in face-down and let them cook. I take a large, ripe pepper, halve it, seed it and cut it into long strips, then add them to the pan. This is followed by a peeled and sliced onion and a large knob of butter. Everything is left to cook, with the occasional stir, until the potatoes are nicely golden and the onion is starting to soften. In goes 400ml vegetable stock, it is brought to the boil, then I let it all simmer enthusiastically for twenty minutes, covered with a lid. Once the stock has almost disappeared and the vegetables are tender and almost falling apart, we tuck in.

## An autumn stock take and a new pear cake

I have never felt a moment's guilt about celebrating life's small, private successes. Those little things that come along (all too rarely, as it happens) to balance the stuff I get wrong.

The two pear trees outside the kitchen door are heartstoppingly beautiful this morning. The Winter Nellis has crimson leaves as slim and fine as a feather; the Doyenne du Comice is a mass of copper and orange, altogether rounder and wider. This has happened in previous years but never a glorious show like this. The lack of autumn winds has kept the trees in full leaf, which is rare at this point in the year. They are normally in the compost bin by now, or still scattered over the hedges and paths like gold and red confetti.

And this autumn is quite the longest I have ever known. The garden seems to have been in this state of assorted ochres and reds for several weeks now. It is rare I stop and look for as long as I have today, but I just cannot take my eyes off it. Did I know my fruit and vegetable patch would ever look this wonderful when I heeled-in those trees and bushes? No, of course I didn't. I don't think it had even occurred to me that I was capable of creating anything quite so beautiful. I didn't know I had it in me. There are those who would declare it all a complete mess, with things left in where they should have been pulled out, tangles of crisp stems where there should be smart, bare earth, and wayward twigs where there should be neatly trimmed bushes. For many, this garden is not a scene of romantic melancholy and rich-hued foliage but an unholy mess in desperate need of weeding, raking, sweeping and pruning. They are wrong, of course, and I celebrate with a hazelnut-scented pear cake.

# A pear and hazelnut cake

butter, softened: 175g
golden caster sugar: 85g
light muscovado sugar: 85g
skinned hazelnuts: 80g
eggs: 2
self-raising flour: 165g
ground cinnamon: half a teaspoon
vanilla extract: a few drops

*For the pears:*
a large, juicy lemon
pears: 750g
caster sugar: 3 tablespoons
ground cinnamon

*For the crumble:*
plain flour: 100g
butter: 75g
demerara sugar: 2 tablespoons
a little cinnamon and extra
    demerara for the crust

Preheat the oven to 160°C/Gas 3. Line the base of a 21–22cm square cake tin with baking parchment.

For the pears, squeeze the lemon into a mixing bowl. Peel the pears, core them and cut them into small chunks, dropping them into the lemon juice as you go. It will stop them browning. Put the pears and lemon juice into a saucepan, bring to the boil and turn the heat down to a gentle simmer. Scatter over the sugar and a good pinch or two of ground cinnamon, then cook, with the occasional stir, till the pears are translucent and tender. They should be soft enough to pierce with a skewer with little or no effort. Try not to let them colour beyond the palest gold or to let the juice boil away. You will need it later.

Make the cake: beat the butter and sugars in a food mixer till light and pale coffee coloured. This will take a good five to ten minutes. Meanwhile, toast the hazelnuts in a shallow pan till they are golden brown, then grind quite finely. Break the eggs, beat them gently just to mix the yolks and whites and add them gradually to the mix with the beater on slow. Fold in the ground hazelnuts, flour and cinnamon, then add a couple of drops of vanilla extract. When all is smooth, scoop the mixture into the prepared tin and smooth it flat.

Lift the pears from their syrup with a draining spoon, reserving the juice. Put the pears on top of the cake mixture.

To make the crumble topping, blitz the flour and butter to crumbs in a food processor. Add the demerara sugar and mix lightly. Remove the processor bowl from the stand. Add a few drops of water and shake the bowl a little – or run a fork through the mixture – so that some of the crumbs stick together like small pebbles. This will give a more interesting mix of textures. Scatter this loosely over the top of the cake, followed by a little more demerara and a pinch of cinnamon.

Bake for about an hour, checking for doneness with a skewer. Remove the cake from the oven and set aside. Bring the reserved juice from the pears to the boil for a couple of minutes till there are 3 or 4 tablespoons left. Trickle it over the surface of the cake and leave to cool.

Enough for 8–12

NOVEMBER 20

# Medlar day

I value the medlar tree for its curling branches and shady canopy; for its single ivory-white blossom and the bronze and turmeric yellow of its leaves in autumn. But, guiltily, not for its fruit. Yes, their unusual form intrigues, the appropriately christened 'cat's arse' tree of medieval gardens. In the hand, the fruit is curiously tactile, like a russet apple, and the advice to pick them hard and let them blacken before using is unusual enough to encourage further investigation. But as a fruit, the medlar has little going for it, save the possibility of making a jar or two of amber jelly to smooth the passage of a cold roast.

For such a rare and difficult-to-obtain ingredient, I have an extraordinary number of pleas for inspiration each year. What are we to do with our crop of medlars other than make jelly? I haven't a clue.

The fruits are small, about the size of a clementine. Skin and pips discarded, there is little to go at. The instructions to bake them as you might a Bramley apple stand good as long as you have the patience to winkle a coffee spoon inside their skin to extract every morsel of flesh. The fruit world's answer to the crab.

This year, the crop is magnificent. Each branch is laden with the plumpest medlars I have seen. With fruits this size, it will at last be worth taking the baking route. Two hours are spent pulling the brown, slightly soft fruits from the tree's spindly twigs, the wet, leaf-encrusted soil under-neath sticking to my feet. The problem is not just how to reach up through the tight tangle of crossed twigs and entwined branches but how to pull the

457

stubborn little baubles from the tree without shaking it so much the other fruits fall off into the mud.

Few fruits have such an ethereal flavour. Part lychee, part overripe apple, there is something Alice-in-Wonderlandish about this fruit. As to its use in the kitchen, well, 'limited' is probably a generous description. This afternoon I had the oven on to make a big, family-style pie, so popped two dozen medlars in to bake. They emerged, almost an hour later, black and soft. We cut the top off each one and scooped the grey-brown interior out with the smallest teaspoons I could find. As each spoonful was removed, a little dribble of cream was poured in. It was an interesting culinary experience and I recommend it to anyone with a laden medlar tree in their garden. It felt like a treat, but it was hardly the culinary moment of the century.

Here's the pie.

## A pie of mushrooms and spinach

*For the filling:*
dried mushrooms: 15g
large field mushrooms: 300g
shiitake mushrooms: 100g
chestnut mushrooms: 300g
butter: a thick slice
rapeseed or groundnut oil:
   3 tablespoons
plain flour: 2 lightly heaped
   tablespoons
vegetable stock or bouillon:
   500ml, hot
spinach: 650g (to give 500g
   prepared weight)

crème fraîche: 3 tablespoons
   (or more if you like)

*For the pastry:*
plain flour: 200g
butter: 100g, cut into small chunks
an egg yolk
Parmesan, grated: 3 tablespoons,
   plus a little extra
a little beaten egg and milk, for
   brushing

Put the dried mushrooms to soak in 100ml warm water and leave for twenty minutes. Drain and reseve the liquid. Thickly slice the large mushrooms, halve the shiitake (unless they are small) and quarter the chestnut mushrooms. Melt the butter in a large, deep pan, add the oil, then add the mushrooms. Cook, covered, over a moderate heat until they start to darken and become tender, giving them the occasional stir to stop them sticking. Scatter over the flour, stir it in and leave to cook for a few minutes before adding the hot stock and the mushroom soaking liquor. Stir well and leave to simmer for ten minutes or so. Check the seasoning, adding salt and black pepper as you wish.

Pick over the spinach, removing any stalks. Rinse the leaves and cook in a large, lidded pan for a couple of minutes, till the spinach has wilted. Drain in a colander and leave to cool, or run cold water through it to bring the temperature down more quickly and keep the colour bright. Squeeze the spinach with your fist to remove the water.

Stir the spinach into the mushroom filling along with the crème fraîche. The amount of cream you add will depend on whether you want a creamy filling or something more robust in nature. I find about 3 heaped table-spoons enough. Tip the filling into a pie dish or baking dish and set aside. Set the oven at 200°C/Gas 6.

Put the flour and butter in a food processor and blitz to crumbs, then add the egg yolk, Parmesan and just enough water to bring it to a firm dough. I start with a couple of tablespoons of water, adding more if it needs it.

Turn the dough out on to a floured board and roll it out thinly. It should be the same thickness as for lining a tart tin. Cut it into approximately 5cm squares. Place the squares on top of the mushroom filling, overlapping them here and there, and brush with a thin layer of beaten egg and milk. Scatter over a small amount of Parmesan and bake for twenty to thirty minutes till the pastry is golden and the filling is bubbling.

Enough for 4

## NOVEMBER 24

# A warming soup in Helsinki market

If ever you find yourself in Hakaniemi market in central Helsinki at lunchtime, you will do well to join the local shoppers in having a bowl of fish soup. If there are no tables left, then perch on a high stool at one of the indoor market's long counters, where you will be jostled by shoppers laden with bags of smoked salmon and crispbreads the size of steering wheels. Whether the colour of a house brick, or ivory hued and topped with a sprig of dill the size of a Christmas tree, these soups are made in the market in kitchens the size of a broom cupboard. The best of them in a week's worth of eating was pale and mild, a beautiful bowl of salmon, swede and leek, its creamy depths spiked with lemon and cubes of tomato.

There were a couple of scallops in there too, possibly as much by accident as by design. The bowls here are deep and generously filled, and come with slices of rye bread as sweet as gingerbread and a little dish of butter scattered with coarse flakes of sea salt.

Market food is rarely disappointing but here it is as good as I have ever tasted it, sold side by side with stalls offering every cure of salmon there is, from beetroot to lemon and pink peppercorn and the ever popular gravlax. You eat to the piercing whine of the meat saw from the adjacent butcher's stall, from where you can pick up your marinated reindeer steaks (juniper, olive oil, dill, bay and onion most in evidence). There are salted fish and cured herrings too, ceramic dishes of Jansson's Temptation, and fishcakes the size of a ball of buffalo mozzarella. Yes, there is raw fish, though not as diverse a selection as you might wish for, but sustainability is very much the word here.

If soup doesn't float your boat, you could lunch on half-moon discs of rye crispbread layered with smoked halibut or a slice of wild mushroom tart made with the ceps that are piled high on stalls beside lingonberries and rosy apples smaller than a golf ball. At the grand Café Kämp they sometimes have deep bowls of cep soup with rosemary as a break from shopping.

Potatoes are a recurring ingredient in Finnish fish soups and they successfully saw off the cold autumn wind that whistled through my thermals throughout my stay. You see whole stalls of them proudly labelled Nicola, Siilkli and Van Gogh. These local varieties are small and waxy and sit happily without turning to slurry in your soup. Any of our small, yellow-fleshed potatoes will work.

## Salmon soup

This is not the classic Finnish *lohikeitto* but the delicious interpretation I ate in the market.

| | |
|---|---|
| a medium to large onion | water: 1.25 litres |
| a leek | tomatoes: 2 |
| butter: 50g | salmon fillet: 600g |
| cauliflower: 500g | double cream: 100ml |
| waxy potatoes: 750g | dill: a small bunch |
| swede: 350g | lemon juice, to taste |

Peel the onion and roughly chop it. Shred and thoroughly rinse the leek. Melt the butter in a deep, heavy-based pan and add the onion and leek. Let them cook over a low to moderate heat, stirring regularly, so they do not colour. They should be soft enough to crush between your finger and thumb, so take your time over this.

Bring a pan of water to the boil. Break the cauliflower into large florets and cook them in the boiling water till just tender. They will get a little more cooking when they are added to the soup. Drain and set aside.

Peel and roughly dice the potatoes and swede. Add them to the onion and leek and cook over a low to moderate heat for ten minutes, stirring regularly. Pour in the water, bring to the boil and season lightly with salt. Turn the heat down to a simmer and partially cover with a lid. Chop the tomatoes and add them to the soup, followed a few minutes later by the cauliflower.

When the swede and potatoes are fully tender, cut the salmon into large pieces and lower them into the soup. Season with pepper and let the salmon cook for about five minutes, until it is just done. Pour in the cream and mix in gently (you don't want the salmon to break up). Chop a couple of tablespoons of dill and stir in, reserving some sprigs for the top. Stir in a little lemon juice to taste, then ladle into bowls and add the sprigs of dill.

Enough for 4–6

Another day, I came across a fish soup so different I could have been in another country. Tomato based and broth-like, it came with Finnish pike-perch, green olives, mushrooms, and – something of a revelation to this cook – sliced gherkins, the sassiest addition to a fish soup I have ever had. Any associations with the Med were slashed with the inclusion of the ever-present chopped dill (it is their parsley) and a last-minute curl of soured cream. The effect was clean tasting and sweet-sharp. In trendier places, fish soup isn't overlooked either; it will just come in a (very) much smaller portion and with a degree or two more elegance. Either way, it's a bowl worth the trip.

## Sour, hot, crisp, soft. A sandwich for the senses

This morning I make fresh, hot vegetable pickles. I thinly slice a raw carrot, 4 radishes and a quarter of a cucumber. I bring to the boil a small wineglass of rice wine vinegar and the same of caster sugar. In go 4 slices of raw ginger and 2 star anise. I then add enough Vietnamese fish sauce to make it interesting, about 2 tablespoons (everyone's tolerance to fish sauce is different; keep tasting as you go), put in the vegetables and let the mixture cool. After an hour in the mixture, they have become crunchy. Two hours and they are full of zingy bite and refreshing crispness.

I get a wok smoking hot, pour in a little oil, then follow it with a few handfuls of minced pork from the butcher. As soon as it is brown on the bottom, I toss it round the pan, let it colour even more, then add 2 chopped garlic cloves and a finely sliced tiny, hot red chilli, followed by a teaspoon of five-spice powder. When all is sizzling and highly fragrant, I chuck in a fistful of coriander leaves.

The hot, garlicky pork gets stuffed into a length of buttered baguette, the pickles are placed on top of the pork and I tuck in 6 whole mint leaves and some more coriander leaves. The resulting sandwich, eaten as a late lunch, was exciting, refreshing, comforting, crisp, soft, searingly hot, blissfully cool. I could go on …

## A piquant soup for a Finnish sky

So grey is the sky this morning at nine, I could be back in Finland. Grey, Nordic-looking skies can be benign or ominous as the mood takes them. (I love them when they are heavy with the promise of snow.) This one is serene and strangely pacifying, without a hint of rain. But the wind has a sting to it, and I decide to have a go at the other fish soup idea I picked up in Helsinki: a brightly coloured broth of tomato, mushrooms and olives, brought to life with the surprising addition of gherkins. The pickles, sliced like pound coins, give a clean, piquant note to the soup.

Acidic ingredients can turn overpoweringly sour if you add them to a recipe too soon. Lemon juice, white wine vinegar, soured cream, yoghurt, gherkins, verjuice and green olives are most successful when added during the last ten minutes of cooking. Added late, they correct the seasoning, slicing through richness and bringing a sauce or stew to life. Introduce them too early and that snap of freshness will go, leaving just a deep, unpleasant sourness. I sometimes add a splash of wine vinegar to my coq au vin to lift the dish's tendency to cloy.

Adding acidity as a seasoning is something I do a lot, but the gherkin idea was new to me. I just thought it worth passing on.

## Tomato fish broth

It was intriguing to come across a soup seasoned with sour ingredients. The version I ate in Helsinki was made with what they call pike-perch but any sustainable white-fleshed fish that holds together well can be used. A thoroughly refreshing fish soup.

| | |
|---|---|
| onions: 2 | water or vegetable stock: 1 litre |
| olive oil | medium gherkins: 2 |
| garlic: a clove | green olives: 16 |
| tomatoes: 6 | parsley: a few sprigs |
| fennel: a small bulb | dill: 3 bushy sprigs |
| button mushrooms: a couple of handfuls | white fish fillets: 500g |
| | soured cream: 4–6 tablespoons |

Peel the onions and roughly chop them. Let them soften in a little olive oil in a deep, heavy-based pan over a moderate heat. Try not to let the onions colour, you want them to be pale and soft. Peel and crush the garlic clove and add to the onions. Roughly chop the tomatoes and add to the pan. Let them cook down to a slush.

Finely slice the fennel and mushrooms and add to the pan. Continue to cook for a few minutes, until the fennel has started to soften a little. Pour in the water or stock and bring to the boil. Turn down the heat and leave to simmer for twenty minutes, adding salt and black pepper.

Slice the gherkins, stone and halve the olives, chop the parsley leaves and dill and set aside. Lower the fish fillets into the stock and continue cooking for three or four minutes, until the fish is just opaque. Stir in the gherkins,

olives, parsley and dill. Correct the seasoning with salt and pepper and, if you wish, a little of the liquid from the gherkin jar.

Ladle into warm bowls and add a spoonful of soured cream to each.
Enough for 4–6

## Putting the garden to bed

There is a moment, round about the last week of November, when the garden appears to breathe a sigh of relief. The leaves, especially those of the fig tree outside the kitchen door, seem to fall off overnight, leaving the paths almost invisible. The greens, golds, red and ochres change to crisp brown and soggy black. The shrubs, trees, bulbs and even fruit canes give the impression that they are tired and ready for bed.

This morning I am out amongst the little vegetable beds with their squishy tangle of trailing nasturtiums, dried bean stems and the last of the wineberries, sweeping, raking, pruning. I am, I suppose, tucking the garden up before it goes to sleep.

There is something deeply satisfying about this moment, even though I don't quite get everything done (a few pots that should be put away before the frost are too heavy to lift and I am tired, hungry and scratched to bits). The one piece of advice I have about these sorts of days is to get something in the oven first. No matter how keen a cook you are, you won't feel like doing anything much when you get indoors. I know I certainly don't.

In my kitchen at least, there are 'dinners' for such occasions that consist of little more than opening a bottle and hacking slices off a lump of cheese. They fly in the face of everything I want a meal to be, but when I'm exhausted they come all too easily. This evening I go one better and make a bowl of deep, savoury soup, adding a few vegetables. It's lazy but good.

I put a couple of cups of water, about 500ml if you are measuring, into a saucepan, then stirred in a couple of teaspoons of vegetable bouillon powder, 2 tablespoons of white miso paste (it is actually more of a pale-yellow ochre) until it dissolved (it is best not boil miso), then I added a few chopped spring onions, a shake or three of toasted sesame oil and a little soy sauce, and gave it all a minute on the stove at a bit of a simmer. Eaten from a deep bowl, it not only warmed and soothed but, curiously, I felt totally replete. Had I had some tofu or some seaweed, I could have added that instead, but you are unlikely to find either in my kitchen very often. Okay, each spoonful was consumed in a 'think more, eat less' kind of way.

And then I attacked the cheese and wine.

## NOVEMBER 30

# Snorkers and a windy night

I am beginning to notice how cosy the new kitchen is. This wasn't planned or even wanted. My first priorities are space and light. Snug and cosy is my idea of hell. It's like clutter. I just don't do it. Yet to go down the stone stairs into the kitchen with its low ceilings and basement light is to enter a space that feels safe and warm – a favourite room where I feel totally at home and exceptionally comfortable, despite its hard surfaces and snow-white walls. To cook in this place has been a pleasure from day one. There is a feel of peace and serenity here, even when in the throes of getting a large meal on the table.

This evening there is a bracingly cold wind blowing. It makes your face prickle. Almost my favourite weather of all. I need a cheap supper that will warm cold guests. We end up with plates piled with beer-braised sausages and mashed potatoes so ridiculously buttery you could almost declare them a soup.

## Slow-baked sausages

The dark-brown beers give an extraordinary depth to any slow-cooked meat dish. I usually use them with beef but they also work well with pork, including sausages, the plumper and more herby the better.

plump pork butcher's sausages: 8
a little oil
large onions: 2
butter: a thick slice
plain flour: 2 lightly heaped
    tablespoons

brown sugar: a heaped teaspoon
stock (vegetable will do): 400ml
dark beer: 200ml
mashed potato, to serve

Set the oven at 160°C/Gas 3. Fry the sausages using a very little oil in a non-stick pan over a moderate heat till lightly coloured on all sides. Remove from the pan. Peel the onions and slice them thinly into rounds. Melt the butter in the pan over a moderate heat, add the onions and let them colour lightly. Stir in the flour and continue cooking for three or four minutes, stirring from time to time, then add the sugar. Return the sausages to the pan, pour in the stock and beer and bring to the boil. Let the mixture boil for a minute or so, then cover with a lid. Place in the oven and bake for fifty minutes, then serve with mashed potato into which you have beaten as much butter as it will take.

Enough for 4

## A Swedish-inspired snack

There is some mashed potato left over. Not the sloppy, velvet-textured mash made almost liquid with olive oil and butter, but the stand-up sort, beaten first with an electric beater and then with a wooden spoon. It heats up well enough in a basin in a pan of simmering water. The microwave would probably work too. (I am guessing. I don't have one.)

The hot mashed potato goes on a thin wrap that I have warmed under the grill, and on top of that a couple of sausages and a dollop of sharp sauce (I used some Swedish lingonberry jam with a few berries from the freezer, but a proprietary Cumberland sauce or even some warm redcurrant jelly would do). The hot mash, sizzling sausage and sharp-sweet sauce are folded up in the warmed wrap. This is, and I will get told off for hinting at this, my version of the Swedish *tunnbrödsrulle* minus the prawns and tomato sauce. It is carb corner, on a nippy night, tucking in like famished Labradors.

December

# The start of it all

I sleep with a nightlight. Not for comfort. I'm a big boy now. I use a night-light because I like the shadows it casts on the dark oak floorboards and the filtered, flickering light it brings into the room. It lasts through till morning, until my alarm wakes me and tells me what the temperature is and whether I will need an umbrella today. It also tells me the date.

The first of December always makes my heart beat a little faster. The day it all starts. The festival that is Christmas has begun. The vulgar commerce of it all may have started weeks ago in the shops, but in this house the season starts today. Over the next few days I will plan the recipes I intend to include in my newspaper column and the food that will be on the table over Christmas. Which bird will be sizzling and spitting in the oven, what the 'other' pudding will be, and who will, or will not, be breaking bread with me over those few, special days. These decisions are momentous only because you tend to remember every Christmas. You don't remember every March 22 or August 7. Unless, of course, it's your birthday. The problem is that every dish that fails or disappoints will be mentioned at every Christmas from now till kingdom come. Unlike so many other meals, Christmas cannot be left to chance. Planning, rarely part of my kitchen life, is essential. December is when I try out new recipes I am thinking of serving at Christmas. Daring is the cook who makes something for the first time on Christmas Eve (daft, more like it).

The vegetable I associate most with this season is not the Brussels sprout, God love it, nor the red cabbage. It is the parsnip. Honey and black, sticky outside, soft within, sitting in the roasting tin, slipped into a pool of pork gravy or tossed with salad leaves. It might be mashed into a soup with curry paste or squished into fritters and fried. Parsnips' inherent sweetness suggests they come with something sharp. Tonight, a dry and bone-chilling evening, I pat mashed paprika-spiced parsnip into croquettes and roll them in fine crumbs. Fried, they get a shot of sherry vinegar in the accompanying sauce.

# Parsnip and potato croquettes

parsnips: 350g
potatoes: 500g
butter: a thick slice
ground cumin: 1 teaspoon
hot smoked paprika: 1 teaspoon
eggs: 2, beaten
fresh white breadcrumbs: 150g
oil for frying

*For the sauce:*
an onion
oil: 2 tablespoons
canned chopped tomatoes: 400g
sherry vinegar: 1 tablespoon
sugar: 2 teaspoons

Peel the parsnips and potatoes and cut them into large pieces. Steam separately (they are unlikely to take the same time to cook), then remove from the steamer. If you don't have a steamer, then a colander balanced over a pan of boiling water and covered with a lid will do.

Melt the butter in a shallow pan over a moderate heat, then add the ground cumin and paprika, followed by the cooked potatoes and parsnips. Fry for ten minutes or so, till lightly golden here and there. Season with salt and black pepper, then crush with a potato masher or a fork. I like a bit of texture left in mine, but others will prefer a smoother mash. Beat for a minute or two with a wooden spoon, then allow the mixture to cool until comfortable to handle.

Take scoops of the mash and pat them into fat cylinders about 10cm long. You should get about eight of them, enough for two each. Put them on a lightly oiled or floured plate and refrigerate for an hour to firm up. (You could skip this step, but your croquettes may fall apart in the frying pan if you do.)

Set the oven at 200°C/Gas 6. Put the beaten eggs in a saucer and the breadcrumbs on a plate. Lower the chilled croquettes, one at a time, into the beaten egg, roll them over so they are fully coated, then drop them into the breadcrumbs. Turn each one, patting the crumbs all over it.

Warm a shallow layer of oil in a non-stick frying pan. When the oil is hot, lower the croquettes in a few at a time and cook till golden on all sides. As each one is ready, lift on to an ovenproof dish. Bake for fifteen to twenty minutes, till hot right the way through.

To make the tomato sauce, peel the onion, chop finely and cook in the oil till soft and pale gold. Tip in the tomatoes, add the vinegar, sugar and salt and black pepper and simmer for fifteen minutes. Serve with the croquettes.

Enough for 4

## A pasta soup for Christmas

'Why don't we keep the chives whole?' says James, as we toss hair-fine noodles with broth made from toasted chicken wings for lunch. 'Then they'll get tangled up with the noodles and make them more interesting to eat.' So we did and he was right, as he often is.

Chicken noodle soup can be good and it can be dishwater dull. The best is when the chicken bits are fried or roasted before simmering in water. That way, they introduce a deeper, more savoury quality to the broth. I've done this for a long time. It takes only minutes more than the traditional method of simmering them from raw.

I only chose angel hair noodles, made from rice rather than wheat, because it's December and I like the corny sentiment. Stellata, the diminutive star-shaped pasta, would work too, as would the barley-shaped orzo. Stars and angels. And it's only December 2.

### Angel hair noodles, chicken broth and chives

groundnut oil: 1 tablespoon
chicken wings: 600g (about 8)
a lemon

angel hair noodles: 100g
chives: 15g

Warm the oil in a large, deep pot. Add the chicken wings and brown lightly on both sides. Halve the lemon, add half to the pan and cook till the cut side colours. Pour in 1.5 litres of water, bring to the boil, then skim and discard any froth that appears on the surface. Simmer for forty-five minutes. Skim once again thoroughly. Season with salt and, generously, with black pepper.

Drop the angel hair noodles into the pan with the chicken, push them down into the liquid, then add the whole chives and cover with a lid. Switch off the heat and leave for four or five minutes.

Divide the chicken wings between four shallow bowls, add the noodles and chives and ladle over the broth. Squeeze in the rest of the lemon.

Enough for 4

# A cake is not just for Christmas

The traditional cake, freckled with nuts and dried fruits, has its fans, though they are fewer than you might imagine. I could eat it at any time of year, but the magic for me is the cake and its almond paste, not the icing. One of the curious things about Christmas cake is that almost everyone likes at least one layer of it but few, I find, like them all.

The modern thing is to find, if not a replacement, an alternative offering. The *bûche de Noël*, the chocolate log so beloved of the French, has recently make a comeback, but it is not something I have ever been able to take seriously. No matter how expertly it is decorated, I always think it looks, well, a bit naff.

The components however – a decently made chocolate sponge and some soft buttercream – are, if nicely made, worth rearranging. With this in mind, I have made a nutty sponge, crunchy with praline, and a buttercream topping flavoured with chocolate hazelnut spread. It is rich, and needs serving in small slices or squares. With its crown of glistening, caramel-coated hazelnuts there is something festive about it, but though this will grace my Christmas table, it is a cake for any autumn or winter's day.

## Chocolate hazelnut slice

I used a standard commercial hazelnut spread for this. There are more upscale versions available, but I am not sure you really need to spend that sort of money in this instance.

*For the praline:*
skinned hazelnuts: 250g
caster sugar: 6 tablespoons

*For the cake:*
dark chocolate (about 80 per cent
   cocoa solids): 200g
butter: 100g
caster sugar: 90g
eggs: 2, lightly beaten

self-raising flour: 120g
cocoa powder: 2 tablespoons

*For the hazelnut buttercream:*
butter: 150g
icing sugar: 150g
soured cream or double cream:
   2 tablespoons
Nutella or similar hazelnut
   chocolate spread: 200g

Set the oven at 160°C/Gas 3. Line an 18cm square cake tin with baking parchment on the base and up the sides. Lightly oil a non-stick baking sheet.

Make the praline. Put the skinned hazelnuts into a non-stick frying pan and toast over a moderate heat until deep gold. Add the sugar and, watching carefully, allow it to melt. Shake the pan occasionally or mix the nuts and melting sugar lightly with a spoon, but take care not to stir too much. As soon as the caramel is dark-honey coloured, tip the mixture on to the lightly oiled tray. Once it is cool, blitz half to coarse crumbs in a food processor.

Break the chocolate into pieces and melt in a bowl set over a pan of gently simmering water. Add the butter in small lumps and leave to melt without stirring. Remove from the heat and gently stir in the sugar and the crushed praline, followed by the lightly beaten eggs. Take care not to over mix. Fold in the flour and cocoa powder. The mixture will thicken and appear a little grainy.

Scrape the mixture into the prepared cake tin and smooth the top lightly. Bake for thirty-five to forty-five minutes, till the cake is lightly firm at the edges but still quite soft in the centre. Remove from the oven and leave to cool in the tin. Don't attempt to take it out of the tin before it is cool.

Make the hazelnut buttercream. Put the butter into an electric mixer and beat till soft and pale. Add the icing sugar and mix till you have smooth buttercream. Mix in the cream, then add the Nutella and continue beating till smooth – a matter of seconds.

Spread the frosting on to the cake. Cut the cake into nine equal squares and top each one with a piece of the reserved praline.

Makes 9

## DECEMBER 4

### A Christmas posset

I have been tinkering with the idea of several sharply refreshing desserts to offer at Christmas, and today I finally get one of them right, a yuletide take on my regular lemon posset recipe. The tiny puddings could be served in shot glasses, used as a filling for a little cake, or sandwiched between biscuits. The scent of clementines is one that I find instantly evokes Christmas, possibly more than any other fruit. I have used them in punches, grated into the icing of a ginger cake, for a sorbet but this year decided to include them in my favourite custard-cup dessert.

double cream: 500ml
caster sugar: 150g

the finely grated zest of
3 clementines
lemon juice: 75ml

Put the cream, caster sugar and clementine zest in a saucepan and bring to the boil, stirring occasionally to dissolve the sugar (you may find a mild tendency to curdle, in which case just whisk it briefly with a small whisk). Lower the heat and leave to bubble for three minutes, no longer, stirring from time to time.

Remove from the heat, stir in the lemon juice and leave to settle. Pour into four small wine glasses or cups and leave to cool. Refrigerate for three or four hours before serving.

Makes 4 small glasses

## DECEMBER 6

# A big, useful casserole

There is a train of thought that says the most useful recipes are those that can be knocked up in fifteen minutes, and to an extent I agree. But even more useful, at least to my mind, are those that might take a while to cook yet last a few days, getting better as they mature, so you come home to find dinner is already made. Big soups fit neatly into this scenario, as do various simple stews and richer casseroles. The best example I have come across is a huge casserole, similar to a French cassoulet, where bits of meat and sausages are held together with a thick, tomato-based sauce and lots of dried beans.

This is a recipe that improves with age, like us, and whose flavours seem to mellow and mature after a day or two in the fridge. I have worked the recipe through for four, but you could easily double it, if you have a pot big enough. You could cook the beans from scratch (I have used canned, to cut down on the cooking time) and use fresh tomatoes too, but this is a recipe whose heart and soul lie in what is known as peasant cooking. The rich tradition of old-fashioned good housekeeping.

## Butter bean 'cassoulet'

A thick, slightly spicy casserole for a winter evening. Go for the plump chorizo the size of a butcher's sausage.

chipolata sausages: 12
sausage-sized chorizo: 6
olive oil: a tablespoon
streaky bacon with plenty of fat:
    6 rashers, cut into large pieces
a large onion, roughly chopped
garlic: 4 cloves, thinly sliced

tomato passata or chopped
    tomatoes: 400ml
butter beans: two 425g cans,
    drained and rinsed
2 bay leaves
grain mustard: 2 tablespoons
coarse breadcrumbs: 50g

Set the oven at 200°C/Gas 6. In a heavy, flameproof casserole, cook the chipolatas and chorizo in the olive oil until their fat runs and they are golden on all sides. Scoop out the sausages and set aside. Add the bacon pieces to the pan and cook until golden. Add the onion and garlic and cook for five or six minutes, until they have softened slightly, then stir in the tomato passata or chopped tomatoes. Cook for a minute or so longer, then stir in the cooked sausages. Bring to the boil, add the drained and rinsed beans, the bay leaves, mustard and a grinding of salt and pepper and then cook over a medium heat at a good simmer for about fifteen minutes.

Remove the pan from the heat. Season the breadcrumbs lightly and scatter them over the top. Bake for twenty-five minutes, until the crumbs are golden. Serve very hot.

Enough for 4

## DECEMBER 7

# A fruit for Christmas

Forget the blueberry, it is the pomegranate that is the fruit of the decade. The fruit that has gone from zero to hero in no time at all, due largely to the bottled juice that is now easily available and the user-friendly cellophane packages of ready-prepared seeds in the supermarkets. They save peeling the tough skin and delicately tearing away the bitter white pith, and prevent the sort of scarlet splatters that Dexter would be proud of. I buy them ready prepared, as chilled juice, and in whole form. They look regal in a bowl. I would insist that they seem to be sweeter than they once were, but then the same has happened with grapefruits, tomatoes and pretty much everything else. The culinary equivalent of dumbing down. That said, the jewel-like seeds still have a bite to them, and are endlessly useful to the open minded. A handful in a salad? Yes, please. In with the breakfast cereal, scattered over grilled lamb cutlets with mint and yoghurt or simply eaten from the hand like peanuts. In many ways, their startling acidity can be used to replace the lemon.

Pomegranate juice can be included in a salad dressing, a marinade (with olive oil and cumin seed), in the icing for a cupcake (stir into icing sugar) or to add a note of astringency to grilled meat, as you might squeeze a lemon. With this in mind, I am using the claret-coloured juice in place of lemon in a Middle Eastern-style almond cake. Outrageously moist, grittily sweet and delightfully tart. The colour is glorious.

## Orange and pomegranate cake

butter: 175g
caster sugar: 175g
large eggs: 3
self-raising flour: 125g
baking powder: 1 teaspoon
ground almonds: 50g
grated orange zest: 2 teaspoons
thick yoghurt to serve

*For the syrup:*
caster sugar: 6 tablespoons
juice of 2 medium oranges
unsweetened pomegranate
  juice: 6 tablespoons

You will need a 19cm x 9cm x 7cm deep loaf tin (measured across the base), lined with baking parchment.

Set the oven at 160°C/Gas 3. Using a food mixer fitted with the paddle attachment, or an electric handheld mixer, cream the butter and sugar together till pale and fluffy. You can expect this to take a good ten minutes. Break the eggs into a small bowl and beat them lightly with a fork to amalgamate the yolks and whites, then add them a little at a time to the butter and sugar mixture. If there is any sign of curdling (and well there might be), then introduce a little of the flour as you go.

Sift the flour and baking powder together, then stir in the ground almonds. Add them, a little at a time, to the butter and sugar mixture. Stir in the orange zest. Be gentle. Spoon into the lined tin and bake for forty-five minutes.

While the cake is in the oven, make the syrup. Put the sugar and orange juice in a small bowl. Stir in the pomegranate juice, but don't attempt to dissolve the sugar. When the cake comes from the oven, and whilst it is still hot, spike the surface with a skewer and spoon over the syrup. Leave to cool and then serve in slices with thick yoghurt.

Enough for 8–10

## DECEMBER 8

### A better canapé

If there is a part of the festivities that depresses me, it is the thought of making 'bits to go with drinks'. It doesn't feel like real cooking, it's fiddly and precious. It's a faff. My answer is usually to throw some olives in a bowl. The nearest I get to 'canapes', said to rhyme with drapes, are the little puff pastry parcels I make tonight, filled with a sort of Welsh rarebit mixture. The only problem is making enough. Warm from the oven, they disappear before you can say rabbit.

### Rarebit puffs

butter: 30g
garlic: 3 cloves, thinly sliced
mascarpone: 100g
Parmesan: 50g, very finely grated
hot, smooth mustard: 2 level
  teaspoons

ready-rolled puff pastry: a 375g
  packet
an egg, beaten

Preheat the oven to 220°C/Gas 7. Melt the butter in a shallow pan, add the garlic and leave over a moderate heat, stirring from time to time, till soft and pale. Tip into a bowl and leave until cool enough not to melt the mascarpone. Mix in the mascarpone, Parmesan (saving a tablespoon for later), a little salt and pepper and the mustard. Set aside.

Unroll the pastry and lay it out flat (if you are using a block of pastry, then roll it out to 30cm x 23cm). Cut into four lengthways, then cut each piece into six equal pieces. You should end up with twenty-four almost-square pieces of pastry. Put a heaped teaspoon of the cheese mixture on twelve of the squares, dampen the edges with beaten egg (milk or water will not seal them tightly enough), then lay a second piece on top of each one. Press tightly round the edges to seal. If some of the filling oozes out, poke it back in and wipe the edges of the pastry. It is essential they are sealed well, otherwise they will leak.

Transfer the puffs to a baking sheet and brush them with the remaining beaten egg. Cut a small slit in the top of each one and scatter over the remaining Parmesan. Bake in the preheated oven for ten to fifteen minutes, till puffed up. Serve straight away.

Makes 12, so double or triple the recipe as you need

## A cheesecake for Christmas

The cheesecakes of northern Europe often contain a few fat sultanas or raisins as relief from the vanilla-scented curd. They can be welcome guests or trespassers, depending on your view. The diminutive British curd tartlets, known as Richmond maids of honour, follow a similar vein, with (in some recipes) chopped peel being used to similar effect.

Looking for ways to use mincemeat outside its short, traditional yuletide window, I have long been wondering whether it would work in a cheesecake, either as a layer between crust and curd or rippled thorough the cream cheese. Today I decide to have a go at the latter. The result is a creamy cheesecake, thick and clarty in the Austrian style, but with a familiar festive note. It is sweet, and good with strong black coffee.

## Mincemeat cheesecake

*For the base:*
butter: 65g
shortbread or digestive biscuits:
   300g

*For the filling:*
full-fat cream cheese: 600g
golden caster sugar: 200g

eggs: 4
an extra egg yolk
finely grated zest of a small orange,
   plus a little extra to finish
vanilla extract: a few drops
soured cream: 300g (2 standard
   142ml pots will do)
mincemeat: 250g

You will need a round cake tin with a removable base, or a springform cake tin measuring 22cm in diameter and about 7.5cm high. Line the base with baking parchment.

Melt the butter in a large saucepan. Crush the biscuits to fine crumbs in a food processor and stir them into the melted butter. Remove from the heat and tip all but a couple of tablespoons of the crumbs into the lined cake tin. Smooth flat, but avoid the temptation to push down too hard; you don't want a tightly packed, impenetrable crust. Put in the fridge for half an hour to set.

Set the oven at 140°C/Gas 1. To make the filling, put the cream cheese and sugar in a food mixer and beat for a couple of minutes, till smooth. Add the eggs and the extra yolk one at a time, beating each one in thoroughly before adding the next. Scrape down the sides of the bowl regularly.

Add the orange zest and vanilla extract. Stop the machine and stir in the soured cream with a large spoon or spatula. Fold the mincemeat in with a spoon, stirring only enough to ripple it lightly through the cheese mixture.

Remove the cake tin from the fridge, wrap it in tin foil and place it in a roasting tin, then pour in the cream cheese filling. Pour hot water into the roasting tin to come half way up the outside of the cake tin. Carefully slide into the oven and bake for an hour. You will find that the middle of the cheesecake will feel uncooked and wobbly, but that is how it should be. Switch off the oven, close the door and leave the cheesecake for a further hour. Remove from the oven, allow to cool and then refrigerate overnight (don't try to skip this step, or your cake won't set).

Scatter the top of the cheesecake with the reserved biscuit crumbs and a little orange zest before serving.

Enough for 8–10

# Consider the prune

A note of liquorice perhaps, a shadow of brown sugar, even a nip of sweet Madeira-type wine, but little hint of the plum it once was. I like prunes, and particularly the way they form a dark and seductive relationship with chocolate (soak them in brandy, dip them in dark chocolate and leave to set to a crisp shell, then serve with tiny cups of slightly bitter coffee).

The prune has a few savoury possibilities. Beef, game, pork and rabbit like to party with it, especially when they are cooked slowly together. I used to make a rich brown sauce with prunes to accompany a paupiette of pork stuffed with mushrooms, though it seems a little elaborate for modern everyday eating. Any slow-cooked dish where prunes have been added will be better (richer, more deeply flavoured) for a night in the fridge.

Rather than cloying, adding cream to a dish containing prunes brings about a rather magical chemistry. A shot of acidity will add even more, and is best in the form of redcurrant jelly or verjuice.

There are two forms of prune worth considering: the fully dried fruit complete with its stone and the mi-cuit – the half-dried prune that needs neither stoning nor soaking. The advantage of the latter is obvious, and I am not sure the lack of a stone makes much difference to the flavour (unlike with a fresh plum, where I feel there is a sympathy between the fruit and its stone, like meat and its bone). Try as I might, I am not sure there is much to be gained by using the fully dried version. We have moved on.

## A casserole of oxtail and prunes

This gives a perfect quantity for two. I would have done the recipe for four, but can't imagine ever getting four oxtail-loving people around the table at the same time.

| | |
|---|---|
| rapeseed or groundnut oil: 2 tablespoons | soft dried prunes: 200g |
| oxtail: 1.3kg | juniper berries: a rounded teaspoon |
| onions: 2 large | red wine: 500ml |
| an orange | |

Set the oven at 220°C/Gas 7. Warm the oil over a moderately high heat in a deep casserole large enough to take the oxtail in a single layer (I use a 24cm lidded casserole). Add the oxtail pieces, cut-side down, and cook for four or five minutes on each side, until sizzling and golden brown. Remove to a bowl or plate.

While the meat is browning, peel and roughly chop the onions. When the meat is out of the pan, add the onions and let them cook for six or seven minutes over a slightly lower heat, till they are pale gold and starting to soften. Return the oxtail to the pan, add 5 strips of peel taken from the orange, plus its juice, the prunes, juniper berries and red wine. Grind in a little salt and black pepper.

Turn up the heat and bring to the boil, then immediately cover with a lid and transfer to the oven. Leave to cook for twenty-five minutes, then turn the heat down to 140°C/Gas 1 and leave to putter away quietly for a further 2 hours.

Serves 2, with generosity

## Roasted roots with vin cotto

When I tip vegetables from the steamer, I tend to toss them in a simple dressing before bringing them to the table. Butter and lemon juice works for members of the cabbage family; olive or walnut oil with a few herbs is often my choice for root vegetables. It is only recently I have taken to making a dressing for baked vegetables too. Roast artichokes with walnut oil and red wine vinegar has become a regular this winter, as has a mixture of sweet root vegetables with a dressing of olive oil, verjuice and dark, mellow vin cotto. My favourite is Maggie Beer's vin cotto, which you will probably have to Google to find a supplier.

Jerusalem artichokes: 600g
parsnips: 350g
carrots: 250g
sweet potatoes: 500g
garlic: 4 cloves
olive oil: 3 or 4 good glugs
thyme: 6 small sprigs

*For the dressing:*
verjuice: 2 tablespoons
olive oil: 8 tablespoons
vin cotto: 2 tablespoons

Set the oven at 200°C/Gas 6. Get a pan of water on to boil for steaming the vegetables. Wash the artichokes and cut them in half. Peel the parsnips and carrots. Cut them into large pieces and place in a steamer basket above the boiling water. Add the artichokes. Steam for twenty minutes or until all the vegetables are just tender. Tip them into a large roasting tin.

Peel the sweet potatoes and cut into large chunks. Add them to the roasting tin with the steamed artichokes, parsnips and carrots. Tuck the garlic cloves, whole and unpeeled, in amongst the vegetables. Pour over the oil, season with salt and black pepper and add the thyme sprigs. Toss the vegetables gently to make sure they are all coated in the oil and seasonings. Roast for about an hour, until they are golden and lightly toasted. Check to see they are soft inside.

While the vegetables are roasting, make the dressing. Mix the verjuice with a pinch of salt, then whisk in the olive oil and vin cotto. As soon as the roasted roots come out of the oven, tip them into a serving dish and trickle with the dressing. Serve warm.

Enough for 4

## DECEMBER 12

# A feast (of sorts)

A sudden attack of deep, carnivorous lust. Not for steak and blood, but for the umami-rich notes of flesh that has been taken to the edge. A cheap pork roast whose crust is as deeply caramelised as it can be without being actually charred. Where the exterior is both sweet-sharp and engagingly chewy and the inside is falling-apart tender. There is salted crackling, a darkly piquant crust and soft, sweet flesh. A feast, but one where the recipe is taken as far as it will go.

The robustness of the recipe is not for everyone, and is certainly not for the fainthearted cook, but it certainly pops my cork – a piece of meat for hacking at rather than attempting any semblance of neatness by cutting into smart slices. Better still, make possibly the best pork sandwich ever by pulling the pork and its dark, sticky undercarriage to rags with a fork, then stuffing it into slices of fresh, warm sourdough or a floury bap with a curl of crisp lettuce and a couple of whole mint leaves.

# Roast pork belly with pomegranate molasses

I suggest cooking the pork on the bone here, but I have also tested this with a thinner, 1kg piece of boneless pork belly. The recipe stands, except for the timing, which needs to be reduced to two hours, with twenty minutes at 220°C/Gas 7.

pomegranate molasses:
    6 tablespoons
water: 2 tablespoons
the juice of a lemon

garlic: 2 cloves
pork belly, a thick piece, bone-in,
    skin scored: 1.5kg

Pour the pomegranate molasses into a glass or china dish slightly larger than the piece of pork. Stir in the water and lemon juice. Peel and chop the garlic, then crush it finely. Mix into the molasses mixture. Lower the piece of pork into the dish, skin-side up, without getting any of the mixture on the scored skin. Set aside in a cool place (the fridge if you must) for a couple of hours. Overnight won't hurt.

Preheat the oven to 150°C/Gas 2. Line a small baking dish or roasting tin with kitchen foil (you will regret it if you don't). The dish should not be too large; you need it to take the piece of meat with just a centimetre or two around each side. Pour the marinade into the dish, then place the pork in it, skin-side up as before, again making sure that the marinade doesn't touch the skin. Rub the skin with a little salt.

Roast for two and a half hours. By this time the pork will be cooked through to the middle and the skin just starting to crackle. Remove the dish from the oven and spoon off most of the oil that has accumulated round the meat (I would keep this for roasting potatoes another time). Turn the oven up to 220°C/Gas 7 and return the pork to the oven. After twenty minutes or so, the skin will be crisp and amber coloured and the underside of the pork will be almost black. Remove from the oven. What is left of the marinade will be very dark. This is as it should be; it has done its work and is not needed. Let the meat rest in the dish for up to ten minutes.

Lift the pork from the foil – if it has stuck, use a palette knife to help release it. The underside will be blackened, sweet and tangy. Slice the pork and its crackling into thick, rough pieces and serve.

Enough for 4

## DECEMBER 15

# Lifesaving soup

Sucker as I am for the holly and the ivy, there are times when December can get the better of me. If I am going to lose it (and I do), then this will probably be the month. When there is too much going on, I have a fast, fail-safe fish soup that seems to make life manageable once more.

I put a couple of lightly heaped tablespoons of white miso paste into a saucepan with 500ml vegetable stock. Over a moderate heat, I whisk in a good teaspoon of Vietnamese chilli paste and bring it to the boil. Just as it approaches, I slide in a large handful of broccoli florets, thinly sliced with their stalks, then about 250g salmon, cut into chunks, and a handful of prawns from the freezer. I finish the dish with a few spring onions, thinly sliced, a handful of coriander and basil leaves and a squeeze of lime juice. It works out at a couple of quid a bowl, and serves two.

## DECEMBER 17

By teatime, the narrow lane outside the house is a sheet of ice. Not grey, as most ice seems to be in the city, but crisp, pearlescent white, as slippery as wet glass. This matters, because most of us walk back from the shops along the road rather than do battle with the uneven stone flags of the pavement. Amazed that I make it without landing on my back, I arrive home with a duck, some prunes and some tight-skinned little citrus fruits.

The clementine, the tiny, seedless Christmas orange, is the one with the tight skin, usually sold with its glossy leaves intact. The one I used for the posset earlier in the month. Unlike its wide-pored, loose-skinned sister the satsuma, it is almost impossible to remove the peel in one piece. Sometimes I dry it in a sieve over the radiator and add it to a pork stew with star anise.

This is the small citrus I choose over any other member of the mandarin family. The skin is easier to grate than the flabby satsuma or, as it is sometimes known, the Japanese mikan. Its clinging skin is more aromatic and, to me, part of the very spirit of Christmas.

When I was a kid, clementines came in thin wooden crates, with every other fruit wrapped in brilliantly coloured foil, like Quality Street. It seems odd now, in the days of supermarket net bags of easy-peel citrus fruits, that the arrival of the Christmas oranges was a special occasion. I value these diminutive fruits more for the spritz of Christmas that lies in their zest than for their flesh. Juicy, sweet and mild, their meat is worth including in a fennel or chicory salad, and makes a spirit-lifting addition to a salad of cold duck or ham, but it's the zest I appreciate most. This is a fruit to pair with fatty meats, such as duck and goose.

## Roast duck with apples, clementines and prunes

a large duck: about 1.5–2kg
Bramley-type apples: 2 medium
    (about 400g in total)
clementines: 2
soft-dried prunes: 100g
onions: 2

a parsnip
bay leaves: 3
stock (duck, see opposite, or
    vegetable): 400ml
brandy, Calvados or dry Marsala:
    3 tablespoons

Take the duck out of its packaging and place in the fridge overnight. The following day, leave it out, uncovered, in a cool, dry place for a couple of hours before cooking.

Set the oven at 200°C/Gas 6. Peel the apples, remove their cores and cut the fruit into large dice. Toss them in a bowl with the grated zest of one clementine and its juice. Cut the prunes in half, discard their stones and add to the apples. Spoon the apple and prune stuffing inside the cavity of the duck. Secure the stuffing by putting the second clementine in the open end of the bird.

Place the duck in a roasting tin and season generously with salt. Peel the onions, quarter them and put them round the duck. Peel the parsnip, chop it into eight pieces and add to the tin, tucking it in around the duck with the bay leaves. Roast for an hour.

Remove the duck from the roasting tin to an ovenproof plate. Turn the oven up to 220°C/Gas 7. Spoon out the parsnips and put them round the duck. Remove and discard the clementine. Scoop out half of the apple and prune stuffing from the duck and add it to the roasting tin. Put the duck back into the oven.

Place the roasting tin over a moderate heat and stir the onions into the apple and prune mixture. Add the stock and keep stirring. Pour in the brandy, Calvados or Marsala, then season with salt and pepper. Bring to the boil and continue cooking for a couple of minutes. If you prefer a smooth gravy, pour it into a blender and whiz to a smooth, thin purée. Pour it into a warm jug.

Remove the duck from the oven, and carve on to two plates. I generally start by removing the legs with a heavy, sharp knife, then carving the breast. Spoon out the stuffing from the duck and serve with the gravy.

Enough for 2, with a little left for later

## To make a quick duck stock

Roughly chop an onion, a carrot and a stalk of celery and put them into a medium-sized pan with the wings, heart, liver and gizzards of the duck. Add a couple of bay leaves and two or three sprigs of thyme. Bring to the boil, turn the heat down and simmer for twenty minutes. Strain and set aside.

## DECEMBER 18

## A useful pâté for Christmas

The Saturday lunch ritual here hasn't changed in a decade or more and remains a testament to shopping over cooking. There may be a bowl of home-made soup but everything else will be pulled from coarse brown paper bags – a sourdough loaf, its flour-encrusted top still crackling; some slices of coppa with their pearlescent splashes of white fat; some hummus, perhaps; a plastic tub of slender purple olives and another of tiny, ribbed cornichons. For dessert there will be warm Eccles cakes and a fat, custard-filled doughnut from St John.

Sometimes there is a terrine too, to eat with the bread and cornichons. A stir-up of minced pork from the butcher, dried figs or prunes, brandy and aromatics such as onion, juniper and bay, these coarse-textured pork pâtés are something to pick at throughout the following week.

French inspired, rough-grained pâtés give the appearance of being hard work when in truth they are anything but. Despite having something of the charcutier's art to them, they are really more a case of stir, season and bake. There is no technique beyond getting the seasoning right. It is easy to forget that food to be eaten cold needs to be more highly seasoned.

A carefully stored terrine will keep for a week or more. I bring it out, in its plain white dish, for lunch on workdays or for when I feel I should offer a 'starter' but haven't got round to making one. For me, it is an indispensable part of Christmas too.

## A coarse pork and fruit terrine

a medium onion
garlic: 2 large cloves
butter: a thick slice, about 30g
minced fatty pork, such as belly:
   400g
pig's liver: 100g
the leaves from a bushy sprig of
   thyme, finely chopped

ground mace: half a teaspoon
hazelnuts: 75g
dried prunes, pluots or figs: 100g
brandy: 2 tablespoons
medium vine leaves, pickled or
   fresh: 8

Set the oven at 180°C/Gas 4. Peel and finely chop the onion and garlic. Melt the butter in a shallow pan and cook the onion and garlic until soft and translucent. Transfer to a mixing bowl. Put the minced pork into the bowl. Finely chop the liver and add it to the pork with the thyme and mace. Season generously with salt and ground black pepper – a good half teaspoon of each. Roughly chop the hazelnuts and the dried fruits. Stir in thoroughly together with the brandy.

Line a 1.5 litre terrine with fresh or dried vine leaves. If you are using fresh ones, pour boiling water from the kettle over them first, both to cleanse them and to make them supple enough to bend round the inside of the tin. Remove their tough stalks. Fill with the mixture, pushing it down into the corners. Cover with a lid of greaseproof paper and foil, then place in a deep roasting tin and pour enough water into the tin to come half way up the side of the terrine. Put into the oven and cook for an hour and a half. Test with a skewer for doneness; it is cooked when the skewer comes out hot rather than just warm. Remove carefully from the oven (the hot water is easy to tip over). Leave to cool overnight, then refrigerate before eating to firm up the texture.

Enough for 6–8

# A cure for Christmas

My key to surviving the unstoppable train that is Christmas cooking is to apply the 'cut and come again' rule. A squirrel-store of recipes that you can make on a quiet afternoon in the run up to Christmas Eve and which will keep in good condition for several days. Useful things such as a vast pork pie, a coarse pork terrine like the one above, a marzipan-flecked stollen and a long-life cake that you can continually cut and come back to. Recipes that, over the course of the festivities, manage to keep this cook sane.

The most useful of these is a side of smoked salmon that I can carve as a first course, a light lunch or as a sandwich on Boxing Day. Just as versatile, but more interesting I think, is a side of raw salmon that you have cured yourself, not in a smoker but in salt, lemon and herbs.

The Helsinki market fish counters with which I became so entranced last month have proved to be an inspiration for this year's Christmas cooking. Several of the open-topped glass cabinets held sides of cured fish to be bought by the kilo and sliced as required. Laid out amongst the tubs of salted herrings were sides of salmon as bright as jewels, flavoured with Norse favourites from fresh dill to juniper berries. While those with pink peppercorns, orange and lemon zest tempted, the star for me was the sweet and earthy beetroot cure, whose dazzling shades of orange, carmine and green seem more than appropriate for the festive table.

A large piece of fish seems an extravagant purchase (well, it is) but, thinly sliced with my longest, sharpest knife, it will go a long, long way. Brought to the table with a sycamore board of dark, moist rye bread, it serves more than a dozen of us.

You need a decent-sized tray or a wide dish long enough to hold the fish (you can cut the piece of fish in two if needs be but it will lack the majesty of a whole fillet brought to the table). Raw grated beetroot, sea salt and citrus zest are needed too, and, as so often in Finnish or Scandinavian recipes, fresh dill. The only real hands-on work comes in grating the roots and patting the marinade over the fish. Salt draws out moisture, and I find you need to pour off the excess beetroot juice that accumulates in the tray over the next twenty-four hours or so. You will also need to secure a reasonable amount of space in the fridge. Until it has finished marinating, your piece of fish will require a whole shelf to itself.

Lightly cured salmon, carved as thinly as you would smoked salmon, is good on shattered sheets of artisan crispbread; perfect as a yule sandwich stuffer (try it with crisp, hot bacon and red-flecked winter salad leaves) but also as a light, elegant starter. Saffron, vermilion and orange, it looks good on a white plate. I find you need something with it too – perhaps a crunchy, bracingly sour salad to nuzzle up against the silky folds of fish. Today I put together a thick dressing of salmon's best friends – capers, soured cream, orange zest, mustard and dill. As a nod to the grated root vegetable in the dry marinade, I tossed the dressing with thick shreds of ivory-white celeriac.

## Salmon marinated with beetroot, dill and orange

Ask your fishmonger to scale and bone the salmon but leave the skin on.

| | |
|---|---|
| a side of salmon, boned (about 800g) | dill: a large bunch, about 30g |
| demerara sugar: 100g | grated zest of 2 lemons |
| coarse sea salt: 175g | finely grated orange zest: 2 tablespoons |
| black peppercorns: 10g | raw beetroots: 600g |
| vodka: 4 tablespoons | |

Check the salmon all over for any remaining bones, keeping an eye open for the tiny, almost invisible pin bones. These can be removed with a pair of tweezers. Lay the salmon skin-side down in a stainless steel or enamelled tin or glass dish. If the fish is too long, you can cut it in half.

Put the demerara sugar and salt in a mixing bowl. Coarsely grind the peppercorns and add to the sugar together with the vodka. Roughly chop the dill and its stems and add to the marinade with the grated lemon and orange zest. Peel and grate the beetroots, then stir into the other ingredients.

Spread the mixture over the fish and rub in well with your hands. Wrap a piece of cling film over the fish and place a heavy weight on it. A small chopping board with a few cans on top will work. Refrigerate anywhere from forty-eight hours to four days.

Pour off and discard the liquid that has seeped from the marinade. Remove the cling film and scrape away the marinade ingredients. You can throw them away; they have done their work. Slice the fish thinly, and serve with the salad below.

Enough for 10–12

A salad of celeriac, soured cream and mustard for the salmon

If celeriac is a step too far, try cucumber or lightly steamed and cooled potatoes instead. The point is to keep the flavours sharp and crisp to contrast with the sweet earthiness of the salmon. This recipe will appeal to anyone who doesn't like their Christmas starters too rich.

soured cream: 200ml
olive oil: 2 tablespoons
gherkins: 4
capers: a teaspoon
wholegrain mustard: 2 teaspoons
grated zest of half a lemon

finely grated orange zest:
    2 teaspoons
lemon juice: 2 teaspoons
caster sugar: a pinch
dill, finely chopped: 2 tablespoons
celeriac: 400g

Spoon the soured cream into a bowl and lightly whisk in the olive oil with a fork or small whisk. Roughly dice the gherkins and stir into the dressing with the capers, mustard and grated lemon and orange zest. Stir in the lemon juice, a little salt, the sugar and the finely chopped dill. Grate the celeriac and fold it in.
    Enough for 4–6


DECEMBER 23

## A long day in the kitchen

### Mincemeat and orange trifle

This is probably the longest and most complex recipe I have ever included in a book. It involves making a mincemeat cake and a batch of orange and lemon curd and will take a few hours of your time. A rainy afternoon type of recipe. You can make life easier by taking advantage of the posher supermarkets' range of ready-made custard (the one made with cream and vanilla is the one to use). I include it because it was part of my Christmas television special and proved very popular.

a little sweet white wine, Marsala
   or dry sherry
ready-made custard: 400ml
double cream: 300ml
physalis (cape gooseberries):
   about 20

*For the mincemeat sponge:*
butter: 250g
caster sugar: 250g
ground almonds: 75g
plain flour: 100g

large eggs: 4, lightly beaten
the grated zest and the juice of an
   organic or unwaxed orange
good-quality mincemeat: 100g

*For the curd:*
   the zest and juice of 5 lemons
      and 1 orange
caster sugar: 300g
butter: 140g, cut into cubes
eggs: 4
egg yolks: 2

You will need a shallow 23cm cake tin, the base lined with baking parchment or greaseproof paper. Set the oven at 180°C/Gas 4.

Beat the butter and sugar in an electric mixer until white and fluffy. Mix the almonds and flour together and set aside. Add the eggs to the butter and sugar a little at a time, with the beater on slow. Turn the machine off and add the zest and a third of the almonds and flour, then turn the mixer on slow until the dry ingredients are incorporated. Add the second and then the third lot, switching the machine off each time. If you do this too quickly you will end up with a heavy cake. Lastly, the machine still on slow, mix in the orange juice and mincemeat. Using a rubber spatula, transfer the mixture to the lined cake tin and bake for thirty-five minutes. Run a palette knife around the edge of the tin and turn the cake out on to sugared greaseproof paper. Leave to cool.

Break the mincemeat sponge into pieces and put them in the bottom of a serving dish. Sprinkle with a little sweet wine, Marsala or dry sherry.

Pour the custard on top, then place in the fridge, covered, for an hour while you make the curd.

To make the orange and lemon curd, put the zest, juice, sugar and butter into a heatproof bowl set over a pan of simmering water, making sure that the bottom of the basin doesn't touch the water. Stir with a whisk from time to time until the butter has melted. Mix the eggs and yolks lightly with a fork and stir them into the lemon and orange mixture. Let the curd cook, stirring regularly, for about ten minutes, until it is thick and custard like. It should feel heavy on the whisk. Remove from the heat and stir occasionally as it cools.

Pour the curd over the custard and chill. Whip the cream, spoon on top, then decorate with a little more orange zest and the physalis.

## The start of the feast

The kitchen is heavy with expectation. Sugar-crusted mince pies, whose sweet, spice-laden filling has spilled out and caramelised on the baking tin; syrup-preserved ginger that I have dipped into bitter chocolate waits on sheets of snow-white baking parchment; oranges spiked with cloves hanging from ribbons make the kitchen smell like something from Hansel and Gretel. Every inch of counter space is home to something for the feast: a bottle of brandy for the pudding, a red cabbage too big for the fridge, and enough sweets and treats, from candy canes to clementines, to fill an army of Christmas stockings.

The fridge, too, is an Aladdin's cave of delights. Links of shiny chipolatas for roasting with the goose; a cracked bowl of apple sauce speckled with cinnamon; the glistening cranberry sauce to bring out for Boxing Day sandwiches with crisps and ice-cold Cox's apples. There is a rolled joint of ham, which I simmered earlier in apple juice and juniper, awaiting its final coat of marmalade, mustard and crumbs; some little carrot patties that will be served to the vegetarians with a sauce of fresh ginger and coriander (see *Tender Volume I*) and a pot of organic cream for the steaming plum pudding.

I want to stop, sit down and pour myself a little drink. Something sweet and seasonal that wouldn't normally get past my lips, such as a glass of golden Madeira, something that smells of Christmas. I want to sit and take it all in, to gloat over what I have done and to calm my suppressed panic about what there is left to do. The tree sparkles with gold and silver, the carols are on and the house is, for once, as warm as toast.

The cabbage is pickled, the marinated salmon is ready to slice, the plum pudding is primed for its second steam in the morning. I have poached a dish of quinces (though I'm not entirely sure why) and have secured the ribbon round the cake with a pin. The pomegranates are peeled and the seeds crumbled into a bowl ready to drop into glasses of champagne; a pineapple is 'panic-ripening' by the Aga.

But then, I have still to climb on the roof to lift the caps off the chimneys (for an open fire, you understand, not for the arrival of some jolly, bearded guy with a sack of toys), make the stuffing for the goose, make mustard sauce for the smoked salmon and knock up some brandy butter for those who insist on it for the pudding. I prefer cream with my pud, but if I am making a sweet Christmas butter, then it will have plenty of finely grated orange and lemon zest in it, and a knife-point of nutmeg, too. Rather than the traditional sage and onion, I am stuffing a chickpea and sausage mixture up the goose's bum as well as roasting some potatoes around it. The fat that pours out will be poured off for roasting potatoes another day.

If all this sounds a bit overexcited, I should explain. I am a relative newcomer to Christmas celebrations. Having fought (and lost) against its non-negotiability for years, I now find I am well and truly hooked up in wrapping, shopping and chopping more than is probably wise for someone of my years. Plum pudding and the laden tree I have always had a soft spot for, but the lure of the rest of the celebrations eluded me until surprisingly recently. Now I think I could eat roast goose and the trimmings every week of the year. The Christmas spirit has slowly, almost unnoticeably, crept up on me, like wrinkles.

One of the most successful of all Christmas desserts has been my habit of passing round a giant plate of edible treasures after, or sometimes instead of, pudding. A vast oval serving plate piled high with all manner of goodies: shelled almonds, expensive chocolates, sticky dates, pistachio nougat, chunks of uncut candied orange peel, huge seedy raisins on the vine, marrons glacés, and even some of those rather naff foil-wrapped liqueur chocolates that one sneers at yet secretly quite fancies. (Listen, if Christmas was solely about good taste, we would have packed it all in years ago.)

I would be lost without the presence of a great fruit-studded panettone. I know there are those who think it's just a big Italian cupcake, but so what? A thick slice, toasted and served with a cappuccino, is a mid-morning treat, and the warm candied peel in it makes the house smell even more Christmassy. The ancient, lightly yeasted bread can also be hauled in to act as an impromptu dessert, either by sandwiching slices of it together with a mixture of lemon curd and cream, or by using it as the carbohydrate of choice in a bread and butter pudding. Its calm spice notes will perfume the egg custard and send the most heavenly wafts of warm vanilla floating through the house.

This is the most magical of all moments – the hour of peace and quiet before we go to bed on Christmas Eve. It is when I put the carols on and pray for overnight snow. This is also the point at which I open the fridge and make a checklist of things to do tomorrow: the bird, of course; slice the red cabbage for stewing with apples and cinnamon; make the batter for some

Christmas-morning blini to eat with slices of smoked salmon and glasses of champagne in lieu of breakfast; squeeze the orange juice. There will, of course, be some sort of Christmas Day drama – there always is – and especially as I have a sneaking suspicion I'm out of tin foil. But I'm not going to look. This is the moment I have been waiting for all year, and I'm going to open a bottle, sit in peace and breathe in the glorious citrus-and-nutmeg scent of Christmas Eve.


## CHRISTMAS DAY


### Roast goose with chickpeas, lemon and stuffing

a goose, 5kg or thereabouts

*For the stuffing:*
large onions: 2
a little goose fat or oil

canned chickpeas: 800g, drained
mint leaves: 10g, chopped
zest and juice of a lemon
the meat from 1kg herby
  butcher's sausages

Peel and roughly chop the onions. Melt the goose fat or warm the oil in a large frying pan, then add the chopped onions and let them cook till they are a light walnut brown. You will need to stir them regularly. Stir in the chickpeas, let them warm through, then partially crush them with a potato masher or fork. Crush so you have some thickly mashed whilst others keep more of their texture. Season with salt, the chopped mint leaves and the grated lemon zest and juice then stir in the sausage meat and season with pepper. You may find the mixing easier, and indeed a rather pleasing thing to do, with your hands.

Set the oven at 220°C/Gas 7. Put the goose in a large roasting tin, stuff as much of the chickpea mixture as you can into the body cavity, then make the rest into balls or patties and place in a lightly oiled roasting tin, or save for another day.

Roast for thirty minutes, then lower the heat to 180°C/Gas 4 and continue cooking for about two and half to three hours, until the skin is dark and crisp. Leave to rest for a good fifteen minutes before carving, taking great care with the hot fat in the tin. Serve with the stuffing.

Enough for 8–10

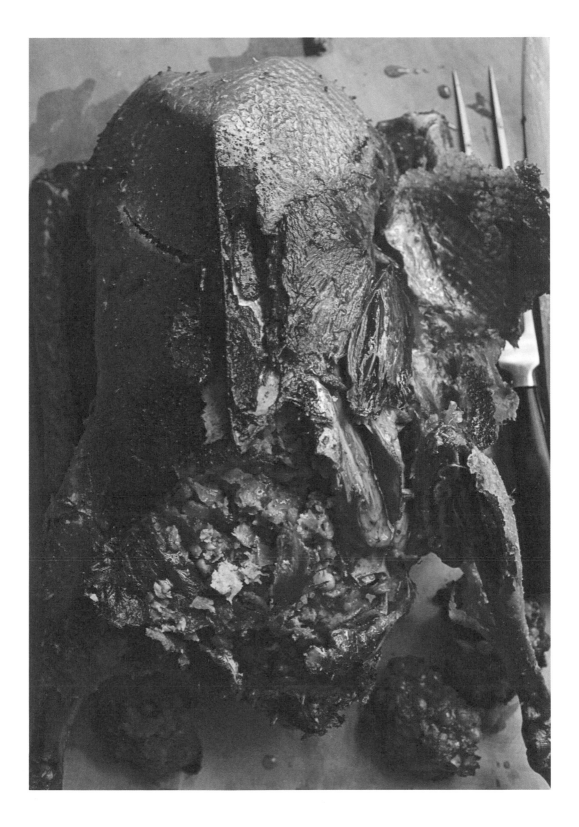

# A hot salmon for Christmas

a puff pastry sheet: 375g
a whole salmon, about 2.8kg,
   skinned and filleted into
   2 long fillets
a little beaten egg and milk, for
   brushing

*For the filling:*
medium cucumbers: 2
dill: 50g, weighed with stalks
Dijon mustard: 5 tablespoons
honey: 2 tablespoons
white wine vinegar: a tablespoon

Make the filling. Lightly peel the cucumbers, removing only the thickest layer of dark green skin. Halve them down their length, then remove the seeds with a teaspoon or your thumb. Finely chop the dill. Chop the cucumbers into small pieces, roughly 1cm square, then put them in a mixing bowl with the mustard, honey, vinegar and dill. Season and set aside.

Roll the pastry out to a rectangle measuring about 40cm x 30cm, making certain it is a little longer than your salmon fillets. Put the pastry on a baking sheet lined with baking parchment. Set the oven at 180°C/Gas 4.

Place one half of the fish on the pastry, pile half the filling on top, then cover with the second fillet of fish. Brush the edges of the pastry with egg wash, then fold the pastry over the fish, sealing the edges that meet by pressing them together. There should be a gap in the centre through which you can see the fish. (If you have a mind to, you could decorate your fish with bits of pastry for scales. Up to you.)

Brush with egg wash and bake for forty-five minutes. Slide on to a baking dish and leave to settle for ten minutes before serving with the remaining cucumber mixture as a cold accompaniment.

Enough for 8

# Potato and onion sauté

A little something to go with the salmon, above.

potatoes: 650g
onions: 250g

a little butter and oil

Scrub the potatoes, but there is no real need to peel them. Cut them into thick slices or small cubes, whichever you fancy. Peel and finely slice the onions.

Warm a little butter and oil in a non-stick frying pan, then add the potatoes, onions and seasoning and cook over a moderate heat for about twenty-five minutes, till they are lightly crisp on the outside and soft inside.

## Another refreshing dessert for winter

To please those who want something fruity to finish their meal, I peel half a dozen clementines, peel and slice a couple of very ripe mangoes and slice three blood oranges. I break open a pomegranate, covering the kitchen walls and my shirt with scarlet juice, and crack it into seeds, discarding every last bit of bitter white pith. I mix the fruits with the juice of a second pomegranate, chill very thoroughly and serve. The fruits would benefit from something crisp at the side – in other words, the brandy snaps below.

## Brandy snaps

caster sugar: 2 tablespoons
golden syrup: 2 heaped tablespoons
butter: 60g
plain flour: 4 generously heaped
   tablespoons

ground ginger: a level teaspoon
brandy: 1 teaspoon
pistachios, chopped: 2 heaped
   tablespoons

Set the oven at 150°C/Gas 2. Very lightly butter a baking sheet. In a small pan, melt the sugar, golden syrup and butter. As soon as the mixture starts to bubble, remove from the heat and stir in the flour, ginger, brandy and pistachios.

Using a teaspoon, place six blobs of the mixture on the buttered baking sheet, each about the size of a large walnut half. There is no need to flatten them, as they will spread naturally in the oven. Bake the biscuits for about ten to twelve minutes, until they are a rich golden brown. Leave them on the baking sheet for five minutes, until they are cool enough to roll. Holding the baking sheet with an oven glove and using a palette knife in the other hand, loosen each biscuit from the tray one at a time – they should still be hot. If the biscuit tears, then leave to set a little longer. Wrap each biscuit round a rolling pin with your hands, gently pressing the biscuit to fit the rolling pin. Work quickly, as the biscuits won't roll once they have completely cooled. Remove each snap once it has set and leave on a cooling rack. Bake the remaining mixture and shape in the same way.

Makes 12–15 large biscuits

# A celebration of frugality

St Stephen's Day, which can be today or tomorrow depending on which calendar you use, is the day those working 'below stairs' would open their presents and count the tips box, while 'upstairs' made do with a simple buffet of soup, stew or cold cuts. As a cook, I have always felt more comfortable below stairs, and relish the thought of getting to pick at the bones of the goose or turkey (or chicken or ham or duck) and turn the nuggets and scraps of roast flesh into lunch.

Removing bits of juicy meat from a carcass can be as enjoyable as any kitchen job (treat it as a challenge). There is much sweet satisfaction to be had in picking the bones clean and boiling them up for a light stock. Stock made from roasted bones can lack body, but adding the scrapings and meat jelly from the roasting tin or carving plate will enrich it.

Stripping the Christmas carcass ranks, along with stirring the Christmas pudding, baking potatoes for Bonfire Night and making pumpkin soup for All Hallows Eve, as one of the great kitchen rituals of the season. I start at the breast, pulling any large pieces away whole, then gradually pull and tug every piece of meat from the breast and legs before turning the skeleton over and starting on the undercarriage. This is not a part to be forgotten. Here lie chubby oysters of brown meat, kept sweet and succulent by the juices that trickle down to the base of the bird as it cooks. A glorious little feast that is all too easy to miss.

In years past, my leftovers from the bird have ended up under a pastry crust (in a tarragon sauce, padded out with onions and mushrooms), as an onion and potato frying-pan hash and in the inevitable, though perfectly acceptable, curry. This year's leftovers are probably the best ever. Mashed potato, a little stuffing, bits and pieces from the goose and some red cabbage cooked with apple. A Christmas bubble and squeak. Perhaps that should be bauble and squeak.

# Christmas bubble and squeak

So good is this that I have given instructions for cooking it from scratch.

potatoes: 1kg
red cabbage: a quarter, or 250g
    leftover cooked red cabbage
butter, oil or goose fat

red wine vinegar: 1 tablespoon
an apple, cored and chopped
juniper berries: about 6
goose or turkey trimmings: 250g

If you are cooking from scratch, peel the potatoes, cut them into quarters, then boil in deep, salted water for ten to fifteen minutes. When they will easily take the point of a knife, drain them, then cover the pan with a cloth while the potatoes lose their steam. Mash thoroughly with a potato masher or use a food mixer fitted with the flat beater attachment.

Shred the cabbage coarsely and fry it in a little butter, oil or, better still, goose fat, till it starts to wilt. Add the vinegar and the chopped apple. Crush the juniper berries and stir them in. Leave to simmer, covered with a lid, for fifteen minutes or so. Drain and set aside.

In a large mixing bowl, stir the mashed potatoes, cooked red cabbage and the bits of goose or turkey meat together. Add a little stuffing if there is some to use up, and season generously.

Get a little butter or goose fat hot in a frying pan. Shape the mixture into small, thick patties and fry till pale gold, turning once to cook the other side. Drain on kitchen paper, then transfer to a hot oven, about 200°C/Gas 6, for forty-five minutes, till crisp and sizzling.

Enough for 4–6

# Sweet soup and a sizzling salad

Sweet potato soup, potato skins and coconut.

sweet potatoes: 1.5kg
rapeseed or groundnut oil

coconut milk: 600ml, maybe a
    little more
a little freshly grated coconut

Set the oven at 200°C/Gas 6. Remove four wide strips from one of the potatoes with a vegetable peeler, place them on a baking sheet, then brush

with a little oil and season with salt. Bake for twenty-five minutes or so, till crisp, then remove and set aside.

Peel the remaining potatoes, cut them into large pieces and place in a roasting tin with a little rapeseed or groundnut oil. Season with salt and black pepper. Roast for about an hour, till soft enough to mash. Tip the potatoes into a blender or food processor and reduce to a purée with the coconut milk, adding enough to bring it to a thick pouring consistency. Put the soup in a pan over a moderate heat and stir gently, checking the seasoning as you go. It should be thick and sweet. Ladle into bowls and place some of the potato skin on top with a spoonful of fresh coconut.

Enough for 4

Another Boxing Day reheat, but this time, spicy, sticky and quick. I make a feature of the fact I am using up the scraps rather than trying to hide it. Frugality in this day and age is, surely, to be celebrated.

## A way with leftover turkey

| | |
|---|---|
| leftover roast turkey: 4–6 good handfuls | grain mustard: a tablespoon |
| garlic: 3 cloves | turkey stock: a cup |
| honey: 2 tablespoons | |
| soy sauce: 2 tablespoons | *For the salad:* |
| chilli sauce: a tablespoon | oranges: 2 |
| tomato ketchup: a tablespoon | a grapefruit |
| | watercress: 4 handfuls |

Set the oven at 200°C/Gas 6. Strip the turkey meat from the bones and tear it into large, irregular pieces.

Peel and crush the garlic and put it in a mixing bowl. Stir in the honey, soy, chilli sauce, ketchup, mustard and turkey stock. No salt, but a little black pepper, then add the turkey meat. Toss gently and tip into a baking dish. Bake for twenty minutes, till glistening, keeping an eye on it so it doesn't burn.

Meanwhile, make the salad. Peel the oranges and grapefruit with a sharp knife, then slice thinly. Toss with the watercress. Pile the hot turkey on the fruit and watercress and serve.

Enough for 4

## Using up the bits

With snow still on the ground and mercifully little to do, three of us sit at the kitchen hob making warm hotcakes of sweet mincemeat and brandy butter. The very essence of Christmas, these diminutive pancakes use up the half jar of mincemeat left in the cupboard and the remains of the clementine-scented brandy butter I made for the pudding.

### Mincemeat hot cakes

mincemeat: 250g
a clementine
eggs: 2, separated

plain flour: 80g
a little butter for frying: about 20g
brandy butter, to serve

Put the mincemeat in a mixing bowl. Grate in the zest of the clementine and add the egg yolks. Add the flour, preferably through a sieve, and mix in gently.

Beat the egg whites till almost stiff – they should be thick enough to hold their shape – then fold them into the mincemeat mixture firmly but tenderly.

Melt a thin slice of butter in a non-stick frying pan. Add large serving spoons of the mixture to the pan and leave to colour lightly underneath. Lift gingerly to check that the underside is golden brown, then flip over with a palette knife or fish slice and let the other side colour lightly. I turn each cake by sliding the palette knife under, then flipping in a smooth but determined fashion. Dithering will end in disaster. Serve on warm plates with a dollop of brandy butter.

Makes about 6; enough for 3

## NEW YEAR'S EVE

Simple, satisfying, almost effortless cooking is all very well. It is, after all, how I cook most of the time. But sometimes I want to grind spices and toast them, make stock, make a bit of a mess, use every pan and bowl in the kitchen.

Tonight, I make my friend Jeremy Pang's curry again, it means making a stock with tamarind paste, toasting cumin and coriander seeds, and frying fish. It's not complicated, but it is more involved than most of my daily cooking. I end the day with a warmingly spicy curry, earthy with cumin and curry powder, refreshing with the sourness of tamarind. A recipe to play with, to tweak, twist and tinker till the recipe is to my taste. A bit more of this, a little less of that. I follow the recipe, but it is about more than that, it's about cooking or the thrill and joy of it all, about having a good time in the kitchen. I can ask for no more.

## Tamarind fish curry

an onion
garlic: 4 cloves
lime leaves: 3
curry leaves: 5
bird's eye chillies: 3
cumin seeds: a tablespoon
coriander seeds: a tablespoon
chilli powder: 2 teaspoons
curry powder: 3 tablespoons
tomatoes: 4, medium sized
white fish fillets: 4

vegetable oil: 2 tablespoons
butter 50g
coriander: a handful
rice, to serve

*For the tamarind stock:*
fish stock: 750ml
tamarind paste: a teaspoon or
    to taste
sugar: a teaspoon

Finely chop the onion and garlic. Crush lime leaves, curry leaves, chillies, cumin and coriander seeds in a food processor, then add the chilli and curry powder and 3 tablespoons of water to form a paste. Roughly chop the tomatoes. Cut the fish into large pieces.

Mix all the tamarind stock ingredients together in a saucepan and bring to the boil, then lower the heat and simmer for ten minutes.

Heat half the vegetable oil and butter in a large saucepan. Add the onions and garlic and brown very lightly, then stir in the spice paste and continue cooking for a minute or two till fragrant. Add the tomatoes and the stock, cover the pan and simmer for ten minutes with the occasional stir until soupy. Check the seasoning, adding salt, pepper and tamarind paste as necessary.

Put the remaining oil in a frying pan, melt the reserved butter with it, then add the pieces of fish. Let them colour and lightly crisp, then add them to the curry, scatter over the coriander and ladle into bowls.

Enough for 4, with rice

# Index

*Numbers in bold type refer to short, simple recipe ideas; those in italics refer to photographs.*

525

## A note on the type

This book was set in Monotype Haarlemmer 11/14pt. The typeface was originally designed by Jan van Krimpen (1892–1958), but was never finished. Working from van Krimpen's original drawings, Frank E. Blokland completed the family for The Dutch Type Library in 2002.